RICHARD WRIGHT: A BIOGRAPHY

Richard Wright

A BIOGRAPHY

by Constance Webb

NEW YORK G. P. PUTNAM'S SONS

CONSTANCE WEBB, a native of California now living in New York, was educated at Fresno State College and the University of California at Berkeley. She has traveled widely and has worked as a copywriter in an advertising agency and as an actress. She is now completing her first novel.

Introduction /Acknowledgments

Although a new generation has discovered Richard Wright, he is still best remembered for his first three books, *Uncle Tom's Children, Native Son* and *Black Boy.* This is due, in part, to his self-exile in France but chiefly because the times are only now catching up with this prophetic writer.

Thirty years have passed since the publication of the short stories *Uncle Tom's Children,* in which the developing history of the black struggle may be traced, and one story, "Fire and Cloud," uncannily foretold almost every aspect of the Negro civil rights movement which began in 1963.

Twenty-six years have passed since *Native Son* exposed the fire in the black community that has erupted in Harlem, Chicago, Detroit, Watts and elsewhere.

Twenty-two years have passed since *Black Boy* revealed the peculiar Fundamentalist/Horatio Alger inheritance common to all Americans—white and black.

12,000,000 Black Voices, inspired by Oliver LaFarge's *As Long as the Grass Shall Grow,* advanced a new form of picture book now common to this generation.

The Long Dream penetrated the class structure within the black community and revealed in fiction the characteristics of the black bourgeoisie the same year as sociologist Dr. E. Franklin Frazier's outstanding book, *Black Bourgeoisie,* appeared on that theme.

So far only Wright has positively revealed the state of mind of a people bursting with energy, untroubled by feudal remains or a feudal past, soaked to the bone in traditions of individual freedom and free association—traditions constantly held before them as the basis of their civilization, yet utterly unrealized in the face of automation and the threat of atomic annihilation. Painstakingly, in *The Outsider,* he demonstrated the effect upon personality when week after week the self-esteem that tradition nourishes and encourages is frustrated and the American citizen is left baffled and unable to grasp the reasons why he failed to attain a genuine democracy. Writing in 1953, Wright groped toward a solution for this existential man who, in failure and death, stretched his mind toward a cosmic unity and came to believe that a bridge had to be found between men, for alone man was nothing.

Black Power in its title preceded by thirteen years the anguished resolution of the black community to stand up as men, to die if need be, and warned ex-Premier Kwame Nkrumah of his nation's vulnerability seven years before Ghana's first independent government was overthrown.

In *Savage Holiday,* a counterpoint to *The Outsider,* he suggested Freudianism as the American version of French existentialism, a last refuge of bewildered white minds, and was critical of analysis, which only pointed to past troubles. Dreams and fantasies might be creative, for "What values would man have," he asked, "were it not for his ability to imaginatively picture the world as being different?"

He was the first man since the great abolitionist Wendell Phillips, who preached: "The Negro for fifty, or thirty years, has been the basis of our commerce, the root of our politics, the pivot in our pulpit, the inspiration of almost all that is destined to live in our literature," to insist that the black "question" was man's matter and linked white and black American as mirror images, warning that if the schism between them is not solved, then America will die.

In *Pagan Spain,* Wright recognized a white Negro in the persecuted Protestant; and in *White Man, Listen!* and *Color Curtain,* the story of the Asian-African conference in Jakarta, he delineated a new group in the rising nations which he called a tragic elite—caught between the old and the new.

Long before Malcolm X, Wright looked at the remnants of the giant Garvey movement and came to believe that black nationalism was a signal that the black man was awakening to a sense of his intrinsic worth. He saw black nationalism as a vital stage toward a different way to live together—the only solution to the American sickness.

In 4,000 unpublished poems in the haiku style he gave a particularly American cast to the fifteenth-century, seventeen-syllable structure. And, as a last work, he demonstrated in *Island of Hallucinations* the extent of CIA activities in Europe eight years before press revelations in 1967.

Although toward the end of his life Wright almost despaired of the future, he kept fighting, putting himself always on the side of those tyrannized, wherever they might be. Almost his last words were "We fret, we feel frustrated, but things are moving on the broad scale. We must never forget that."

The list of his books alone is impressive enough to make him one of the world's important writers. He combined a profound political insight with a poeticism and lyricism which lifted his social ideas beyond protest or "cause." He was a genius, a skilled, dedicated, meticulous craftsman, an example of the very best that America can produce, whose audacity of insight and masterful style left Europeans breathless.

I met Richard Wright and his family when he was at work on *Black Boy* and we became friends. It was a friendship which lasted until his death. At *Black Boy's* completion he gave me the galley sheets of the unpublished last third of the book, which I printed privately. Many of the quotations in the first part of this biography are drawn, in large part, from this material. Then, when I decided in 1945 to write a study of his work, he began to give me notes, letters, telegrams, manuscripts and ideas for new books and talked to me hour after hour in New York, Long Island and Paris. After his sudden death in 1960, his wife, Ellen, came to the United States and we made tape recordings in which she talked of their life in France. In 1966 I went to Paris and Ellen opened to me all of Richard's files, which included two diaries—day-by-day records for the years 1945 and 1947. I have also had the assistance of Alan Wright, Richard's brother; of Joe C. Brown, a close boyhood friend; of Paul R. Reynolds, Jr., his agent; and reference to hundreds of letters to his editor, Edward C. Aswell; to his translator in Holland, Margrit de Sabloniere. Chester Himes, a close friend of Wright's, loaned me his autobiography, consented to taped interviews, and wrote me detailed letters over a five-year period. Ralph Ellison read the manuscript, offered suggestions, corrections, new information from his own personal life and details of his friendship with Wright. Theodore Brown, Jack Conroy, Arna Bontemps, Dorothy Norman, Langston Hughes, Herbert Hill, Jean Blackwell Hutson, Oliver Swan, Jan Wittenber, Chester Aaron, C. B. Cobbins, Daniel Guérin, Hélène Bokanowski, Walter Goldwater, William French, Jacqueline Lavalle, and Richard P. Cecil have given critical aid or information. I wish to thank Michel Fabre for the use of material gathered for his thesis; and Edward Margolies for help during research and the loan of letters collected for a forthcoming book in association with Fabre. The author also thanks Fabre and Margolies for permission to use their bibliography contained at the end of this volume.

It was felt that a constant reiteration of the citation "conversation with Richard Wright" would become burdensome to the reader; therefore most material thus obtained is not indicated in the footnotes even though quotation marks have been retained in the text. For the same reason, where the source is Wright's diaries, unless quotation is lengthy, the source has not been footnoted. In the interest of style, the author has taken occasional sequential liberties, although not with actual facts.

I wish to thank Ellen Wright for her aid in what has often been a painful task. Without her generosity it is doubtful whether this book could have been completed.

I wish also to express appreciation to the following publishers for the use of quotations from Wright's published works: Harper & Brothers, Doubleday and Company, The World Publishing Company, The New American Library, Avon Publications, Dobson Books, Ltd., *Twice a Year*.

Contents

Illustrations follow page 128.

"It's them goddamn rebels . . ."

I

On most pleasant days, Richard Wright's grandfather sat behind the house at 20 Woodlawn Street, Natchez, Mississippi, in an old chair near the spread branches of a locust, far enough from its trunk so that the sun's light shone upon his bent white head, and far enough from the house to establish his isolation. Hour after hour, the lean black man, with angular features in a long narrow face, sat whittling on a block of wood, whistling quietly or maybe, if he was feeling good, humming some strange tune. Sometimes he paused and stared across the field at the flitting yellow and white butterflies, or bent forward and with the point of his sharp knife drew lines in the hard clay at his feet. When he had finished the intricate design it resembled a relief map of an area—which, in fact, it was—the scene of a river battle. Carefully, he marked crosses, stabbing them into the drawing at various places.

Occasionally his solitude was interrupted by one of his grandchildren, and he would lift his head briefly, bare his snow-white teeth and hiss: "You, git 'way frum me, you young'un." A second admonition was never needed. His wife said that he had developed the habit of hissing when he had been fighting in the Civil War. He was later to continue his own private "civil war" with the United States government.

Of unknown parentage, Richard Wright's grandfather was born into slavery on March 21, 1847, on a plantation in Wilkinson County, near Woodville, on Percy's Creek, Mississippi. When news of the assassination of President Lincoln reached the South, Richard Wilson ran off from his owner, John C. Alexander, and groped his

11

way through Confederate lines until he reached Mound City in Cairo, Illinois. There, the eighteen-year-old, slightly built young man enlisted in the Navy and was attached to the Mississippi Flotilla. "He darkly boasted of having killed mo'n mah fair share of them damn rebels while en route to enlist in the Union [Navy]." Militantly resentful of slavery, and bitterly disappointed that after the war's end he had served only ninety-seven days before being mustered out, he returned home to guard ballot boxes with an Army rifle so that Negroes could vote.

Jackson had been a center of political ferment and the headquarters for Generals Grant and Sherman during the war. After the war ex-slaves seized the large estates, armed themselves, and declared: "We have but one master now—Jesus Christ and He'll never come here to collect taxes or drive us off"; a commander of a Negro regiment in Jackson told Negroes they had to defend their rights "to the click of the pistol, and at the point of the bayonet."[1] Every detail of that period Richard Wilson described to his wife, Margaret Bolden, whom he married before the Reverend William Haynes, on February 26, 1871, at Woodville, Mississippi. His courtship of Margaret took place against a background of battles, ranging from the bloody murder of the Great Emancipator to the virulent political fights in the Constitutional Conventions, when a Southerner ascended to the Presidency. The Conventions accepted the freeing of the Negro people as a political necessity only, and for practical purposes passed the vicious "Black Codes."

Wilson's own state had taken the lead in the enactment of the Codes, and "rifle clubs" had been formed for the restoration of white supremacy. At the moment of the Army's withdrawal from the state terror began as the Ku Klux Klan, riding under the slogan "Campaign for Liberation," began systematically to murder Negroes and white Republicans, with the most violent battles to occur in Mississippi, Louisiana and South Carolina. Richard Wilson had two heroes: Abraham Lincoln and Frederick Douglass, one of the great Abolitionist leaders. In 1883, Douglass declared:

The citizenship granted in the 14th Amendment is literally stamped out in face of government. The old master class is triumphant, and the newly enfranchised class in a condition but little above that in which they were found before the rebellion.[2]

That statement and the year marked an end to the hopes of Richard Wilson—he was then thirty-six-years old.

His few months in battle had taken their toll. He became blind in the right eye, the result of a wound suffered in the war, and chronic rheumatism began to warp his body. When he applied for a veteran's disability pension he discovered that the Navy had no record of his ever having served under the name of Richard Wilson. The shock was traumatic; it was an erasure of the most important part of his life.

Wilson persisted in an investigation until he discovered that during the discharge process a white officer had filled out the papers misspelling his name, making him Richard Vincent.[3] "It was possible that [his] southern accent and his illiteracy made him mispronounce his own name. It was rumored that the white officer had been a Swede and had had a poor knowledge of English. Another rumor had it that the white officer had been a Southerner and had deliberately falsified [his] papers." Whatever may have been the reason for the error, Richard Wilson began a lone crusade for justice which gradually turned into a private and intricate assault on the War Department.

"For decades a long correspondence took place between [Wilson] and the War Department; in letter after letter [he] would recount events and conversations (always dictating these long accounts to others) ; he would name persons long dead, citing their ages and descriptions, reconstructing battles . . . naming towns, rivers, creeks, roads, cities, villages, citing the names and numbers of regiments and companies . . . giving the exact day and the exact hour of the day of certain occurrences, and send it all to the War Department in Washington."[4]

Year after year the old man pursued his lone battle, and as time passed, first the government, then all white people, became synonymous in Richard Wilson's mind with the rebels. And he began to live under a delusion that the war between the states would be resumed. He hated white people so passionately that no one ever heard him speak of them except as "goddamn rebels."

Richard Wilson's wife "was as nearly white as a Negro [could] get without being white, which [meant] that she was white." Margaret Wilson had been a house slave and her maiden name of Bolden had been given to her at birth in Woodville, Mississippi, about 1853, by the white man who owned her. She ". . . came of Irish, Scotch and French stock in which Negro blood had somewhere and somehow been infused." As a young girl, Margaret had been described as handsome, with long black hair parted in the middle above a wide creamy forehead and pulled back in a thick knot on her neck. For true beauty, however, her chin was too long and square and her lips too thin and straight. Hidden by an outward appearance of fragility was a wiry strength. As she grew older, Margaret's mouth became even narrower because she developed a habit of holding her lips clamped into a tight line. Scanty eyebrows added to the severity of her expression. But the few times that she relaxed, her smile was surprising—gentle, wide and innocent.

When angry, she had the peculiar mannerism of her husband of hissing her words. But her hisses came between shouts and at the peak of rage she collapsed into tears. When she prepared for a trip outside her home, her poised, brittle mask was complete as she hooked the thin gold pin into place above a flowing black tie and under her starched collar. She was calm; she was virtuous; she was the Lord's vessel, and thus superior. In the neighborhood or at church, acquaintances were greeted by a faint upturn of the lips meant for a smile; and a nod of the head dismissed or encouraged, depending upon the social class or staunchness of moral conviction in the acquaintance. Sometimes a perverse, secret humor possessed Margaret when she took her grandchildren up Farish Street to its intersection at Capitol, where it bisected the business district racially. She swept in and out of the stores, apparently enjoying the amazed stares of people who saw a white woman holding black children by the hand. A haughty contempt was transmitted in the arch of her neck, the ramrod stiffness of her slender back and quick little footsteps under the sweep of a black bombazine dress.

Within her own home, however, no emotion was masked. Never deliberately cruel, she was given to outbursts of rage. A "crime" might be as simple as a child's speaking when he had not been asked for an opinion; or saying, What? or worse still, Hunh?—instead of the proper Yes, ma'am or No, ma'am. Punishment was not graded in vigor—each blow was equal in force—and the difference was only that for most serious infringements of rules her strength increased with her indignation and the beatings lasted longer. She was convinced that she, personally, was the standard-bearer for God put on earth to discipline the wrongdoer. It was not the meek who would inherit the earth; it was the righteous.

To help support the household, Margaret Wilson boarded local schoolteachers and gave them two sparse meals a day. She was a poor cook and everyone often took bicarbonate of soda. Her favorite dish was composed of ground peanuts held into place with lard and meal and molded into the shape of a roast beef. While it was cooking— usually once a week—no member of the family stayed in the house if he could avoid it. Some of them claimed that the "roast" smelled burned; others were not so moderate—it smelled dead and then burned. While it cooked on a Sunday, lovely odors of pork parts or crisp local catfish wafted toward the Wilson home from the kitchens of their neighbors.

On summer evenings, Mrs. Wilson brought a hard straight chair to the porch and sat erect with her backbone pressed against the seat from hip to shoulder. Even then neither her mind nor her hands rested. Her thin fingers jumped a needle in and out of white fabric and made neat tiny stitches in ruffled curtains for each room in the house. All the while, she argued obscure points of dogma from the Bible, which she knew from memory, beginning at Genesis and ending with Revelation. It was the Old Testament rather than the New that she quoted most often.

As her husband stepped up his assault on Washington Margaret retreated into the primitivism of the Seventh-Day Adventists. She had been raised in the Methodist church but she left it in her late teens for one more suited to her intense temperament. The Adventists claimed to be the one and only true church of God and castigated all other denominations as bearing "the mark of the beast." Only it and its believers would attain everlasting life; everyone else would be annihilated.

During church services Mrs. Wilson permitted herself to nod her head in cadence with the minister's voice and occasionally to sway lightly with the music. Only at such times did the tense nerves in her wrinkled white face open. She lived in an atmosphere that urged her to expect a miracle someday, and she contributed toward that future by maintaining rigid religious discipline in her home. Only Richard Wilson was exempt from his wife's strictures, partly because of his creative engagement in the letters, and still more because his authority was unquestioned.

Religion and war notwithstanding, the Wilsons gave birth to nine children. All but one survived, almost a miracle in the nineteenth century among poor Southerners. The children not only survived but grew to fulfill a small portion of the dreams of their parents. All were educated. And to the Wilsons book learning was almost more important than food. By 1908, the children were grown: Cleo was married and lived in Chicago; Margaret, named for her mother and called "Maggie" by the family, was married to a prosperous saloon-keeper in Arkansas; Charles worked in Mobile; Edward was in Carters and Thomas was a schoolteacher in Hazelhurst. Clark had a talent for design and worked as an independent carpenter and building contractor in Greenwood; Addie, the baby, was in school in Huntsville. Ella, Richard's mother, taught school in Cranfield within ten miles of Natchez.

Richard is born, 1908

II

Ella Wilson, born in 1883, the second-eldest girl and fourth child born to Richard and Margaret, became a country schoolteacher. Though outwardly tractable, Ella possessed an unyielding determination to think her own thoughts and to act upon them. Instead of sitting beside her mother in the evening or entering into long religious discussions, Ella often stood on the porch and leaned against the wall of the house. Usually she just stared up at the sky or into the dark night and watched the kerosene points which flickered from lamps in distant houses. At times she closed her eyes and seemed to be listening to the most ordinary sounds—crickets, or the wind in the grass, or the tree tap-tapping against the house. Mooning, her mother called it, but nothing she said made a difference or changed Ella except for a moment. If Mrs. Wilson spoke tartly and told her to sit down or asked what she was doing, she replied, "Nothing, Mama, just thinking," and obediently seated herself on the edge of the porch.

In every respect Ella differed from her mother. Instead of crying when she was angry, Ella's tears fell down her cheeks when she was happy or when she saw a beautiful sunset. A deceptive, softly sensual façade concealed a temperament so nervous that she appeared to be burning her strength to its limit all the time. Eyelids drooped slightly at the outer corners in resemblance of her mother, but her eyes were large and rounded and she had the thick, arched eyebrows of her father.

No one could say that Ella was not unusually intelligent, but then that was not a quality her mother praised—it could lead too easily to trouble in the South, where a sense of one's place was paramount. Margaret and Richard could maintain an anonymity in the heart of the black community but a schoolteacher might come to the attention of a black overseer principal, or even of a white supervisor. Ella gave no indication that she was fully aware of the intricacies of Southern protocol. In fact, she ignored racism as if it did not exist. All men and nature were part of a whole, she felt, and there should not be so much friction in the world.

Ella taught spelling, arithmetic and geography in a one-room country school, four months a year for twenty-five dollars a month. All of the schools for black children were geared to the growing schedule of cotton. School opened in November, once the crops had been gathered, and closed early in March for the replanting. As a schoolteacher and woman who did not work in the fields, Ella had community status. Less rigidly than her mother but in similar fashion, Ella assumed a proud, reserved carriage and expression outside the home.

At a Methodist church social in Cranfield, Ella met Nathaniel Wright. She had noticed him before because he was so tall and always surrounded by friends, and because he seemed carefree and laughing. On the evening of the social he stayed at her side the entire time, and before she went home he declared that he loved her. Ella was then twenty-four, she had been teaching for several years and was bridling at the narrow confinement in her home. Nathaniel was a romantic figure and, impulsively, all the poeticism in her heart went out to him. They married a month after they met.

Ella's family, particularly her mother, were not pleased with her choice of a husband. Nathaniel was illiterate and a sharecropper. "He's not our kind," they told Ella. Probably the worst blow to Mrs. Wilson was that Ella left the Adventists and joined the Methodist church of her husband. Thoroughly disgusted, she warned her daughter that sinfulness was always punished.

Nathaniel was of Indian, white and African ancestry. His father, Nathaniel, had been a slave and received the name Wright from his owner. Nothing is known of Nathaniel's mother or grandparents except that they had been slaves who had, in some way, mingled with Mississippi's first family, the Choctaw Indians in Neshoba County. Nathaniel was indeed handsome, with high cheekbones inherited from his Indian forebears and a face kept from starkness, softened, by his African heritage. He had a long narrow-bridged nose and deep wide-apart eyes of an unusual light brown with green and yellow flecks in them. Against his reddish-brown skin the lightness of his eyes was startling. When he was not laughing or teasing he sat quiet and observed the world around him and at such times he had an appearance of madness or genius.

The young couple went to live in a sharecropper cabin near the river. It was a gray, weathered shack but it had a floor and Nathaniel put in windows and painted round the doorway and the panes of glass with white. Unlike most of the sharecropper cabins, which opened directly upon a dirt yard, it had three steps which led down from a narrow front porch. Ella continued to teach and also took over the care of a vegetable garden behind the shack. All her life she had dreamed of such days and nights. There was laughter and eating and singing. There was ". . . cooking and sewing and sweeping and the deep dream of sleeping gray skies in winter." During the days when she taught at school and Nathaniel worked in the cotton fields she was sustained by the excitement of seeing her husband in the evening. When there was no school she took his lunch to him in the field and they sat on a spread cotton sack and ate as if it were a picnic day. Nathaniel would not let her help him with the heavy work and after they had eaten she returned to the house and worked in the yard or sewed a new white cotton shirt for her husband. He did not like to wear a blue workshirt—the material was too coarse—and always wore a white shirt under the rough blue overalls which were the uniform of the area. On Sundays they rode to church in a wagon drawn by a mule and Ella ignored, yet secretly enjoyed intercepting, the stares of women at her husband. If he noticed them, he laughed easily and looked at his wife as if it were a secret they shared. Sometimes she believed that there must have been an empty black hole in her heart that Nathaniel had come to fill.

A plantation owner had furnished Nathaniel with land, seeds, tools and a mule, plus the cabin, firewood to be cut from his woods, water from a well in the backyard. In return, Nathaniel had agreed to grow cotton and give half of his yield to the owner, keeping the other half himself. It was a common arrangement in Natchez. Nathaniel and other croppers who worked under the same arrangement called themselves "halfers." Nathaniel knew, if his wife did not, that at the end of the year he would owe the landlord more than he realized on the sale of his half of the cotton. The landlord, of course, kept all the records and since Nathaniel could neither read nor write—he had never even been inside a schoolhouse—each year would see an increase of debt. But the soil was all that Nathaniel knew. When the harvest was ready he went down the rows dragging a long coarse canvas sack slung over his shoulder. He was young, but his back already had a permanent ache because cotton could not be picked on one's knees nor standing straight up. And after the fluffy white stuff was picked he was not finished. Again he followed his mule down the unending turnrows and prepared the ground for the next crop.

A year passed quickly for Ella and Nathaniel and then, one sweltering day, September 4, 1908, a son was born. He was named Richard for his grandfather. The exact hour of his birth is not known: birth certificates for Negroes in Natchez were not recorded until 1911. Both of his parents were happy that their first child was a son. He would not be a farmer, Ella said to herself, with a slight pricking that this was disloyal to her husband. Aloud, Nathaniel said he would have a son to help him someday.

Richard grew into a sturdy, tall boy. He had the unusual eyes of his father, except that his were darker, luminous, with the lids drooped at the corner; he inherited the long upper lip of his grandmother and a strong jaw, but his mouth was fuller and modeled like Greek sculpture. A high forehead ended in an inverted widow's peak which began his hairline, and his mother kept his hair clipped so short that his rounded skull showed through. Sometimes when she watched her son at his most concentrated play, she felt like laughing and crying simultaneously; a puzzled expression was on his face, and if he was distracted, he looked up at her with a wary perceptiveness, as if they were equals instead of mother and baby. At such times Ella grabbed him up and hugged while he stiffened his arms against her and kicked to get down and back to his interrupted games.

Her son was in almost perpetual motion and even nighttime was difficult. When he was tucked into his iron white-painted bed in a corner of the room he frowned and talked and caught hold of his mother's dress to keep her from leaving him. In the night Richard often awakened his parents by calling out or sometimes shrieking; his mother worried about his bad dreams but his father said he would outgrow them.

Sights stirred him to action; he would run for the sheer joy of running and throw himself into the air with open mouth to feel the wind whistle through his lips and then scream, enveloping himself in sheer sound. His mother would hurry from the house and ask: "What is it? What's the matter with you, child?" Silent, he stared at the ground. He was too young to explain that his eyes were filled with the moss-drooping trees, the green grass and his own aliveness bursting to be released. Ella would look at him, and insist through her silence that he answer. Richard would mumble that nothing was wrong . . . he was just playing. As often as she could, Ella stayed in the garden and kept watch on her son. He liked to wander. As soon as she was out of sight he followed a powerful desire for new sights and sounds and colors and headed most often for the river. When he was two years old his mother found him a half mile from home, sitting on a bluff over the Mississippi, immersed in a small island of solitude. Later on, at four or five years, the river still claimed most of his time. By then, he climbed and slid down the cliff until he reached the water's edge. Sticks and grass made good boats; and hurled rocks dashed up small geysers. Often he sat quietly and watched the water; he drowned in its motion—"it was going somewhere." He saw cows sleeping on the levees or eating grass; there was the drip, drip of water from the paddlewheels on the steamboats. He looked across the river to the shores of Louisiana drooping green from the willow trees along the bank.

Never was there such a river, the child thought. After Sunday service came homage to the town's other power as white and black Southerners, joined in their concern, went to the levee to see how high the water had risen. Hernando de Soto named the Mississippi the River of the Holy Ghost and like all viable religions it had its own rituals. Mud flats appeared one day where water flowed deep the day before. Endless sandbars rose to test the piety of the steamboat navigators. And year after year stern waters preyed upon the land, leaving behind layer upon layer of fine black silt, and created a new soil—the richest in the nation. When the church bells warned of a flood the townsfolk worked frenziedly piling sandbag offerings along the levees.

Badness and gladness in almost equal parts composed Richard's first six years. When he was four he burned up his grandmother's house. Granny lay ill, under the constant care of a doctor and nursed by her daughter. Richard and his brother Alan, who had been born two years later, on September 24, 1910, played in the front room. All morning Ella had been scolding Richard, telling him to keep still, warning him that he must make no noise. And he was angry, fretful and impatient. His picture books bored him because he wanted to be outside running and shouting.* "[He] wandered listlessly about the room, trying to think of something to do, resentful of being neglected. The room held nothing of interest except the fire and finally he stood before the shimmering embers, fascinated by the quivering coals. An idea of a new kind of game grew and took root in his mind. Why not throw something into the fire and watch it burn? He looked about. There was only his picture book and his mother would beat him if he burned that. Then what? He hunted around until he saw the broom leaning in a closet. That's it. . . . Who

---

* The following account is made up of quotations from *Black Boy*, confirmed in conversation with Richard Wright.

would bother about a few straws if he burned them? He pulled out the broom and tore out a batch of straws and tossed them into the fire and watched them smoke, turn black, blaze, and finally become white wisps of ghosts that vanished. . . . His brother came to his side, his eyes drawn by the blazing straws.

"Don't do that," he said.

"How come?" Richard asked.

"You'll burn the whole broom," he said.

"You hush," Richard said.

"I'll tell," Alan threatened.

"And I'll hit you," Richard answered.

"An idea was growing, blooming. Now Richard wondered just how the long fluffy white curtains would look if he lit a bunch of straws and held it under them. He pulled several straws from the broom and held them to the fire until they blazed; he rushed to the window and brought the flame in touch with the hems of the curtains. His brother shook his head. "Naw," he said.

"He spoke too late. Red circles were eating into the white cloth; then a flare of flames shot out. Startled, Richard backed away. The fire soared to the ceiling and he trembled with fright. Soon a sheet of yellow lit the room. He was terrified; he wanted to scream but was afraid. He looked around for his brother; he was gone. One half of the room was ablaze. Smoke was choking him and the fire was licking at his face, making him gasp.

"He made for the kitchen; smoke was surging there too. Soon his mother would smell the smoke and see the fire and beat him. He had done something wrong, something which he could not hide or deny. Yes, he would run away and never return. He ran out of the kitchen and into the backyard. Where could he go? Yes, under the house! Nobody would find him there. He crawled under the house and crept into a dark hollow of a brick chimney and balled himself into a tight knot. His mother must not find him and whip him for what he had done. Anyway, it was all an accident; he had not really intended to set the house afire. He had just wanted to see how the curtains would look when they burned. And neither did it occur to him that he was hiding under a burning house.

"Presently footsteps pounded on the floor above Richard. Then he heard screams. Later the gongs of fire wagons and the clopping hoofs of horses came from the direction of the street. He was stiff with terror. The thunder of sound above him shook the chimney to which he clung. The screams came louder. He saw an image of his grandmother lying helplessly upon her bed and there were yellow flames in her black hair. Was his mother afire? Would his brother burn?

Perhaps everybody in the house would burn! Why had he not thought of those things before he fired the curtains? He yearned to become invisible, to stop living. The commotion above him increased and he began to cry. It seemed that he had been hiding for ages, and when the stomping and the screaming died down he felt lonely, cast forever out of life. Voices sounded nearby and he shivered.

"Richard!" his mother called frantically.

"He saw her legs and the hem of her dress move swiftly about the back yard. Her wails were full of an agony whose intensity told Richard that his punishment would be measured by its depth. Then he saw her taut face peering under the edge of the house. She had found him! He held his breath and waited to hear her command him to come to her. Her face went away; no, she had not seen him huddled in the dark nook of the chimney. He tucked his head into his arms and his teeth chattered.

"Richard!" The distress he sensed in her voice was as sharp and painful as the lash of a whip on his flesh. "Richard! The house is on fire. Oh, find my child!"

Richard was determined not to leave his place of safety. Finally he saw another face peering under the edge of the house; it was his father's. His eyes must have become accustomed to the shadows, for he pointed at Richard.

"There he is!"

"Naw!" Richard screamed.

"Come here, boy!"

"Naw!"

"The house is on fire!"

"Leave me 'lone!"

"Nathan crawled to Richard and caught hold of one of his legs. The child hugged the edge of the brick chimney with all of his strength. His father yanked his leg and he clawed the chimney harder.

"Come outta there, you little fool!"

"Turn me loose!"

He could not withstand the tugging at his leg and his fingers relaxed. It was over. He would be beaten. He did not care anymore. He knew what was coming. Nathan dragged him into the back yard and the instant his hand left Richard he jumped to his feet and broke into a wild run, trying to elude the people who surrounded him, heading for the street. He was caught before he had gone ten paces.

No one had died in the fire. Richard's grandfather and an uncle had lifted Granny from her bed and carried her out using the mattress as a stretcher. For a while Richard's absence and long silence had made everyone think that he had perished in the blaze. His cousins, the Hoskins, who lived on Prentiss Street, two blocks away, thought it was something of a joke as long as no one had been injured. "That child! What will he do next?"

Ella grimly stripped the leaves from a tree branch to prepare it for his back. "You almost scared us to death," his mother muttered. He was lashed so long and so hard that he lost consciousness. He was literally beaten out of his senses and later found himself in his bed at home, screaming, . . . tussling with his mother and father who were trying to keep him still. He was lost in a fog of fear. A doctor had to be called—and he ordered that the child should be kept in bed and quiet, that his life depended upon it. A high fever engulfed Richard and packs of ice had to be placed on his forehead. Nightmares of huge wobbly white bags, like the full udders of cows, suspended from the ceiling, made him awaken and scream. He was afraid they would fall and drench him with some horrible liquid. Day and night he begged his parents to take away the bags, pointing at them and shaking with terror because no one saw them but Richard. Several weeks passed before he was well again. All of his life he remembered that his mother had come close to killing him.[1]

Young Richard could be cruel and inordinately sensitive—both at the same time. One day, in Natchez, "something itched on his naked black arm and when he looked he saw a reddish brown ant crawling in frantic haste, its tiny antennae quiveringly trying to find its way in a strange land of flesh. He shook his arm and the ant paused, bewildered. He laughed, touched the ant gently with a finger, brushing it softly from his arm to the ground. He stooped and watched it crawl over the earth in wild fear. Then the ant slowed, feeling at home once more; it picked up a white mote and carted it off on some mysterious errand. . . . He stood and smiled."[2]

Whenever Nathan took Richard fishing and they returned home with their catch he burned with a desire to see them slit open. "Kill them, Mama," he urged his mother. Then he stood on a chair and watched her slit a fish down the side and take out its insides. The first time he saw this happen he was faintly disappointed. "There's no blood," he said.

As Richard neared six years "each event spoke with a cryptic tongue. And the moments of living slowly revealed their coded meanings." There was the wonder he felt when he first saw a brace of mountainlike, spotted, black-and-white horses clopping down a dusty road through clouds of powdered clay.

There was the delight he caught in seeing long straight rows of red and green vegetables stretching away in the sun to the bright horizon.

There was the faint cool kiss of sensuality when dew came on to his cheeks and shins as he ran down the wet green garden paths in the early morning.

There was the vague sense of the infinite as he looked down upon the yellow, dreaming waters of the Mississippi River from the verdant bluffs of Natchez.[2a]

On a day always remembered, Richard's mother told him that they were going on the Mississippi in a boat. They were going all the way to Memphis, Tennessee, and he would sleep overnight on the boat. His eagerness made the remaining time seem endless. Each night he went to bed hoping that they were leaving the next morning.

The day eventually arrived. A neighbor, who had purchased their wagon, took them with their possessions down to the levee. As soon as the wagon stopped at the massive rampart of dirt, Richard climbed out and ran to see the boat. The *Kate Adams* was a tiny, dirty-white boat squatting like a hen in the yellowish-brown water. Richard burst into tears when he saw the side-wheeler. Ella had prepared her imaginative son for a floating palace. When he sobbed and did not want to embark she simply thought he was sad at leaving home.

Nathan led his children down into the engine room of the broad-beamed side-wheeler to watch the powerful boilers. They stayed for several hours and watched the men working, and by the time they climbed back on deck Richard had forgotten his disappointment. All the excitement of the trip returned and Ella had difficulty getting him to sleep. She told him stories about Memphis—a giant city—where they were to live, until finally he fell asleep, cuddled between his parents, with his head in Nathan's lap.

Richard did not know why his parents moved to Memphis. All he remembered was talk of "the eveel boll weevil." The weevil blocked out the sun when it swarmed into Mississippi following a path through the South like an automated machine gone wild as it systematically denuded the land of every leaf. The entire nation was an essentially rural-agricultural society up until 1920. The Southern states were dependent mainly on cotton. And of all Southern states Mississippi was probably the most enslaved by its major crop. Prior to the voracious weevil, Mississippi averaged a crop of approximately 1.5 million bales. After the weevil struck, seven of the next ten crops were below a million bales and one was only 604,000 bales.[3] The economy of the state was disrupted. And, since cotton was grown more for export than for domestic consumption, the crisis in Europe added to the catastrophe in the United States.

On June 28, 1914, the Archduke Ferdinand, heir to the Hapsburg throne, was shot by a Serbian nationalist. A month later, Russia began to mobilize its military forces. These events hardly registered in the minds of Southerners; but on July 31, 1914, the cotton exchanges closed and frightened investors dumped stocks, bonds and commodities. Thousands of bales of cotton that had been sold to Central Europe and Russia could not be shipped and contracts were canceled.[4] Cotton prices fell to five cents a pound from an average of between twenty-five and thirty cents per pound. As a result, a great exodus from the cotton area began and Nathan Wright was one among the thousands who left their homes in 1914. Being a sharecropper, Nathan had nothing to offer but his labor; now there was no product.

Many families went to Northern industrial centers such as Chicago, Detroit and New York. Richard's father took his family to Memphis. Richard did not know why his father stopped at Memphis but he believed that his mother may not have wanted to leave her large, close-knit family in Mississippi, or that they lacked the money to travel any farther. Memphis was then a famous center for the cotton and banking empire and had a reputation as the metropolis of Mississippi, Arkansas and Tennessee. The state also produced textiles, coal, pig iron, copper, marble, lead, clay products and grew wheat, oats, hay, tobacco, peanuts and corn. Nathan may have believed that if he failed to find work in the city he might again work on a farm.

Memphis, Tennessee,
Dread and distrust . . .

III

Quite early in the morning, Richard awoke and stood at the rail of the *Kate Adams* asking questions. How soon would they get to Memphis? How high were the buildings? Would the boat go right up to the city? Where would they live? An expectancy he sensed in his parents wound him to a greater pitch of excitement. From a Natchez bluff the water had seemed to move slowly, with sluggish inevitability. Now, it eddied and whirled alongside the ship.

At last Nathan pointed out Memphis in the distance, and as they approached the first thing Richard saw were shanty boats moored under willow trees at the bank of Mud Island, which rose up right in the center of the harbor. Rafts and other boats, men singing and carrying bundles across swaying tote-planks to the decks of flat rafts met his eyes. Front Street was crowded and bustled with people. Huge drays drawn by heavy-footed horses or sinewy mules, four and six to a team, were lined up along the street, and sweet-smelling woodsmoke from steamboats fled with the wind, first toward the buildings and then out across the water.

Carrying their bundles, the Wrights walked up Beale Street, which rose out of the Mississippi River and ran a mile straight through the busy center of Memphis. Richard was awed and happy but as they continued the long walk toward East Street, in the Negro section, he began to feel frightened. From his mother's description he had envisioned the city as a fairyland with tall buildings similar to trees and beauty everywhere. Unconsciously appended to his mother's stories had been his own experiences of green or black fields, animals and birds in the pine woods, and the bald cypress dangling strands of moss. Square, squat, stone and dilapidated wooden buildings fenced him all around and noxious odors came from alleyways. He drew close to his mother's side and clutched her skirt. Only after he noticed that his brother was holding to the other side did he drop his hand. He was not a baby. On they walked, past vendors in front of their stores with racks of clothing, or piled vegetables, or junk, who called out as they passed. Concrete and gravel hurt his feet. And each step they took led him deeper into squalor. Long rows of shacks and shambling outhouses packed close alongside the street closed him in.

In 1914, the eastern part of Memphis was ugly. White landlords had built houses in swamps, over bayous, in the most unhealthy part of the city. The rampancy of tuberculosis and other diseases was such that six years before the Wrights arrived newspapers had advised white people not to hire Negroes as household servants. The death rate among whites was low in 1914; among blacks it was very high.

Garbage lay in the streets and crawled with maggots. There was gambling, narcotics addiction, prostitution, drunkenness and an air of hopelessness. Memphis shared a reputation with Chicago and New York as being one of the most violent cities in the nation.

Thousands of black men, women and children came to the city each year hoping to find work. Salaries for both skilled and unskilled work were higher than what they had known, but the cost of living was higher. A few middle-class Negro families lived in Klondyke, the northeast section. These were for the most part physicians and dentists trained at Meharry Medical College, one or two lawyers, a few teachers. Skilled black men worked in candy factories, broom factories, lumberyards and slaughterhouses.

Near East Street the Wrights stopped in the New Era Pharmacy and Nathan inquired about vacant apartments. They were directed to a brick tenement building just off Beale Street. Honky-tonks and saloons were everywhere. Doors sagged open crazily on bent and broken hinges and revealed littered interiors. The stone building where Nathan rented a kitchen and bedroom apartment looked bleak and hostile to his son. Two rusty metal beds took up most of the space in the small bedroom in which all four would sleep. In the kitchen the whole family would eat, live and play. The cabin in Natchez had been small but there had been acres of land and sweet-smelling air; every breeze in Memphis wafted in the scent of sulphur and garbage. Small paved squares in front and in back of the one-story tenement would be the only play areas for the children.

Nathan found work as a night porter in a drugstore on Beale Street and "in what seemed a matter of weeks" underwent a total change of personality. In Natchez, even when he had staggered with weariness, Nathan had customarily greeted Richard by lifting him high in the air, over his head. "How's my boy!" his father hailed him. Night work and the city killed his joy in life, destroyed his love and loyalty and erased a sense of tradition drawn from working his own land, among friends from childhood, in his own town.

On the farm, space had given an outlet to diverse personalities. Now, confined within what amounted to a room and a half, each need or idiosyncrasy impinged upon another. Nathan grew exhausted and shouted at Ella to keep the children quiet. Their mother's most frequent words became, "Hush! Stop that noise! You daddy is sleeping!" When Nathan began to drink beer on Sunday, his day off from work, and refused to attend church with Ella and the children, Richard sensed his mother's disapproval and growing hostility. Gradually fear and desperation seeped into the child. In self-defense he grew defiant of his father.

One morning Richard and Alan were playing in the rear of the building when a stray kitten, mewing loudly, wandered in from the alleyway. His father, clad in underwear, stumbled sleepily to the back door and demanded quiet. Richard answered that they were not making noise, it was the kitten. Nathan shouted, "Scat!" several times but the kitten lingered and meowed plaintively. At last Nathan shouted: "Kill that damn thing! . . . Do anything, but get it away from here!"

When Nathan went back in the house Richard thought of how he could get back at his father for always shouting at him. He took a piece of rope, made a noose and slipped it over the kitten's head. Then he "pulled it over a nail, then jerked the animal clear of the ground. It gasped, slobbered, spun, doubled, clawed the air frantically; finally its mouth gaped and its pink-white tongue shot out stiffly."

Richard felt triumphant; he had taken his father's words literally and believed that Nathan could not punish him without risking his authority. When Ella saw the kitten's body she paled: "What in God's name have you done?" she asked. This time his mother did not beat him. Instead, all afternoon she talked to him about invisible demons who would exact vengeance for his cruel deed. When it grew dark Ella gave Richard an order that paralyzed him: "Get out there and bury that poor kitten." When he screamed that he was afraid she asked: "And wasn't that kitten scared when you put that rope around its neck?" Richard said that he was doing what his father had ordered and Ella slapped him across the mouth with the palm of her hand. She knew that her son was aware of his lie.

Ella forced Richard out into the night alone, and stood just out of his sight so that her words floated toward him from the menacing darkness. After the kitten was buried she forced him to kneel and pray for forgiveness. Richard's vivid imagination dredged up an image of himself gasping for breath like the kitten and he could not repeat the end of the prayer. His mother's lesson blotted out his triumph over his father.

Nathan deserted his family and went to live with a woman he had met in a saloon. For the first few days after his disappearance Richard paid little attention. By this time, an absent father meant freedom to play and shout and he was glad. But after a week passed there was no food to eat, and when Richard said he was hungry his mother gave him tea sweetened with a little molasses. Richard began to suffer from acute hunger pains and pleaded constantly for food. One day when her son had been especially persistent to know why he could not eat Ella asked: "Where's your father?"

"I don't know," Richard said.

"Who brings food into the house?"

"Papa," Richard said. "He always brought food."

"Well, your father isn't here now," Ella said.

"As the days slid past the image of [his] father became associated with [his] pangs of hunger, and whenever [he] felt hunger [he] thought of him with a deep biological bitterness."

Ella went to work as a cook and left Richard and his brother alone in the flat each day with a loaf of bread and a pot of tea. "When she returned at evening she would be tired and dispirited and would cry a lot. Sometimes, when she was in despair, she would call us to her and talk to us for hours, telling us that we now had no father, that our lives would be different from those of other children, that we must learn as soon as possible to take care of ourselves, to dress ourselves, to prepare our own food; that we must take upon ourselves the responsibility of the flat while she worked. Half frightened, we would promise solemnly."

Richard did not know why his mother worked as a cook and not a schoolteacher. It may have been because the few middle-class professional Negroes in Memphis had been educated at Meharry, Howard or the University of West Tennessee. Ella had a more rudimentary education and in addition lived in the slums. Her environment of poverty did not permit any meeting with the population that lived across the town in Klondyke. At a later time she found another job, as a cleaning woman in a doctor's office. So it would appear that in a sharecropper milieu in Natchez her education was sufficient but not in a city the size and sophistication of Memphis.

Gradually, Richard's mother changed. When he misbehaved she

made him stand silent before her for a few minutes before administering punishment. This was intended to force Richard to judge himself—he knew when he was "bad," she insisted. It had an opposite effect to that she desired: Richard grew angry and restive. He believed it was because her silence made him feel guilty and when that happened all he wanted was to run away.

As she became more unhappy she turned toward the church and became ardently religious. Yet, religion was not answer enough. Ella grew more frustrated than ever and struck out at Richard, beating him for the slightest deviation of rules that became ever more strict.[1]

A constant source of friction between them was Ella's attitude toward neighbors in the community and her attempts to keep Richard from playing with their children. "Son," she told him, "they are your color, but they aren't your kind." His mother was called a snob, and a ". . . high-toned bitch." Although Ella inhibited her son, among his playmates he was free, lively and somewhat spoiled, because he could usually get his way with guile or a wide smile. Sometimes Ella took Richard to work with her and stood him in a corner of the kitchen while she cooked. That did not work out very well because he was too hungry and Ella had been told that she was not to feed her child anything but leftover scraps from dinner plates. Richard could not understand why some people could eat and he could not. And Ella could not bear to watch his suffering.

In Memphis Richard continued his habit of wandering and exploring and became fascinated by a saloon on Beale Street. It had a dim, alcoholic smell, and the shouts of laughter were intriguing. From staggering drunks he could beg pennies or tease them into chasing him. Vomiting drunks were horrifying and yet he could not keep from watching them when they clutched their stomachs or lay facedown, retching. A tall black man caught him peeping under the swinging door one day, and dragged him into the saloon. Everybody gave him sips of liquor and taught him to shout obscene words. It was a great game. Richard loved the attention he got and the nickels handed to him by one or two men.

Many nights Ella searched for him when she came home from work and found him dazed and wandering or shouting obscene words at women he passed. She beat him, prayed over him, cried—but nothing could keep him from going to the saloon as soon as she left the house for work. Ultimately, a woman nearby promised to watch Richard and keep him in the house. But it was many months before the craving for alcohol left him.

In 1915, Richard learned to read. He had not yet attended a day of school because his clothing was ragged. Ella was ashamed to send him in such a condition, and did not even send him to Sunday school during that time. He had grown taller during the year and his skinny arms and legs stuck out of the poor but clean clothing in a comic fashion. Ella's earnings barely paid for rent and a little food and coal and rarely lasted through an entire week. When they used up their meager supply of coal she took one child to work with her and left the other at home in bed to keep warm and to pay the delivery man when he came with more coal. One day when the man arrived and saw Richard shivering in bed he felt sorry for the child and stayed to build a fire. When he discovered that Richard could not count he sat with him until he had taught him to memorize from one to a hundred. All afternoon Richard counted the numbers over and over, afraid that he would forget, and when Ella came home he demonstrated his new accomplishment before she had time to remove her coat. His mother was amazed and proud; it was the first pleasurable moment she had had for almost a year. She began to teach Richard to read. Every Sunday he would read the words aloud from the newspaper as she listened and corrected and approved. Books left lying on the sidewalk while children played in the street became Richard's new passion. Reading became even more of an obsession than alcohol had been, and day after day he sat at the edge of the street puzzling out the strange marks upon paper and looking at the pictures.

By January, 1916, Richard could read and he entered Howard Institute, a local grammar school. One of his mother's sisters had sent clothing for the children, knickers made of wool, black stockings, and new high-button black shoes. Ella had made new white middy shirts—which Richard hated, but had to wear. Some of the neighborhood boys took him to school the first day. The children in his class were a year younger but when he was asked to recite he was paralyzed by fear even though he knew the lesson. During recess he attached himself to the older boys and learned all the four-letter words describing sexual functions and discovered that he had known them before, in the saloon. When school let out that day, he raced home "with a brain burdened with racy and daring knowledge, but not a single idea from books. [He] gobbled [his] cold food that had been left covered on the table, seized a piece of soap and rushed into the streets. . . ." He was eager to display all that he had learned in school that morning. Richard went from window to window on Beale Street, printing in huge block letters his newly acquired four-letter words. That night a neighbor visited his mother and told her what Richard had done. Before she allowed him to go to sleep Ella made him take a bucket of water and a towel and scrub the words from every window. Never again did he write such words on windows.

Just when Richard had settled into school, in January, his mother became ill and had to stay in bed. He stayed home from school to look after her and learned to cook "mush" with lard topping and tea, which formed the basis of their diet. While Ella was ill the family for whom she worked hired another cook and when she was strong enough to leave her bed, she could not immediately find a job. Ella forced herself to make the rounds of the charitable institutions in Memphis but was not able to get help.

Then a morning came when Ella, half-sick and desperate, visited Settlement Home, an orphanage supported by the C.M.E. Church, south of Memphis. She spoke to ". . . a tall, gaunt, mulatto woman who called herself Miss Simon," who agreed to take charge of Richard and his brother provided Mrs. Wright worked and made small payments.

"The orphan home was a two-story frame building set amid trees in a wide, green field." When Miss Simon saw Richard she took an immediate fancy to him while he, in turn, was afraid of her the moment he saw her. The institution was like a prison and Miss Simon was the jailer. Added to a personality corrupted by absolute control over the children was a frustrated sexuality. Her first maneuver was to get rid of Mrs. Wright; and she forbade her visits to the children with the excuse that they were being spoiled by so much attention. After that she tried to win Richard's confidence. Night after night she would take him to her apartment on the second floor and talk to him. Would he like to be adopted by her if his mother gave consent? Then he could live with her; they would live together always. But her words only frightened Richard still more. Then she informed him that he would help her in the office each day and they would have lunch together. The job she had manufactured for Richard was to blot each envelope as she finished writing an address and she made him stand close beside her. There was a wart on her chin with threads of stiff black hair bristling out, which Richard kept watching in horror. A fetid odor wafted toward his face when she said: "Take the blotter." The child tried to reach for it but succeeded only in twitching his arm until Miss Simon thrust it into his hand. Finally, he began to cry and twisted away when the repulsive woman reached her hand to his face. In angry defeat, she drove him from the room.

"The house was crowded with children and there was always a storm of noise. The daily routine was blurred to [him] and [he] never quite grasped it." Hunger and fear were dominant. The meals consisted of some cooked cornmeal with lard, or greens prepared with lard, served twice a day. At bedtime, in place of supper, the children received one slice of bread smeared with molasses. "The children were silent, hostile, vindictive. . . . There was an over-all atmosphere of nervousness and intrigue, of children telling tales upon others, of children being deprived of food to punish them.

"The home did not have the money to check the growth of the wide stretches of grass by having it mown, so it had to be pulled by hand. Each morning after [they] had eaten a breakfast that seemed like no breakfast at all, an older child would lead a herd [of orphans] to the vast lawn and [they] would get to [their] knees and wrench the grass loose from the dirt with [their] fingers. At intervals Miss Simon would make a tour of inspection, examining the pile of pulled grass beside each child, scolding or praising according to the size of the pile." Many times Richard was so weak from hunger that he grew dizzy and fainted—when he came to his senses he thought he had been dreaming.

Once during the six weeks Richard ran away but was returned to the home by a policeman and beaten sadistically by Miss Simon. He began to distrust everything and everybody. His mother, like his father, had disappeared into the unknown. And the feeling of abandonment grew:

Dread and distrust had already become a daily part of my being and my memory grew sharp, my senses more impressionable; I began to be aware of myself as a distinct personality striving against others. I held myself in, afraid to act or speak until I was sure of my surroundings, feeling most of the time that I was suspended over a void.[2]

A great, happy day arrived which was not unlike awakening in a familiar bed after a nightmare. Ella arrived one afternoon with the news that they were going to live with her sister in Elaine, Arkansas, and en route they would visit Granny, who had moved from Natchez to Jackson, Mississippi. Their aunt had sent money for the trip. Trembling with excitement, Richard ran about gathering his ragged clothes. "[He] was leaving the hated home, hunger, fear, leaving days that had been as dark and lonely as death."

IV

Granny lived in the heart of the black community, six or seven miles from where Farish Street crossed Capitol, in Jackson. Clay Wilson, Richard's uncle, purchased the home at 1107 Lynch Street for his parents in about 1915. Lynch was unpaved, but then few streets were built of anything but gravel, or occasionally vitrified brick, at that time in the capital city of Mississippi.

Clipped grass grew to the very edge of the road and protected Granny's house from the dust of the unpaved street, and green fields to each side coaxed a sometime-breeze to cool off the porches at night. Birds sang, chirped and cawed in fragrant pines or jumped and pecked the blossoms of the magnolia trees. It was a two-story, white-painted frame structure of seven rooms, but it gave a thin, somewhat up-thrusting aspect under a barely slanted roof which clamped its soaring like a lid.

Behind the house the rich black soil was weathered smooth and blotched with scrubby grass and leaf mold under the trees. Two long straight rows of vegetables stretched over half the yard and a large locust sweetened the air at the back, hidden slightly from the house by smaller trees of peach and sweetgum and chinaberry. Inside the house were long narrow hallways, a curving staircase with round columns and banisters, and dark polished floors beneath white-plastered ceilings and walls. Richard was enchanted.

The days and hours began to speak now with a clearer tongue. Each experience had a sharp meaning of its own.

34

There was the breathlessly anxious fun of chasing and catching flitting fireflies on drowsy summer nights.

There was the drenching hospitality in the pervading smell of sweet magnolias.

There was the aura of limitless freedom distilled from the rolling sweep of tall green grass swaying and glinting in the wind and sun.

There was the drugged sleepy feeling that came from sipping glasses of milk, drinking them slowly so that they would last a long time, and drinking enough for the first time in my life.[1]

And there was intoxication when the first words of fiction fell upon his wide-open ears. Granny was boarding a young schoolteacher —named Ella like his mother—of a singularly dreamy and remote manner. Richard was attracted to the girl and intimidated by her at the same time because she was always silently reading. One afternoon he found her sitting on the front porch, with a book in her hands, as usual. Curiosity and desire overcame Richard's timidity and he begged, ". . . please tell me what you are reading." Ella looked toward the front door of the house apprehensively—Granny believed that all books except the Bible were works of the Devil—and said: "Your grandmother wouldn't like it if I talked to you about novels." But the intent eight-year-old child persisted until Ella closed the book and began to whisper the story of "Bluebeard and His Seven Wives." At her first words he ceased to see the porch, the sunshine, her face. Everything fell away; he was left with a new world "peopled with magical presences." Imagination blazed, "enchanted and enthralled, [he] stopped her constantly to ask for details. . . . The sensations the story aroused . . . were never to leave [him]."

Just at the most exciting part of the story, when Richard's interest was at a height, his grandmother stepped harshly onto the porch. "You stop that, you evil gal!" she shouted. "I want none of that Devil stuff in my house!" Richard protested that he had not heard the end of the story and Granny bared her teeth and slapped him across the mouth with the back of her hand. "But I want to hear what happened!" he wailed and dodged another swooping blow.

Not to know the end of the story filled him with a sense of loss and incompletion. He vowed that as soon as he was old enough he would buy all the novels there were: "So profoundly responsive a chord had the tale struck in me that the threats of my mother and grandmother had no effect whatsoever. They read my insistence as mere obstinacy, as foolishness, something that would quickly pass; and they had no notion how desperately serious the tale had made me. . . . No words or punishment could have possibly made me doubt. I had tasted what to me was life, and I would have more of it, somehow, someway." Whenever his grandmother was not on the second floor of the house, Richard sneaked into Ella's room and stole one of her books. Actually, he only borrowed it for a day or two and took it behind the barn, where he laboriously deciphered words—usually too few to make any meaning out of the story. Granny drove Ella from the house and claimed that she had taught her grandson evil things he should never know.

Then one day they were at the train station with their bags, waiting for the train to Elaine, Arkansas; and for the first time Richard noticed two lines of people at the ticket booths. One was a "white" line, the other a "black" line. After they boarded the trains Richard watched the door and stuck his head out the window to see what was happening. It was a curious affair, mysterious and intriguing. Soon he saw that white people went into a different section of the train and asked Ella if he could go and peep at them. "You keep quiet," his mother answered. How could Richard keep quiet about something so odd? He merely subsided until the train left the station and then began to question his mother: "Mama, is Granny white? Do white people think she is white? Granny looks white. Why does she live with us colored folks? Did Granny become colored when she married Grandpa? Why didn't Granny marry a white man?" Grudgingly, she answered some of his questions in a matter-of-fact, offhand way. "What will I be when I grow up?" he finally asked his mother. Ella mocked him: "They'll call you a colored man when you grow up. . . . Do you mind, Mr. Wright?" No, he did not mind, but he was angered by his mother's teasing. There was a vague uneasiness about it all, but when he was big he would handle it when he came to it.

When they arrived in Elaine, Richard saw a wooden bungalow weathered silvery gray, with a fence around it; it looked like home and he was glad. Aunt Maggie was his favorite relative; she had been present at his birth and always sent presents and money whenever she could. Maggie, born in 1886, was three years younger than Ella and among the eight Wilson children these two were the most intimate. Maggie, the daredevil, was tied to Ella, who was more conservative, and she, in turn, was happiest and most herself in her aggressive sister's presence.

But Maggie's power was camouflaged by a kind of voluptuous, sinuous grace. Her movements were quick, yet smooth, and she had her father's long, angular face. Childless all her life, Maggie claimed

Richard as her own. He was her son, too—look at his curved eyebrows and the beautiful mouth—they were hers; Ella had a thin, narrow mouth, "just like Mama."

Maggie's husband, Fred Hoskins, owned a saloon that catered to the hundreds of Negroes who worked in the surrounding sawmills. Hoskins' broad, handsome face was somewhat flat in contour, with observant eyes half covered most times by sleepy-looking eyelids. Fred was devoted to Maggie, who was his second wife, and Richard watched covertly the affectionate teasing between them; he had not seen demonstrable love between adults since his father had gone away.

At mealtimes Maggie's table was loaded with food. Yet even after eating until his stomach hurt, Richard was apprehensive. There might not be anything for the next day so he secreted some biscuits in one of his pockets. When, in washing his clothing, Mrs. Wright discovered gummy wads of bread in his pockets she scolded him and threatened whippings to break his habit. Her admonishments only drove her son to secrecy. Richard found different hiding places. There were biscuits and bread hoarded all over the house—behind dressers, under a tabletop in the space left for extra leaves and in a corner under a loose floorboard. It was many weeks before his faith that food would appear at each meal was established.

Every evening Uncle Hoskins tended his saloon, returning home early the following morning. And during the day, while he slept, a revolver lay near his head—white men who coveted his thriving saloon had offered him a price far below the value of the business and he had refused to sell. They then had threatened to kill him.

One morning [Richard] awakened to learn that Uncle Hoskins had not come home from the saloon. Aunt Maggie fretted and worried. She wanted to visit the saloon and find out what had happened, but Uncle Hoskins had forbidden her to come to the place. The day wore on and dinnertime came.

"I'm going to find out if anything's happened," Aunt Maggie said.

"Maybe you oughtn't," [Ella] said. "Maybe it's dangerous."

The food was kept hot on the stove and Aunt Maggie stood on the front porch staring into the deepening dusk. Again she declared that she was going to the saloon, but [her sister] dissuaded her once more. It grew dark and still he had not come. Aunt Maggie was silent and restless.

"I hope to God the white people didn't bother him," she said.

Later she went into the bedroom and when she came out she whimpered:

"He didn't take his gun. I wonder what could have happened?"

[They] ate in silence. An hour later there was the sound of heavy footsteps on the front porch and a loud knock came. Aunt Maggie ran to the door and flung it open. A tall black boy stood sweating, panting, and shaking his head. He pulled off his cap.

" 'Mr. Hoskins . . . he done been shot. Done been shot by a white man," the boy gasped. "Mrs. Hoskins, he dead.' "

Aunt Maggie screamed and rushed off the porch and down the dusty road into the night.

"Maggie!" [Ella] screamed.

"Don't you-all go to that saloon," the boy called.

"Maggie!" [Ella] called, running after Aunt Maggie.

"They'll kill you if you go there!" the boy yelled. "White folks say they'll kill all his kinfolks!"

[Ella] pulled Aunt Maggie back to the house. Fear drowned out grief and that night [they] packed clothes and dishes and loaded them into a farmer's wagon. Before dawn [they] were rolling away, fleeing for [their] lives.

Richard's mind reeled in terror: "Why had we not fought back?" he asked his mother and "the fear that was in her made her slap [him] into silence."

"There was no funeral. There was no music. There was no period of mourning. There were no flowers. There were only silence, quiet weeping, whispers, and fear." Richard never learned where his uncle was buried; his aunt was not allowed to claim the body nor any of his assets.

"Uncle Hoskins had simply been plucked from our midst and we, figuratively, had fallen on our faces to avoid looking into that white-hot face of terror that we knew loomed somewhere above us."[2]

Two years later, in 1918, Elaine sharecroppers organized a society and asked plantation owners for an itemized accounting of their indebtedness and refused to allow their cotton to be moved or sold unless they knew the price. Plantation owners declared that a state of insurrection existed and, aided by wagonloads of people from all over Arkansas and part of Mississippi, systematically shot down men, women and children—in their church, in the streets and even in the cotton fields.[3]

Ella and Maggie took a room in West Helena and huddled inside, day and night, with the shades drawn. They were afraid to be seen on the streets so Richard was sent out for food. But, except for these shopping trips, he, too, stayed in the darkened room. Gone was any desire to run or play; dread made his legs feel weak as he silently listened to his aunt and mother whispering and crying. A paralysis of fear gripped his mind: if his mother and aunt could not protect him from that unknown force named "white," then who could? He was lost.

"Finally Aunt Maggie defied her fear and made frequent trips back to Elaine, but she went in secret and at night and would tell no one save [Ella] when she was going." Both women remained in a state of shock for several weeks and lost confidence in themselves. They had no money, husbands, relatives or friends, they were afraid to look for work so, after much discussion and hesitation, they decided to return home to Jackson. There they could rest and reorganize their lives.

Three or four months in their mother's house were long enough to make the sisters restive. Granny's strict religious routine—the daily family prayers and long Bible readings, the Adventists' dietary limitations—made Ella and Maggie yearn for a home of their own again; and they packed and moved back to West Helena. They rented one half of a double corner house in front of which ran a sewage ditch. "The neighborhood swarmed with rats, cats, dogs, fortune-tellers, cripples, blind men, whores, salesmen, rent collectors and children." Across the street from the flat was a roundhouse, where locomotives were repaired. "There was an eternal hissing of steam, the deep grunting of steel engines, and the tolling of bells. Smoke obscured the vision and cinders drifted into the house, into . . . beds, into [their] kitchen, into [their] food; and a tarlike smell was always in the air." Richard loved it. As soon as his mother and aunt left for their cooking jobs each morning he ran over to the roundhouse:

. . . yes there's that roundhouse Mama don't want me to go down there he shot a glance over his shoulder for she'd told him a thousand times to stay away from those trains for he'd get hurt but I'm a man he told himself as he rounded a bend in the road and saw the giant shed where black beautiful locomotives stood Lawd there was a big brand new one oh Jesus he'd like to drive it he looked around nobody was in sight he grasped hold of the steel bar and hoisted himself up into the cab gee whiz levers wheels handles he timidly caught hold of a jutting bar and pulled it and the locomotive began to throb and move slowly at first and then with increasing speed as it plunged forward bumpbump bumpbump bumpbump and he looked out the window seeing a solid wall of black telephone poles flying past and the sky had red sparks for stars and the locomotive rocked left right up down with mighty explosions of breath. . . .[4]

Richard's imagination took him on long trips when he sat in the cab of a locomotive after eluding the train guards. At other times he pretended the stagnant ditch of water in front of the house was the Mississippi and sailed cigar-box boats or waded in the stream, stepping over an occasional dead cat or dog and bits of broken bottles. He was nine years old, still not in school; but he had learned to leave old places without regret and to accept new ones for what they looked like. He could read and count and that was about as much as most of the people in his environment could do, grownups or children. And slowly, he was gaining a fearsome knowledge of reality.

Something had been happening in the house of which Richard— for once—was not aware; Maggie had a new friend, a Professor Matthews, who visited every evening after the children had gone to sleep. Matthews was an austere, tall man with thin lips and eyelids that never seemed to blink. He wore dark suits, shirts with high, stiff, snow-white collars and cuffs, and rimless octagonal-shaped glasses. One Sunday morning Matthews paid a daytime visit and was introduced to Richard as the man who would be his new uncle. Apparently Matthews sensed Richard's distrust so he gave him a dime and then knelt and said prayers for the "fatherless young man." Aunt Maggie said that she was going north, to Detroit, to live when they married and Richard was sad because he did not want to lose his second mother. But the professor cheered him up by leaving presents on the kitchen table when he visited Maggie at night.

A few weeks passed and Matthews began to visit the home during the daytime, but each time he came all the shades were drawn and the children were not allowed outside until he left. One night Richard heard his aunt crying and climbed out of bed and went to the front room and peered around the jamb of the door; ". . . there was 'uncle' sitting on the floor by the window, peering into the night from under the lifted curtain." Maggie and Ella were hurriedly packing a trunk. Richard was terrified. "Was my mother leaving? Why was Aunt Maggie crying? Were the white people coming after us?" "Mama!" Richard cried and darted into the room. Matthews leaped to his feet and whirled on Richard with a gun in his hand. Ella caught her son in her arms and put her hand over his mouth to keep him quiet. She held his arms so tightly that he stopped crying because of the pain. Ella put him back to bed and he lay in the dark listening fearfully to all the strange noises. Maggie came into his room and kissed him good-bye and whispered through sobs that he was to be a good boy and not to forget his aunt, who loved him. Then she was gone.

Richard later learned that Professor Matthews had been "keeping company" with a well-to-do white woman in West Helena for several years before he met Maggie. When he tried to break off his previous relationship the woman threatened to say that he had raped her. To avoid possible lynching he had to leave town quickly. He stole some money from the woman, hit her over the head, knocking her unconscious, and then set fire to the house, hoping to destroy the evidence of his assault.[5]

A few days after Maggie left, a white sheriff came to the house and questioned Ella for a long time but made no attempt to search the house or question Richard. "A dread of white people now came to live permanently in [his] feelings and imagination. . . . Nothing challenged the totality of [his] personality so much as this pressure of hate and threat that stemmed from the invisible whites."

With Maggie gone, Ella could not earn enough money to feed her children, and Richard's stomach was so consistently empty that it gave him headaches almost every day. After months of near-starvation Ella luckily found work in a doctor's office for five dollars a week. At once she announced that the children were to go to school. Ella bought pants and new shoes for Richard and once again he entered a classroom, happy yet paralyzed by shy embarrassment. During recess he attached himself to a group of older boys and listened to their conversation. His admittance into their company was gained by the degree of his hate for white folks. "None of this was premeditated, but sprang spontaneously out of the talk of black boys who met at the crossroads."

It was degrading to play with girls and in our talk we relegated them to a remote island of life. We had somehow caught the spirit of the role of our sex and we flocked together for common moral schooling. We spoke boastfully in bass voices; we used the word "nigger" to prove the tough fiber of our feelings; we spouted excessive profanity as a sign of our coming manhood; we pretended callousness toward the injunctions of our parents; and we strove to convince one another that our decisions stemmed from ourselves and ourselves alone. Yet we frantically concealed how dependent we were upon one another.[6]

Often the talk turned to the First World War, which was then being fought: " 'Them white folks sure scared of us, though.' . . . 'Yeah, they send you to war, make you lick them Germans, teach you how to fight and when you come back they scared of you, want to kill you.' . . . And the talk would weave, roll, surge, spurt, veer, swell, having no specific aim or direction, touching vast areas of life, expressing the tentative impulses of childhood. Money, God, race, sex, color, war, planes, machines, trains, swimming, boxing, anything. . . . The culture of one black household was thus transmitted to another black household, and folk tradition was handed from group to group."

Behind the house in which the Wrights were living, near the railroad terminus, was a skimpy yard paved by black cinders. The only touch of green Richard could see was beyond the tracks, where the white neighborhood began. His side of town was called "the wrong side of the tracks." But cinders were good weapons: "You could always have a nice hot war with huge black cinders. All you had to do was crouch behind the brick pillars of a house with your hands full of gritty ammunition. And the first woolly black head you saw pop out from behind another row of pillars was your target. You tried your best to knock it off. It was great fun."

During one fight Richard and his friends engaged in a "war" with white boys who lived beyond the tracks. It was his belief that cinder weapons were invincible, but the white boys retaliated with a bombardment of broken bottles. They had the advantage over Richard's gang because they hid behind trees, bushes and hedges on their lawns. When the black children retreated to the narrow pillars of their homes there was little protection, and a broken milk bottle caught Richard behind the ear and opened a deep gash which needed three stitches to close. In the evening when Ella returned from work she examined his wound and then slapped him. When she learned that he had been fighting white boys she stripped him naked and beat him with a barrel stave. While she hit him she lectured between blows ". . . gems of Jim Crow wisdom." He was never, never to fight white folks again; they were right in clouting him with a bottle; she worked hard every day to make enough money to take care of him. When was he going to learn to be a good boy? She couldn't be bothered with his fights. All that night Richard had nightmares of monstrous white faces looming over him suspended from the ceiling. From that day on the ". . . green trees, the trimmed hedges, the cropped lawns grew very meaningful . . . became a symbol." Years later when he thought of white people, the hard, sharp outlines of white houses surrounded by trees, lawns and hedges were present somewhere in the background of his mind. "Through the years they grew into an overreaching symbol of fear."

In November, 1918, two months after his tenth birthday, Richard was sitting in school one day when he heard whistles blowing and bells ringing. All of the children rushed to the windows and the teacher left the room. When she returned she announced:

"Everybody, pack your things and go home!"

"Why?"

"The war is over," the teacher said.

Richard went into the street and for a minute was frightened. "White and black people were laughing and singing and shouting." A soldiers' band played music and there was singing and dancing in the street. Everyone talked about the "Fighting Black Devils," the Negro soldiers who had broken through the Hindenburg line.

But in a few months the holiday spirit ended. Richard saw headlines in the newspapers telling of lynchings of returning Negro soldiers, most of whom were still in uniform. At night before going to sleep he lay awake and wondered how to get even with the South. Whenever he caught sight of a group of people talking together he sidled quietly up to its fringe and listened to the talk about race. Though he never personally witnessed any physical attacks against black men or women, he ". . . had already grown to feel that there existed men against whom I was powerless, men who could violate my life at will." And because his environment was bleak and bare he lived through his imagination: no one would kill him. He would kill as many whites as he could if he were attacked.

These fantasies were no longer a reflection of my reaction to the white people, they were a part of my living, of my emotional life; they were a culture, a creed, a religion. The hostility of the whites had become so deeply implanted in my mind and feelings that it had lost direct connection with the daily environment in which I lived; and my reactions to this hostility fed upon itself, grew or diminished according to the news that reached me about the whites, according to what I aspired or hoped for. Tension would set in at the mere mention of whites and a vast complex of emotions, involving the whole of my personality, would be aroused. It was as though I was continuously reacting to the threat of some natural force whose hostile behavior could not be predicted . . . as though I had been the victim of a thousand lynchings.[7]

V

Ella aged before her time. Each day her face seemed more sunken and the skin loosed its hold on her square jaw and sagged like a double chin into her neck. Lines developed between her nose and mouth and down into her chin. Whenever she looked at Richard tears began to form in her eyes and she kneeled for longer intervals, praying that God would give her strength to raise her boys. Some days she could not drag herself to her job and lay huddled in bed weeping and talking to Richard about her mother's house. "Already there had crept into her speech a halting, lisping quality that, though [he] did not know it, was the shadow of her future, [he] was more conscious of [his] mother now than [he] had ever been and [he] was already able to feel what being completely without her would mean. . . . Then real fear came as her illness recurred at shorter intervals. Time stood still." Richard waited, hungry and anxious.

One morning the shouting voice of his brother awakened him; Ella was very sick. Richard went into her room and found her lying on her back on the bed fully dressed. She had tried to go to work and had fallen back in a paralytic stroke. Richard thought she was dead and was afraid to touch her. Finally he went to Ella and shook her arm; she moved slightly and groaned, but did not speak. Utter fright engulfed him and he ran into the hall and hammered at a neighbor's door. A tall, black woman bustled into the apartment and felt one of Ella's hands. Then she called five or six other women in the neighborhood, who came and undressed his mother and put her to bed. A doctor was called and after an examination of Ella he told Richard that his mother had suffered a stroke, her entire left side was paralyzed, and she would need constant care.

Later in the day Richard rummaged through drawers and found his grandmother's address. He wrote, asking her to come at once. The neighbors took charge and watched Ella day and night, fed the children and washed their clothes. Richard refused to eat but when the women prevailed upon him he ate as little as possible, ashamed of charity, ashamed that he had to be fed by strangers. Mrs. Wilson arrived and dictated letters to all her children asking them to send money so that she could take Ella home. Money arrived and Ella was taken by stretcher to the train for Jackson.

Maggie came from Detroit to help nurse her sister, followed by Cleo from Chicago, Edward from Carters, Clark from Greenwood, Charles from Mobile, Addie from Huntsville, Thomas from Hazel-hurst. Richard caught whispered words: "What is to become of her children?" Long conferences were held and it was decided that Richard and his brother would have to be separated; it was too much of a burden for any one aunt or uncle to take both boys. Richard became more anxious than ever, wondering what was to become of him.

At night my sleep was filled with wild dreams. Sometimes I would wake up screaming in terror. The grownups would come running and I would stare at them, as though they were figures out of my nightmare, then go back to sleep. One night I found myself standing in the back yard. The moon was shining bright as day. Silence surrounded me. Suddenly I felt that someone was holding my hand. I looked and saw an uncle. . . . "You were walking in your sleep," he said.[1]

Granny gave him more food and made him take naps in the daytime and gradually his sleepwalking and nightmares passed.

One evening Richard and his brother were called into the front room following a family conference and were told that Alan would go to Detroit with Aunt Maggie and Richard would go to Greenwood with his Uncle Clark. It was a deep disappointment; Richard had wanted to live with Maggie. But he stayed only a few months in Greenwood before he was able to persuade his uncle to send him back to his grandmother's—another term of school was broken but Richard did not care. He would be with his mother and her presence made him feel less afraid even though she was still seriously ill.

Ella improved slightly and an operation was recommended. Edward returned from Carters, Mississippi, to take his sister to Clarksdale, where the operation would be performed in the doctor's

office. After surgery Ella was taken to a rooming house by stretcher—
there were no hospital facilities for Negro patients in Clarksdale. As
soon as she had recovered slightly she was carried aboard a train,
where she lay in the baggage car for the trip to Jackson. "Back home,
she lay for days, groaning, her eyes vacant. Doctors visited her and
left without making any comment. Granny grew frantic. Uncle Edward, who had gone home, returned and still more doctors were
called in." A blood clot formed in Ella's brain and she had another
paralytic stroke.

Richard crept silently through the house and helped care for his
mother. Once, in the night, she called to him and whispered that she
could not bear the pain, she wanted to die, and her young son held
her hand and pleaded with her to keep quiet.

That night I ceased to react to my mother; my feelings were frozen. I
merely waited upon her, knowing that she was suffering. She remained
abed ten years, gradually growing better, but never completely recover-
ing, relapsing periodically into her paralytic state.

My mother's suffering grew into a symbol in my mind, gathering to itself
all the poverty, the ignorance, the helplessness; the painful, baffling,
hunger-ridden days and hours; the restless moving, the futile seeking, the
uncertainty, the fear, the dread; the meaningless pain and the endless
suffering. Her life set the emotional tone of my life, colored the men and
women I was to meet in the future, conditioned my relation to events
that had not yet happened, determined my attitude to situations and
circumstances I had yet to face. A somberness of spirit that I was never to
lose settled over me during the slow years of my mother's unrelieved
suffering, a somberness that was to make me stand apart and look upon
excessive joy with suspicion, that was to make me self-conscious, that was
to make me keep forever on the move, as though to escape a nameless fate
seeking to overtake me.[2]

At the age of twelve, Richard had not yet had one full year of
formal schooling but he had ". . . a conception of life that no
experience would ever erase, a predilection for what was real that no
argument could ever gainsay, a sense of the world that was [his] and
[his] alone, a notion as to what life meant that no education could
ever alter, a conviction that the meaning of living came only when
one was struggling to wring a meaning out of meaningless suffering."

Addie, Richard's youngest aunt and the baby of the family, graduated from the Seventh-Day Adventists School in Huntsville, and
returned home to live. Addie was a slender pretty girl, with intense
brown eyes but a permanent suspicion of the world gave her a
peculiar habit of kicking doors open before she went. She always

paused before a partly opened door and kicked it open; if the door swung in, she flung it back with her foot, or, if the door was shut, she opened it with her hand for an inch or two, then opened it the rest of the way with her foot. "She acted as though she wanted to get a glimpse into the room beyond before she entered it, perhaps to see if it contained anything dreadful or unholy." If anything, Addie was even more religious than her mother. She was hired to teach in the Adventists' school and became secretary of the church. This gave her an opportunity to save her nephew, whom she believed was a dangerous sinner. Richard's position in the household was a delicate one; he was a minor, a dependent, and what little religion he had came from his aunt's enemies, the Methodists. "Granny intimated boldly, basing her logic on God's justice, that one sinful person in a household could bring down the wrath of God upon the entire establishment, damning both the innocent and the guilty, and on more than one occasion . . . interpreted [Ella's] long illness as the result of [Richard's] faithlessness."

For the most part, Richard grew adept at ignoring these threats; he simply turned off his ears when his aunt and grandmother began to rail at him. But schooling provided Addie with a weapon. She proposed that he be enrolled in her class when the fall term began and thus two goals would be met: he would get an education and be brought to religion at the same time. Richard protested, but his mother sided against him and he was forced to give in to his aunt's wishes.[3]

At the end of September, 1920, the religious school opened and Richard was enrolled. There were twenty pupils in his class, ranging in age from five to nineteen and in grades from primary to high school, all crowded into one room. Addie was the only teacher for the school and she was roused from a normally nervous state to a feverish intensity by an acute desire to prove her teaching skill and her devotion to Adventism. From the start she made it clear to all the other pupils that Richard would not receive any special consideration just because he was her nephew. She went even further: he was a Godless sinner of whom she did not approve and she wanted no one else to give him friendship or sympathy.

"The pupils were a docile lot, lacking in that keen sense of rivalry which made the boys and girls who went to public school a crowd in which a boy was tested and weighed, in which he caught a glimpse of what the world was. These boys and girls were will-less, their speech flat, their gestures vague, their personalities devoid of anger, hope, laughter, enthusiasm, passion, or despair." Richard had nothing in common with his classmates: he had come from a milieu of alcoholism and saloons, railroad yards, street gangs, an orphan home; he had shifted from town to town and house to house, had known the murder by white people of an uncle and the murder of a white woman by another uncle. Before the first day of school had ended Richard had shocked half the students with his cursing and four-letter words.

As the first week of school drew to an end the acute antagonism between Richard and his aunt flamed into the open. One afternoon she walked down the aisle and stopped at her nephew's desk.

"You know better than that," she bit out from between clenched teeth, loud enough for the rest of the class to hear and rapped him across the knuckles with a ruler.

"Better than what?" Richard asked in amazement and rubbed his injured hand.

"Just look at that floor," she said.

Richard looked down and saw bits of walnut meat strewn about and smeared into grease on the white pine floor. Richard had nuts in his pocket but he had not eaten any. At once he knew that the mess had been made by the boy seated in front of him so he waited for a confession. That righteous God-fearing young man did not speak. A gang code, learned in the streets, kept Richard from "squealing" but at the same time the code demanded that one did not sit idly by and let someone else take punishment. Still the boy in front of Richard sat silent. Addie forced Richard to the front of the class and beat his hand with the ruler until it was red and then lashed him across his bare legs until welts rose. He gritted his teeth to keep from crying and stared unblinkingly into her eyes to show her that she could never really touch him.

After school was out Richard reached home before Addie and sat brooding, waiting for her return and vowing that she would never beat him again. It had always been his feeling that only a mother or a father had the right to beat a child. His body was off limits to anyone else and he was old enough to enforce a private code. Addie was strange and unhappy, but he was not going to be her scapegoat.

The moment Addie walked into the house she yelled for him to come into the kitchen; and when he did he saw that she was holding switches from the peach trees in the yard.

"You're not going to beat me again!" he told her.

"I'm going to teach you some manners!" she said.

In an attempt to calm his aunt, Richard told her again that he had not thrown the nutmeats on the floor and, throwing his gang loyalties aside because they were alone, gave her the name of the boy who had dirtied the floor. But Addie could not be stopped. Wildly she began to strike at him in the face. Richard fell and then scrambled to his feet, the blows cutting his skin open, and ran to a drawer for a weapon. He grabbed up a knife and threatened to cut her if she did not leave him alone. Addie screamed and attacked again and Richard lunged at her with the knife. He missed and threw his leg around her legs as she fought to wrest the knife from his hand. They crashed to the floor and rolled, kicking, scratching and fighting like deadly enemies.

Granny came running into the kitchen; Ella came limping to the door and Grandpa came down from upstairs. Addie ran out of the room, still kicking the door before her in spite of her rage and there was shouting, crying and pleading. Richard would not relinquish the knife but hid it under his arm until the tumult ended. She took her defeat so hard that she never spoke directly to Richard again for many years, although they ate at the same table and slept under the same roof.

It was not utterly settled in Richard's mind whether he believed in God or not. His existence or nonexistence did not concern him. God revolved around how successfully he could protect his own personality from the contrary religious demands of Granny and Addie and his mother. Sometimes he longed so much for peace in the household that he wondered whether he could allay their fears for his soul and yet maintain his own integrity. It was with that in mind that he blundered, hurting his grandmother and bringing her shame before her congregation. Since he was forced to attend the long prayer meetings, and since his grandmother always watched to see their effect upon her grandson, he told her one day that *if*, like Jacob, he ever saw an angel, then he might become a believer. Granny, in her eagerness to believe in miracles, told the Elder and members of the church that her grandson had seen an angel. When Richard blurted out that he hadn't she replied: "You shouldn't've spoken to me," . . . in a breaking voice that revealed the depths of her disillusionment. Later, Richard was able to convince her that he had not intended to hurt her feelings and she seized upon his apology to make him promise to pray, really to pray, to pray hard, to pray until tears came, and then he might find God.

Trapped, Richard went upstairs every day to his room, knelt and tried to pray. Everything he said sounded silly and seemed absurd. But he kept his failure a secret and began to make the hours in his room pass quickly by trying to write verses from the Bible into hymns. If he wrote a really good hymn, perhaps his Granny would forgive his irreverence. But he failed in that and finally thought up a story about Indians. He had been reading a volume of Indian history and wrote a story about an Indian girl who was beautiful and reserved, ". . . who sat alone upon the bank of a still stream, surrounded by eternal twilight and ancient trees, waiting. . . . The girl was keeping some vow which [Richard] could not describe. . . ." Like many young writers, he solved the problem by killing off the heroine. She walked into the stream, and kept walking until the water covered her head. "Not a murmur or a gasp came from her, even in dying."

Now, to whom could he show his first story? Not to his relatives; they already thought him peculiar and Godless. A classmate, Alberta Osborne, might listen to it. Of course, she was only a baby, just twelve, and girls did not have much sense but he would read it to her anyway. When Richard finished reading aloud Alberta was astonished.

"What's that for?" she asked.

"Nothing," Richard answered.

"But why did you write it?"

"I just wanted to."

"Where did you get the idea?"

For some unaccountable reason he did not understand he was gratified by her response. His story belonged to him and to him alone; it was something he had created.

Granny did not discover how Richard actually spent his hours of prayer but in a few months she gave him up as lost. Henceforth, she would not speak to him at all and he was given an ultimatum: "Wash and iron your own clothes!" she told him. But Richard's resentfulness was blotted from his mind because his mother promised that he could enter a public school.

At the end of September, 1921, Richard awakened before the sun rose one morning and leaped out of bed. The wood was cool under his bare feet and he curled his toes against the polished floor, enjoying the texture as he walked to the window that overlooked the back garden. Should he dress? Naw, it was too early. And he was too excited to read. Small trills of excitement blending joy and dread came and went in the pit of his stomach. He leaned on the windowsill and gazed toward the tiny lines of the Jay Railroad which divided College from Washington section. The sun would glint on the steel tracks a quarter of a mile behind the house and then he would dress; then it would be time. Restless, he walked to the bureau and picked up a cheap, brand-new straw hat and smoothed the grosgrain ribbon which circled the flat-topped crown. He tried it on for the tenth or fifteenth time, tilting it over one eye, then pushing it back toward his hairline while looking in the mirror. Carefully, he placed it beside a new tablet and two pencils and wandered back toward the window.

He heard his grandmother going down the stairs and anxiety gripped him. He would be late! The sun was shining at the back of the house! Rushing into his clothes, he buttoned the knickers over long black stockings, put on his shirt, tied his shoes and rushed into the bathroom to wash.

Before going downstairs he went back in his room, picked up the new hat and his school supplies and tiptoed down the hall to his mother's room. Ella was propped by two pillows into a semi-sitting position. She smiled when she saw Richard and then cautioned him to be careful and to study hard and pay attention to the teacher at the new school. Her admonitions were so familar that Richard barely listened; only a vague irritation arose in him at her tone of voice. After all, he was thirteen and she still acted as if he were a baby.

Richard raced down the stairs and into the kitchen, where Granny served him a bowl of mush. When he had finished the cereal Granny gave him a paper bag containing a couple of baking powder wheat-flour biscuits, a boiled egg and a baked sweet potato for his lunch and he hurried down Lynch Street to the Jim Hill Public School.[4]

At the school Richard was assigned to the fifth grade, which was taught by Miss Katie Mae Wilson, a woman of medium height who wore glasses. Standing before her class of between twenty and twenty-five pupils—boys seated on one side and girls on the other—Miss Wilson made it clear that "She would settle for nothing less than the best in her classes." Before turning to the blackboard behind her desk Miss Wilson explained that she could see every pupil and what was happening in her classroom reflected in the sides of her glasses.

"That's a lot of stuff!" Richard whispered to his seatmate, Richard "Squilla" Jordan, who smothered a laugh.

Within two weeks Richard was promoted to the sixth grade, although he still remained in Miss Wilson's class. Overjoyed, he ran home with the news. "The family had not thought it possible. How could a bad, bad boy do that?" Richard told them that he was going to study medicine, engage in research, make discoveries. Since he had leaped a grade in two weeks, everything appeared possible and the family did not discourage him: "Get an education was the byword. The male image of greatness was Booker T. Washington to some, and Dr. W. E. B. DuBois to others. . . ."

Richard, "the bright boy of the class, always astonished . . . Miss Wilson with his unusual questions and answers. It was always, 'If so why so' and 'If not why not?' [Richard] always finished his test papers before the rest of the class got started. A lot of times he was smart enough to slip and help [Joe Brown] and his other jug buddies."

As his confidence burgeoned Richard became chief instigator of classroom disruption. He was usually very careful because Miss Wilson was highly skilled with a leather strap which she kept in a desk drawer. "Miss Wilson's favorite little method of using the strap on the boys [was to call them] up to her desk in the presence of the whole class. You were instructed to put your hands into the pockets of your knickers, push your hands in tight and then slightly bend over. . . . Miss Wilson had a slow way of taking her time in applying licks. It was a feeling you never forgot."

Richard was always afraid of a whipping "and when he did get a licking he was very sensitive and would quickly shed a few tears and then pout but he never . . . sassed the teachers." His greatest fear was to be sent to the principal's office. Professor Sam Brinkley, principal of the Jim Hill school, had a deformed left hand which he always kept in his pocket. "Whenever he did his whipping he would first remove his coat and [the students were instructed to do the same]. He didn't use a strap. There was a certain kind of a shrubbery bush which limbs were taken from and they were called rat-tans. Mr. Brinkley would take his own good time, sit back in his chair, and slowly apply the licks with his good hand and in the meantime he talked while whipping and he would address the boys as 'Mister' and the girls as 'Miss.' "All the children knew that after getting a thrashing from Professor Brinkley he would then notify their parents. And Richard always worried about what his Granny would do to him when he reached home.

"In [the] class was a tall, black, rebellious boy who was bright in his studies and yet utterly fearless in his assertion of himself; he could break the morale of the class at any moment with his clowning and the teacher never found an adequate way of handling him." His name was Joe Brown and Richard nicknamed him "Gowdey" and "Big Mama." Joe and Richard "Squilla" Jordan[5] were Richard's favorite friends and all three boys sat at the back of the classroom at double wooden desks with slots underneath for their books.

One morning Richard, Joe, Squilla, Lewis Anderson and another of his buddies, Perry "Conkey" Booker, were making a disturbance in the back of the room. Richard was talking out loud about a Western he and Squilla had seen at the Alamo Theatre downtown on Farish Street. The star of the film was William S. Hart, a favorite of Richard's, and he and Squilla were imitating the actor's use of his two guns, complete with sound effects. The rest of the boys were listening, laughing and keeping an eye warily on the teacher, who had called for silence. Squilla could always re-create every part of a motion picture and Richard urged him for the dramatic details.

Finally Miss Wilson gave a second warning which was final. "I want you boys in the back of the room to remain in your seats when the noon recess bell rings," Miss Wilson said, singling out Richard, Squilla, Joe, Perry and Lewis. "You all will remain in your seats and no one will be excused during the recess hour. Richard Wright! I want you to take down the name of any person who leaves the room."

During the recess Lewis Anderson wanted to go to the lavatory. "I got to go," he said. "I can't hold it." Richard warned his friend: "Boy, you will get your butt whipped if you leave the room!"

"I have it!" Squilla said while Richard urged him on. But Squilla did not immediately give his solution. Instead, he kept asking Lewis if it was not possible to wait until after recess was over. "No! No!" Lewis squirmed in his seat. Richard suggested that they find a bottle in the room for Lewis to use and then he would hide it under his desk. "Or," he said, "you could just pee on yourself and with your long drawers it wouldn't show through your clothes and nobody will know it but us. We swear to keep it a secret."

Squilla suddenly guffawed and pointed to the front of the room at the huge iron potbellied coal stove which stood next to the windows. Resting on top of the stove was a gallon-size container which held water to humidify the air in the classroom. Then Squilla pointed to a big pot of flowers near the window, but Conkey spoke up: "You can't do it in the pot, that strong stuff will kill the flower." Squilla had everyone's attention and Richard listened avidly for his friend's final brilliant idea. Carefully, Squilla laid out the plan. Conkey, who was in charge of the stove that day, could remove the gallon container, let it cool for a while, let Lewis urinate into it and place it back on top. Richard protested: "When that ole water starts to boil it will be real smelly in the room."

But Squilla's creative mind was still at work. He told Conkey that when he put the next scuttle of coal into the stove he should take two or three of the large-sized rocks which lay in a box near the stove and mix them with the coal. When the rocks were heated they made a loud popping sound and Miss Wilson would believe that the coal was faulty and gave off strange odors.

When the recess period was over the students began to file into the room, and as soon as they took a breath small frowns appeared on their faces. As soon as Miss Wilson entered the room she assigned two boys to open all the windows. "There must be something wrong with this last shipment of coal," she said to the students. Soon the heated rocks began to pop loudly; the teacher nodded briskly and class began.

Richard's friends named themselves the "Dick Wright Klan" in a humorous parody of the KKK. It was an exclusive club and consisted of boys from middle-class families who had a certain status in the community but very little money. They were also the brightest in the class and the most mischievous.

Richard's Klan brought lunch from home consisting almost unvaryingly of two soda-wheat biscuits, a hard-boiled egg, a piece of fried fatback and a yam. But one day the Klan put their nickels together, which made twenty-five cents, and then Squilla added one more. With thirty cents they went to the little grocery store next to the school. The store smelled wonderful to Richard with the big barrels of sour pickles, pickled pig's feet, hoop cheddar cheese, barrels of gingersnaps and huge peppermint candy sticks. His mouth watered while he watched Mr. Jordan, the owner, prepare a treat for the Klan. The grocer took a whole loaf of unsliced bread, cut a block from the top, poured in a can of sardines, added slices of raw onion and finally poured vinegar over the whole until the bread was soaked. Then he put the cut block into place, cut the loaf into portions and handed it to the boys, who rarely could afford such a meal.

During the same year that Richard was at Jim Hill the two sons, Perry Jr. and Lucas, of lawyer Perry Howard, a National Republican Committeeman for the State of Mississippi, attended the school. The Klan did not become friendly with the Howard boys, who lived on West Pearl Street, which led to downtown Jackson where Negro families were mixed in with whites: "This street was considered the street where the big Niggers lived." But another boy from the same neighborhood, Frank Sims, who was directly related to the Mississippi Senator B. K. Bruce, was eventually permitted membership in Richard's club.

Richard nicknamed Frank Sims "Bay-bay" and it was in the basement of his home on Pearl Street that the Dick Wright Klan held meetings. Members of the club had a password and a secret knock and no one else was admitted. To ensure complete privacy Richard "advanced the bright idea of how to keep out the undesirables. There were two or three steps down to the basement door that led into the club room. With [Richard's] idea [they] placed a gallon bucket of water on a ledge above the door with a long string attached from the inside to the bucket. If it wasn't the right member, [Richard] would pull the string and dump the water upon the head of the intruder."

Another favorite game of the members of the club was to hide themselves from view of the street just as it grew dark. They would take a long black ribbed stocking of the type worn with knickers, and stuff it with rags to shape it into a long black snake. To this the boys would attach a long piece of black string. They would hide in the grass by the sidewalk and when people passed by they pulled the snake directly across their path. In their hiding place the boys held their sides with laughter when they heard people scream and run or jump with fright. Richard especially liked to frighten the little girls.

A few times Richard's friends went to his house but Granny made them uncomfortable. She always lurked in their vicinity and asked: "What are you boys doing?" There was a coldness in the house which kept the children away. But just down Lynch Street, west of the house, were two Negro colleges: Jackson, which had been established by a missionary Baptist group during Reconstruction, and Campbell, which was founded by the African Methodist Church. At Jackson College there was an outdoor tennis court and a croquet field, and in Barret's Hall, the men's dormitory, there was a pool table. Richard and Joe made friends with some of the students in the co-educational school, who loaned them tennis rackets and let them play pool or croquet occasionally.

A great rivalry existed between the two colleges, which became extreme during the baseball and football season. Richard and Joe were always trying to find methods by which they could see the games and often acted as bat boys or carried water to the players during practice. In this way they were sometimes permitted to attend the play-offs. When these methods failed Richard and Joe went to the athletic field, which was enclosed by a tall board fence, and pried loose a couple of boards. During a game they peered through the crack they had made and waited for a fight to erupt. Then they slipped through the boards and in the confusion made their way to unoccupied seats.

On hot days the Dick Wright Klan walked way down below Washington section about a mile southwest of Granny's house to Rock Bottom Creek's swimming hole in Barrett's pasture.[6] Barrett's pasture was heavily wooded and the winding creek ran about two and a half miles through his land. Sometimes while the boys were swimming Old Man Barrett would arrive at the large pool with his gun and threaten to shoot their "black butts if they did not get out of his pasture, stinking up the water that his cattle had to drink. Old Man Barrett never shot his gun. [They] never stopped slipping in his pasture for a swim." Occasionally, poorer-class white boys threatened them by hurling rocks or hiding their clothes. But Richard and his friends were adept at gathering and throwing rocks in return. And one afternoon the white boys were at the pool swimming when

Richard and his friends arrived. They slipped into the bushes, located the white boys' clothing and concealed it carefully. The white boys never returned. Richard used to say: "Even though they're poor white trash they can go to Livingston Park and swim in the public lake but we niggers can't. We got to dive out of trees like black monkeys and swim with the water moccasin snakes, and bull frogs." He would tell his friends of the news stories he read in the Chicago *Defender:* in Lake Michigan Negroes and white folks swam together and black men could sit beside white women in streetcars and go to the libraries and take out any book one wanted to read. Pensively, he ended his stories, "I'm gonna leave Mississippi and be long gone up North one of these days."

All of Richard's friends, with the exception of Frank Sims, worked at part-time jobs after school each day and on Saturdays, but Granny would not permit him to work on the Adventists' Sabbath. It was an insoluble dilemma because no one would hire a boy unless he could work after school and on Saturdays and Richard cursed himself for living in such a crazy and different family.

One afternoon Squilla took Richard home with him to show him a way to earn money. He explained that he would have something to read at the same time that he earned over fifty cents a week selling a newspaper which contained supplements. Squilla loaned Richard a paper that was running a serialization of *Riders of the Purple Sage* by Zane Grey. Walking home from the Jordan house, he began to read the story with the same excitement he had felt when Ella, the schoolteacher boarder, had recited the tale about Bluebeard. Now, at last, he could have reading material in his own home because Granny could not object to what constituted a job. She always burned books he brought to the house and branded them as sinful.

The cheap pulp stories in the supplements enlarged his knowledge of the world; Richard felt "they were revolutionary, [his] gateway to the world." But he had been selling the papers for only a few weeks when the stepfather of a classmate, Essie Lee Ward, Richard's only rival for class honors, came to speak to him. Jake Ward, a small soft-spoken black man, lived in a little "shot-gun house" on Poindexter Street. The house resembled the weapon it was named for in that it had two bedrooms, one on each side of the kitchen, through which one looked into the backyard while standing on the front porch—just as one sighted between the barrels of a shotgun. Richard liked "little black Jake," which was his unspoken nickname for the man, because his wife Willie was always ordering him around. It amused Richard to observe the way that both wife and stepdaughter henpecked the man who worked silently at his trade as a carpenter.

Jake had purchased a paper from Richard a few weeks before and then in his shy fashion asked him: "Son, who told you to sell these papers? Was it a white man?" Then Jake showed Richard a picture of ". . . a huge black man with a greasy, sweaty face, thick lips, flat nose, golden teeth, sitting at a polished, wide-topped desk in a swivel chair. The man had on a pair of gleaming yellow shoes and his feet were propped upon the desk. His thick lips nursed a big, black cigar that held white ashes an inch long. In the man's red-dotted tie was a dazzling horseshoe stickpin, glaring conspicuously. The man wore red suspenders and his shirt was striped silk and there were huge diamond rings on his fat black fingers. A chain of gold girded his belly and from the fob of his watch a rabbit's foot dangled. On the floor at the side of the desk was a spittoon overflowing with mucus." Under the picture was a sentence that claimed ". . . the only dream of a nigger is to be president and to sleep with white women!" It was a publication of the Ku Klux Klan and called upon all white men to organize in defense of Southern white womanhood. The gentle carpenter then explained the role of the Ku Klux Klan to Richard and showed him another article which stated that lynching was the only solution for the problem of the Negro. On his way home that night Richard threw the papers into a ditch and later told his grandmother that the company already had too many agents in Jackson and did not need him to sell.

Richard burned at his studies: during the first weeks of each semester he read his civics, English and geography textbooks from cover to cover. He solved all his mathematical problems in advance and then, during school hours, he read secondhand copies of *Argosy All-Story Magazine* and *Flynn's Detective Weekly*. If he ran out of magazines, he wove stories of his own in his mind.

At the end of the school year in June, 1922, Richard got a job with Mr. Mance, a next-door neighbor, a janitor who had decided to change his profession and become an insurance salesman. Since he was illiterate, he offered Richard a job filling out policies for the insurance company. The pay was five dollars a week—a fantastic sum. All of the money could be saved and given to Granny, Richard calculated, because he traveled into the Delta region with Brother Mance and slept on corn-shuck mattresses and ate salt pork, black-eyed peas and milk on the plantations they visited.

The trips were hard and the poverty depressed Richard. It was worse even than Granny's and under the sympathy he felt for the farmers was a sense of superiority; they were yokels and sometimes bought insurance because they felt that they were connecting them-selves with something that would make their children " 'write 'n speak lak dat pretty boy from Jackson.' " He had all but forgotten that he had been born on a plantation. At the end of the summer Richard returned home "with a pocketful of money that melted into the bottomless hunger of the household." Ella was proud, Granny felt that he had accomplished a miracle and even Addie temporarily seemed less hostile. But Mr. Mance died during the winter and the insurance company would not accept a minor in the position even though Richard had been doing the actual work.

School opened and Richard began the seventh grade. And again hunger returned so sharp some evenings that when he was studying the scent of frying meat from a neighboring home would make his mind wander. His clothing grew so shabby that he was ashamed to go to school. Many of the boys in his class were wearing their first long pants while Richard still wore knickers with long black stockings. He grew so bitter toward his grandmother that he packed a bag and threatened to leave the house if she did not relent and let him work on Saturdays. "That old church of yours is messing up my life," he told his Granny. She snatched the suitcase out of his hands and told him he could work. If he wanted to go to hell, then he could go. God would know that it was not her fault.

The next day at school Richard asked his friends about jobs, and Frank Sims gave him the name of a white family who wanted a boy to do chores. As soon as school was let out Richard went for an interview. A tall, sour-faced white woman talked to him. "Yes, she needed a boy, an honest boy. Two dollars a week. Mornings, evenings, and all day Saturdays. Washing dishes. Chopping wood. Scrubbing floors. Cleaning the yard." He would get his breakfast and dinner. The woman asked if he wanted the job and said that she had a question to ask and she wanted him to tell the truth.

"Do you steal?" she asked . . . sternly.

Richard started to laugh but caught himself quickly.

"What's so damn funny about that?" she asked.

"Lady, if I was a thief, I'd never tell anybody."

"What do you mean?" she blazed with a red face.

He had made a mistake during his first five minutes in the white world. He hung his head and mumbled that he did not steal, "No, ma'am," and he was not sassy. Promising to report for work at six o'clock the next morning, Richard walked slowly home musing at the strangeness of the white people. The following morning when his work was completed he was served a breakfast of stale bread and a plate of molasses. When he lifted the dish to his lips he saw circlets of green and white mold floating on the surface of the heavy syrup. The food was not even clean! He put on his coat and left the house. Scum-covered food, added to the insults of that morning, was more than he could accept. The white employer had asked why he still attended school and what he would be when he grew up. Almost without volition Richard had answered: "A writer."

"You'll never be a writer," she said. "Who on earth put such ideas into your nigger head?"

Scuffing his feet, kicking at stray stones, Richard walked toward school. He would not go back to that house. Perhaps he would never be a writer but she had no right to say so. She had assaulted his ego by assuming that she knew his place in life, what he felt, what he ought to be and he resented it with all his heart. A few days later he found another job doing chores for a white family which he kept until the end of the school year. But summer came with bright hot days and he was out of work again.

After a morning spent in looking for a job, he thought he would go to Joe Brown's house at the end of Washington section and then help him with his job at four o'clock. It was Joe's job to hang up the mail by the side of the railroad track on an iron upright frame, hoisting it high with a long wooden pole with a metal hook on the end. The train would swoop past, pluck the mail off the stand without stopping, and then toss out the local mail sacks.

At the train stop, Gowdey, a black woman named Mrs. Julia Humbles, and her husband, owned a small grocery store. Mrs. Humbles was also the postmistress for Gowdey's second-class post office; it was a job she held for eighteen years. Richard was always curious about Mrs. Humbles. How had she gotten a "white" job? He found out later that before Mrs. Humbles took over there had been a white woman, Mrs. Mathis, who had operated the post office in the Delta Cotton Oil Mill. When she gave up the position Mrs. Humble took over and the post office moved into her grocery store. It was said by the old-timers that "the whites didn't like the idea of niggers having to come into the white oil mill's office, being served by a white woman."

Richard liked to help Joe with the mail; it seemed more fun than work. And both boys dreamed that one day they would be trainmen. It was thrilling to watch the colored switchmen walk on top of the cars, turn a steering type of wheel and then get down to uncouple the cars. Richard and Joe surreptitiously hopped on and off the trains, stealing rides, and learning to hobo for the day they would go north. When the club members got together they talked of how to get past Fulton, Kentucky, which was notorious for its police attacks against those who stole rides. "Someday," Richard told his friends, "I'm going to take all the Negroes in Mississippi on the number four cannonball all the way up to Chicago! I'm gonna make that old train run a hot box and pass that ole Panama Limited like a bat out of hell. I'll show them rich white folks something, sitting in their fine parlor cars and drawing rooms."

Richard learned that Bullard's Brick Yard on Dalton Street, not far from his home, was hiring boys for fifty cents a day for ten hours' work. Richard was growing tall but he weighed only a hundred pounds and he wondered if he could do the heavy work in a brick-yard. The strongest boys sat on the side of a large two-wheeled barrow taking off the green bricks as they came out on a conveyor belt. When they had loaded forty on the barrow they rolled them to a shed where they were stacked to dry out before being set in a kiln for firing. Joe worked on the barrow job. Richard was given the job as driver of a two-wheeled dump cart pulled by a mule. He was to drive to a pit that was about three-quarters of a mile from the main plant and wait while men loaded the cart with fresh red clay.

There remained only one problem: Richard was timid about the mule. But he watched the other mule drivers and soon learned how to treat the animal he was in charge of. Her name was Kate, and he grew fond of her. Each morning he would rub her behind the ears, pat her gently on the behind, or slip her an ear of corn he stole from the barn. While he slipped on the harness he cajoled, "Come on, sweet baby"—and soothed the skittish animal.

After the carts were loaded with clay they were driven back to the plant and the dirt was dumped into a giant open hopper, and then mixed with water and oil. When he had been on the job only a few weeks Richard began to have trouble with the straw boss named Short. Richard and his friend Conkey Booker, who drove another cart, livened up the work by racing their animals back to the main plant. It became a daily free-for-all until one day when Richard was too eager to win the race. Conkey was ahead so Richard left the driver's seat and climbed onto the poor mule's back to urge her on to victory. When the straw boss saw the dripping, heaving sides of Richard's mule he threatened to fire him on the spot and allowed him to remain only because he put on his most sheepish, innocent face and hung his head.

It was at the brickyard that Richard and Joe met the local "tough guys." "Big bad Biggy Thomas (Bigger Thomas), and his brother William, August Harding and his brother T. J., Bill and Frank Newsome, Hopey and Eddie Willis; these were considered some of the rough guys.[7] Biggy was the fiercest of the group: he was always fighting and using foul language. But Richard always managed to get along with them without fighting. He told Joe that he helped them with their lessons and at other times simply stayed out of their sight. And secretly he enjoyed listening to them play the "Dirty Dozens."

In September, 1923, Richard enrolled in the Smith-Robertson Public School on the opposite side of the city from his grandmother's home. To reach school he had to walk ten or twelve miles—there were no buses or streetcars—cross the downtown section of Jackson at Capitol and Farish until he came to the corner of Bloom and East Oakley Streets and the two-story brick structure.

Erected in 1894, it had been the first and only public school for Negroes until 1912. At the time of Richard's enrollment there were seventeen teachers for about 1,500 pupils in nondepartmentalized grades from one through nine. There were no high schools for Negroes; if a student wished to continue his education he had to attend the one Negro Catholic school or one of the Negro colleges— Jackson or Campbell. Tougaloo, one of the AMA colleges established after the Civil War by Northern whites, had an all-white faculty and only those considered "big Niggers" sent their children there. Money alone was not sufficient: at the time, there existed a "blue-vein" society in Jackson, and if skin tone was not mixed sufficiently with white so that blue veins clearly showed in the wrists a Negro was excluded.

The principal of Smith-Robertson was Professor W. H. Lanier, a handsome broad-faced brown man with military bearing. Professor O. B. Cobbins was Lanier's assistant as well as a ninth-grade teacher.

There was no cafeteria, no assembly hall, no library, no gymnasium and no science laboratories at Smith-Robertson. Since Richard's previous school had been even less well-equipped he was not worried about Smith-Robertson's limitations. It was the harshly militant personality of the principal that bothered him.

Professor Lanier was a great lover of Army discipline. Although he had never been a regular soldier, he had drilled men during the Spanish-American War, and the verve and enthusiasm of Theodore Roosevelt's "Rough Riders" had influenced Lanier's entire personality.

Every morning the entire student body, with the exception of the lowest grades, lined up in front of the school building in formation like Army cadets. At 9 A.M., the recess periods, dismissal at noon and after school and for fire drills the students had to march to the clank, clank, clank of Mr. Lanier's bell, keeping time with every clap. When Lanier looked out over the crowd and saw someone out of step he singled him out. "Fall out!" he told the culprit. Then the missteppers were put through a fifteen-minute drill—halting and about-facing—before they were allowed to attend their classes.

Lanier had a unique method by which he disciplined the bullies in the school. "He would say, 'All right, mister, stretch out your arms.' He would then stretch out his towards you. He would then count one . . . two . . . and on to three [when] you would grab each other's arms and somebody would kiss the dust."

Another of Lanier's methods of handling recalcitrant pupils frightened Richard even more. "He would put his arms on your shoulders and then butt your forehead like a big bull."

A short time after Richard entered Smith-Robertson, Lanier, always on the lookout for unusual aptitude, discovered that he was a brilliant student. Calling him to the office, he held long conversations with Richard and encouraged him to go on to college, told him of his own son, who had been unable to take books from the all-white local library but was attending an Eastern university.

One morning Professor Lanier walked into the classroom where the students were struggling with sentence diagramming. Lanier waited until it was Richard's turn to recite. No one else in the class had been able to break up a particular sentence: "Of all the saws I ever saw I never saw a saw saw like this saw saws." As Richard effortlessly reeled off the sentence he saw the faintest smile on Lanier's face. "He's proud of me!" Richard thought to himself.

For several months, morning and afternoon, Richard walked with Joe the ten or twelve miles to school, though most of their friends had bicycles. As they took the long hike, they vowed to each other that they would find jobs and buy their own bicycles. Richard went to work for the wife of the foreman of the sawmill, Mrs. Bibbs. Working before and after school, he finally saved up enough money to buy a second-hand bicycle. Granny did not approve and began to throw out hints that it was nearing the time for him to be on his own; but when he contemplated his future it looked bleak: "What had he learned that could help him to make a living?"

On a long hot Saturday afternoon Richard sat upstairs in his room. He was resentful that Granny would not let him go out with his friends on her Sabbath. At last he finished reading all of the magazines, comic books and papers that he and Joe had taken from garbage cans in white neighborhoods and became restless. He took out his ruled composition book and began to write a story about a villain who was trying to take the home of a poor widow. When it was partially completed he thought up a title: "The Voodoo of Hell's Half-Acre." "It was crudely atmospheric, emotional, intuitively psychological, and stemmed from pure feeling." "Voodoo" took Richard three days to write and was approximately 3,000 words in length. At its completion he experienced a strange sense of elation. He felt satisfied and full—better even than when he had eaten one of Jordan's sardine specials. He felt as if he could run and shout and fling himself in the air like a small child.

Richard's joy made him feel bold. On Tuesday, after school, he went to the office of the Negro tabloid, the *Southern Register,* on North Farish Street. Malcolm Rogers, the editor, together with Mrs. Lillian Perkins, gathered news, operated a linotype machine, wrote copy and edited, and delivered the final paper.

Mrs. Perkins took Richard to see Rogers and he almost shoved his composition under the surprised editor's nose. "What is that?" he asked.

"A story."

"A news story?" the editor asked.

"No, fiction."

"All right. I'll read it," Rogers said and pushed the composition book to one side of his desk.

"But I want you to read it *now,*" Richard protested.

Rogers blinked at the tall, thin youngster's audacity but he spoke without irritation: "I'll read this and let you know about it tomorrow."

"Voodoo" was accepted for publication in 1924 in the *Southern Register,* divided into three installments of a thousand words apiece. Rogers suggested that Richard continue to write stories and to see him when school was ended for a possible job.

Only Rogers gave him any encouragement. Richard had never mentioned his writing to the Dick Wright Klan and when the story appeared in the newspaper the teachers, his classmates and his friends wondered out loud how he could manage to tell such a big lie about a terrible villain and how he had made the character so alive.

The story got him into difficulty at home: his Uncle Tom, a schoolteacher, was surprised, highly critical and contemptuous; Granny called it a lie because he had made it up; Ella worried that he would not be able to get a job if people thought he was weak-minded enough to write stories; Aunt Addie said it was a sin to use the word "Hell." Richard became angry and silent. Someday, he vowed, he would go north to write books and novels.

Summer returned and with it the problem of another job. Ella's care and a bottomless pit of need at home swallowed every penny. So he had to refuse an offer from the editor of the *Register* to work as a news collector, which might have paid less than three dollars a week. Besides, the Bibbs family, for whom he worked part-time, paid three and it was steady and familiar. He had been with them since October, 1923. Mrs. Bibbs, a round-faced young blond woman, encouraged Richard in his studies and sent him to see her husband, a foreman at the sawmill. Mr. Bibbs swung Richard off the floor as if he were a bundle of feathers. "You're too light for our work," he told him. The hot empty days dragged on; late mornings after he finished at the Bibb's, Richard looked for work and read during the afternoons. He heard of friends who had found jobs but was unsuccessful no matter how hard he tried.

One morning he was walking on West Pearl Street to downtown Jackson when he passed the home of Carl T. Robinson, a classmate. Carl was sitting on the front porch and as soon as Richard spoke to him he began to sob. "You've heard, haven't you?" he asked. "About what?" "My brother, Bob?" "No, what happened?" "They killed him," he managed to say. "The white folks?" Richard asked in a whisper, guessing. Bob Robinson was dead, murdered by a group of white men who had taken him in a car into the country and after cutting off his penis and testicles had shot him. The lynchers had accused him of sleeping with the white prostitutes in the hotel where he had worked as a bellhop. Richard could taste the brass savor of fear on his tongue; his mind reeled and he stifled a desire to weep. No, it could not be true—not Bob, twenty-four years old, who was the hero of all the boys in the neighborhood, a tall brown-skinned young man who laughed and joked and made friends with everyone.

Richard did not search for a job that day. He returned home and sat on the porch staring into nothing—"Bob had been caught by the white death, the threat of which hung over every male black in the South."

What I had heard altered the look of the world, induced in me a temporary paralysis of will and impulse. The penalty of death awaited me if I made a false move and I wondered if it was worth-while to make any move at all. The things that influenced my conduct as a Negro did not have to happen to me directly; I needed but to hear of them to feel their full effects in the deepest layers of my consciousness. Indeed, the white brutality that I had not seen was a more effective control of my behavior than that which I knew. The actual experience would have let me see the realistic outlines of what was really happening, but as long as it remained something terrible and yet remote, something whose horror and blood might descend upon me at any moment, I was compelled to give my entire imagination over to it, an act which blocked the springs of thought and feeling in me, creating a sense of distance between me and the world in which I lived.[8]

Toward the end of July, 1924, Richard went back to work for Mrs. Bibbs and bought schoolbooks for the ninth grade—his last year in school. He was now definitely decided upon leaving home when the ninth-grade term ended. There were many days when he spoke to no one in the house except his mother, and he was trying to build a wall behind which to live, to protect himself from events inside and outside the home. An awareness of why he attended school was becoming acute; his life depended not so much upon learning as upon getting into another world of people.

Richard's brilliance in the eighth grade impressed his teacher, Mrs. M. L. Morrison, who often turned her English and arithmetic classes over to him as a practice instructor. Professor Cobbins, his ninth-grade teacher, would excuse Richard from class so that he could assist Mrs. Morrison. Altogether, Richard studied two years of American history, civics, botany, English, first-year Latin, first-year algebra, general science, civil government and a little physiology and anatomy. An ability to rattle off the names of all the bones in the body when he could not earn enough money to put flesh on his own skeleton made him smile wryly. But he was grateful to his teachers and realized that they "were doing their best to pump knowledge into their pupils; they knew that this was all the schooling colored children would receive in Jackson. So they gave all that they had."

Toward the end of April Richard was selected class valedictorian, his friend Richard "Squilla" was salutatorian, and three other honor students—Essie Lee Ward, Minnie Farish and Hattie Crawford—were to make speeches. As soon as he knew that he was to make the leading speech for graduation Richard chose a topic he called "Attributes of Life."

One morning he was summoned into the office of Professor Cobbins, whom he had nicknamed "Peanut Head" and "Goober Head" because the young assistant principal wore his hair shaved close to the scalp and two small cowlicks made lumpy impressions above his forehead.

"Well, Richard Wright, here's your speech," Cobbins told him, handing a paper across his desk.

"But, Professor, I've written my speech already," Richard said.

Cobbins laughed indulgently.

"Listen, boy, you're going to speak to both *white* and colored people that night. What can you alone think of saying to them? You have no experience. . . ."

It was not the first time that Richard had disagreed with Professor Cobbins. It had been raining one day, a steady unremitting torrent, and Cobbins had remarked to the class that it was the work of God. Richard's hand shot up and without waiting to be recognized he asked: "What does God have to do with making it rain?" He then went into a long explanation of the chemical changes, moisture, hot and cold air, wind currents, to prove that God did not make it rain every time the farmers needed it.

Cobbins' suggestion that Richard give a speech he had not written made him furious. But he tried to keep his voice low and quiet when he answered:

"I know that I'm not educated, Professor, . . . but the people are coming to hear the students, and I won't make a speech that you've written."

No matter how much the assistant principal argued, Richard clung to his own notions of honesty. More and more, stubborn refusal was becoming a way to preserve his own integrity. Finally, Cobbins made an inverted threat: he had been considering Richard for a position in the school system, he said, but he wondered whether he would fit in. Smith-Robertson was to be permitted the use of a newly built, city auditorium for its graduation exercises, and a white man, Mr. Bailey, the superintendent of schools, would be attending. It was necessary to make a good impression on Bailey and to show him that the black man was grateful for the rare opportunity of the use of a city auditorium.

Gradually, as he listened, Richard grew sickened. But when Cobbins suggested that unless he changed his attitude and accepted the speech he might not graduate at all, he had to fight his emotions to keep his temper. "But I passed my examinations," he told Cobbins. Then he turned toward the door to leave, but the professor called him back: "Have you talked to any white people about this?" he asked. And he seemed to sigh and relax slightly when Richard told him no. Winking at Richard, he said that he would help him go to college if he stopped being stubborn. "I want to learn, Professor, but there are some things that I don't want to know."

He left Cobbins' office puzzled, disgusted and hurt. Would he graduate or would Cobbins stop him? An uneasiness filled his body, bringing dread and the feeling that he had witnessed something unclean, sordid. Squilla was waiting for him in the hallway; he had accepted a speech on Ethiopia which Cobbins had written. News of Richard's clash with Cobbins spread through the senior class and even his friends were critical of his position. Squilla told Richard that it was foolish to take a chance: he might not graduate and then what would happen? Only Joe Brown gave him encouragement.

When Richard's Uncle Tom, a nervous man who twitched when he walked, heard what had happened he lost his temper: "You're nothing but a child," he told Richard. Even Ella complained: "You're trying to go too fast." Richard clenched his teeth, kept his mouth closed, and smiled. The more he was hurt the wider he smiled. At last Cobbins relented and sent word that he could graduate and could make his own speech.

There was one more problem to settle before graduation. Richard had nothing to wear. Finally, his employer, Mrs. Bibbs, loaned him the money to buy a pearl-gray suit. On the night of May 29, 1925—before streamers of the class colors pea-green and peach, surrounded by the class flowers fern and sweetpeas, under the class motto "We Finish to Begin"—Richard spoke positively and abstractly about life. Not one member of the honor student's family was present. Richard heard the applause and left the auditorium before the presentation of the school play: *Climb Though the Rocks Be Rugged*. Someone had invited him to a party but he did not accept. The hell with it! he thought. "With almost seventeen years of baffled living behind [him] he faced the world. . . ."

The white South has never known me . . .

VI

As a grammar school graduate and in uneasy circumstances at home, Richard's life almost depended upon his finding work. He accepted the first offer, a job as porter in a clothing store on Farish Street. "The shop was always crowded with black men and women pawing over cheap suits and dresses. And they paid whatever price the white man asked. The boss, his son, and the clerk treated the Negroes with open contempt, pushing, kicking, or slapping them." No matter how often Richard watched his employers' behavior toward Negroes, he could not see it happen without becoming enraged. Afraid that his white boss would see his anger, he kept nervously on edge trying to hide his emotions.

One morning while I was polishing brass out front, the boss and his son drove up in their car. A frightened black woman sat between them. They got out and half dragged and half kicked the woman into the store. White people passed and looked on without expression. A white policeman watched from the corner, twirling his night stick; but he made no move. I watched out of the corner of my eyes, but I never slackened the strokes of my chamois upon the brass. After a moment or two I heard shrill screams coming from the rear room of the store; later the woman stumbled out, bleeding, crying, holding her stomach, her clothing torn. When she reached the sidewalk, the policeman met her, grabbed her, accused her of being drunk, called a patrol wagon and carted her away.[1]

Fearful, yet pressed by curiosity, Richard went to the back of the store, presumably to get a mop. Blood and wisps of hair and clothing were scattered on the floor and the boss and his son were washing the red liquid off their hands at the sink. One of the men slapped him on the back: "Boy, that's what we do to niggers when they don't pay their bills," he said.

In a few weeks Richard noticed that whenever he raised his eyes from the floor the boss was watching him. One morning the son asked: "Why don't you laugh and talk like the other niggers?" Richard smiled; his heart contracted, his eyes widened to show more of the white and he softly answered that he did not have anything to smile or talk about. His answer made his employers uneasy and he was fired.

Dick "Squilla" Jordan got Richard a job with the American Optical Company on Capitol Street a few weeks later. The Illinois-born manager had been looking for a schoolboy to work full-time during the summer months and part-time when school reopened. A knowledge of algebra was necessary and a chance to learn the optical trade was offered. The pay was five dollars a week and the hours were 8:30 A.M. to 7:30 P.M. Richard's spirits rose—he would learn an occupation and Squilla worked nearby on Capitol in a jewelry store and Joe Brown worked for "Fair," a general merchandising store in the same neighborhood.

Mr. Crane, the manager, a tall red-faced brisk white man, questioned Richard about his schooling and was pleased to learn that he had had two years of algebra. American Optical was a small factory filled with strange machines all smeared with red rouge. Richard was the sole Negro employee. He swept, mopped, dusted and ran errands. When his work was completed he stood and watched two white men grinding lens on the machines. They had been introduced to Richard by Mr. Crane but never talked to him. A month passed. Richard was not learning the trade as he had been promised so one afternoon he asked Reynolds, one of the white men, to tell him about the work. "What are you trying to do, get smart, nigger?" was his answer. Then Richard walked over to speak to Pease, the other worker. But Pease was even more violent than Reynolds: he shook his fist in Richard's face and told him, "This is *white* man's work around here." From then on both men changed toward Richard. They called him a lazy black sonofabitch, refused to say good morning or good evening and sometimes taunted him: "Nigger, you think you'll ever amount to anything? . . . What do niggers think about? . . . If I was a nigger, I'd kill myself . . . But I don't reckon niggers mind being niggers." Richard kept silent and tried to hide his anxiety under a nervous smile.

Day after day the men harassed Richard, until a climax came one noon. Mr. Crane and his secretary were out of the office—Reynolds and Pease had timed it that way so that Richard would be more intimidated and they could, in turn, deny any report he might make to the boss. Pease called Richard to his workbench. To get there he had to go between two narrow benches and stand with his back against the wall. When he reached Pease, Reynolds walked over and blocked the narrow passageway between the benches, folded his arms and stared at Richard. Pease looked up and spoke slowly, so there would be no possibility of his not understanding. "Richard, Reynolds here tells me that you called me Pease," he said.

Richard was trapped. If he denied the crime of omitting "Mr." in front of a white Southerner's name he was then calling Reynolds a liar. There was no neutral course to resolve such a dilemma. "I don't remember calling you *Pease,* Mr. Pease," he said cautiously. The words barely left his mouth when the man shouted that he had just that minute called him Pease! And he slapped him until he fell against the bench. Reynolds stood over him with a steel bar in his hands and threatened to rip his gutstring loose with the bar. They gave Richard a minute in which to leave the factory and warned him not to show up again nor to tell the boss. The following day Richard returned to collect money owed for the week's work and waited until he was certain that Crane was at his desk before entering the office. The manager was sympathetic and asked Richard to tell him what had happened and which man was at fault. Visions of the two men waylaying him, killing him, appeared in his mind and memories of the murder of his friend's brother kept him from speaking freely. There was no use to complain—he would never learn to operate the machines as long as the two white men remained in the small plant. Crane gave him more than he had earned for the week, shook his hand and walked him to the door. Richard ran down the steps fighting tears, then paused and looked back. Crane stood at the head of the stairs, shaking his head helplessly.

For many weeks after his experience at American Optical he felt numb. A heavy cloak of exhaustion lay over his limbs and he went to bed tired and arose tired. There was no one he could talk to because he knew that he would hear a justification of the behavior of white people. He would be told that he was wrong, that he had to adjust to their ways that, as a matter of fact, he brought these incidents onto his own head because he would not accept an unalterable way of life. Squilla told him: "Dick, look, you're black, black, *black,* see? Can't you understand that? . . . You act around white people as if you didn't know that they were white. And they *see* it." Certain of his mannerisms enraged white people: he walked erect, with his chin level with the ground and his eyes often abstracted so that he looked white people in the eye; his feet were lifted and placed precisely without any self-abnegating shuffle—and the swing of his entire body showed an unself-conscious pride.

. . . it was simply utterly impossible for me to calculate, to scheme, to act, to plot all the time. I would remember to dissemble for short periods, then I would forget and act straight and human again, not with the desire to harm anybody, but merely forgetting the artificial status of race and class. It was the same with whites as with blacks; it was my way with everybody.[2]

Richard's next job was a helper in a drugstore and he began work apprehensively, determined to watch his every action and facial expression. It was the noontime rush that defeated him. Timing had to be split-second so people could return to work or go shopping on their lunch hours. Orders were shouted and snapped and a general frenzy prevailed. Richard could not keep his mind on not offending white people while at the same time trying to anticipate the orders of his boss and the two countermen. On Wednesday he dropped a huge jug of orange syrup in the middle of the floor. On Saturday he was fired.

Again he was idle for weeks and as the summer passed he knew he could not possibly go to college or even finish high school. By autumn jobs became more numerous and Richard heard that hall-boys were needed at the Edwards Hotel and applied. He was hired to mop long tiled hallways and worked with a Negro gang. Some of his fears were forgotten because he could laugh and joke and not watch every word or action. But in a few days he was almost in trouble again. One evening he walked out of the building with one of the young maids and when they passed the white night watchman he slapped her playfully on the buttocks. The girl twisted away and walked on down the street but Richard stopped and stared at the guard, amazed. "Nigger, you look like you don't like what I did," the watchman threatened Richard. "Don't you like it, nigger?" "Yes, sir," Richard whispered with a dry throat. "Well, talk like it, then, goddammit!"

An urgency to leave Jackson and, ultimately, the South pounded inside Richard. He would be killed sooner or later if he remained. Slowly, out of his salary, he began to save a few dollars and gave up cigarettes, soda and even food, but it was exasperating: it would take forever to earn his fare to another city. Almost his entire pay went to feed the family at home and the goal of one hundred dollars which he had set himself would take two or three years to amass. Would he survive that long? He became a bellboy and added a few extra dollars to his salary by smuggling bootleg whiskey in to the hotel prostitutes. It was still not enough to bring closer his timetable for going North.

About nine o'clock one evening after work, Richard met two of his friends who were known as "the Hubert boys." Their father was Z. T. Hubert, president of Jackson College. Zack, Jr. and Giles Hubert were community models: "the image of the upper middle class, they wore nice clothes, had spending money, both were stockily built, brown-skinned average good-looks, well mannered and good mixers with the boys who lived outside of the college campus."[3]

"The Hubert clan, which produced college presidents Benjamin Franklin Hubert and Zachary Taylor Hubert, and several cousins and brothers scarcely less notable, sprang directly from bondage. Paul, the founder of the line, had been a leader among the slaves of Warren County, Georgia, and his sons, Zachary and Moses, immediately after the Emancipation purchased land in Hancock County. Hardly had they built their log cabin when they created a brush-arbor church and a log school. All twelve of Zack Hubert's children made their way to college and notable careers."

Zack Jr. and Giles always greeted Richard with "Man! How much you got stashed away now?" And whenever they met they tried to think of ways to help Richard leave the South. They finally came up with a plan: in the Jackson College cellar large quantities of tinned food were stored. It would be a lark, an adventure, to steal the food, sell it to local restaurants and give Richard the money.

A night was set for the robbery, a small wagon was borrowed, sacking material for covering and chisels and screwdrivers were collected and a time arranged. Richard was terrified but he could not let Zack and Giles know how he felt as they crept through the night to the school. The three boys were overcome with fits of nervous giggles and Richard was certain that they would awaken the entire neighborhood. At the school they broke through a window and into the storeroom, from which they lugged away a few cases of fruit and tinned meats and fish. Putting on a bold face, the Hubert boys visited a few restaurants and sold the tinned goods for much less than their value, but a certain amount was collected and given to Richard for his trip. From their own allowances Zack and Giles contributed what they could spare but it still was not quite enough.

An impatience that grew into a feeling of torture plagued Richard day and night. Just a small amount of money would free him. The household and his relatives grew more onerous—they had not changed, but his sensibilities had become so supercharged that every glance, every word was a direct affront that rubbed on raw feelings.

Just when he thought that he could not stay another day in Jackson, Arthur Leaner, who was a year or so younger than Richard, offered him a way out.

Leaner lived on the east side of Jackson on Church Street, which was considered one of the "best" streets. Arthur's parents were musicians—his father and three brothers had a Dixieland jazz band which played for "white" dances. Arthur was "the Mr. Fix-It type fellow. He had an in with Professor Lanier and Professor Cobbins . . . always able to make a dime when the rest . . . didn't know how. Arthur had an in with the Jewish fellow, Abe Lehman, who owned the only Negro theatre in Jackson."[4]

The tall, skinny, rather handsome young Arthur Leaner was always on the move, and poured his energies into "wresting every dollar from a world he was convinced would never change." He watched for students with talent and persuaded them to appear, without payment, in an annual black-face minstrel show at the Catholic School for Negroes. His partner in the affair was Abe Lehman with Arthur acting as the go-between with the head of the school, Father Height.

Arthur Leaner had a talent for showmanship similar to that of Billy Rose.[5] Before every show Arthur rehearsed his performers, provided costumes made of vividly colored cheesecloth and marched them through every section of the black community. "Some of his top showmen were Collie Lennoard, he was a funny guy who always played the end man; Zeke Bradley blew the cornet, Julius Carter (Ditty Boy) beat the drum. Sometimes Arthur's brother George would play the piano. [Richard, Joe Brown], Richard Jordan, Conkey Booker, Lewis Anderson and others would fill in to make up the show."

Although Richard appeared in Arthur's shows he was not friendly toward him; he told his friend Joe that they were being used, "sold down the river" by performing without payment while Arthur and Abe Lehman pocketed all the money. But when Arthur explained a method by which he could earn money fast Richard momentarily forgot his antagonism. Arthur, who knew everything that was happening anywhere in their community, sent him to see Abe Lehman, the owner of the Alamo on Farish Street, to ask for a job. He explained that the girl in the ticket office was using a "system." "If you get the job," he said, "you can make some good gravy." But Arthur would not give any details; he simply smiled mysteriously, snapped his fingers as if he had performed a miracle, and walked away.

Richard spent five minutes resisting temptation, which meant thrusting to the back of his mind the moral strictures of his mother and Granny and one stab of fear that he might be caught, and walked across to the Alamo. Richard made a pledge of honesty to the owner, feeling no qualms about what he intended to do.

During the first afternoon the girl in the ticket office watched Richard closely and he knew that she was trying to determine whether or not to include him in the graft. Abe Lehman also watched him for a few days. During this time a tension as great as any he had known made his hands perspire but he gave no outward sign. More and more he was learning to master his inner distress and fear.

While he was eating dinner in a café near the Alamo one evening, a strange black man walked in and sat down beside him. When he called him by name Richard became wary: was he one of the boss' spies? The man explained that he was a friend of the girl in the box office and he looked at Richard searchingly: "We start tonight," he told him.

"It'll work this way," he explained in a low, smooth tone. "A guy'll come to you and ask for a match. You give him five tickets that you'll hold out of the box, see? We'll give you the signal when to start holding out. The guy'll give the tickets to Tel; she'll resell them all at once, when a crowd is buying at the rush hour. You get it?"

By the end of the week the money had been split four ways and Richard had fifty dollars to add to his "going north money." But when he dropped a hint to the man he had met in the café that he wanted to leave the job he grew violently angry. Quickly, Richard reassured him and agreed to remain. Well, he thought, I'll have to sneak away one night without saying anything to Lehman or this gang.

On a Saturday night Richard waited until Granny and the rest of the family left for church and then took his packed cardboard suitcase from its hiding place. Trying to armor his emotions against a desire to weep, he walked down the hallway to his mother's room. Ella cried; told him to take care of himself and to send for her as soon as he could. She was not happy living in her mother's house. What would she do without her big son? Then Richard walked out the back door and started toward the little Jay Railroad lines a quarter of a mile away. He tramped along the railway ties and when he reached Gowdey's oil mill he lifted his head and sniffed the air for one more smell of the good cottonseed being pressed into cakes—it always smelled like a ham baking—but it had begun to rain and the scent he loved was blotted out. He waited downtown at the I. C.

Railroad Station for an hour. Later, Richard sat in a Jim Crow coach headed for Memphis. A heavy weight seemed to lift from his body but when his cheek itched and he put up his hand to scratch he discovered tears.

One Sunday morning in November, 1925, Richard's train rolled into the Memphis station. It was a cold gloomy day as he carried his suitcase down Beale Street in search of a rooming house. Ella had cautioned him about the giant river city; it was full of danger from thieves, prostitutes, pickpockets, drunkards and confidence men, but he was prepared. He had sewn a small cloth bag for his money and pinned it toward the front of his underwear. A thief would have to kill him first because no one could remove his clothing unless he was dead.

After walking several blocks he saw a large frame house with a sign advertising rooms for rent. Richard examined it closely to see if it was clean and respectable and then, stepping lightly on the balls of his feet, he walked up its steps. At his timid knock, a big jolly brown woman opened the door and invited him to enter. She introduced herself as Mrs. Moss, the owner and landlady, and volunteered that her husband worked in a bakery.

Mrs. Moss questioned Richard closely, often punctuating her words with gales of laughter, and finally explained that the rent for a room was three dollars a week. "That's a little high," Richard said and explained that he was unemployed. "Then give me two dollars and a half till you get yourself a job," Mrs. Moss told him.

His new landlady was one of the warmest, friendliest persons Richard had ever known. When she had shown him to his room he fell asleep, his mind relaxed, after promising to eat dinner with her when she returned from church. Later in the afternoon, Mrs. Moss called him to dinner and introduced him to her young daughter Bess, who was a giggling seventeen-year-old eager for marriage. When Mrs. Moss indicated that she was willing to have Bess marry Richard he retreated, feeling awkward and embarrassed but most of all amazed. Upstairs in his room, he lay across his bed and thought about the two people whom he had met; he was already accepted by strangers more than he had ever been by relatives in his own home. But was it wise to remain in a house with a seventeen-year-old girl eager for marriage and a mother equally anxious to have her daughter fall in love with him? "To Bess and her mother, money was important, but they did not strive for it too hard. They had no tensions, unappeasable longings, no desire to do something to redeem themselves. The main value in their lives was simple, clean, good living and when they thought they had found those same qualities in one of their race, they instinctively embraced him, liked him, and asked no questions."

On the day after Richard's arrival he found a job as a dishwasher in the Lyle, a drugstore at the corner of Main Street and Beale. The salary was ten dollars for the first week, twelve dollars thereafter, and he would be given two meals during the night hours that he worked. One problem would be how to eat during the day and yet save money to send for his mother. The solution was easy: he had accustomed himself to worse conditions when he lived at Granny's, and he purchased a can opener and some pork and beans. When he awakened the following morning he sat on the bed and ate beans out of a can, scooping them up with his fingers. Afterwards he slipped out of the house and walked to the waterfront, where he sat on a knoll and watched the Mississippi River.

In his mind was the constant memory of his mother's plea that he send for her as quickly as he could. As soon as he was accustomed to Memphis he decided to look for another job which would pay more money. And while wandering around one afternoon, killing time and eating bags of popcorn, he remembered that the American Optical Company had a large office in Memphis. Why not apply? Memphis was not a small town like Jackson and no one would hold the trivial quarrel he had had with Reynolds and Pease against him. Besides, Mr. Crane, the manager, would give him a good recommendation. Richard went to the office on the fifth floor of a building at the corner of Madison and Second Avenue, rode boldly up in the elevator and asked for a job. With meticulous honesty Richard explained everything that had happened at their branch office in Jackson and he was hired. His salary was only eight dollars per week with a promise of another dollar a week until it reached ten, which was less than he was making but he was happy to get away from the stench of dishwater. He was happy also to spend more time away from his boarding house because young Bess Moss nagged for his attention.

In American Optical he was assigned to run errands and wash eyeglasses after they came from the rouge-smeared machines. Every evening he took large sacks of mail to the post office, but they never seemed too heavy and his energy revived with a better diet. At noon he often ran errands for the white men employed in the company and began to earn enough in tips so that he could put away his salary toward his mother's fare from Jackson and a room or apartment when she arrived. It took almost a year but finally he was able to send for her and for his brother Alan, who had returned home from

Detroit. The three set up housekeeping in two rooms only a few blocks from where they had lived when Richard was a small boy.

A measure of objectivity and an ability to contain his tensions grew in Richard as he worked alongside the white men in his company. Memphis had an air of urbanity and he was sometimes invited to enter into their discussions. It was a shop which consisted of about a dozen men who ranged "from Ku Klux Klanners to Jews, from theosophists to just plain poor whites." Although he discerned hatred or disdain in the attitudes of some of the men, no one abused him openly or shouted at him.

Richard began to patronize secondhand bookstores and discovered periodicals like *Harper's Magazine,* the *Atlantic Monthly,* and the *American Mercury.* He would buy back issues for a few pennies, read them, and then resell them to the bookdealer. Another habit he developed by which he satisfied his need to read everything and yet save money was to arrive at the office building at eight in the morning. He did not have to report for work until nine and had made a friend of a janitor in the downstairs bank. There he read the early edition of the Memphis *Commercial Appeal,* thus saving five cents a day.

One morning he read an editorial attack in the *Commercial Appeal* against H. L. Mencken. The name was familiar to him as the editor of the *American Mercury,* but he had not read any of Mencken's writings. "The article was a furious denunciation of Mencken, concluding with one, hot, short sentence: 'Mencken is a fool.' " Richard wondered what Mencken had done to call the wrath of the South down upon his head; he knew he was a white man but the editorial cursed him as if he were black. Were there, then, people other than Negroes who criticized the South? Richard's sympathies and curiosity were aroused. How could he get hold of books by or about Mencken? He had often gone to the library for white men at work but it was segregated and there were no facilities for black men.

The only white people with whom he had any contact at all were in American Optical; carefully he weighed each man in his mind to see whom he could approach to ask for the loan of a library card. It would be dangerous: he had to be careful, but he was determined to get his hands on a Mencken book. Over and over he went down a mental list of the personalities in the shop: Don was a Jew, and his position was not much better than Richard's—uneasy and insecure, he had a frantic desire to demonstrate a racial solidarity with the Southern whites; Olin, a young white man, subforeman of the shop, pretended to be a friend in the same way that most white Southerners fancied they were friends to Negroes and the epithet "nigger" fell out of his mouth with regularity; Bill assumed that Negroes were put on earth to be slaves; the boss was a Baptist and would never understand why a black man would want to read Mencken; all the other men on the job showed in their talk that they were sympathizers, if not members, of the KKK. There remained only one man who was difficult to categorize—Mr. Falk, whom the men in the shop hated and called a "Pope lover." As an Irish-Catholic he was an object of hatred in the South and Richard thought he might be refused but not betrayed if he asked to borrow a library card.

Well, Richard thought, here goes! and with weak knees he approached Mr. Falk's machine and whispered: "I want to ask you a favor." When Richard explained what he wanted Falk looked at him suspiciously. "My card is full most of the time," he said. "You're not trying to get me into trouble, are you, boy?" he asked. Richard reassured him and then stood silent. He could not argue—that would be placing himself on the same level as a white man—but he could persist through his quiet presence. Finally, Falk asked what book he wanted and when Richard told him he asked, why Mencken? He was not an author who wrote "the right things."

A few days later Falk called Richard over and, after making him promise not to mention it to any of the white men at work, loaned him a library card. "Do you think you can manage it? If they suspect you, you'll get in trouble," he said. Richard explained that he would write a note, presumably from Falk and forge his name, and the white man laughed and gave his permission.

At the local library Richard stood a respectful distance from the desk and assumed a stupid expression, seeking to look as unbookish as possible, while the librarian read the note. She was suspicious and cross-examined him. Mr. Falk never wrote such vague notes—what books by Mencken did he want? "You're not using these books, are you?" she asked pointedly. If the woman had turned her back for a moment Richard would have run out the door in fright but he reassured her that he could not read. She stamped the card and handed Richard the books.

A block away from the library Richard stopped to look at the titles; one was *A Book of Prefaces*—at nineteen he could not even pronounced the word—and the other was *Prejudices*. He frowned at that one, disappointed; the word was known to every black man and stained with race hate. Why would Mencken use such a word? Perhaps he had misread the editorial about the author. "A man who had prejudices must be wrong."

That night Richard began to read *Prefaces* and was shocked and jarred by the style. "Why did he write like that? And how did one write like that? [He] pictured the man as a raging demon, slashing with his pen, consumed with hate, denouncing everything American, extolling everything European or German, laughing at the weaknesses of people, mocking God, authority. What was this? [Richard] stood up, trying to realize what reality lay behind the meaning of the words. . . . Yes, this man was fighting, fighting with words. He was using words as a weapon, using them as one would use a club. Could words be weapons? Well, yes, for here they were."

Amazed and half-frightened, Richard looked around the room to reassure himself that he was alone. The names of Anatole France, Joseph Conrad, Sinclair Lewis, Sherwood Anderson, Dostoevski, Tolstoy, Twain, T. S. Eliot, Thomas Mann, Dumas, Poe, Dreiser and dozens of others beamed through his mind like an arc light. Who were these men? Did they exist or had Mencken made them up; and how did one pronounce some of their names? When he ran across words he did not know he stopped reading and looked them up in the dictionary. A strange and exciting world he was avid to know was rising before his eyes and he lead the entire night, finishing the book at dawn. It was difficult to keep his eyes open and he felt drowsy at work but the mood of the book he had read stayed with him all day.

Reading grew into a habit; he made more and more trips to the library. As soon as he read two books he took out two more, using Mencken as a guide to discover new authors. The first work of serious fiction he read was *Main Street* and afterwards he discovered a new use for a novel: it made him see Mr. Gerald, his employer, as an American type and he would smile when he saw him lug his golf bags into the office. Sinclair Lewis had lessened the distance between them, only, of course, in Richard's mind, but he felt he knew Gerald and the narrowness of his life. It was the delineation of character that held his attention; he read to find the point of view of the author. After *Main Street* he began on Dreiser and took from the library *Jennie Gerhardt* and *Sister Carrie*. There in those pages lay all his mother's suffering. Again he was overwhelmed. "All my life had shaped me for the realism, the naturalism of the modern novel, and I could not read enough of them." He was reading the literature of the twentieth century, the literature of rebellion, and each author seemed to be telling him that he was not queer or strange to rebel. Other men were fighting too.

Whenever he took a book with him to work he wrapped it

carefully in newspaper—a habit that was to persist for years in other cities and under other circumstances. But when he went out on an errand some of the white men in the shop took off the paper to see what he was reading and questioned him when he returned. "Boy, what are you reading those books for?" . . . "That's deep stuff you're reading, boy." . . . "You'll addle your brains if you don't watch out." No one at work, with the exception of Mr. Falk, read anything except newspapers or pulp magazines and some of the white men began to watch him with suspicion. Richard's tension returned and his fear made him feel guilty. Were the men aware that he looked at them with new eyes, that he understood character and relationships and had entered a dangerous and forbidden area? He would have to guard his every act and force himself to smile and laugh easily, to play dumb. Each day he fought to maintain a sunny disposition and each day it became more difficult.

I held my life in my mind, in my consciousness each day, feeling at times that I would stumble and drop it, spill it forever. My reading had created a vast sense of distance between me and the world in which I lived and tried to make a living, and that sense of distance was increasing each day. My days and nights were one long, quiet, continuously contained dream of terror, tension, and anxiety. I wondered how long I could bear it.[6]

Anxiety overpowered him some days and he stopped reading for a while, hoping that he would regain his balance, but a vague hunger would swell until there seemed an irritation in his muscles and he would forge another note and take home the drug "that opened up new avenues of feeling and seeing. . . ." And as he read, a nimbus formed around the word "North" he had to get out of the South; his life depended upon it.

Aunt Maggie came from Detroit to pay her sister and nephews a visit. Professor Matthews, with whom she had fled the South, had deserted her and she was undetermined about what she would do next. It was during her visit that the vague dreams of going north congealed into action . . . after she teased him for saying "I wish . . ." all the time. Ella, Maggie and Richard held long conferences about job prospects, the cost of rent and food and how they could make the move. Maggie wanted to go to Chicago, where she had never been, instead of returning to Detroit. In that city, she had been told, there were more jobs in factories and small shops; she was tired of cleaning or cooking and wanted to learn a new skill. She thought she might study to be a lady barber in Chicago and then, whatever her circumstances and wherever she lived, she could earn a better living. But after each conference Richard became more depressed—

the whole family could not leave at once because there was not enough money.

"Finally sheer wish and hope prevailed over common sense and facts." They would have to gamble. Richard and Aunt Maggie would go first, find work and a place to live, and then send for Ella and Alan. Between Richard and Maggie they had $150—he would work another month and save as much as possible. And he would not tell his employer he was leaving until two days before so that the white men on the job would not become hostile. Then he would pose as an innocent whose aunt was taking his paralyzed mother to Chicago and say that he had to accompany her.

Three and a half weeks dragged to an end and the day arrived to quit his job. Richard went into Mr. Gerald's office and when his boss heard the news he leaned back in his swivel chair and watched Richard's face closely as he questioned: "You think you'll do any better up there?" Why not stay in the South and work and send money to his mother if it was necessary for her to go? When word reached upstairs in the factory the white men went to Richard to give him advice. "The North's no good for your people, boy . . . You'll come back here where your friends are . . . How're you going to act up there? . . . Would you speak to a white girl up there? . . . You'll change. Niggers change when they go North." Richard was going North so that he could change but he tried to behave stupidly. Only Mr. Falk gave him a secret smile of encouragement when Richard slipped his library card under some papers on his machine.

On a northbound train, in full flight the following day, Richard thought of his nineteen years in Mississippi and Tennessee. He could not fully account for the divers experiences that had resulted in a rejection of the South—for he was leaving without a single regret— and yet, from the heart of that terrible culture there had blossomed in him a sense that life could and should and had to be different.

The white South said that it knew "niggers," and I was what the white South called a "nigger." Well, the white South had never known me —never known what I thought, what I felt. The white South said that I had a "place" in life. Well, I had never felt my "place"; or, rather, my deepest instincts had always made me reject the "place" to which the white South had assigned me. It had never occurred to me that I was in any way an inferior being. And no word that I had ever heard fall from the lips of southern white men had ever made me really doubt the worth of my own humanity . . . Not only had the southern whites not known me, but, more important still, as I had lived in the South I had not had the chance to learn who I was. The pressure of southern living kept me from being the kind of person that I might have been. I had been what my surroundings had demanded, what my family—conforming to the dictates of the whites above them—had exacted of me, and what the whites had said that I must be. Never being fully able to be myself, I had slowly learned that the South could recognize but a part of a man, could accept but a fragment of his personality, and all the rest—the best and deepest things of heart and mind—were tossed away in blind ignorance and hate.[7]

Yet, Richard knew that he was a Southerner: his personality had been formed by that culture; it belonged to him as much as it did to the white man. Transplanted in the North, he would see if life could be lived with dignity . . . if the personalities of others would not be violated . . . if men would be able to confront other men without fear or shame. If this could happen, then he "would know that there was yet hope in that southern swamp of despair and violence, that light could emerge even out of the blackest of the southern night."

And exhausted by his thoughts, by the strain of his efforts, he listened to the sound of the clicking wheels of the train and fell asleep.

Chicago seemed an unreal city . . .

VII

Richard's first glimpse of "the flat black stretches of Chicago" depressed and dismayed him. "Chicago seemed an unreal city whose mythical houses were built of slabs of black coal wreathed in palls of gray smoke, houses whose foundations were sinking slowly into the dank prairie. Flashes of steam showed intermittently on the wide horizon, gleaming translucently in the winter sun."[1] It was December, 1927, and a frozen wind was blowing snowflakes over the city.

It was five in the morning and still dark when Richard and Maggie got off the train. They walked slowly along the runway between tracks toward the station. People were jammed together like cattle and they moved and jostled and made noises like animals. Richard had never been so enclosed by such a variety of bodies, white and black, impatient, pushing at their confinement. An impersonal fury pervaded the atmosphere. Twice his cardboard suitcase was almost torn from his hand and Richard had an impulse to laugh hysterically as he imagined the bag traveling to the station alone, held up and moved along by the press of human bodies.

Relief came when he reached the station. Automatically, Richard looked all about for signs: FOR WHITE, FOR COLORED but he saw none. "It was strange to pause before a crowded newsstand and buy a newspaper without having to wait until a white man was served." The noise was incredible, a din seemed to enter Richard's mind and body. No one strolled or even walked. People appeared to be nearly running and Richard wondered how they avoided colliding with one another. The station was like a scene from a silent movie—people running, their legs, arms and heads jerking, doors whizzing in a dizzy circle, lights flashing, whistles sounding, bells ringing.

Outside the station Richard drew a deep breath and almost choked when the icy air struck his unaccustomed lungs; he began to gasp and cough as tears from the paroxysm froze on his cheeks. While they waited for a streetcar Richard "looked northward at towering buildings of steel and stone. There were no curves here, no trees: only angles, lines, squares, bricks and copper wires." Occasionally the ground beneath their feet shook from some faraway pounding and Richard felt that the city, despite its massiveness, was somehow dangerously fragile. Even the speech was strange. It was clipped and rapid and shrill. And after the slow, accented speech of the South it was difficult to understand what people were saying.

As Richard stood in the icy wind he began to grow tense again, although it was a different feeling than he had known before. This iron city had its own rules and laws—whould he ever learn them? What would happen to him here? He was seized by doubt. Should he have come here? But going back was impossible; he would have to cope with the unknown that lay ahead. He turned to his aunt to reassure himself, but her lips were compressed and her face and eyes seemed frantic.[2] Richard kept silent.

When the streetcar came Maggie pushed Richard ahead of her and motioned him to a seat next to a white man. He sat nervously on the edge and stared straight in front of him. Richard was not afraid of the white man but he dreaded the scene he thought would take place. After a few blocks, when nothing had happened, Richard peered at the man from the corner of his eye without moving his head and saw that he was staring out of the window oblivious to everything around him. A few stops along the man got off and another white man sat beside Richard and buried his face in a newspaper. How strange, he thought. "How could that possibly be? Was he conscious of my blackness?" There had been a terrible intimacy in the South and in his Granny's home; here he was just a part of the landscape.

Southward, toward Indiana Avenue, the streetcar screeched on its steel tracks headed toward the city within a city, the black metropolis of Chicago. When they reached the poor South Side neighborhood and Richard looked around it seemed to him that all the black faces he saw looked stricken and frightened. At Aunt Cleo's, whom Richard called Aunt Sissy, in a soot-blackened building, Richard had a disappointment. She was living in one room instead of an apartment but luckily the landlady had a small room empty on the same floor as Cleo which Richard rented. His aunt looked older than her years;

her body sagged under a cotton dress and gray wool sweater; her eyes had a wild and beaten look and her hair was already specked with white. Her husband, a Southern sharecropper, had deserted her when they reached Chicago, just as Nathan had deserted Richard's mother.

Richard was so exhausted from the trip and the myriad impressions of the new city that he went to bed immediately after dinner and, for once, slept without dreaming. Early the next morning he rose from bed feeling that he was going to freeze—the temperature had dropped below zero—and dressed, doubling his clothing. The house was as cold inside as a Southern street was in midwinter. A gray day showed through the curtained window and Richard hoped that the wind would stop blowing because his clothes were too light. He was still wearing his pearl-gray graduation suit but his arms had grown and bony wrists protruded way below the edge of his sleeves. His height had increased to five feet seven inches but he still weighed little over one hundred pounds and a skinny neck sprang out of his white collar. When he sat he tended to hunch his neck forward so that the ill-fitting suit rode up and engulfed him to the chin. Aunt Cleo gave him a wool scarf to tie around his neck under the thin topcoat, for regardless of weather Richard had to find a job.

From the vestibule he stepped onto an ice-glittering street and for a moment the sun and cold blurred his vision so he was momentarily dizzy. Then, wanting to run so that his blood would stir faster, he edged cautiously down the slippery steps and walked as rapidly as he dared to the corner to catch a trolley. On the streetcar he rode and rode until there were no more black faces on the sidewalks; he "had now crossed the boundary line of the Black Belt and had entered that territory where jobs were perhaps to be had from white folks. [He] saw a sign in a delicatessen: PORTER WANTED."

Richard went into the store and a short, stout white woman with neatly combed black hair approached him and asked what he wanted. The voice jarred him. She was Jewish and spoke with an accent that changed a *w* into a *v*. For a moment Richard could not speak; he remembered with shame the obscenities he and his friends used to shout at Jewish storekeepers in Mississippi:

> Jew, Jew,
> Two for five
> That's what keeps
> Jew alive.

There were many more folk ditties, some mean, others filthy, all of them cruel. No one ever thought of questioning our right to do this; our mothers and parents generally approved, either actively or passively. To hold an attitude of antagonism or distrust toward Jews, was bred in us from childhood; it was not merely racial prejudice, it was a part of our cultural heritage.[3]

Afraid to look into her eyes for fear that she would read his embarrassed thoughts, Richard spoke quickly and asked if she needed a porter. The woman asked him to wait until her husband arrived and offered him a seat, but Richard said he would wait outside. The woman protested that it was too cold but he would not stay inside and went to the sidewalk, regretting that he had not remained in the warm store but unable to face the woman and say he had changed his mind. It was easier to walk up and down for half an hour in the cold than for Richard to explain—he would have felt uncomfortable and defensive.

At last a bald, stoutish white man entered the store and took off his coat so Richard went in and asked for the job. He was hired. The work was easy and the owners, Mr. and Mrs. Hoffman, were kind, but he was appalled that he could not understand a third of what was said to him. "My slow southern ears were baffled by their clouded, thick accents." One day Mrs. Hoffman asked him to go to a nearby store owned by her cousin and get a can of chicken à la king. Richard had never heard the phrase before and asked her to repeat it. He still could not understand—she was speaking some foreign language. At last, after several attempts to make him understand, she asked: "Don't you know nosing?" Thoroughly abashed, Richard suggested that she write it down for him and, in sudden fury, Mrs. Hoffman shouted that she could not write. All the way to the store he said the separate sounds of the phrase and hoped that he could make himself clear. "Cheek Keen Awr Lar Keeng," Richard said slowly, hoping that the Hoffmans' cousin would not think he was being offensive. The cousin stared at him for a few minutes then put a can into a paper bag and handed it to him. Out of sight of the store Richard peeked into the bag and read the label. Some of the curses he had learned long before came involuntarily out of his mouth. How could he have been so stupid? He knew those words.

But Richard wondered why Mrs. Hoffman had been so impatient with him. Why had she shouted at him? She could have explained quietly. It was because he was black, that could be the only reason. She did not care, he decided. Then he grew angry. Life was certainly mixed up. "Though English was my native tongue and America my native land, she, an alien, could operate a store and earn a living in a neighborhood where I could not even live. I reasoned further that

she was aware of this and was trying to protect her position against
me."

Some months after he began his job in the delicatessen the
counterman in a luncheonette near his aunt's room told him that
examinations were going to be held for postal clerk and Richard at
once filed an application and waited. But in the meantime he wondered how he could take a day off without losing his job and began to
speculate about Mr. Hoffman's personality. In the South people fit
more readily into categories in relation to Negroes than in the
North. The Hoffmans were bewildering to him and he could not
accurately predict their behavior. If he asked for a day off, would
Hoffman tell him he was fired? "In the South it would have been an
unwise policy for a Negro to have gone to his white boss, and ask for
time to take an examination for another job. It would have implied
that the Negro did not like to work for the white boss, that he felt he
was not receiving just consideration and, inasmuch as most jobs that
Negroes held in the South involved a personal, paternalistic relationship, he would have been risking an argument that might have led to
violence."

Notification arrived that the examination was scheduled to take
place on a Monday and since Richard had been working seven days a
week he decided to take off Saturday and Sunday to rest. Afterwards
he would tell Mr. Hoffman that his mother had died and that he
had gone to Memphis to her funeral. Punishment after the fact was
preferable to an argument in advance. Richard took the examinations and returned to work on Tuesday. His employer was astonished
to see him, and had simply assumed that he had taken another job.
Neither of the Hoffmans accepted his story about Ella's death so
Richard piled lie on top of lie until he was hopelessly entangled. As
the untruths wrapped him round he hated himself and hated the
Hoffmans too. Mrs. Hoffman hammered at him that they understood
how he felt; he came from the South; he could not have an honest
relationship there, but he could tell them the truth. "We treat you
nice, don't we?" she asked him. Richard's shame and anger grew
because he felt he had revealed a sense of insecurity. He did not want
anyone to know how he felt and when the Hoffmans pitied him it
increased his self-consciousness. At the end of the week he quit his
job without telling them he was leaving.

It was not until I had left the delicatessen job that I saw how grossly I
had misread the motives and attitudes of Mr. Hoffman and his wife. I
had not yet learned anything that would have helped me to thread my
way through these perplexing racial relations. Accepting my environment

at its face value, trapped by my own emotions, I kept asking myself what had black people done to bring this crazy world upon them?

I was persisting in reading my present environment in the light of my old one.[4]

After a fruitless week looking for work Richard met on the street a girl he had known in Jackson. She was glad to see him and when he told her that he could not find a job she suggested that he go with her to a restaurant in the Patricia Hotel on Fullerton Street and she would vouch for him. The North Side Café had been recently opened by Mrs. Crooks, the mother of Richard Crooks, the New York tenor. Mrs. Crooks, a woman with cool gray eyes and a somewhat sardonic manner, hired Richard as dishwasher and general helper for fifteen dollars a week plus meals.

In addition to Richard and his friend from Jackson, who was the salad-maker, there were Tillie, an elderly rawboned Finnish woman with a sharp face, and several young white waitresses. The girls were brisk and comparatively free of racial prejudice, at least on the job. One morning when Richard was making coffee, Cora, one of the waitresses, came toward him carrying a loaded tray of food and squeezed against him to draw a cup of coffee. The encounter was casual and innocent but it was something that had never happened to Richard in his life. If he had not been born in the South the incident would have been as trivial to him as it was to the girl. But as Cora stood against him he contrasted her action with that of a Southern woman. If she had wanted coffee she would have ordered him to stand aside so that she would not touch him—the work of the hectic kitchen would have stopped for a moment. Cora's unaware body, which pressed so intimately, contained no hysterical, irrational fright and Richard felt an emotional safety in the knowledge.

Another time, one of the waitresses came late to work and was afraid that Mrs. Crooks would be angry. She went into the ladies' room to change into her uniform and a second later called urgently to Richard to tie her apron strings. For a second he was immobilized and then went forward, took the two loose strings, carried them around her body and to the back, where he tied a knot. As the girl ran to her station she grasped his hand for a moment and thanked him. Richard's mind filled "with all the possible meaning that that tiny, simple, human event could have meant to any Negro in the South where [he] had spent most of [his] hungry days."

Around three o'clock each day after the noon rush Richard had an hour for lunch and he usually sat on a bench in a nearby park. Most of the waitresses joined him there and sat with him talking of their home lives, their boyfriends or husbands, their sex problems, their finances. As he listened Richard wondered at their inexperience and naïveté—their problems appeared superficial. They seemed to live on the surface of life and wanted to avoid any situation which might arouse pain or fear or dread or even passion. All his life Richard had cultivated and probed his own emotions; for him the world could never be reduced to the good and the bad, the holy and the evil, the white and the black. A conviction began to grow that for the ignorant white girls to understand his life, Negro life, would require a vast revolution in theirs. And that what they needed to make themselves complete and mature personalities was a knowledge of lives such as he lived and suffered.

One afternoon Mrs. Crooks walked into the kitchen and saw Richard sitting on a box reading the *American Mercury*. "What on earth are you reading?" she demanded. At once Richard was on guard, even though he knew there was no reason to be. "Oh, just a magazine" that he had found, he told his boss. "Do you understand it?" she asked. "Yes, ma'am." "Well," she exclaimed, "the colored dishwasher reads the *American Mercury!*"

Tillie, the Finnish cook, was an expert and Richard enjoyed her cooking. As he passed the stove one day he heard her cough and then spit. At the same time he wondered where her spittle had gone because she was bent over a steaming pot of soup. His senses claimed that she spat into the pot, but his mind could not accept that any human being could be so dirty. He decided to keep watch and an hour or so later he observed while Tillie again cleared her throat, coughed and spat into the boiling soup. Richard's stomach revolted and he felt its contents start up in his throat but at the same time he did not want to believe what he had seen. Meal after meal he had eaten with relish and now in his own body was the cook's phlegm.

For a day Richard stopped eating and wondered if he dared complain to his white boss about her white cook—would Mrs. Crooks take his word if Tillie denied it? Well, he would have to have another witness but he felt uneasy about speaking to the white waitresses. Instead, he took aside his friend who made salads and asked her to say nothing, just to watch the cook. Half an hour later the girl rushed to Richard and sank into a chair but in a minute she jumped up and ran into the ladies' room to vomit. When she returned she said she could not work in the restaurant under such conditions but she, too, was afraid to complain about a white woman. It was an impasse and each time Richard picked up a tray to serve a customer he felt like vomiting. Finally, the Negro salad girl came to

work one morning and handed her coat and purse to Richard instead
of putting them in her locker.

"I'm going to tell her and quit, goddamn," she said.

"I'll quit too, if she doesn't fire her," I said.

"Oh, she won't believe me," she wailed in agony.

"You tell her. You're a woman, she might believe you."

Her eyes welled with tears and she sat for a long time; then she rose
and went abruptly into the dining room. I went to the door and peered.
Yes, she was at the desk, talking to the boss lady. She returned to the
kitchen and went into the pantry; I followed her.

"Did you tell her?" I asked.

"Yes."

"What did she say?"

"She said I was crazy."

"Oh, God!" I said.

"She just looked at me with those gray eyes of hers," the girl said.
"Why would Tillie do that?"

"I don't know," I said.

The boss lady came to the door and called the girl; both of them went
into the dining room. Tillie came over to me; a hard cold look was in her
eyes.

"What's happening here?" she asked.

"I don't know," I said, wanting to slap her across the mouth.

She muttered something and went back to the stove, coughed, spat into
a bubbling pot. I left the kitchen and went into the back areaway to
breathe. The boss lady came out.

"Richard," she said.

Her face was pale. I was smoking a cigarette and I did not look at
her.

"Is this true?"

"Yes, ma'am."

"It couldn't be. Do you know what you're saying?"

"Just watch her," I said.

"I don't know," she moaned.

She looked crushed. She went back into the dining room, but I saw her
watching the cook through the doors. I watched both of them, the boss
lady and the cook, praying that the cook would spit again. She did. The
boss lady came into the kitchen and stared at Tillie, but she did not utter
a word. She burst into tears and ran back into the dining room.

"What's happening here?" Tillie demanded.

No one answered. The boss lady came out and tossed Tillie her hat,
coat, and money.

"Now, get out of here, you dirty dog!" she said.

Tillie stared, then slowly picked up her hat, coat, and the money; she stood a moment, wiped sweat from her forehead with her hand, then spat, this time on the floor. She left.

Nobody was ever able to fathom why Tillie liked to spit into the food.[5]

All spring Richard worked at the café and then, three months before his twentieth birthday, he was called for temporary work in the post office. His pay was higher than in the restaurant—seventy cents an hour, or approximately twenty dollars a week—and his confidence grew. If he eventually became a regular clerk his salary would increase. The problem involved in a permanent appointment was a physical examination—he had received 94 percent on the written test out of a possible one hundred. More substantial meals had increased his weight to a bare 110 pounds but the minimum at the post office was 125. Every dollar that could be spared went for food; he ate steak, drank milk, ate dozens of bananas, rice, and yet his body did not respond. His aunt persuaded him to visit a doctor, who told him that there was nothing organically wrong, he was malnourished and should continue to eat and sleep long hours. Like an automaton he followed the medical man's orders but his weight remained the same. At last he admitted to himself that he would fail the examination but continued to eat, determined not to quit until defeat was certain.

Autumn came and he was called for his physical, preparatory to becoming a regular postal clerk. Still fighting for weight on the morning of the examination, he drank two quarts of buttermilk and ate six bananas. His stomach groaned under the pressure but the needle on the scales remained way under the required amount. Richard walked home, disconsolate, hating himself and wondering where he would find another job. Waves of doubt crept into his thoughts. Was he always to hang on the fringes of life? Was it too much to ask for, just a modest job? Would life ever grow any easier? It was unfair that only a few pounds kept him from security, especially when his written test had been among the highest of the applicants. But he did not spend a long time brooding—that's life, he said to himself, and went to see his old employer, Mrs. Crooks, who gave him back his job at the café.

Aunt Maggie had rented an apartment in which Richard shared a rear room. His mother and brother came from Memphis and all three slept in the windowless chamber. And under the pressures and tensions created by four people in two rooms—and at least two, Maggie and Richard, highly individualistic—an explosion came. Maggie sensed that Richard had kept something from her when he did not admit he had failed the post office test. She questioned him until he told her what had happened. Then, almost abruptly, everything changed between them. Suddenly, Richard was a failure, he would never "amount to anything," it would be her fate to look after her sister and the two young men for the rest of her life, she was not getting any younger, what would become of them if she got sick, on and on. His aunt seemed to be perpetually scowling or nagging.

At first Richard simply drew into himself when Maggie began to lament; he did not want to argue or say anything to hurt: "I loved her, next to momma she was the only one close to me." Sometimes he quietly left the house when she began fighting or buried his face in a book, trying to close mind, ears and heart. But this apparent calm only enraged his aunt. In a challenging voice she said: "Boy, are you reading for law?" "No." "Then why are you reading all the time?" "I like to." "But what do you get out of it?" "I get a great deal out of it."

Richard attached a small lamp to a chair next to his bed and shielded the light with newspaper so that it would not disturb his mother and brother. Every night or early in the morning, whenever he returned home from work, he read for a few hours. Maggie complained that his habit increased the electric light bill. When her complaint had no effect on her nephew she reached such a peak of frustration that she slipped into the room when he was reading and turned out the light, leaving him in darkness. Until Maggie developed that habit Richard had maintained his neutrality and had acquired the deafness of children whose parents shout; but this was beyond endurance and represented a complete invasion of his rights and person. And the ugly hysteria in the atmosphere kept him on edge.

Although he had saved no money, Richard decided to rent his own apartment and exclude Maggie. He invited his other aunt, Cleo, to live with them and moved his mother and brother into a tiny, dingy two-room place. In the kitchen was a rusted metal bed; one of its legs had to be supported with a box or chair, its mattress was thin, scarred by use and dirty. Richard beat it thoroughly and washed the bed with Lysol and then covered the mattress with a clean sheet. A thin worn sheet was not much protection against dirt but it made him feel that he was not lying in the sweat and grime of strangers.

Cockroaches ran out of every crack and corner and an odor of grease hung in the air day and night. But Richard was glad to have his own place and at night the kitchen became his private room. He could read or write or just stare at a wall and think; no one would bother him. Writing was beginning to be the single aim of his existence and he spent hours writing out disconnected sentences and paragraphs.

He grew to love the sheer beauty of words and his reading took on a different character. Richard began to study an author's style. He read Crane's *Red Badge of Courage,* Dostoevski's *The Possessed, Crime and Punishment, The Brothers Karamazov,* and then discovered *Three Lives* by Gertrude Stein. *Three Lives* shocked and excited him—suddenly, in his ears was the speech of his mother, his grandmother and his friends in Mississippi. Stein's winding snakelike sentences slowly ate their way into his feelings. Rose's remark about suicide made him feel like laughing out loud—"If I ever killed myself Melanctha it'd be by accident, and if I ever killed myself by accident Melanctha, I'd be awful sorry"—it expressed his own philosophy exactly. For weeks after he read the book he played with single sentences and phrases but the results were so poor that he would tear up the sheets and try again.

On the other hand, when he discovered Proust and read *Remembrance of Things Past* it crushed him and made him feel hopeless. The strong lucid prose awed Richard and the "vast, delicate, intricate, and psychological structure of the Frenchman's epic of death and decadence" made him yearn to write of the people in his own environment with an equal power. Proust's burning example before his eyes made him feel that he never could.

Another postal examination was scheduled for spring and Richard gave up writing temporarily. His obsession was to gain weight so that he would have security in a Civil Service position and then he would learn to write. He ate when he did not want to eat and drank milk and buttermilk until he hated the sight of the frothy white liquid. To relieve tension and fill the emptiness of not writing, he occasionally went to rent parties. Throughout the South Side, every night in the week, there were such parties; they were a device by which urban Negroes survived. Rent money was raised by having a party. Food, soft drinks or beer were served and a small charge was made, either for admission or food. Out-of-work musicians performed in exchange for something to eat or drink or a phonograph would provide dance music.

Richard enjoyed some of the parties in a quiet way; they were a new and different experience and he had made no friends in Chicago at all. Although he talked and laughed with girls, he did not dance and never asked to take anyone home or follow up an acquaintanceship. Sometimes a bold girl walked up to him, cupped her palm under his chin and exclaimed to the room at large that he had the *sweetest* face, or the most innocent, or that he was pretty. Then everyone would laugh and at such moment Richard wanted to wipe out everyone in the room. He knew he looked younger than his twenty-one years but he resented being touched and made fun of; he would lower his eyes, a tight smile on his lips and tremble with anger. As he grew more self-conscious he deliberately lost his Southern accent and began to speak in a terse, cynical manner designed to rebuff anyone who tried to approach him intimately. All of his timidity was hidden behind a superficially friendly mask. He began to make fun of things that hurt him and as too many things hurt him he was usually laughing. It was his defense. If he was lonely, he was not aware of it because all of his energy was channeled toward supporting his family and learning to write.

In a quest for emotional experience he took walks in the neighborhood during the day or at night after work, following fire engines and watching the reactions of the people around him. Sometimes he stopped on a street corner and listened to individual speech. Jive talk fascinated him. He had not heard it in the South—it was the speech of urban Negroes. To Richard jive meant fun, play, kidding, hiding things with words and stepping up the tempo of living through talk. He loved it because it was made up day after day by people on the South Side; made up on the spur of the moment during talk, picked up and tossed from one person to another, enriched, expanded or thrown away. It had a secret side he enjoyed; black men could carry on a conversation among themselves within earshot of whites, who would not know what was said.

" . . . as though offering libations of forgiveness to my environment."

VIII

In the spring Richard took a second Civil Service examination and passed. The months spent cramming himself with food had increased his weight to 125 pounds and he qualified for a permanent appointment as a postal clerk. Added weight lessened his long-jawed, hollow-faced appearance; his cheeks became fuller. A deep indentation under his nose at the bow of his upper lip became more prominent and, when abstracted, Richard touched its upper curve with the index finger of his left hand as if feeling a pimple.

On his first night of work Richard took a Loop-bound train to the post office. Before reaching Roosevelt Road the El curved underground and Richard stood up, swaying with the motion of the train, and walked through each coach until he reached the first car. There he leaned his head against the glass and watched the silver rails rush under the train. Far ahead lights glinted, and the motion, the roaring sound and a sense that the walls of the tunnel were fleeing past the train released Richard's tensions and he felt a will-less omnipotence.

At his station, Richard got off and walked toward the post office, a square of stone with yellow windows shining. The wind had disappeared and the April air was beginning to warm slightly. Inside the post office Richard was given a badge with a number which would be his right of entry and exit in the future. His job was to sort mail into designated cubbyholes as rapidly as possible. In the beginning he was conscious of reading each envelope before tossing it in its correct slot but within a few days he could take a batch of mail and while talking in low monotones from the side of his mouth to fellow clerks work automatically. Suddenly his hands would be empty and he had no knowledge of how it had been accomplished. The mail just disappeared into its correct pigeonhole.

Working nights, Richard spent his days in experimental writing, filling endless pages with stream-of-consciousness Negro dialect, trying to depict the dwellers of the black belt as he felt and saw them. But he was always dissatisfied and ripped up page after page; something was missing and he failed to get onto the paper what he felt. At the library he veered from fiction and looked up books on psychology and sociology, and the same fever of recognition that he had experienced in reading Gertrude Stein engulfed him when he recognized his and his family's behavior. Next he studied tables of figures "relating population density to insanity, relating housing to disease, relating school and recreational opportunities to crime, relating various forms of neurotic behavior to environment, relating racial insecurities to the conflicts between whites and blacks."

Sociology and psychology enabled him "to discern many strange types of Negro characters, to identify many modes of Negro behavior; and what moved [him] above all was the frequency of mental illness, that tragic toll that the urban environment exacted of the black peasant." A need Richard did not understand drove him toward sketching out warped, lost, baffled types—the religious fanatic, the pyromaniac, the murderer, the sex fiend. And he struggled "to master words, to make them disappear, to make them melt into a rising spiral of emotional stimuli, each greater than the other, each feeding and reinforcing the other, and all ending in an emotional climax that would drench the reader with a sense of a new world."

At the library one afternoon Richard and a well-dressed young student simultaneously reached for the same volume on a shelf and their shoulders bumped. After they both apologized the young man suggested that they have a cup of coffee together. Over coffee his new acquaintance told Richard about a Negro literary group in his neighborhood whose members were trying to write and invited him to come to their meetings. Since they were academically trained Richard went to the meetings hoping to learn something about method and technique. But he was repelled by a childish immaturity and middle-class bohemianism and especially by an inverted Puritanism: "their ideas were but excuses for sex, leads to sex, hints at sex, substitutes for sex. In speech and action they strove to act as un-Negro as possible, denying the racial and material foundations of their lives, accepting their class and racial status in ways so oblique that one had the impression that no difficulties existed for them." Though Richard had never been past the ninth grade he discovered that he had made a harder and more intensive attempt to write than any of them. They could not teach him anything—he would learn more from his own dogged experimentation and from books.

An ability to endure tension was growing in Richard and he was becoming conscious of what was happening to him.

I knew that my attitude of watchful wonder had usurped all other feelings, had become the meaning of my life, an integral part of my personality; that I was striving to live and measure all things by it. Having no claims upon others, I bent the way the wind blew, rendering unto my environment that which was my environment's, and rendering unto myself that which I felt was mine.

It was a dangerous way to live, far more dangerous than violating laws or ethical codes of conduct; but the danger was for me and me alone. Had I not been conscious of what I was doing, I could have easily lost my way in the fogbound regions of compelling fantasy. Even so, I floundered, staggered; but somehow I always groped my way back to that path where I felt a tinge of warmth from an unseen light.

Hungry for insight into my own life and the lives about me, knowing my fiercely indrawn nature, I sought to fulfill more than my share of all obligations and responsibilities, as though offering libations of forgiveness to my environment. Indeed, the more my emotions claimed my attention, the sharper—as though in ultimate self-defense—became my desire to measure accurately the reality of the objective world so that I might more than meet its demands.[1]

With a promise of steady employment and some security through a Civil Service rating Richard moved his family to a three-room apartment on the South Side. An extra room was its only advantage; the slum hallway which led to their fourth-floor apartment was dank and gloomy and smelled of coal-oil, which tenants burned for warmth. But a room of his own made the place seem luxurious to Richard. As soon as he helped Ella clean the entire apartment he scrubbed a wood table, placed it away from the distractions of a window which overlooked the street, piled paper and pencils neatly upon it and arranged his books and magazines on the floor against the wall. Now he could study or write without any distractions from the household.

From time to time rumors of unemployment came but Richard did not listen to them. He had grown up in complete ignorance of economics and matters of employment, and just as the years of inflationary prosperity had not affected his life it seemed a matter of no concern that a crisis was building in the United States. But when the time came for verification of his appointment as permanent clerk he was told that it would be held up temporarily. The volume of mail dropped, Richard's hours were cut back and his paychecks became smaller.

On November 13, 1929, en route to work from the library, Richard passed a newsstand and stopped to glance at the gigantic headlines on all the papers: STOCKS CRASH—BILLIONS FADE. For a moment he sensed that something terrible had happened, but stocks and bonds were a mystery belonging to a life he did not share so he put the news out of his mind. But the volume of mail proceeded to fall so low that he worked only one or two nights a week.

> In the post office canteen the boys stood about and talked.
> The cops beat up some demonstrators today.
> The Reds had a picket line around the City Hall.
> Wall Street's cracking down on the country.
> Surplus production's throwing millions out of work.
> There're more than two million unemployed.
> They don't count. They're always out of work . . .
> There'll be a revolution if this keeps up.
> Hell, naw. Americans are too dumb to make a revolution.[2]

Finally the post office job ended completely and Richard was again out of work. Within two weeks his worries reached a peak. Aunt Cleo had a heart attack, his brother developed stomach ulcers and Ella also became ill. Richard felt he was supporting a hospital and in addition to searching for work had to cook, clean, shop and care for his sick family. Alan went to live and work in Toledo, Ohio, with his Uncle Charles. As Richard tramped the street looking for work he began to realize the extent of the national crisis. "Unemployed men loitered in doorways with blank looks in their eyes, sat dejectedly on front steps in shabby clothing, congregated in sullen groups on street corners, and filled all the empty benches in the parks of Chicago's South Side."

At last Richard swallowed his pride and went to see a distant cousin of his mother's who was superintendent of a Negro burial society; he was hired as an insurance agent. The thought of lending himself to such an enterprise sickened him but his cousin shrugged his shoulders: "Well, if you don't sell them, somebody else will . . . You've got to eat, haven't you?"

With few exceptions burial societies were rackets. They existed because the majority of poor Negroes could not afford to buy insurance from legitimate companies and the societies issued policies for as little as ten cents a week. In most cases the owners of the societies were leaders in the black community and often received protection from white city officials in exchange for a weekly or monthly payoff. At the end of twenty-five years a policyholder received a sum of money presumably sufficient for burial. However, the money collected always exceeded that paid out because most Negroes were so poor that after a few years they were forced to let their policies lapse and lose all they had paid in.

Richard's salary was fifteen dollars for every dollar's worth of new premiums he signed for the company, but for every dollar's worth of old premiums that lapsed he was penalized fifteen dollars. Since that arrangement just about equaled out he received an incentive commission of ten percent on total premiums collected. "This gambling method of remuneration was practiced by some of the burial companies because of the tremendous 'turnover' in policyholders, and the companies had to have a constant stream of new business to keep afloat. Whenever a black family moved or suffered a slight reverse in fortune, it usually let its policy lapse and later bought another policy from some other company." Richard considered himself fortunate if, after subtracting lapses from new business, there remained fifteen dollars that he could call his own.

Each day Richard visited flats filled with hungry men, women and children, many of them broken or defeated. He tramped up and down tenement staircases and after a few months became emotionally drained by the sight of people who were "lost, ignorant, sick in mind and body." When he returned home at night taut nerves and physical exhaustion kept him from reading or writing—and when he could not write a restlessness, an agitation in the blood, enveloped him and he had nightmares. Each morning he awoke feeling that he had not been to sleep at all and a sexual irritation became insistent. Every day he was meeting pretty housewives who tried desperately to keep up their insurance payments and when they could not were willing to pay the ten or twenty-five cents due with their bodies.

One morning at a flat on Champlain Avenue Richard met a voluptuous young black girl, the mother of an illegitimate child even though she herself was not yet eighteen, who invited him inside "to sit on the couch and have a cup of coffee." A table made from a wooden crate and covered by spotlessly clean blue-and-white checked oilcloth stood next to a window that overlooked the avenue; two straight chairs held a laundry basket in which a tiny baby was sleeping and the only other furniture was a wide-armed puffily sagging couch and one other wooden kitchen chair. The kitchen was small, as if constructed out of a former closet, and on an open shelf above the sink were a few dime-store dishes. But the whole apartment was clean and scrubbed and white curtains hung at the window.[3] When Richard finished drinking his coffee the girl took the dishes into the kitchen and washed them, humming to herself and swaying her high full hips in time with the song. Then she returned to the couch and in a childish openhearted way nestled against Richard and began to wiggle her body. When he kissed her she fell back on the couch limp and soft and pulled him on top of her young squirming body.

From that day on Richard visited the girl once a week and paid ten cents each time, marking the payment carefully in her premium book before leaving the house. The only request the girl ever made of him was to take her to see a circus. She could not read or write and was always simple and sweet and uncalculating when he called. "Sex relations were the only relations she had ever had; no others were possible with her, so limited was her intelligence." But within a few months the visits left him in a state of self-disgust. After each sexual encounter he went away resolved not to return; he was angry with himself and his restless loneliness and angry at the girl because she was ignorant and he could not talk to her. He listened to some of the other agents describe their sexual victories over black women too poor or sometimes too frightened to defend themselves or find the money for their miserable premiums and was sickened—he had not forced himself on the girl on Champlain but felt as if he were taking as much advantage as the others. Another worry was that he knew she saw other men besides himself and the idea of a venereal disease revolted him.

As an insurance agent Richard took part in a swindle prepared by his company. The society had originally issued a policy that was too liberal in its provisions from their point of view and they decided to exchange the policies for others with stricter clauses. A superintendent of the company accompanied Richard on his rounds and claimed he was making a routine inspection of the individual policies. While Richard distracted the client by marking a payment in his book the superintendent exchanged a new, inferior, policy for the one originally held. The new one was identical in color, serial number and beneficiary but carried much smaller payments. Since many of the policyholders were unable to read or write they did not learn that the insurance benefits had decreased. It was dirty work and Richard wondered if he could expose the fraud. "And when [he] could think of no safe way [he] would curse [himself] and the victims and forget about it."

By spring of 1931 the Depression had grown severe and Richard could not sell insurance to hungry people even for a dime. He sold his watch and some books—all that he had to sell—and looked for a cheaper apartment. At 4804 St. Lawrence he found a second-floor apartment in a two-flat rotting building. "The place was dismal; plaster was falling from the walls; the wooden stairs sagged." When Ella saw it, she wept.

Election time was approaching and a Negro Republican precinct captain asked Richard to help round up votes for William Hale Thompson ("Big Bill, the Builder") to retain him in office as mayor.

As mayor of the city . . . , he was hailed as "Big Bill, the Builder," Chicago's greatest booster, the defender of the weak, the champion of the people, while at the same time in certain newspapers the word "Thompsonism" came to be a symbol for spoils politics, police scandals, school-board scandals, padded pay-rolls, gangster alliances, betrayal of the public trust, bizarre campaign methods, and buffoonery in public office.[4]

Richard had no interest in Thompson or any of the other candidates but he needed the money. But as he went from door to door with the precinct captain he discovered that politics was bribery, ". . . people voted for three dollars, for the right to continue their illicit trade in sex or alcohol." On Election Day Richard went into the polling booth and unfolded a wad of ballots; the whole sordid, dishonest process went through his mind. What he hated worst of all was that Thompson was using the bloc of South Side votes to control city hall. With his pencil Richard scrawled I PROTEST THIS FRAUD across the ballot.

I knew that my gesture was futile. But I wanted somebody to know that out of that vast sea of ignorance in the Black Belt there was at least one person who knew the game for what it was.[5]

Some of the fraud Richard objected to was that he felt that he had been used by B. Doc. Huggins, the political captain in his local ward. Huggins, who owned a barbership in Richard's neighborhood, looked like a diplomat or foreign minister. He was short, with olive skin, straight hair, a well-groomed goatee in which flecks of silver shone, and he had a habit of throwing out his chest when he uttered sentences in an authoritative manner. He was extremely popular both in his barbershop and in the ward but it was Richard who had done the legwork and brought in the highest number of votes ever polled in Huggins' district. Out of it Huggins received a political appointment as Inspector of Police Personnel. All the job involved was an occasional visit to police headquarters on 11th Street and State to look over the files. He was supposed to read the complaints made against the police. At first Richard had been amused: Doc was no more qualified for that job than a monkey. But he would walk into his barbership, throw out his chest to display his police badge and then whip out a big .38 revolver from a hip holster. Richard, too, had been promised a job but it was an offer to be a street attendant with the City Parks Department. On the job he was to wear a white uniform and cap, push a handcart and sweep up trash in the downtown Loop area. Richard did not even consider such a job. Dress up like that in a monkey suit! Not me!, Richard swore to himself. He had hoped to receive one of the clerical jobs in City Hall, a public library or some other office. Resentful, he pocketed the few dollars he had received for days of tramping up and down stairs and vowed to have nothing more to do with politicians.

Relief kitchens were opened all over Chicago but Richard had avoided them. Ella and Maggie felt that there was something shameful in charity; to beg would rob them of self-respect; to ask for help was an admission of guilt. But one morning Ella awakened her son and told him that there was no food left at all. The quiet woman avoided looking at him and he in turn kept his eyes turned from his mother's face. He did not want to embarrass her and he did not want to begin an argument. She would see what he thought about her kind of pride if she looked into his eyes. A desire to laugh came over him and he dressed quickly and left the house to walk to the Cook County Bureau of Public Welfare.

Hell, he thought to himself, poor people are not responsible for their sudden plight. The United States government owes this little ration to black people and a lot more. Black men slaved for years without receiving a dime and he was damn well not going to sit by and left his family starve! It was all right to be proud but false pride was stupid.

At the Cook County office Richard had to wait several hours for an interview. He was curious to see how people reacted when they begged for food. Did all black men feel like his mother and aunt, or were they smarter? He noticed that newcomers entered the room shyly but after sitting for a while they began to exchange experiences and seemed more confident.

Across the room from where he sat were middle-class relief officials, their desks carefully guarded by a waist-high wooden counter. Richard watched their faces as they spoke to clients. They appeared resentful and somewhat contemptuous as they snapped out questions and wrote down answers for personal histories. They appeared to be so identified with their petty jobs it had become their personal possessions they were giving away instead of government surplus foodstuffs. Clients were looked upon as shiftless people who could work if they really wanted to; these were the "idle ones" referred to in the *Daily Tribune*.

On Richard's side of the barrier were the shabby idle ones, hollow-cheeked, eyes sharp and anxious from hunger. He listened and became aware of something happening in the room. "The black men and women were mumbling quietly among themselves; they had not known one another before they had come here, but now their timidity and shame were wearing off and they were exchanging experiences. Before this they had lived as individuals, each somewhat afraid of the other, each seeking his own pleasure, each staunch in that degree of Americanism that had been allowed him. But now life had tossed them together, and they were learning to know the sentiments of their neighbors for the first time; their talking was enabling them to sense the collectivity of their lives, and some of their fear was passing."

As Richard left the relief station new impressions flickered in his veins like electrical charges. He was not alone—society had cast out millions of others along with him. And all over the country these millions of defeated people were coming together in relief stations and talking. Black minds were shedding illusions. "These people now knew that the past had betrayed them, had cast them out; but they did not know what the future would be like, did not know what they wanted . . . [but] out of their talk was rising a new realization of life. And once this new conception of themselves had formed, no power on earth could alter it."

Richard's mind swam with questions. How could he be with the people in the black community? How many other individuals understood what was happening? Could what he was feeling, this new experience, be what had been missing in his writing. Had his flights of imagination been too subjective, too lacking in reference to social action?

I was slowly beginning to comprehend the meaning of my environment; a sense of direction was beginning to emerge from the conditions of my life. I began to feel something more powerful than I could express. My speech and manner changed. My cynicism slid from me. I grew open and questioning. I wanted to know.[6]

From May to December in 1931 Richard was unemployed, and each week he walked to the relief depot for the sacks of flour, prunes, cornmeal, wedges of cheese—whatever surplus food was handed out. There were not even pennies for carfare and he sometimes staggered from exhaustion when he walked home with the food. When his shoes wore into holes he stuffed their insoles with several thicknesses of paper.

Christmas came and Richard was called back for temporary work at the post office. An enormous change had taken place in the personalities of the white men with whom he worked as a result of the Depression. He had to shift the pictures in his mind to take in white victims as well as black. All conversations centered around the American catastrophe; they talked about unemployment, their own privation, and the relief demonstrations in the city. For the first time, Richard was invited to white homes and he saw a new camaraderie developing between black and white men. At the end of January the work in the post office ended.

As the Depression deepened, old friends began to leave Jackson and arrive in Chicago: Joe Brown, Richard "Squilla" Jordan, Arthur Leaner and Julius "Ditty Boy" Carter. Richard was especially happy to see Joe and Squilla. Joe moved in with his aunt, who lived on 4700 South Langley Avenue, not too far from Richard. Joe's aunt, Mrs. Lola Penn Green, worked as a pastry cook at Mandel Hall Cafeteria in the University of Chicago, and it was his job to act as baby-sitter for eight-year-old John. Mrs. Green often brought food home from the cafeteria which Joe shared with Richard.

Through his Aunt Maggie, who had found a job as a power machine operator at LipSon Brothers, Inc., west of the Loop, at 337 South Franklin Street, Richard got Joe some work in the shipping department and as a deliveryman. LipSon's was the largest silk dress factory of its kind in the Chicago garment district and Maggie did piecework. Joe was hired as non-union labor and during the four months he was there a fierce strike erupted in the garment center. As soon as Joe finished work each day Richard met him to find out what had been happening. He roared with laughter that closed his eyes and caused tears to squeeze between the lids while listening to his friend. Joe, a quiet young man with a humorous twist to his lips, was a poet; and when he told a story he brought to it a poet's eye for nuance and imaginative, loving use of words. Strikers were throwing rotten eggs on the scabs, stench bombs from shop windows, and Joe told Richard how he had to pour citronella oil on the silk material he was delivering to remove the odor. Maggie was not as amused as Richard and persuaded Joe to leave the plant. She was afraid he would be doused with acid.

Richard and Joe went everywhere looking for work. For a short time they tried writing insurance policies for the *Herald-American* newspaper on a subscription plan but no one could afford to take one out; since they were paid on commission they gave it up. There were little "hole-in-the-wall employment offices with a cover charge of $5 to $10 for these select positions . . . the usual nigger jobs, dish-washers, porters, houseboys and the like." Then they tried building up an industrial insurance fund for a Negro-owned and -operated company, Supreme Liberty Life on 35th and South Parkway, but, again, no one had any money to spend on insurance.

Late one afternoon Richard and Joe sat around drinking some homemade brew. Joe's aunt made wine from blue grapes and liquor from white potatoes and malt. Richard felt a little fuzzy but he was relaxed; they had been laughing and talking about "those damn Southern peckerwoods." Inevitably, the problem of finding work came up and they decided to visit Arthur Leaner.

It was mid-zero weather when Richard and Joe went to Leaner's "Red Cross Home." He, his wife and two children had been evicted from their apartment because they could not pay the rent and were being cared for by the charity organization. The tall skinny man was bitter: "There is no pity in this naked city. And one of these days I'm going to get stinking rich. And I'm going to step on the toes of every son-of-a-bitch that crosses my path! Jews and white folks get the niggers' money and I'm gonna get me some too."

Richard argued quietly: "Down South you were always talking about being a preacher and about spiritual values. What's spiritual about going around stepping on people?"

"Man, the Holy Ghost is free, but you have to pay for the piping!" Leaner answered, breaking into a laugh. He walked back and forth across the room in short steps, pausing in deep thought, then, suddenly stopping, he gazed up at the ceiling and clicked his fingers. He had caught an idea.[7]

Richard and Joe sat watching "like two dumb lambs" who still believed in good and evil and an inherent value in ideals. Arthur had a plan to make some real cash money: A mail-order business covering the entire United States. They would call themselves the "Three Wise Men of the East"[8] and would serve as spiritual advisers to all the lonely hearts and solve their problems. Richard tried to speak but Arthur would not let him complete a sentence because ideas were blooming one on top of the other and he grew more enthusi-astic. Finally Richard cut Arthur short with a demand to speak: "We can't play with Uncle Sam's post office because we could easily get our butts into trouble and be sent to Sing Sing."

Arthur would not listen: "I work at that crummy post office too, you know. We can get away with it—just let me finish!"

Arthur outlined his plan in more detail. First a small outlay of cash would be required. Richard gave Joe a secret look, his eyes half closed, as if saying that Arthur had something fishy to propose. They all agreed, however, that it would take about $15 to start the company. Each man had to raise $5 to chip into the pot. The money would be used to have their pictures taken. They would all wear Indian turbans and perhaps clergymen's collars. The pictures would be portraits with their heads turned three-quarters and they would ask the photographer to underexpose so that they would appear slightly light-skinned, and present a foreign look.

Richard began to play along enthusiastically: "Then we could take three big turkish bath towels and wrap it around our heads with a few different twists and then when people see our picture, they'd never know whether we were niggers or not." Arthur said: "Now, we are seeing eye to eye. Then when we get the pictures we will have a cut made at the engraver's and you could write the copy and we will set up an ad for the newspapers and magazines. First, we will run our ad in some Southern country news or agricultural magazine and then we'll just sit back and see what happens. Dick, how do you think we should word the ad?"

Richard looked out of the corner of his eye, giving Joe another secret look before he answered: "Well, Arthur, this is a technical question, a different style of writing than I am used to, but I'll give it a try." He studied the floor and for once Arthur kept silent. Then he said such an advertisement could invite people to ask as many questions as a dozen and that if they would care to they should include information about themselves and send it back with one dollar for the cost of mailing an answer. In this fashion they would receive money and enough information to enable them to give personal advice. But, Richard insisted: "I'm not clear as to what legitimate steps we will have to take to keep ourselves straight with postal regulations."

But Arthur had the answer: "I've got that all covered. You see, I have a friend from India over on 47th and State. He sells Lucky John the Conquer Root, Badminton Oil, Lucky Dusk Incense, Lucky Charms and Goofey Dust. We'll buy a couple of pounds of powdered incense and in the ad we will say that we will send a small envelope of spiritual dust which is of the spirit mother Edith. Mother's dust will be working the two-week period they are waiting for an answer. In this way we'll be giving folks something for their cash and if things don't turn out as we expect, then we could always claim that they didn't use the spirit dust as instructed."

A decision was made to use Arthur's place for a mailing address and they agreed to meet with the $5 apiece the following week; then,

about two weeks later, they would meet again to count the money
that was coming in and write up answers for their customers.

"The evening had grown old now, [they] had spent about five
hours together making plans to develop [their] new venture. Arthur
went back to his icebox and got three bottles of home brew. [They]
drank a toast to [their] future success with the blessings of the spirit
Edith. Arthur gave [them] that warm fellowship handshake, [they]
put on [their] seedy overcoats, adjusted [their] ear muffs." Arthur
then placed his hands on their shoulders; he stood in the middle as if
in silent prayer, and Richard and Joe left.

No sooner had Arthur put the chain on his door when Richard
stopped, turned to Joe and said: "Big Mama Joe, this is not our
bottle of brew. I still don't trust that Arthur—he's tricky. And we're
going to catch hell raising that $5. Besides, a business like that is
phony. I couldn't live with myself if I took advantage of everybody
in a plot like that."

That was the first and the last meeting of "The Three Wise Men
of the East." "In later years Arthur Leaner [under an alias] became
one of the outstanding radio disc jockeys in Chicago. He started out
on . . . a station that was losing money . . . He got the station out
of the red, by designing a program geared to the Negro audience. He
did get filthy rich. He posed as a minister by night, the Reverend
Arthur B. Leaner and by day [as a jazz expert]. He went into all
kinds of business enterprises, record mats, the publishing of a weekly
newspaper, advertising agency, night club business, Bar-B-Q huts,
spiritualist churches, promoter for live stage show attractions at the
largest . . . theatre . . . He had a showplace home . . . He sold
everything on the air from goats milk to Canadian Ace Beer. He was
the teenage idol of the airlanes. With his fast speaking voice, over the
air he was mistaken as being from the Islands . . . he developed a very
peculiar accent. Arthur is retired now and [engaged in a new business entirely].[9]

Once a week a caseworker, assigned by the Cook County Welfare
Office, visited Richard's apartment. At first he was resentful toward
an invasion of his family privacy by a prying white official. But Mrs.
Mary Wirth did not snoop in corners as if doubting their word but
simply asked perfunctory questions and noted them down in a
leather book. Gradually, he grew to anticipate Mrs. Wirth's visits.
When she discovered that he wanted to become a writer she was
enthusiastic. No one in his whole twenty-four years had encouraged
him, with the exception of the Negro editor in Jackson. This was
really a remarkable woman. Soon he was telling Mrs. Wirth about

his interest in sociology and psychology as tools toward understanding character. He did not know that she was the wife of a famous sociologist, Dr. Louis Wirth, of the University of Chicago, and when she told him he asked eagerly if her husband would give him a reading list. A thrill leaped in Richard when Mary Wirth suggested that he go to the University and talk to Dr. Wirth personally. She would make the arrangements.

A few weeks later Richard went to the University and walked along the corridors until he found Dr. Wirth's office. After he tapped on the door heavy footsteps approached and it was opened rather abruptly by a heavy-faced, nearly white-skinned Negro who asked: "What do you want?" The greeting was curt but Richard explained that he had an appointment with Dr. Wirth, made by his wife, and the man invited him inside. He rather proudly informed Richard that he was Horace Cayton, research assistant to Wirth, and asked him if he was a student. "I'm trying to be a writer," Richard replied. Cayton's eyebrows shot up and he appeared about to smile but he kept silent and rather condescendingly offered to show Richard some of the work being done. When Wirth came in he gave Richard a list of ten or twelve books and suggested that he return to the University for a discussion when he had completed his reading. Within a space of weeks Richard had gone through all the books and returned for the promised talks. Dr. Wirth was amazed by his rapidity and the extent of his knowledge and easy grasp of difficult sociological questions.

In February, Mary Wirth had Richard assigned, through the relief bureau, to Michael Reese Hospital as an orderly. On the first morning he reported to work he noticed the sharp racial division maintained by the hospital. As he walked along the basement corridor he saw two lines of women approaching. "A line of white girls marched past, clad in starched uniforms that gleamed white; their faces were alert, their step quick, their bodies lean and shapely, their shoulders erect, their faces lit with the light of purpose. And after them came a line of black girls, old, fat, dressed in ragged gingham, walking loosely, carrying tin cans of soap powder, rags, mops, brooms, . . . [he] wondered what law of the universe kept them from being mixed? The sun would not have stopped shining had there been a few black girls in the first line, and the earth would not have stopped whirling on its axis had there been a few white girls in the second line."

Richard worked with three other men and cleaned operating rooms, dog, rat, mice, cat and rabbit pens, and fed guinea pigs. Of Richard's co-workers only one, Bill, was near his own age. Bill straightened his hair and the grease he used was repellent to Richard. But even worse was a brooding hate which poured out of his half-closed eyes and he did not like Richard, who tried to conceal his own dislike of the young man. Bill listened in sudden silence whenever Richard talked to him, trying to convey in simple terms some of his ideas. Then one day he interrupted to tell Richard his own point of view.

"I got it," he said.

"You've got what?" Richard asked.

"This old race problem you keep talking about," he said.

"What about it?"

"Well, it's this way," he explained seriously. "Let the government give every man a gun and five bullets, then let us all start over again. Make it just like it was in the beginning. The ones who come out on top, white or black, let them rule."

From then on Richard decided to stop pumping his ideas into Bill's head—his simplicity was terrifying.

The two other men who worked as orderlies were quite old and had been in the Michael Reese Hospital for fifteen or more years. "One was Brand, a short, black, morose bachelor; the other was Cooke, a tall, yellow, spectacled fellow who spent his spare time keeping track of world events through the Chicago *Tribune*." Brand and Cook hated each other and spent most of each day arguing. And all three men ridiculed Richard because of his interest in the experiments conducted by the doctors. An adolescent dream had been medical research in a laboratory so Richard was continually asking questions and followed the work of the interns avidly. But one day when he asked a question a doctor answered: "If you know too much, boy, your brains might explode."

On Saturday mornings Richard assisted a young doctor who cut the vocal cords of dogs so they would not disturb the patients in the hospital. Nembutal was injected as anesthesia and when a dog was unconscious a scalpel was thrust down its throat to sever the vocal cord. The operation fascinated Richard but he did not like to see the dogs awaken. They would suffer pain from the severed vocal cords and lift their heads to the ceiling in a soundless wail. All the rest of his life those animals became for him a symbol for silent suffering.

In June, hospital authorities instituted a time study throughout the building, and one morning while Richard was cleaning a young man came to stand over him with a stopwatch in his hand. Angered, and feeling like a machine, Richard sprayed a room with disinfectant, scrubbed the coagulated blood from tables, floors and walls, scraped and washed hardened dog, rat and rabbit feces, and finished the room in seventeen minutes. He heard the snap of the stopwatch but the time-study man did not comment. From seven in the morning until twelve noon Richard scrubbed laboratory rooms followed by the click, click, of the watch. He was staggering with exhaustion when he finished and waited for the man's report. The time study showed that he had cleaned one room in seventeen minutes so that was the norm established, even though Richard protested that it had been the least soiled. After lunch he was to scrub five flights of stairs and finish by six o'clock. No time was left in the study for rest breaks or even a drink of water.

All four men brought their lunch each day and ate in the laboratory and rested briefly afterwards. Richard read a book while eating or listened to the interminable arguments between Brand and Cooke. One winter noon the two men began to quarrel over which was the better or more accurate paper: the Chicago *Tribune* or the *Herald-Examiner*. Richard sat unconcerned. He expected the argument to dwindle out as it always had before, but suddenly Brand and Cooke were screaming at each other. Then Cooke pulled a switchblade knife from his pocket and Brand caught up an ice pick and both men began to circle each other—hands out from their sides, knees bent, palms up with their fingers curled about their weapons.

Richard and Bill jumped to their feet in alarm and called: "Cut it out!" In a moment the two were slashing at each other, charging back and forth across the room. Finally, one was thrown against a tier of animal-filled cages.

Like kingpins, one steel tier lammed into another, then they all crashed to the floor with a sound as of the roof falling. The whole aspect of the room altered quicker than the eye could follow. Brand and Cooke stood stock-still, their eyes fastened upon each other, their pointed weapons raised; but they were dimly aware of the havoc that churned about them.

The steel tiers lay jumbled; the doors of the cages swung open. Rats and mice and dogs and rabbits moved over the floor in wild panic. The Wassermann guinea pigs were squealing as though judgment day had come. Here and there an animal had been crushed beneath a cage.[10]

We'll all lose our jobs, Richard thought, and all four men stared at each other. Richard looked up at the clock and saw that it was twelve-thirty—just half an hour remained before the doctors returned. They worked frantically and as they righted the steel cages and replaced the tiers they agreed to keep the fight a secret. They would tell anyone who asked that they had not been in the laboratory during lunchtime that day.

Once all the cages were in order the men were faced with an impossible task of sorting out the animals. They knew in general that rats or mice went into certain cages but between a cancerous mouse or a tubercular mouse they had to guess. The white doctors had never taken the time to answer a single question and all four men were ignorant of the meaning of the experiments. Animals that had been squashed were replaced by healthy stock from the storage cages and when the room was in order Richard unlocked the door and they waited nervously for the doctors' arrival.

All afternoon the doctors came and went and Richard slipped in from his step-scrubbing job to ask if anyone had noticed any change in his test animal; there were no repercussions. "Another day went by and nothing happened. Then another day. The doctors examined the animals and wrote in their little black books, in their big black books, and continued to trace red and black lines upon the charts." A week passed and Richard felt out of danger.

When it was certain that no one was aware of the accident Richard wondered whether or not he should have gone to the director's office and confessed. But he put it out of his mind by arguing that it had been the director who initiated the time study which made him a slave and he could not risk his thirteen dollars a week pay by acting idealistically. Occasionally he wondered whether new scientific discoveries were made or hypotheses discarded because of unexpected findings from the mixed-up animals.

Work at the hospital ended and Richard was assigned by the relief office to the South Side Boys' Club, but his wages were barely enough to provide rent and food for his family. Fortunately, he found the work engrossing. Boys between the ages of eight and twenty-five came to swim, draw and play games at the Club. For hours Richard ". . . listened to their talk of planes, women, guns, politics, and crime. Their figures of speech were as forceful and colorful as any ever used by English-speaking people." Richard kept a pencil and paper in his pocket so he could jot down their word rhythms and stories. After he finished work he went home and began to write sketches, sometimes only a long paragraph which blended a Southern environment, which he knew best, with the characters and personalities of the Northern boys.

Again Richard was transferred by the relief office, this time to work as a publicity agent in the Federal Negro Theatre, one of the many projects established by President Roosevelt's New Deal administration. On the morning he reported to work Richard was introduced to about forty Negro actors and actresses and to the theatre's white director. She was a skinny medium-sized woman with sharp features and a nervous mannerism of adjusting wisps of graying hair every few minutes. A motherly yet domineering quality in the woman typed her in Richard's mind as soon as he watched her work with the actors—missionary type! In a few days he knew that his first impressions were correct. All of the plays selected by the director were revamped to "Negro style" instead of being played straight. Jungle scenes, spirituals, dialect, the rolling of eyes and a shuffling walk were superimposed on plays by Molière, Jonson, Ibsen and Chekhov. Contemporary plays were refused as too controversial.

For a few weeks Richard studied the situation and wondered what could be done about the director's "quaint aesthetic notions." What a waste of talent, he thought, when he looked at the actresses and actors lolling about in their chairs. Here was an opportunity for the production of serious Negro drama and no one was aware of it. At a meeting to discuss publicity Richard met a young white director, Charles DeSheim; they went out together for coffee and Richard explained what was happening in the Federal Negro Theatre. A few days after their meeting he read a new play, *Hymn to the Rising Sun,* by Paul Green. It was a one-act play about a Southern chain gang, powerful and poetic, and Richard wanted it produced.

Through Mary Wirth, Richard had met some people influential in the Works Progress Administration and he went to see them and asked if the white director could be replaced by someone more sensitive to the needs of a new black theatre. They promised him that they would investigate for themselves and then take action if they considered it necessary. At the same time Richard suggested that if the director was transferred he would recommend Charles De-Sheim as a replacement.

Within a month the white director was transferred, DeSheim became director and the cast was housed in the Princess Theatre in the Loop. Happy at last, Richard handed out copies of Green's play and sat back in his chair to listen to a first run-through. But something went wrong. The Negroes stammered and faltered in their lines. Finally they stopped altogether. DeSheim looked frightened. One of the Negro actors rose.

"Mr. DeSheim," he began, "we think this play is indecent. We don't want to act in a play like this before the American public. I don't think any such conditions exist in the South. I lived in the South and I never saw any chain gangs. . . ."

Richard could not believe his ears but when he tried to defend the play he was heckled and shouted down. After the rehearsal broke up Richard went into the office and looked up the past experience of the actors and discovered that most of them had played only in vaudeville. And to his mind vaudeville was a cheap, low form of entertainment. Legitimate theatre was art—and these actors had not wanted to test themselves through dramatic realism.

When Richard arrived at the theatre a few mornings later he found that the company had drawn up a petition demanding the ouster of DeSheim. After he and the white director had held a frantic conference, DeSheim talked to the cast and assured them that it was their right to petition against him if they wanted to but that he believed any misunderstandings could be settled smoothly. "Who told you that we were getting up a petition?" a black man demanded. "There's an Uncle Tom in the theatre!" a black girl yelled.

Most of the difficulties were eventually smoothed over and the play went into rehearsal. Twice the play was scheduled to open but at the last minute orders were sent down that it was not to go on. After the second failure a meeting was held on the South Side in protest and a delegation was assured by George Kondolf, director of the federal theatres, that the play would open in October. But on the night of October 14 police-laden squad cars patrolled the Loop streets and intimidated the crowds that stood in front of the Princess Theatre hoping to see *Hymn to the Rising Sun*. The play was banned. Again a South Side committee protested and this time they were answered by Robert J. Dunham, "Relief Czar for Illinois." The play was described as immoral and Dunham claimed that Negroes themselves had been opposed to it. When the actors and actresses continued to demand they be allowed to perform the play Dunham told them it was out of his hands. Washington would have to decide. Richard heard from friends in the Works Progress Administration that Harry L. Hopkins, national administrator of the program, instructed the Chicago office to "Go slow; the play is too 'sexy.' "[11]

After a brief period with a white experimental theatrical company as publicity agent he was transferred again. Mary Wirth had become Chief Social Worker at the Seventh Chicago Works Progress Administration and she helped Richard to get an assignment on the Illinois Writers' Project, the "Guides." It was his first professional writing assignment and Richard felt confident and enthusiastic. Within a few months he was made acting supervisor of essays.

All my life I had been full of a hunger
for a new way to live . . .

IX

As often as he could—spring, summer and fall—Richard walked east on 37th or 39th Street, then cut across South Parkway over to 51st, still heading in the direction of Lake Michigan, until he reached Washington Park. Unless he was very tired he rarely sat down on a bench, instead, he wandered through crowds of unemployed Negroes, pausing here and there to listen to speakers. Every day was a pageant and Richard had never heard or seen such extreme orators.

Followers of Marcus Garvey, the imprisoned and then deported leader of the Universal Negro Improvement Association, stood on park benches or boxes and passionately declared that their leader would return in the wind and the rain to trouble the white man and lead the black man to victory.[1] Richard stood entranced as he listened to their words: the white man was a liar, a fornicator, a drunkard, a cheat. From his reading he knew that their hopes to return to Africa were forlorn. Africa was owned by white nations in Europe whose economies rested upon the diamonds, gold and cocoa they raped from black soil; and if these countries permitted an "Africa for Africans" he was certain that black men in those territories would not welcome strangers attempting to take over their land even if those newcomers had black skins. But he loved their passionate rejection of America ". . . for they sensed with that directness of which only the simple are capable that they had no chance to live a full human life in America. Their lives were not cluttered with ideas in which they could only half believe; they could not create illusions which made them think they were living when they were not; their daily lives were too nakedly harsh to permit of camouflage. [He] understood their emotions, for [he] partly shared them."

Some of the Garveyites noticed that Richard listened intently to their speakers and invited him to their homes. He discovered that their totally racialistic outlook gave them a dignity he had not seen before in black men. "On the walls of their dingy flats were maps of Africa and India and Japan, pictures of Japanese generals and admirals, portraits of Marcus Garvey in gaudy regalia, the faces of colored men and women from all parts of the world." When they asked Richard to join their organization he tried to explain that he was trying to be a writer, letting down his own reserve, admitting them to personal territory, because he had not the heart to say they would never succeed. They could not understand his excuses. But it was through the Garvey movement that he ". . . caught a glimpse of the potential strength of the American Negro."

Occasionally Sufi Abdul Hamid spoke in the park and Richard was drawn toward his flamboyant attire and mannerisms. Hamid dressed in a turban and wore a colorful cape and high black Russian boots, but his brilliance as a speaker was overweighed by the limitations of his proposals: More Jobs For Negroes—Buy Where You Work. He had heard about Hamid's boycott against all white businesses in the South Side which would not employ Negroes. And he knew that Woolworth's had capitulated to the ragged pickets and finally hired twenty-one Negro girls, but what was that when thousands of black women were unemployed? And there was an element of mysticism in Hamid that Richard did not like.

Prior to Roosevelt's Administration there were spontaneous parades of as many as 5,000 Negroes which left the park in silent columns, three abreast, and marched to the Illinois Free Employment Agency's main office in the Loop. Other times men and women marched quietly to addresses on the South Side to reinstate families who had been evicted for not paying their rent. Then, before dispersing, they set up guards to keep marshals or the police from throwing them out again. As the number of evictions increased "flying squadrons" developed and groups of men dashed from tenement to tenement to prevent the removal of families. While sitting on furniture people sang "We Shall Not Be Moved"; and Richard laughed aloud when someone told him of "deals" that were made by marshals in one neighborhood. After removing furniture from apartments on high floors four or five times and having it replaced by squadrons, they arranged to take out a token—one chair, a small table or a lamp. This arrangement saved the strength and the tempers of both sides.

Richard's favorite group in Washington Park was called the "Bug's Club." Here he met intellectuals, most of whom were from the University of Chicago. The group engaged in forums on art, literature, music and politics, and Richard could not seem to hear enough about questions of style versus content, the techniques of naturalism and the responsibility of the artist toward society. He also made it his business to meet white intellectual girls, around his own age. Most of the Negro girls he had met in Chicago seemed to irritate him. All of them seemed to be trying to emulate white women, unlike the Southern girls, who, he was convinced, were more confident and aware of themselves as black and took pride in the fact. And for men or women friends he was always in search of those who could enjoy ideas. ". . . there just were not too many Negro girls who could fill the bill."

Most of the black Communist intellectuals in the Park amused and sometimes angered Richard. "When they walked, their stride quickened; all the peasant hesitancy of their speech vanished as their voices became clipped, terse. In debate they interrupted their opponents in a tone of voice that was an octave higher, and if their opponents raised their voices to be heard, the Communists raised theirs still higher until shouts rang out over the park."

A large silent crowd caught Richard's attention one afternoon when he crossed South Parkway at 51st Street to enter the park, and he stopped to listen. A Communist was speaking about a bonus march to Washington—President Hoover would drive out the workers and the people would then rise up across the nation and make the revolution. When the speech ended Richard edged through the crowd until he reached the speaker. A superior smile turned up Richard's mouth when he told the Communist that even if the United States Army drove the bonus marchers from Washington and even killed one or two there would not be a revolution. "You don't know the indignation of the masses!" the man exploded. Richard, who had been in and out of the homes of poor families when he worked for the insurance company and for B. Doc. Huggins, had seen no sign of revolt. Instead, he had been shocked by the fear and bewilderment he saw on the faces of starving people.

But when Richard attempted to explain his own experience the Communist ended their conversation abruptly: "You're an intellectual," he spat out disdainfully and turned away. A few days later, after President Hoover had driven the marchers away from the White House by bayonet, Richard went back to the park and hunted for the Communist. It would be fun to needle him and see what kind of explanation he came up with. He found the man sitting on a bench talking to a friend: "What about that revolution you predicted if the bonus marchers were driven out?" Richard asked. "The prerequisite conditions did not exist," he muttered and shrugged.

One night Richard was invited to a forum by a girl he had met in the park, who had been part of the circle around the "Bug's Club." She was a pretty girl, warm and friendly, and even more important to Richard, an intellectual. Thyra Edwards was a social worker who lived at the Oakland Unitarian Community Center on Oakland Boulevard. Thyra had arranged a joint meeting between the John Reed Club and the Community Center, whose minister was a liberal.

During the evening a tall, thin young man with a sturdy, kind face and a shock of bristling hair was introduced to him as Jan Wittenber,[2] a painter and member of the John Reed Club. Richard liked him immediately. The man's comfortable with me, Richard thought. It's probably because he's some kind of foreigner. Jan looked squarely into Richard's eyes when he spoke and although he seemed a man of great tension by nature, he was comfortable and at ease with a black man. He was neither too friendly nor evasive and radiated a warm interest in everything and everyone around him.

While the two men drank beer and ate salami sandwiches Richard described his attitude toward the Communists he had met at Washington Park. He had discovered that Jan was a Canadian Jew; surely he would see the extravagance in the behavior of the black radicals. But Jan was sympathetic toward their antics and seemed to grow critical of Richard's questioning. These were merely "tactics" which were necessary to arouse interest in revolutionary politics. Richard was still dubious but before he left he made an appointment with Jan so they "could talk art, literature and politics."

At a second Thursday night meeting Wittenber told Wright about the John Reed Club and asked him to attend one of the discussions—they would teach him to write. It was the wrong approach. "Nobody can tell me how or what to write," was his answer. Furthermore, he was cynical and felt that Communists could not possibly be sincerely interested in Negroes. He preferred a white man to say that he hated a black man, which he could accept as an honest statement, but not that he respected him. A few weeks later, when Richard was sitting at home idle, restless and bored with reading, he decided to visit the John Reed Club as an amused spectator.

The John Reed Club was founded in New York in 1929 just after the collapse of the stock market and was nationally organized by the Communist Party in 1932. The Clubs were not conspiratorial or "front" organizations like those developed after 1935 through which the Communists manipulated public opinion. By 1932 the Club had active chapters in many small towns across the country as well as in all major cities and published several magazines which featured the work of unknown writers and artists and provided a stimulating milieu for talented young people.

Wittenber had explained the history of the Clubs to Richard and had reassured him that he could pay as many visits to their office as he wished. There would be no compulsion on him to join. Richard walked one block north to 47th Street and caught a streetcar going west, then transferred to a bus which took him to 1427 South Michigan. "A dark stairway led upwards; it did not look welcoming. What on earth of importance could transpire in so dingy a place?" Half-tempted to take a walk instead of attending a meeting, Richard paused halfway up the stairs, but when he heard a hubbub of voices he wanted to find out what was going on. On the second floor he paused for a moment, uncertain whether or not to knock, then put his hand on the knob and stepped quietly inside the room. For a moment no one noticed Richard and he looked around the strangest room he had ever seen. "Paper and cigarette butts lay on the floor. A few benches ran along the walls, above which were vivid colors depicting colossal figures of workers carrying streaming banners. The mouths of the workers gaped in wild cries; their legs were sprawled over cities."

A friendly, slightly gray Swedish man with a moustache welcomed Richard and told him that the Club was not having a regular meeting that night but he could sit in on an editorial meeting of their magazine, *Left Front*. Still wary of their hospitality, he sat in a corner of the room and listened to their discussion. Despite the layers of dirty grime that almost obscured the original color of the walls there was a sense of electricity in the room. A quickening excitement ran through Richard and he pulled himself up mentally and vowed to judge the white strangers coldly and objectively, and watch to see how they really regarded Negroes.

After the meeting was over Grimm, the gray-haired man, introduced Richard to Nelson Algren, "who was to create some of the best novels of his generation"; to Ben Shahn, "who was to become one of the nation's leading painters"; Jackson Pollock; and to a girl who worked for an advertising agency; another who was a schoolteacher; and to the wife of a university professor. Then, going to a closet, Grimm brought out armloads of back issues of *The Masses, Anvil, Left Front* and *International Literature* and gave them to Richard.

While he waited for the streetcar to take him home Richard stared at the streetlamps gleaming dully in the night's mist and felt an elation he could not explain. On the trolley he opened one of the magazines and began to read. Thoroughly engrossed, he jolted along and then suddenly roused himself, wiped a clear spot on the window and saw that he had gone past his stop. He rushed to the front of the car and swung off clumsily with the burden of magazines. At home he opened the door quietly and tiptoed into his room, where he spread the magazines out on the bed. Then he lay across the bed and began to read. As he finished one magazine he started on another and the night passed and it grew light without his knowledge.

When he had waited in the relief station and watched strangers united by a common suffering become friends he had wondered if the poor and hungry could be organized in some way. Now he knew; there "did exist in this world an organized search for the truth of the lives of the oppressed and the isolated. . . . It was being done in one-sixth of the earth already." The words of revolution leaped from the pages and struck Richard blindingly.

It was not the economics of Communism, nor the great power of trade unions, nor the excitement of underground politics that claimed me; my attention was caught by the similarity of the experiences of workers in other lands, by the possibility of uniting scattered but kindred people into a whole. It seemed to me that here at last, in the realm of revolutionary expression, Negro experience could find a home, a functioning value and role. Out of the magazines I read came a passionate call for the experiences of the disinherited, and there was none of the lame lispings of the missionary in it. It did not say: "Be like us and we will like you, maybe." It said: "If you possess enough courage to speak out what you are, you will find that you are not alone." It urged life to believe in life.[3]

An immense feeling of freedom flashed through Richard's mind, followed by ripples of energy which engulfed him and brought him off the bed. He took up paper and wrote "a wild, crude poem in free verse, coining images of black hands playing, working, holding bayonets, stiffening finally in death." When he read the poem over he knew it was clumsy but he had merged white and black, expressed a common experience; there was a logic in the universe, and he, Richard, belonged somewhere. Black hands were raised in fists of revolt, side by side with the white fists of white workers. "And some day—and it is only this which sustains me—Some day there shall be millions of them, On some red day in a burst of fists on a new horizon!"[4]

It was morning. In the kitchen he heard the sound of water running and was suddenly ravenously hungry. Ella called to him: "Richard, are you ill?" When he answered no, that he was reading, she opened his door and stared curiously at the magazines that littered the top of his bed. "You're not throwing away money buying those magazines, are you?" she asked. Ella hobbled to the bed on her crippled legs, pushed her rimless glasses against the bridge of her nose and picked up a copy of the *Masses*. On the cover of the magazine was a cartoon, a Communist idealization of a worker who represented all workers of the world. "My God in heaven," Ella gasped. "What's wrong with that man?"

Slowly, unwillingly, Richard reentered his mother's moral world of a gentle Jesus on a Cross, of a God who had fixed a meeting place where they could live without fear in heaven. He sighed quietly and stood beside her looking at the magazine she held out to him. Through her eyes he stared at the cartoon; "it was the figure of a worker clad in ragged overalls and holding aloft a red banner. The man's eyes bulged; his mouth gaped as wide as his face; his teeth showed; the muscles of his neck were like ropes. Following the man was a horde of nondescript men, women, and children, waving clubs, stones, and pitchforks."

"What are those people going to do?" Ella asked.

"I don't know," Richard hedged.

"Are these Communist magazines?"

"Well . . ."

"What do Communists think people are?"

"They don't mean what you see there," Richard fumbled.

"Then what do they mean?"

"This is symbolic."

"Then why don't they speak out what they mean?" Ella demanded.

Clumsily, because his mother's down-to-earth remarks struck against the feelings he experienced when he had looked at posters of workers in the John Reed Club, he tried to defend the cartoon. He knew that she would change her tactics in a moment and attempt to direct him. Stumbling slightly, Ella turned to leave but she paused at the door. Her son's uncertainty had left an opening. "That picture's enough to drive a body crazy," she stabbed. "You're not getting mixed up with those people?"

"I'm just reading, Mama," Richard evaded but when she left he knew that he had not been able to answer her criticisms. He looked at the magazine again, to see it through his own eyes this time, and he knew that she was right. The cartoon in no way reflected understanding or revealed ideas shared by the average person. But he would not give up what the meeting and then reading the magazines had given him. He sat down and began to look through the material again. Communists had an ideal, a purpose, a program, but they did not know how to express them. He was reminded of the speakers in the park who were so remote in their words from the people they hoped to influence.

Gradually, his sense of elation returned. Here was a task he could perform. Communists had conceived of individuals too abstractly; he would write and through words show how the average person felt. At the same time, he would tell the story of Communism to people like his mother—the idealism, the self-sacrifice, the hope of a future—all this he would translate into simple words which everyone could understand. The sense of elation returned; he had a task, a goal, a purpose.

A few nights later he joined his new friends at a tavern on State Street, and showed them his poem. Jan read silently and when he had finished he spoke enthusiastically: "Dick, this is good! Let me send it to Jack Conroy, in Moberly, he's the editor of the *Anvil*. It should be published!" A thrill of excitement spread through Richard but he had one more test: "If you're going to publish this to recruit me to the Party, then nothing doing." But Jan told him the poem would be published whether or not he ever joined; he had communicated a deep emotion, a primary function of art, and that was its importance.

Then Richard told Jan of his mother's reactions to the cartoon on the cover of *Masses*. "She'll have to learn the symbolism of the revolution," Jan explained. A long discussion followed which went nowhere, but Richard left the tavern after promising to attend the next meeting of the Club. Maybe there he could persuade the members that Ella's reaction was representative of ordinary people.

An openhearted acceptance was building in Richard toward the people he was meeting, but he held his emotions down until a final test. He would watch them closely; he would see the faintest anti-Negro gesture. But after the meeting he marveled: "How had these people, denying profit and home and God, made that hurdle that even the churches of America had not been able to make?" He saw no prejudice.

Richard attended several Club meetings and afterwards spent the night writing poems. Each time a sensation of vitality took over every cell in his body; a limitless freedom, a daring dream of human unity which was more important to him than bread. For he ". . . felt that without a common bond uniting men, without a continuous current of shared thought and feeling circulating through the social system, like blood coursing through the body, there could be no living worthy of being called human.

I hungered to share the dominant assumptions of my time and act upon them, I did not want to feel, like an animal in a jungle, that the whole world was alien and hostile. I did not want to make individual war or peace. So far I had managed to keep humanly alive through transfusions from books. In my concrete relations with others I had encountered nothing to encourage me to believe in my feelings. It had been by denying what I saw with my eyes, disputing what I felt with my body, that I had managed to keep my identity intact.[5]

The editor of *Left Front* accepted for publication two poems, "Rest for the Weary" and "A Red Love Note," and sent a third poem to Jack Conroy, editor of *Anvil,* in Moberly, Missouri; "I Have Seen Black Hands" was sent to the *New Masses,* the successor of the *Masses.* Suspicion flared in Richard briefly: "Don't send them if you think they aren't good enough," he told the editor, "They're good enough," he said. "Are you doing this to get me to join up?" Richard asked again.

There were not many reservations left and the Communists seemed to be the only political organization that was expressing the country's widely felt need for a drastic change. Richard had collected votes for the Republican Party, and he had served as Assistant Precinct Captain in the regular fourth ward Democratic organization. In the headquarters, at 47th Street and Cottage Grove Avenue, he had watched the same political manipulations that had disgusted him in the Republican election campaign. Both parties were essentially the same and as far as a black man was concerned they were identical.

The scope and seriousness of the Club's activities impressed Richard and its optimism in the midst of the Depression was a sharp contrast to the Republicans and Democrats. "The Club was demanding that the government create jobs for unemployed artists; it planned and organized art exhibits; it raised funds for the publication of *Left Front;* and it sent scores of speakers to trade-union meetings. The members were fervent, democratic, restless, eager, self-sacrificing."

By the end of January, 1932, Richard joined the Chicago John Reed Club and committed himself wholeheartedly—morally, intellectually and artistically—in the fullest gesture of his life. Quietly, and to himself, he made another vow: he would make black men and women understand Communism and accept its philosophy and he would accomplish it through his writing. He planned a series of biographical sketches of Negro Communists. At the same time he would work with Club members and teach them the dreams and everyday realities of Negro life.

He had attended only a few meetings when he noticed that a bitter fight was going on between the painters and the writers in the Club. Richard asked Jan Wittenber to explain what was happening but he seemed evasive. Arguments broke out at every meeting and from a sense of loyalty because of his own interests Richard sided with the writers. One evening a special meeting was called and Richard was astonished when the writers of the *Left Front* group accused the painters of not fairly representing the total Club. They called for a new election of executive secretary and Richard's name was put in nomination. This is crazy! Richard thought and, getting to his feet, he explained that he had been a member only a few weeks and was not familiar enough with the aims of the Club to accept the nomination. The debate lasted all night and early in the morning, by a show of hands, Richard was unanimously elected executive secretary.

As the Club's secretary he learned that he had been used in a factional fight. Most of the painters were secret members of the Communist Party. "They would meet outside of the Club, decide what policies the Club should follow; and when they put forth their proposals in open meetings, the sheer strength of their arguments usually persuaded non-Party members to vote with them. The crux of the fight was that the non-Party members resented the excessive demands made upon the Club by the local Party authorities through the fraction. For example, the fraction demanded that the *Daily Worker* and the *New Masses,* official periodicals of the Communist Party, be put on sale at all meetings. The non-Party group declared that this would limit the Club's membership to those who already believed in Communism."

Without Richard's knowledge the writers had ousted the painters from leadership by nominating a Negro. One of the rallying cries of the Party was equality and freedom for the black man and no Communist dared vote against Richard. As the Club's new leader Richard tried to keep the antagonism between the painters and writers at a minimum. But his inexperience sometimes overwhelmed and tired him so that he did not look forward to the meetings. Both sides continued to batter at him and he worked out compromises. Sales of the *Daily Worker* were withdrawn in the Club but the *New Masses* remained. Richard thought that this would satisfy the writers since there was some justification for the sale of *New Masses* as a more literary expression of the Club than for the newspaper. But neither side was pleased.

Toward the end of March Richard noticed a lessening of tension in his relations with the painters' fraction. Friendliness was in the air and Richard wondered why. He had not long to wait; he was informed that if he wanted to continue as secretary of the Club he would have to join the Communist Party. Without hesitation he signed a membership card.

In May, 1932, the First National Conference of the John Reed Club was held in Chicago and Wright attended, although Jan Wittenber was delegate for the city. It was with a feeling of anticipation that Richard entered the Lincoln Center Auditorium. It would be the first time that he had met delegates from all over the United States. After speaking to a few people he knew Richard slid quietly into a seat and looked around. Up near the front of the room was a dark-skinned, rough-hewn man with tousled hair. Now and then he made the room resound with his deep laughter, and others standing around lifted their heads for a minute and smiled. "That's Mike Gold," someone told Richard.

The meeting was called to order and the first point on the agenda was the election of the presidium by the thirty-eight delegates in attendance. Jan Wittenber was selected from Chicago, Joseph Freeman (New York), Jack Walters (Newark), Maurice Sugar (Detroit), Harry Carlisle (Hollywood), Conrad Komorowski (Philadelphia), Charles Natterstad (Seattle), George Gay (Portland), Kenneth Rexroth (San Francisco), Carl Carlson (Boston). Then honorary members of the presidium were nominated: Langston Hughes, Romain Rolland, John Dos Passos, Paul Vaillant-Couturier (France), Maxim Gorky (Russia), Johannes Becker (Germany), Seikichi Fukimori (Japan), Lu Hsün (Chou Shu-jên) (China).

Even the dull election of a presidium charged Richard with emotion—he was part of a truly international organization. Despite its occasional petty bickering, the Club was meaningful—why, the bloodstream of the world was represented in those names. He heard the nomination of Louis Aragon turned down because he had protected himself from a jail sentence by pleading poetic license in a poem in the *Magazine of Revolutionary Literature*. Others nominated but not elected were Theodore Dreiser, the Mexican painter D. A. Siqueiros and Malcolm Cowley. The Club had power and importance far beyond anything Richard had realized.

Following the nominations each member club discussed the work in its area, which revolved around film and photographic leagues, workers' schools for writing and painting, organizing art exhibits, participating in strikes or demonstrations, giving dance concerts; and then a long time was spent on discussing agitation and propaganda techniques. Some of Richard's exhilaration began to lessen and he leaned forward in his seat, one arm across his body, the elbow of his other arm resting on it as a cushion, and idly felt his upper lip, concentrating on the speakers. There were overtones and under-currents of friction that he could not analyze but he began to watch the faces of Mike Gold, William Gropper and Joseph Freeman, the New York delegates.

The New York delegation had brought with it three staff members of the *New Masses,* which made it the most high-powered representa-tion at the conference, and it carried added power since it was the oldest and the largest of the John Reed Clubs in the country. Hints were made that New York was trying to run the conference and outright criticism was made "for [New York's] failure to provide effective and responsible leadership to the other clubs throughout the country." Richard was somewhat at sea for he sensed an attack from the Party against the John Reed Clubs—some policy change was in the making. He was pleased when Gold stated that he sensed a strong sectarianism among the delegates, and glancing at Chicago's delegate, he saw Wittenber compress his lips and lower his eyebrows in silent antagonism. But later on in the sessions, Gold, with a whimsical sneer, declared the purpose of the Clubs was not to run a school for young boys and Richard became antagonistic. He himself was a fledgling writer and warmly supported all young, working-class artists for whom the John Reed Clubs were a center where they could learn their craft and have access to publications in which they might be published. It was becoming "almost a religion" with Richard to help young unknown writers.

When the conference ended Richard put out of his mind the uneasiness caused him by friction between the Clubs and the Party and began work again on the sketches of Party members. He had met a Negro Communist, David Poindexter, who had been born in Tennessee in the heart of the black tobacco belt in 1903. David had come North when he was seventeen and worked in hog-killing plants, pie factories and on the open hearth in a steel mill in Chicago. He had been recruited into the Party by Sol Harper and Richard had met him in Unit 205 on the South Side. "Distrustful but aggressive, he was a bundle of the weaknesses and virtues of a man struggling blindly between two societies, of a man living on the margin of a culture." Richard felt that if he could get David's story he would illustrate the difficulties encountered by a folk people in their adjust-ment to an urban environment. In David's life of only thirty years lay the history of the 300-year development of the American conti-nent—from peasant to urban dweller. A man who came from an area without electric lights or running water had learned to handle with ease the machines of the most industrially advanced country in the world. If he could show this, then each stage of development would reveal the dramas of hope, fear, love and hate that existed in the Negro people.

I would make these lives merge with the lives of the mass of mankind. I knew I could. My life had prepared me for this.

Poindexter was agreeable and invited Richard to his home and introduced him to his Jewish wife and his young son. Richard talked for hours, explaining his ideas, and it was arranged that he would visit David every morning and take notes for two hours. Everything worked well for a few weeks until word spread in the Party that the two men were meeting every day and that notes were being taken.

After supper one night Richard sat in his room reading when Ella called to him that someone was knocking at the door. When he opened the door he saw one of the members of the South Side branch standing stiff and quiet with his hands in his pockets and his cap pulled down low over his eyes. Signaling to Richard mysteriously with a backward bob of the head, he indicated that he wanted him to come outside and not let Ella know what was happening. Intrigued and somewhat mystified, Richard took up his coat and called to his mother that he was going out for a few minutes.

Looking straight ahead and not answering his questions, the man led Richard all the way down the steps into the cold street. At the pavement he pivoted slowly and his black eyes stared into Richard's:

"Intellectuals don't fit well into the Party, Wright," he said solemnly.

"But I'm not an intellectual," I protested. "I sweep the streets for a living." I had just been assigned by the relief system to sweep the streets for thirteen dollars a week.

"That doesn't make any difference," he said. "We've kept records of the trouble we've had with intellectuals in the past. It's estimated that only thirteen percent of them remain in the Party."

"Why do they leave, since you insist upon calling me an intellectual?" I asked.

"Most of them drop out of their own accord," he said.

"Well, I'm not dropping out," I said.

"Some are expelled," he hinted gravely.

"For what?"

"General opposition to the Party's policies," he said.

"But I'm not opposing anything in the Party."

"But you have to prove yourself."

"What do you mean?"

"You'll have to prove your revolutionary loyalty."

"That's what I'm trying to do through writing."

"That's not the way to do it," he said. "You must act."

[Then he explained to Richard that a practical way to demonstrate his loyalty to the Party was through militant resistance to the police and cited the case of a Communist who had been hit over the head by the police in an unemployment demonstration. Richard told him it was a primitive way to express loyalty and that he would not be of much use to the organization if he suffered a brain concussion and became insane from a cop's blows. The man did not answer for a minute and then he shook his head as if Richard were a lost soul.]

"The Soviet Union has had to shoot a lot of intellectuals," he said.

Richard was aghast: "Good God!" [he] exclaimed. "Do you know what you're saying? You're not in Russia. You're standing on a sidewalk in Chicago. You talk like a man lost in a fantasy."[6]

Richard walked back into the house feeling as if he were in a dream world—what had motivated that comrade to seek him out with such dire predictions of his future? And his comrade's parting words had been to ask him if he had heard of Leon Trotsky, who had been banished from the Soviet Union. It irritated him to think that his reading was questioned or limited in any way. He had not read Trotsky's works; it had been Stalin's *The National and Colonial Question* that interested him, but he did not want anyone to tell him what he could or could not do.

A few mornings later Richard sat at Poindexter's house scribbling notes when the doorbell rang and a square-shouldered, tall black man was admitted. He was introduced as Ed Green and he nodded stiffly at Richard before turning to Poindexter. "What's happening here?" he asked bluntly. David explained and then Green began to cross-examine Richard. His manner was so abrupt and rough that Richard did not feel like answering but he saw that the Poindexters were nervous and uncomfortable so he answered quietly. Green wanted to know what he was going to do with the notes he was making; what he did for a living; what school he had attended, and how far he had gone in his education; and to whom he had shown the material. Green left the room as brusquely as he had entered.

"Who does he think he is?" Richard asked Poindexter. He was told that Green was a member of the Central Committee of the Party, a very important man. In addition, he was the representative of the International Labor Defense for the South Side.

For a few more weeks Richard self-consciously continued taking notes but each morning David became more withdrawn and did not seem able to speak as freely as he had, so he put away his pad and pencil, hoping to allay his fears. Then Richard sat and listened to David and his friends tell of their experiences, as boys, in the South until he became steeped in the details of their lives. Putting away the biographical notes, he decided that he would use the material he had gotten from David and his friends for a series of short stories.

As leader of the John Reed Club, Richard did not attend regular unit meetings of the Party and this freedom gave him time in which to evaluate his experience with his comrades. Their suspicion of him—that he might be a traitor; might inform the police; and their refusal to understand or accept his words—temporarily blocked his feelings. He felt frozen, suspended in air, but the Club needed his attention so he pushed the episode out of his mind. Besides, the whole philosophic concept of the Clubs was in question and, although Richard did not know it, this larger problem was reflected in the local meetings.

Two factions in the Club were assuming rigid outlines different from the simple division between painters and writers that had placed Richard in leadership a few weeks after his initiation. And to most of the members those who were actually antagonistic toward the original intent of the Club appeared most progressive. These were the people who attacked sectarianism, bureaucratization—the last bourgeois hangovers—and cried for bolder methods and an end to sloganized diatribes disguised as poetry and fiction.

Abetting the disorganization in the Club, local Party leaders put so many demands upon it for speakers, sign painters and money that little time or energy remained for work on its magazine, *Left Front*. Instead of writing stories, or poems, or articles, writers were making speeches before meetings arranged by the Party through which they hoped to recruit new members. Bills piled up, the rent was past due and meetings dissolved into political wrangles. Richard tried to mediate between the opposing groups because at all costs he wanted the John Reed Club to continue and he could see young writers becoming discouraged.

One meeting night the Party, operating through its members in the John Reed Club, proposed that publication of *Left Front* be dropped and all efforts directed toward the *New Masses*. Richard and all the other writers voted down the proposal, which the Party viewed as a hostile act. In a few weeks the Party called a conference, and Richard supported the idea—now there would have to be clarification of the role of writers in relation to Communism. When the steering committee met to discuss an agenda for the conference Richard argued that it should deal with craft problems. He asked for

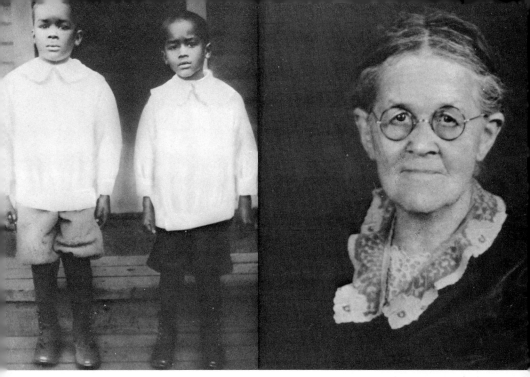

Richard Wright (left) and his younger brother, Alan, in 1916, when they were living in Elaine, Arkansas.

Richard's grandmother, Margaret Bolden Wilson.

Ella Wright, about 1920.

Richard's father, Nathaniel, when he was about fifty-five.

Addie Wilson, Richard's aunt.

Richard's graduation picture.

The Faculty and Members of the Senior Class
of the

Smith-Robertson Public School

Request the honor of your presence
at the

Graduating Exercises

Friday, May Twenty-Ninth
Nineteen hundred and twenty-five
at the

City Auditorium

eight o'clock p. m.

Compliments of_____

Photo by Togo Oyama

Richard Wright (standing sixth from the right) worked in 1931 as assistant precinct captain for B. Doc Huggins (front row second from the left), who was working for a political appointment as inspector of police personnel. Joe C. Brown, Richard's boyhood friend, is standing fourth from the right.

hard Wright, during his
ngry days in Chicago" just
r his arrival there in 1927.

Richard Wright, fall of 1932.

In September, 1933, Wright was elected executive secretary of the John Reed Club in Chicago.

His first wife, Rose Dhima Meadman, was a ballet dancer.

Maxwell Bodenheim (top left), and friends, with Richard Wright when they were all members of the Creative Writers Project (WPA) in New York in 1938.

(Right) Mexico, 1940, when he left Dhima.

A doting father, he read to his elder daughter, Julia, almost every day. She was three when this picture was taken in 1945.

Photo by Studio Gallery, Stockholm

With Ellen Poplar in 1945, four years after their marriage.

Photo by Carl Van Vech

Julia in 1943.

Photo by Studio Gallery

With Ellen in their Brooklyn apartment
on Middagh Street in 1944.

At the time of the completion of
Native Son.
Photo by Bernard Cole

Knobby.

Photo by Studio Gallery

Simone de Beauvoir was a close friend.

George Padmore, the "father of African emancipation," and his wife, Dorothy, during one of their visits to the Wrights.

Rachel (left), Wright's younger daughter, was born in France, January 17, 1949. She is seven years younger than Julia, with whom she is shown at the beach in Trouville-Deauville in 1961.

Richard Wright, Julia and Ellen at the American Artists and Students Center, Paris, in 1946.

Ellen remodeled the Norman farmhouse where the Wrights spent their summers.

A scene from the film. Bigger Thomas (played by Richard) is taken to a restaurant in Southside Chicago by the Communist Jan Erlone (played by Gene Michael) and Mary Dalton.

Some of the cast.

Photo by Gisele Freund

ative Son was filmed in Argentina in 1950.
loria Madison (left) played Bessie and Jean Wallace played Mary Dalton.

Bigger murdering Bessie.

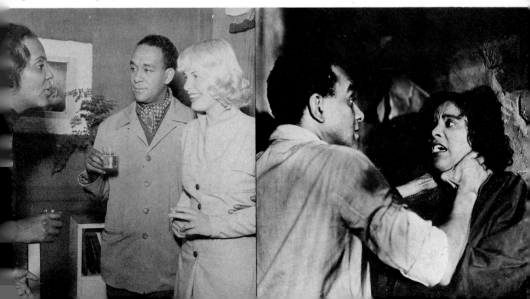

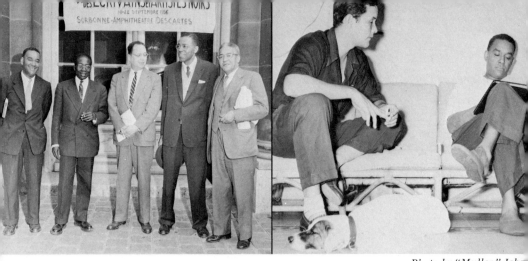

Richard Wright with Leopold Senghor, President of Senegal (second from the left), and other speakers at the Présence Africaine Congress of Black Writers and Artists, September 19, 1956.

Photo by "Muller," Jaka

Interviewing an Indonesian student in Jakarta, April, 1955.

In Rome, June, 1957, when he was a guest of the Italian publisher Alberto Mondadori.

Photo by Anders Holmquist, F

Three weeks before his death.

Photo by M. J. Beraud-Villars, Paris

At a panel discussion of American writers, in Paris.

a definition of what was expected from writers—books or political activity? Both, was the answer. It was simply a question of organizing one's time—a certain number of hours could be spent writing and the rest of the time on Party tasks.

At the conference Jan Wittenber acted as adviser, and the major part of the day revolved around a debate: What did the Communist Party expect from the Club? When Richard opened the discussion he began by appealing for an organizational structure that would emphasize that the work of a writer was to write, that this was as valid and important as any other form of revolutionary activity. And he explained that a novel, a work of art, was more important than pamphlets or speeches because it would endure. He pointed out the importance of *Left Front* to young writers and ended by warning that the future of the Club was in doubt if a clear policy could not be found.

Arguments continued throughout the day, and the Party leader's ideas that the Club members must become disciplined and responsible workers for Socialism won out. Writers would have to produce pamphlets for use in Unemployed Councils and union organizing, and they would have to, at times, distribute leaflets, walk picket lines and continue to make speeches whenever the Party deemed it necessary. *Left Front,* after only four issues, was judged to be of no use to the Party; all efforts must be channeled to the *New Masses,* and *Left Front* was voted out of existence.

As Richard watched the hands go up in support of the dissolution of the magazine an angry pain went through him. And he asked for the floor to make a final speech. Since the conference had only exacerbated the problems within the Club and increased the tensions which led to constant bickering and fights over strategy and tactics, he recommended that the Club be dissolved and all efforts be directed toward Party work. Otherwise, the dichotomy would eventually tear the Club apart. His short speech brought sharp words from the Party leadership, who called him "defeatist."

An invisible wall was building slowly between me and the people with whom I had cast my lot. Well, I would show them that all men who wrote books were not their enemies. I would communicate the meaning of their lives to people whom they could not reach; then surely, my intentions would merit their confidence.[7]

On September 8, 1933, Richard organized an open forum on the "Literature of the Negro" and was the leading speaker. The Party had been enthusiastic when he proposed the meeting and Richard hoped that, through his own speech, he would be able to clarify his point of view and educate the members who were antagonistic toward his ideas. After the success of the forum the Party sent Richard to union meetings, neighborhood groups and colleges in and around Chicago to speak in his melodious and convincing voice.

Occasionally, he met Negro Communists on the South Side who continued to regard him with suspicion and made jokes to each other in his presence. "Man, there's that writer, Wright, he's got a book under each arm!" Sneers and laughter about his reading spread through the various Party units until it refined itself into ridicule about his concern for style and craftsmanship and the comment grew precise: "Whenever you see Wright he's carrying William James under one arm and Waldo Frank under the other."[8]

On one occasion Richard was asked to show a newspaper-wrapped book that he carried under his arm.

The comrade looked at it and shook his head.
"What're you reading this for?" he asked.
"It's interesting," I said.
"Reading bourgeois books can only confuse you, comrade," he said, returning the book.
"You seem convinced that I'm easily confused," I said.
"You know," he said, his voice dropping to a low, confidential tone, "many comrades go wrong by reading the books of the bourgeoisie. The Party in the Soviet Union had trouble with people like that."
"Didn't Lenin read bourgeois books?" I asked.
"But you're not Lenin," he shot at me.
"Are there some books reserved for some people to read, while others cannot read them?" I asked.
"Comrade, you do not understand," he said.[9]

Richard learned to accept gibes philosophically; it was not viciousness on the part of black Communists in Unit 205, and he felt they did not mean to hurt. "They just did not know anything and did not want to learn anything. They felt that all questions had been answered, and anyone who asked new ones or tried to answer old ones was dangerous. The word 'writer' was enough to make a black Chicago Communist feel that the man to whom the word applied had gone wrong."

A large increase in membership in the John Reed Club, largely due to his efforts, and a lessening of tension with Party leaders had begun to restore his enthusiasm. With doubters, he argued that the workers' movement was the last best hope of this earth. "But for a writer to get hold of it is the thing, the task, the fun, and the grief.

. . . Really the revolutionists have not come home to us; they do not as yet act or live within the folk consciousness of our lives. . . . But they have something! They are in the vortex of the events of our time, the focal events of our day and age; they are living in the heights of our times."[10] The Party had assigned him as full-time organizer to the John Reed Club and paid him a few dollars a week; although it was little more than enough to pay his expenses, the money gave him a feeling of security.

Club organizing did not interfere with writing and he was wrestling with a set of short stories that he knew would be published in one of the Party publications. A large readership was assured.

Indeed, we felt that we were lucky. Why cower in towers of ivory and squeeze out private words when we had only to speak and millions listened? Our writing was translated into French, German, Russian, Chinese, Spanish, Japanese . . . Who had ever, in all human history, offered to young writers an audience so vast?

And Richard wrote what he felt:

Confronted with a picture of a revolutionary and changing world, there spilled out of our hearts our reaction to that world, our hope, our anger at oppression, our dreams of a new life; it spilled without coercion, without the pleading of anyone.[11]

Earl Browder, Party chief, ". . . valued writers for their prestige and popularity rather than for the purity of their Marxism or intrinsic literary merit. Mass movements, labor, unemployment—these were the throbbing issues. The writers who believed their work mattered a continental to the 'ninth floor'* were deluding themselves; the party distrusted them always as putative defectors and sentimental moralizers. 'Oh, we could preach sermons on Sunday,' Earl Browder remarked, 'but for the intellectuals, every day was Sunday.' . . . Disagreements involving art and politics were to be settled amicably within the family circle. . . ."[12] And Richard passionately and uncritically supported the Party in public.

In September, 1934, another John Reed Club conference was held in Chicago and Richard was one of forty delegates representing a membership that had grown to 1,200. When Richard entered the hall and looked around, a sense of being anchored in life, in the flow of the universe, filled him; the room glowed with intellectual intensity so sharp it made his throat feel constricted. Jack Conroy caught sight of him and darted up with a look of Ozarkian boyish

* Browder's office on the ninth floor of 50 East Thirteenth Street.

innocence and Richard grinned in pleasure. He loved that man! Nelson Algren in corduroy pants, a shabby jacket and a shirt without a tie gave him a rough, enthusiastic greeting even though they saw each other regularly. There were Emmet Gower and Merlin Bower, young writers; Marion Perkins, a sculptor; and friends from the post office, Abe Aaron and Sam Gaspar. And he met Alexander Trachtenberg, the head of International Publishers, a short, thick, dark-skinned man with a heavy moustache. A dramatic man, Richard thought; with scimitar and fez he could lead a whole Turkish army.[13]

At some point during the session Richard shifted in his seat and was aware that a feeling of restlessness had descended upon him. When he looked around the room, paying most attention to the young writers who were his responsibility as organizer, he saw bewilderment, dissatisfaction and looseness in posture as they lounged in their seats. Richard saw that the speakers were not holding their interest and he was concerned. Most of the men were young, eager and on the verge of doing their best work. He looked at the speaker, concentrating until his figure receded far off, as if through the lens of a camera, and focused all of his attention on the words of the speech. It occurred to him that the problem was that no one had brought forth a single unifying idea and it was impossible to decide what was expected of a writer.

Interest quickened when Alexander Trachtenberg began his speech; he was incisive, yet humorous, and made clear the position of the Party in relation to the John Reed Clubs. Their purpose was to win writers and artists to the revolution. A creative revolutionary literature was of extreme importance in the fight against capitalist society. Sectarianism toward the cultural movement had to be weeded out of the Party. And he ended by proposing that the national committee be instructed to organize a nationwide congress of writers within six or eight months. The suggestion was unanimously endorsed by the conference.

As the congress drew to a close, I attended a caucus to plan the future of the clubs. Ten of us met in a Loop hotel room and, to my amazement, the leaders of the club's national board confirmed my criticisms of the manner in which the clubs had been conducted. I was excited. Now, I thought, the clubs will be given a new lease on life. Writers would now be free to make their political contributions in the form of their creative work.

Then I was stunned when I heard [Trachtenberg] announce a decision to dissolve the clubs. Why? I asked. Because the clubs do not serve the new People's Front policy, I was told. That can be remedied; the clubs can be made healthy and broad, I said. No; a bigger and better organization must be launched, one in which the leading writers of the nation could be included, they said. I was informed that the People's Front policy was now the correct vision of life and that the clubs could no longer exist. I asked what was to become of the young writers whom the Communist party had implored to join the clubs and who were ineligible for the new group, and there was no answer. This thing is cold! I exclaimed to myself. To effect a swift change in policy, the Communist party was dumping one organization, scattering its members, then organizing a new scheme with entirely new people![14]

Richard had "sacrificed energy to recruit writers who subscribed to a revolutionary point of view, and now [his] feelings fought against the waste and meaninglessness to which [his] efforts were being reduced." It was his first experience with a Communist policymaking body and he naïvely thought that there would be discussion of Trachtenberg's proposal. Everyone sat silent. Richard looked around in amazement; he knew that others agreed with his point of view. He filled his lungs with air, sighed deeply and argued alone against the Party's cultural boss. No one supported his arguments, the decision had been made in New York prior to the conference and Bolshevik discipline demanded total acceptance.

It was not courage that made me oppose the party. I simply did not know any better. It was inconceivable to me, though bred in the lap of southern hate, that a man could not have his say.[15]

When Richard argued with friends in the Club that the Party was making a mistake in its new direction they insisted that in the face of Hitler's aggressions the Party had to broaden out. "Trachty," they told him, knew what he was doing and had access to information of an international character. But Richard was unconvinced. Independent, revolutionary literary clubs that could develop writers from Negro and working-class communities would form the nucleus for an indigenous American movement. By abandoning the Clubs the Party was demonstrating that it thought it could gain more from "name" writers, that this was cynical, self-seeking, and that control from the top, which he had already tasted in his interviews with David Poindexter, would be increased. No one, no party, should tell a writer what to write; most writers were unconscious revolutionists because the character of their work forced them always to seek the new, that which was beyond the world around them. And a black writer was the most revolutionary of them all.

But on November 23, the Party sent Wright to lecture in Indianapolis. He went happily to share the platform with Langston Hughes, who had recently looked him up when he came east from Carmel, California, because he admired some of Richard's poems. Langston, with a collegiate zest for life and his warm jokes, made Richard feel as if he were the elder. He liked Langston's poetry, and Langston had the same passion for helping new writers as Richard.

Spring came and plans went ahead to recruit anti-Fascist writers. In March, Germany denounced the Versailles Treaty, reintroduced conscription and announced that her army would be increased. France and Russia joined in an agreement of mutual defense in the event that the Fascists moved against either country. "The revulsion inspired by the Nazis in American liberals and radicals antedated the revelations of Belsen and Auschwitz; to them, Hitler was a forerunner of a new and bloody 'dark ages.' The reports, official and unofficial, flowing out of Germany after his triumph, the stories of pogroms and book burnings and concentration camps, enforced the image of the Third Reich as a medieval hell."[16]

A call for an American Writers Congress—written by Granville Hicks and issued by the *New Masses*—invited all writers of reputation who were in sympathy with revolutionary ideals to create a League of American Writers. The new League would be an affiliate of the International Union of Revolutionary Writers (I.R.R.W.). Richard signed the call along with sixty-three other writers. Theodore Dreiser, Waldo Frank, Erskine Caldwell, Lincoln Steffens and his wife, Ella Winter, Nelson Algren, James T. Farrell, Michael Gold, Jack Conroy, Malcolm Cowley, Edwin Seaver and Earl Browder were among the supporters. And in preparation for an International Congress of Writers conference were listed the names of some of the most distinguished literary figures in the world: André Gide, Boris Pasternak, Anna Seghers, Bertolt Brecht, E. M. Forster, Aldous Huxley, André Malraux, Louis Aragon, Isaac Babel, Alexis Tolstoy, Heinrich Mann, Leon Feuchtwanger, Ilya Ehrenburg.

Named as a delegate, Richard got a ride to New York with Paul Romaine, Nelson Algren and one or two others for the April 26–27, 1935 meeting to be held in Mecca Temple. On the first day, at the only public session, Earl Browder made the opening speech before a huge, enthusiastic audience. Richard sat quietly in his seat, unimpressed by his leader's assurances that the Party had no desire to put them into uniforms nor dictate what they should write. Writers were to be good writers, not bad strike leaders. A good work of art would ultimately be judged by the masses and there was no fixed Party line on the form it would take.

Early the next morning Richard dressed and looked out of the window on an April day in New York. During breakfast in a Horn and Hardart automat he went over in his mind what he planned to say in defense of the John Reed Clubs. A feeling of ennui came and went in his body—what was the point of his stubborn resistance toward the new line, it was hopeless, no one else would support him. But he fought his inertia and attended the meeting that was to make the final decision to dissolve the Clubs. When his turn came to speak Richard described the loneliness of the Negro author and explained what the John Reed Clubs meant to all young writers. Applause broke out spontaneously at the end of his speech, but Richard smiled inwardly, cynically. They would clap for him but they would not support his position. Debate was closed and the vote was called. Hands went up all over the room to dissolve the Clubs. When the call came for those who disagreed, Richard's hand was raised alone. He knew that his opposition would be interpreted as unconscious antagonism to the ideals of Marxism. The hell with it, he said to himself.

With the Clubs dissolved, Richard was freed from routine duties and he did not attend unit meetings on the South Side for fear of being disciplined. Occasionally, he heard from comrades that he was being called a "smuggler of reaction," a "petty bourgeois degenerate," a "bastard intellectual," and an "incipient Trotskyite with anti-leadership tendencies."

During summer and fall Richard worked on the series of short stories he had begun and on a novel about post office workers. He was certain that the Party would not approve of an honest portrayal of Negroes—they had to be heroes, not human beings. Working all day and writing all night brought on a serious illness. It descended upon him suddenly one night after work. An acute constriction and shooting pains in his chest made breathing difficult. Ella made him lemon tea, which he forced through parched lips. He was forced to stay in bed for several weeks, for he had worried and worked himself into pneumonia.

At the end of September Richard's chest had healed and he received word that the *New Masses* wanted him to write an article on the Joe Louis–Max Baer fight. When the fight was over Wright stood on Prairie Avenue and 47th Street and stared all around him, touched to his depths by the joy that burst from the black community at the great fighter's victory. Pressed by bodies on every side, Richard edged his way across 47th Street toward South Parkway and watched people form into snake-lines and dance in the street. Twenty-five thousand people were in the streets singing, talking, dancing and shouting. And Richard noticed that white policemen had been with-drawn; he had never known that Chicago had so many black cops. And they were careful not to antagonize the triumphant crowd.

At home, Richard sat at his writing table and words poured out almost as fast as he could move his hand. In two hours the article was finished and when he read it over he changed one or two lines, crossed out a word and substituted another and it was ready to mail. This time he spoke directly to fellow Communists—they had to see the dynamite that lay close to the surface in the black community.

Say, comrade, here's the wild river that's got to be harnessed and directed. Here's that *something,* that pent-up folk consciousness. Here's a fleeting glimpse of the heart of the Negro, the heart that beats and suffers and hopes—for freedom. . . .[17]

Not long after Wright's article appeared in the *New Masses,* James W. Ford, a member of the highest body of the Party, the Communist International, was in Chicago and sent for him. Ford met Richard alone and after they shook hands he said that he had heard about him. As he smiled and parried the remark, Richard looked closely at the famous leader whose life had taken a course similar to his own. Behind Ford's smile Wright sensed bitterness and a conscious attempt to appear utterly at ease. He, too, had been born in the South, in Alabama, had worked as a water boy, carrying water to men on the railroads and had, at one time, been a postal worker in Chicago.

Ford waved Richard to a chair and opened their conversation by praising the Louis article in the *New Masses.* It was the first political treatment of sports the Party had ever had and it indicated that Richard was a man needed by the Party, especially in the anti-Fascist work ahead. But it developed that the work the Party had in mind was organizational; they wanted to make him a mass leader and pro-posed that he begin by organizing a committee against the high cost of living. In this way he would become familiar to Negroes on the South Side. When Richard protested that he was in the midst of a novel,[18] that he was twenty-seven and had not yet written anything worthwhile, and needed six months more to prove he could write, it made no impression on Ford. "The Party can't wait," Ford told him. Twenty million people were on relief and capitalism was crumbling. The danger of Fascism and the march toward war were speeding up. Being a Communist was not easy; it meant sacrifice and Bolshevik discipline. Wright was not indispensable simply because he was black. And implicit throughout was a threat that he would be branded a counterrevolutionary if he did not accept Party law.

"Dick"—Ford crossed his legs and leaned back in his chair as he spoke—"the role of the creative writer is to serve the interests of the people by inspiring them and helping them to prepare and organize their struggle. The Party has made its decision; you are to accept this task."

Richard agreed to take on the work of initiating a committe on the South Side to study food prices and the daily cost of living for a six-month period. After it was well organized he would turn it over to another member to continue. Whether Ford accepted his terms or not Richard did not know because he became genial and terminated the discussion. Instinct told him that Ford did not have to answer, and that whether or not he would let him off the committee at the end of six months would depend upon the wishes of the organization. Richard left the room angry at himself, angry with Ford and angry with the Party. In principle, he felt that the Party was right—"A decision was the highest injunction that a Communist could receive from his party, and to break a decision was to break the effectiveness of the party's ability to act . . . it was impossible for working people to forge instruments of political power until they had achieved unity of action." And Richard wanted to remain a Communist, ". . . to shape people's feelings, awaken their hearts."

In a month Wright had the committee under way among men and women on the South Side. But every night was spent in meetings and he could not work on his novel. One night, determined to write, he came home from a meeting and sat at his desk. It was no use, his mind fogged over and rebelled at the strain and he fell into bed. Then the Party offered him a trip to a youth conference in Switzerland as a delegate. From Switzerland, he would go to the Soviet Union to study.[19] Richard refused; he wanted to travel—it was one of his dreams—but he knew that the Party wanted to make a black leader out of him and he was determined to prove himself as a writer.

By spring of 1936 "Big Boy Leaves Home," a long short story based on the information he had collected from David Poindexter, was accepted by Alfred Kreymborg for publication in *New Caravan*, a collection of writing by Negroes. And his poems, articles and fiction were appearing regularly in all of the Party magazines and newspapers. When the League called a conference of Midwestern writers Richard attended with the aim of presenting ideas that would lessen the antagonism of political functionaries toward the creative individual. A new category existed in literature because the modern petty bourgeois writer was being driven toward producing revolutionary work in the crisis of Fascism and capitalism. Richard called it "Personalism."

The great difficulty arises when we seek to grasp this new expression in positive terms. There is among the petty bourgeois writers no class solidarity, no economic interests to preserve, no ideology or psychology to maintain. They have only themselves and that consciousness of themselves as being between two worlds, one rising and the other falling; and the consciousness that their values and hopes are receding. Therefore, the only expression possible in the initial stages is one of personal protest, or *personalism.*

Richard had not read any of the existentialist philosophers but there were overtones of that philosophy in *personalism.*[20]

Personalism as a medium of literary expression will emphasize tendency rather than form or content.

Personalism will foster expression of protest; in terms as individual and personal as possible.

Personalism will represent the highest intensity of social consciousness possible.

Having no values other than negative ones, it will be detailed in its presentation of material; it takes nothing for granted.

It represents all forms of revolt in writing.

Personalism represents the revolt of the petty bourgeois against the petty bourgeois.

Personalism represents the revolt of the petty bourgeois against the bourgeois.

Personalism will be anti-aesthetic insofar as it will seek to push art beyond mere contemplation. In short, its expression must become an objective act, having immediacy as its aim. Though using a high emotional content, its aim and end will be beyond the mere power to move. It will seek to make those who come in contact with it take sides for or against certain *moral* issues, and these issues will be elementary ones.

In summation, Richard presented a "Personalist Aesthetics" and continued the argument which had been raised by James T. Farrell at the first League meeting in New York: the reason that most revolutionary or proletarian writing ended with a forced revolution which was not successful was that the writer ignored his own traditions; and from a misconception as to what is the purpose of creative writing.

No repercussions descended upon Richard from the Party leaders but his own unit regarded him with even greater suspicion and he avoided them as much as he could. In all fairness, he admitted to himself, and to his old friend Joe Brown, who was not interested in politics, the new Popular Front program had increased opportunities for young Negroes on the South Side. It was "a road out of the black belt."

A few months after the Midwest conference, in July, 1936, General Franco, in alliance with the military, the aristocracy, monarchists and Fascist Falange, attacked the legally elected government of Spain and the disastrous Civil War began. In every section and branch of the Party a fervent unification occurred. And the Party's quick rallying to the support of an anguished Spain was supported overwhelmingly by a majority of the American intelligentsia—doctors, lawyers, artists, teachers and writers regarded the Spanish war as "a testing ground for war with Fascism in general."

Causing almost as much excitement, but without any ennobling effect on individual Party members on the South Side, was the announcement of a public trial instituted against sixteen Communists of a "Trotskyite—Zinovievite Terrorist Centre." The Centre, acting under orders of the isolated and exiled Leon Trotsky, had planned to assassinate Stalin and his supporters in the Kremlin and had, indeed, murdered Sergei Mironovich Kirov, Stalin's favorite, in Leningrad. "In four days, the Sixteen were judged without proof, condemned by order, and executed."[21]

Word reached Richard that a campaign had been launched to rid the Communist Party of all its "Negro Trotskyite elements." And one evening a group of comrades called at his home and asked to speak to him in a private. Wright took them into his narrow room and closed the door—snow had begun to fall when he had been on his way home from work and he was not going out into the freezing air for anyone. One of the visitors, a short, round-faced brown man, assumed a serious expression and said that there were rumors that Richard was in league with a Trotskyite group and plotting to make a secret appeal to influence members to leave the Party. Astonished, Richard said that he did not even know one Trotskyite, and that he was tired of hearing such accusations. If they continued, then he would resign from the Party, even though, ideologically, he had no differences with it. "You can't resign from the Party," another comrade said. "People would think something was wrong with our organization if you resigned."

A guffaw burst from Richard, but he checked it when he looked at the serious faces around him. He sighed and looked out the window at the blowing snow. Why do I persist in antagonizing them? They don't know any better—and I have to maintain a double vision—it is the ideals of Communism that weld me to the Party. I'm a Communist that can't stand Communists.

Sensing a lessening of antagonism in Wright's face, the comrades told him they had come to invite him to a meeting on Sunday, a trial of a Trotskyite, Ben Ross.* Again, Richard almost lost his temper. He asked them why they spent so much useless effort attacking each other instead of fighting landlords or discrimination. He told them to forget Ross, that he was a minor street agitator and in two weeks would not be an issue at all. But as they spoke about their intentions of making Ross an example to the rest of the membership and to the working class his old love of witnessing something new overcame him and he agreed to attend.

Ross' trial took place the following Sunday afternoon at Party headquarters. Richard entered the hall and took a place near the back of the room. When he looked around he saw sneering or hostile expressions on the faces of some of his comrades, and alternate waves of dread and keen excitement went through his body. His nerves were jumping and he was anxious for the trial to get under way. While waiting, he envisioned himself in Russia, where real trials were being held. If he were there, he might be shot for his stubborn independence.[22]

A member of the Central Committee, the fourth rank of leadership, stood up to make the opening speech, and another wave of crawling anticipation ran up Richard's neck. The leader "painted a horrible but masterful picture of Fascism's aggression in Germany, Italy, and Japan." It was a vivid speech and the audience's emotions were roused. Then two other speakers followed. One described Russia's struggle toward industrialization, ringed by a hostile world, sacrificing herself in the struggle to achieve socialism for the workers of the world. Next came a speech which put the world struggle in perspective with the work being accomplished in the United States. "This was done in a leisurely, painstaking manner, yet the people in the hall were charged with passion; a sense of human destiny lived; an atmosphere of human frailty was present."

Still another speaker talked of the Party's work in Chicago and finally on the South Side so that the world, the national and the local

* Name is fictitious.

pictures had been ". . . fused into one overwhelming drama of moral struggle in which everybody in the hall was participating."

This presentation had lasted for more than three hours, but it had enthroned a new sense of reality in the hearts of those present, a sense of man on earth. With the exception of the church and its myths and legends, there was no agency in the world so capable of making men feel the earth and the people upon it as the Communist Party.

I knew, as I watched, that I was looking at the future of mankind, that this way of living would finally win out. I knew that in no other way could the emotional capacities, the passional nature of men be so deeply tapped. In no other system yet devised could man so clearly reveal his destiny on earth, a destiny to rise and grapple with the world in which he lives, to wring from it the satisfactions he feels he must have. I knew, as I watched and listened, that but few people understood the essence of Communism, its passional dynamics; but few people knew that Communism was more important than any of its individual parties, than the sum of all its tactics, strategies, theories, mistakes, and tragedies. I knew that once this system became entrenched on earth, for good or bad, it could not fail, that all Europe and her armies could not destroy the Soviet Union, that the spirit of self-sacrifice that Communism engendered in men would astound the world.[23]

The charges directed against Ross were made toward the end of the evening, not by leaders of the Party, but by his emotionally aroused friends. Richard listened to each person as he recited dates, places and conversations, at the end of which Ross crumpled. "I'm guilty of all the charges, all of them." In confessing, he was the sinner finding redemption. No one threatened him; he could have walked from the hall and never seen his comrades again. But he did not want to. "The vision of a communal world had sunk down into his soul and it would never leave him until life left him."

A gigantic tension arose in Richard; it was so great that he rose to his feet before the meeting had ended and left the hall. He walked slowly down the stairs and out into the street. A stinging wind struck him in the face and blurred his eyes. On his way home he again thought of the trials taking place in Moscow and knew that if his comrades held state power he would be executed.

"What kind of a mind is this which accepts and waits, watching, and examining the texture and tissue of the feelings produced . . . by these social and political explosions, not afraid for the simple reason that I am a part of this too deeply to be either wildly hopeful or panicky with fear?" Richard mused. "But, regardless of tactics, what is there to *go back* to?"[24]

New York, 1937

X

Spring came slowly to Chicago in 1937, but for the first time in his life there Richard did not feel the bite of the wind or huddle into the collar of his coat when he stepped along the street. He felt as if he were skimming along the pavement and familiar landmarks seemed withdrawn into a new perspective outside of his life. James Ford and Benjamin Davis, in the name of the Central Committee, had offered him the post of Harlem Editor of the *Daily Worker*.

Carrying three manuscripts of novels, half a dozen short stories and assorted poems tucked in a briefcase under his arm, a portable typewriter and a cardboard suitcase containing his meager wardrobe, Richard took a train at the La Salle Street Station bound for New York. As the dreary blocks of Chicago passed before his window he felt wrapped in a dream. Now he was really leaving the Black Belt, plunging into the unknown, into a freedom which was widening and deepening.

Once before he had been in New York but his eyes were still used to flat Western plains, and when he saw the city again he was startled. "But where was the smoke pall? The soot? Grain elevators? Factories? Stackpipes? The flashes of steam on the horizon? The people on the sidewalks seemed better dressed than the people of Chicago. Their eyes were bold and impersonal. They walked with a quicker stride and seemed intent upon reaching some destination in a great hurry." Arriving in Grand Central Station, he headed for the IRT-Lexington Avenue subway, downtown platform. People bumped him from every direction and even though his left arm dragged from the weight of both suitcase and typewriter he would not loose his fingers clutching the portfolio under his right armpit. Anything could be lost or stolen, he would not care. But not the pages of words torn from his mind and emotions.

At Twenty-eighth Street and Lexington Richard emerged from the subway and looked around to get his bearings. He put the suitcase and typewriter on the ground, shifted his briefcase to the left arm and stretched his long fingers and thumb to relax their tension. After a minute or two he started off briskly, down Lexington until he reached Twenty-sixth, then left and east, to Number 235 and Apartment 2B, where he would stay with white comrades.[1]

On his second day in New York Richard met Benjamin J. Davis, Jr., who took him to the Harlem Bureau of the *Daily Worker* and assigned him a desk. Davis, a Harvard-trained lawyer, still had the physical self-confidence from the years he played varsity football and a warm intelligence in his face. At last he was meeting a black leader without antagonism, one he could respect and with whom he could talk, and Richard sensed that Davis was taking him under his influential wing. Davis' Marxism was not reeled out in memorized clichés but formed the substantive basis from which new approaches to ideas seemed to come. And he had a sense of humor, which Richard had not found in many leaders in Chicago.

Davis told Richard, over coffee on Lenox Avenue, that first afternoon, that the Party wished him to work with two women, Dorothy West and Marian Minus, who were putting up the money for a new publication to be called *New Challenge*. Taking a sip of his coffee, Davis paused in his description of the proposed magazine and then said that Richard was to edit, write and provide direction. As an opener, it might be well for him to write an article anywhere from two to five thousand words in length giving a revolutionary history and prospectus of Negro literature. This would be valuable for Party use; it could be given out to sympathizers or used in the recruitment of writers. Perhaps even more important would be its educational value in bringing black writers to the point of development of black militant workers. So far, the educated Negro spent most of his time pleading with white America and seeking handsome awards instead of working side by side with the working class.

By the end of May Wright had written a twenty-page draft which he entitled "Blueprint for Negro Literature." When Richard showed it to Davis he was enthusiastic. The Party, at that time, claimed that the Negro was a victim of economic exploitation and not racial prejudice. His problems were merely one aspect of the general oppression against workers, women, trade unions and radicals. "Equal rights for Negroes" were to be realized through a type of colonization in the Black Belt—the establishment of a Negro republic in the South. However, Ben Davis may have approved "Blueprint for Negro Literature" because while it seemed to encourage an independent black nationalism, it limited the struggle by confining it within the Communists' classic position of "black and white, unite and fight" against capitalism. The old line was freedom for the Negro; and the new toward the end of the decade was an emphasis against war and Fascism and the Negro was put aside.

Negro writers must accept the nationalist implications of their lives, not in order to encourage them, but in order to change and transcend them. They must accept the concept of nationalism because, in order to transcend it, they must possess and understand it. And a nationalist spirit in Negro writing means a nationalism carrying the highest possible pitch of social consciousness. It means a nationalism that knows its limitations, that is aware of the dangers of its position, that knows its aims are unrealizable within the framework of capitalist America; a nationalism whose reason for being lies in the simple fact of self-possession and in the consciousness of the interdependence of people in modern society.

With the decline of the moral authority of the Negro church and the irresolution of the black middle-class leadership, a new responsibility developed upon the black writer.

They are being called upon to do no less than create values by which their race is to struggle, live, and die. They are being called upon to furnish moral sanctions for action, to give a meaning to blighted lives, and to supply motives for mass movements of millions of people. By their ability to fuse and make articulate the experiences of men, because their art possesses the cunning to steal into the inmost recesses of the human heart, because they can create myths and symbols that inspire a faith in life, they may expect either to be consigned to oblivion by the silent judgment of workers who ignore their writing, or to be recognized for the valued agents they are, as has been done to the socialist writers of the Soviet Union. . . .[2]

For almost six weeks, Richard ignored the petty bickering between functionaries in the Harlem office. Whenever he was at his desk his head was bent over the typewriter as he rapidly pounded out sentences with two fingers, a cigarette hung to his lips, its smoke making him squint. And if he raised his eyes they were unseeing; their gaze rippled beyond the immediate view. It seemed that all of his waking hours were filled. There were various meetings involving the *Daily Worker*, articles to write for that publication each week and for *New*

Challenge, people to see uptown and downtown, and his job with the Works Project Administration writing "Negroes in Manhattan" for the *American Guide* by which he earned his living of $23.86 per week.

In the bottom drawer of his desk were all of Richard's writings—short stories, novels and poems—except for work in progress, which he carried with him everywhere he went like an extension of his right arm. And he had invited everyone, but particularly young writers, to read his work. He was never too busy to discuss technique or craft questions and the work of Conrad, Joyce, Dostoevski and Ford Madox Ford with youngsters, but he noticed that only one young man consistently opened his drawer to read from the stack of his manuscripts. From the beginning, Richard was aware of the hostility of other leaders[3] and a coolness toward him on the part of the organizer and her coterie from the Nat Turner branch of the Party in Harlem. He spoke to a new friend of the hostility he sensed, although the telling never seemed to ease it from his mind.[4] As an appointee of the Central Committee he was not required to attend unit meetings so on the surface he chose to ignore their attitude. Antagonism appeared on such a picayune level—an occasional snide remark within his hearing, "the big man," "the big Chicago writer," or the dumping of stacks of papers on his desk when he was out of the office or silence when he entered the room. Temperamentally conditioned to discord, Richard often simply erased it from his mind.

In addition to the friendliness of Ben Davis, who worked out of the Harlem Bureau, and the support of the unseen Central Committee, Richard had his own group of admirers. Chief among these, and the one of whom Richard was most fond, was the nineteen-year-old, college-trained music student Ralph Ellison. Before coming to New York Richard had heard from Langston Hughes that he had had an inquiry from a youngster asking if he knew of a poet named Richard Wright. Hughes had given Richard the inquirer's address and Richard had dropped him a postcard saying he would be living in New York and would be glad to talk with him.

Ellison had turned up the second day after Richard's arrival and had willingly become his "legman."[5] And Richard always found extra time to listen to the young man's ideas about music and sculpture. "He really wanted to be a sculptor but he found that he could not say what was hotly in him to say with stone and marble."[6] Richard saw that Ralph was "terribly curious about art, the meaning of experience and especially Negro experience" and had an unusual facility for expressing his ideas. One afternoon, he pushed a book toward Ralph and said: "I'd like you to write a review of this for the first issue of *New Challenge*." Ralph demurred, saying that he had been studying music from his eighth year and was not a writer. In fact, Ralph had completed three years on a Mus.B. degree. He had also taken the highest grades in a class in the nineteenth-century English novel, given to seniors, when he was only a freshman. But Richard was oblivious to his "pupil's" academic background and believed that his own enthusiasm and confidence won the young man over. The review was written by Ellison and accepted for publication.[7]

Then when Richard began to collect material for a second issue of *New Challenge* he asked Ralph to write a short story and overcame his disinclination by describing the process of creation. "He talked about it not in terms of mystification but as writing know-how. 'You must read so-and-so,' he'd say. 'You have to go about learning to write *consciously*. People have talked about such and such a problem and have written about it. You must learn how Conrad, Joyce, Dostoevski get their effects. . . .' He guided [Ralph] to Henry James and to Conrad's prefaces, that type of thing."[8]

In a very short time Ralph handed a short story to Richard while they were having coffee in a café. Circlets of shadows drooped under his sensitively wary eyes and Richard believed that the handsome youngster was between anguish and joy—a state where he could as easily tear the story to shreds or exult that it was approved. Richard put the story away in his briefcase to read later and he kept it for two months. When Richard finally read "Hymies Bull," an imaginative story in the style of Hemingway, he was very satisfied and warmly enthusiastic.

When, a few weeks later, Ralph told Richard that he had written another story and would like him to read it he agreed that he would but put it aside because of other work. Ralph was persistent and kept pressing Richard for an opinion. "You are the master—I want to know if it's any good." At last Richard sat down to read. Halfway through he realized what was wrong and had an impulse to stop and explain. Instead he went through to the end and then raised his eyes. "Ralph," he exploded, "this is my story, my style. You have copied my ideas, my words and my structure! You must find your own symbols—you must tap the content of your own unconscious and use it! You must dig it out of yourself and not duplicate someone else." Astonishing to Richard was the young man's admission that he had "naturally" used his work as a model, that it was deliberate, but he made no other defense. Richard did not realize that Ralph would no sooner argue with him than he would have argued with one of his music teachers as to whether his phrasing of a trumpet solo or his arrangement of a spiritual was "theirs." He felt that he was not a writer and wrote many things which he had no intention of submitting for publication. As one long apprenticed to music Ellison knew how long it took one to achieve his own voice and thus had no illusions, even at nineteen, that he would *not* be influenced by those whose work he admired. But the young man saw that Richard was upset and since he had not developed any vanity about writing— convinced of his future as a musician—he did not answer back. Richard was a master and he was also a good friend.[9]

Preparations for the Second Congress of the League of American Writers were made for Carnegie Hall on June 4, 1937. Since the first Congress other writers had joined the list and signed the Call. Included were Upton Sinclair, Van Wyck Brooks, Clifford Odets, John Howard Lawson, Archibald MacLeish, Paul de Kruif, Vincent Sheean, Donald Ogden Stewart and the out-of-favor chairman of the League, Waldo Frank. Excitement filled Richard; all his nervous system felt as if it were shirred to a long straight band as he anticipated an attack against Frank. In Davis, and even in Ford, he sensed dismay at a letter the chairman of the League had written. Richard watched Ford's yellow-tan face tighten with rage; his mouth narrowed under the thin moustache as he hissed: "Renegade!"

Waldo Frank's letter, addressed to the Soviet ambassador in Washington, questioned the Moscow Trials and the accusations against Leon Trotsky. Moderate in tone, the open letter did not attack the USSR nor Communism, but asked for clarification and indicated that he personally found it difficult to accept Trotsky's charges of a frame-up. Enemies of the Party, however, might use the Trials to attack the morale of people sympathetic toward Russia. Despite the Communist adherence to its new line of collaboration with all anti-Fascists, when Frank suggested that an international commission of Socialists and Communists be established to study Trotsky's charges he was branded an enemy.

At Carnegie Hall, Richard listened to speeches made by Ernest Hemingway, against the Fascist bullies; Earl Browder, against writers who had no right "to go free-lancing in the field of sharpest political struggles without accountability to anyone"; Joseph Freeman, criticizing Trotskyites whose behavior aided the Fascists; Granville Hicks, praising Communists who had been active workers in the literary United Front. Although some of the speeches were boring, Richard had no doubts about his attitude toward those attacking the Party. Who needed them? What was important was to change the limits of life under which men lived. Nowhere in the world were people to be found who demonstrated such tense will and devoted striving toward that goal than among Communists. Stalin was right: "We Communists are people of a special mold."

In July, a member of the Young Communist League darted into the office and breathlessly reported to Richard that a fourteen-year-old Negro boy had been violently attacked by a white butcher in Brooklyn. The YCL unit in that borough wanted him to cover the case for the *Daily Worker*. Richard jumped up, grabbed his briefcase and left for Brooklyn by subway. When he arrived he saw a large picket line around Philips' Butcher Shop at 1592 Fulton Street. He was pleased at its size and the fact that the line was composed of both white and black adults as well as members of the Young Communist League. One of the members of the Brooklyn unit told him that John Wilson had gone to the store to buy fifteen cents' worth of hot dogs. He had forgotten to wait for change of twenty-five cents and when he had returned to ask for it he had been beaten and knocked down by one of the white butchers. Leon Toscona, the butcher, had been arrested and taken to the Pennsylvania Avenue Court and then released on $500 bail.

Late in the afternoon the picket line had grown so large that the store was forced to close. No one was entering anyway and it was impossible to carry on business. The following day a sign was posted in the window: "Because of yesterday's occurrences and complying with the demands of the Communist Party, the Young Communist League, the Citizens Civic Affairs Committee, we are closing this store until the people of this neighborhood decide otherwise."[10]

Indignation in the mixed neighborhood was so great that the manager of the store attended a mass meeting, publicly apologized, offered to pay John Wilson's medical expenses, send him to the country to recover and discharge Toscona. A Negro butcher would be hired to take the place of Toscona and his salary would be in accord with union wage scale.

Back at his office Richard typed up a story for the *Worker* and marveled at the power of the Party and its influence. Who else could have united Italians, Negroes, Jews, Poles and Irish—traditionally hostile in the United States—into a common and successful cause! Italians, whom Richard believed to be the most clannish of people, had taken a stand against one of their own in support of a black child.

While Richard worked on a weekly column he polished the stories he had written in Chicago and two appeared in the *New Masses*. And when one of them won the *Story Magazine* prize, party leaders congratulated themselves on their acuity in bringing Richard to New

York and in having allowed him to develop. James Ford, secretary of the Harlem Division of the Party, cautioned that he tended to be aloof and was headstrong. In Harlem Richard kept up a constant pressure for a cultural program which would develop artists, writers, musicians and actors within the black community. More of his energy, Ford thought, should be spent in bringing new members into the Party instead of concentrating on individual development.

When Horace Gregory, the poet, fell from favor with Party leaders Richard was appointed as his replacement on the board of the *New Masses*. A large reception was held in his honor at the International Workers Center, 317 West 124th Street, with three hundred in attendance. Thank God he had not allowed the stupidities of the Chicago branch to drive him from the organization, Richard thought, when he looked around the hall. Mike Gold, Samuel Sillen and Ben Davis made speeches lauding his work and a whole stream of important people crowded up to talk to Richard during the evening. Among them were Arthur Schomburg, James Ford, Eugene Gordon, Lester Granger, Dr. Max Yergan, Mr. and Mrs. Leroy Wilkins, William Chase, Langston Hughes and Clarence Hathaway.

As Richard's reputation outside of Communist circles grew he became more valuable to the Party, and at the Third Congress of the League of American Writers he was elected to the board. A fourth Congress was scheduled to be held in New York two years later, in June, 1941. Between the two Congresses the Soviet-German Pact was signed on August 23, 1939, and an ill-prepared American leadership floundered from side to side like an injured pigeon. Intrigued by the dismay in many comrades, Richard amused himself by listening to various rationalizations. Even leaders, he thought, lacked an understanding of the true essence of Communism. And changes of policy seemed to stimulate and expand knowledge of his own strange personality and that of others.

The rightness or wrongness of a given set of tactical actions by the Communist Party does not strike me as being of any great ultimate importance. What does fasten my attention upon communist action is whether it overcomes settled and ready-made reality, whether it effectively pushes outward and extends the area of human feeling, not like a book or a work of art, but *really* whether it illuminates new possibilities for human life (sometimes I find myself most deeply attracted to it when most people are repelled—that is, for instance, when the USSR signed the pact with Nazi Germany) and creates incalculable surprises, when it disrupts the established hopes and despairs and notions of millions, when it achieves transformations in the patterns of human feelings so deep and sharp and sudden that no mechanical inventions or industrial processes which we have known can equal or surpass them.[11]

An exodus of intellectuals began and Richard spent more time at national headquarters in Manhattan. It was fascinating to watch Mike Gold, V. J. Jerome and Samuel Sillen swing their intellect, voices and pens into action against Granville Hicks, Waldo Frank, Archibald MacLeish, Ralph Bates, Lewis Mumford and Malcolm Cowley. Mike had a positive genius for picaresque epithets when roused in defense of the Party. Who else could have so aptly called the defecting writers "coffee-pot intellectuals" or "migratory intellectuals?"

Among some comrades Richard discovered a need for rationalization that was foreign to him—in himself was an element of adventure and self-revelation—he was not afraid of illogical explanations. What was important was to dream up new forms of organization which would make Communist strength felt anew and more strongly. In the midst of the furore he did not enter into any of the name-calling directed against the people leaving the Party but privately analyzed the difference between them and himself.

It takes a more integral order of feeling to accept what is happening in Europe from the angle of the USSR than the Hicks, Sheeans, and Bateses possess. They are rebels against capitalism; the ones who stick, who are contemptuously referred to as the "faithful," are rebels against the limits of life, the limits of experience as they know it. They are (and not in a mystical or religious sense) striving against the world. For work of that caliber there is no right and no wrong; words and theory are but faint reflections of their struggle. Just as Lenin turned from the men who went mystic after the failure of 1905, just as the Bolsheviks pushed on relentlessly after the first war and set up a dictatorship to retain power for the common masses (set up power in one country which is as vast as twenty American countries!) so the men who today stay do so because they are living more meaningfully (as they *must!*). They tense themselves for another push. Those who left make it easier.[12]

In September, the American Peace Mobilization was formed in Chicago and Richard was elected a vice-president together with Theodore Dreiser, Joseph Curran, Paul Robeson and Vito Marcantonio, among others. The organization was dedicated toward keeping the United States out of war, and an innocent—the Reverend John B. Thompson of Oklahoma—was selected to serve as president. Frederick Vanderbilt Field, a lawyer and member of the well-known family, became national secretary. A dramatic "Peace Vigil" picket

line walked before the White House twenty-four hours a day and
Dreiser flew to Washington to address a mass rally.

"Writers Don't Want War" claimed Richard in a statement issued
to the *New Masses* in June and went to lecture at the Schomburg
Collection of the New York Public Library. Surrounded by sculp-
tures representing famous black men from many parts of the world,
he declaimed that "only a revolution on the Marxist line of the
Third International will solve the social and economic problems of
the United States." And at the Fourth Congress of the League of
American Writers Richard followed the isolationist line of the Party
and spoke movingly, in a sweet voice, of the dogged reluctance of the
Negro people to accept President Roosevelt's drive toward war.

"The men of Wall Street are driving us to war. . . . With cold
ruthlessness they tell us we must fight or else. . . . Congress grinds
on reactionary wheels to repress and enslave those who dare question
and protest. . . . Today unless the people intervene we are on our
way to participate in another war, the conflict between British and
German imperialism, and those same regular Jim Crow practices all
Negroes suffer are being repeated, even intensified in the Army and
Navy. The same rich who impose lynch discrimination on us want to
take us into war."[13]

Only a week after the League meeting, Richard wrote a follow-up
to his speech entitled "Not My People's War." The article had been
requested by Party leadership to coincide with the launching of a
National Peace Week on June 21, 1941, but printers' schedules
prevented its appearance until June 25. Hitler's army, estimated at
over three million, had its own timetable and opened a violent attack
against Russia on June 22, and by the time "Not My People's War"
appeared the American Communists were mobilizing in support of
the USSR.

Well, Richard thought, it seems like we are all in for it. He had
not thought the war would come so quickly but since it had there
was nothing to do but knuckle down and see it through, hoping that
the world that survived would be a better one. Though his draft
status was 2A–F, based upon his dependents, he was anxious to serve
the national democratic cause through his writing if such could be
useful in helping to defeat the Axis powers. In an attempt to clarify
and popularize the Administration's war policy and war aims among
Negroes and the American people as a whole he wrote a foreword to
a condensation, in *Coronet* magazine, of his book, *12,000,000 Black
Voices,* indicating his support of the war. Then he wrote to Paul
Green in Chapel Hill, North Carolina, with whom he had collaborated on a play and told him that any guidance or advice, or sugges-

tions along this line would be appreciated.[14] Finally, Richard paid a visit to his local draft board and asked for information toward getting a commission in the United States Army. The board sent him to see a Captain Kelly at Selective Service Headquarters and Richard explained that he thought he could be of service to the War Department through writing or making films. Kelly, a friendly Irishman, had heard of Richard and promised to write to Washington and send the necessary papers for application for a commission. With single-minded concentration Richard then asked his literary agent to use his influence to get him into the Army and submitted an outline, "Mobilization of Negro Opinion"[15] describing "a three-fold program of propaganda to consolidate the bulwark of world colored opinion to the cause of the United Nations . . . against the Axis powers."

I love my people . . .

XI

When Richard heard that A. Philip Randolph, President of the Brotherhood of Sleeping Car Porters, planned to assemble a hundred thousand Negroes to march on Washington and demand employment of Negroes in defense industries he put aside a new novel on which he was working and called Ben Davis to make an appointment to see him. Davis told Richard that he would be up at Party quarters in Harlem during the afternoon and could see him then.

Just as he reached the office Richard met James Ford, who was leaving. "Hello, comrade," Ford greeted him in his lugubrious manner. After shaking hands with the older man, Richard continued into the room to the desk of Davis, who looked up and smiled as he approached. "What's all the excitement, Dick?" he asked. Out of the corner of his eye Richard saw Ford pause and then return to his desk, as if he had forgotten something, but he pretended not to notice and pulled a chair up to Davis' side.

Sometimes Richard enjoyed needling Ford because he reacted bitterly and lectured him, using tired, old, stereotyped pseudo-Marxist phrases. Only a week before, Richard had gotten him furiously angry by suggesting that the government hire an old slew-footed Negro named Sam and ask his advice on every detail of foreign policy as it affected race. If asked about the Oriental exclusion act, Sam would say, "That'll make the Orientals mad and we shouldn't do it." The government would reply: "But we exclude you and you don't get mad." Then Sam would answer: "Yessah, boss, but that's because I don't have any army or navy." Ford had not been amused.

It was Ben Davis who usually kept peace between the two men, although he, too, had cautioned Richard and criticized his approach toward Negroes after *Native Son* was published. Negro and white masses were excluded from the novel, with the exception of a white mob scene, and Davis said it resulted in giving the reader an incomplete, and thus untruthful, picture of the reality of the American movement. Davis also denied the existence of white chauvinism in the Party—"Communists burned it out." While it irritated Richard that even an intelligent man like Davis was unable to understand a different, and what he felt to be a more revolutionary, conception of the Negro, at least he was reasonable and listened and his sincerity was ingratiating. Probably no one else in the Party would see the importance and significance of Randolph's proposed march except Davis.

Enthusiastically, Richard began to describe an article he wanted to write explaining and supporting the march on Washington. If Randolph could propose such a course of action, it was a barometer, a weather vane indicating the mood of the black mass. Thousands—millions—of black men were angry because they were allowed to fight in the war only as servants in the Navy or in segregated units in the Army. Jobs were opening up in war industries for the white man but the black man was excluded. Even his blood was segregated! At first the Red Cross Blood Banks had refused "black" blood entirely; then when a shortage developed it had been accepted but kept separate from "white" blood. The Party would never recruit Negroes unless it fought on two fronts—in Europe against Hitler's racists theories and at home against the capitalists' racism. If the Party took a stand, it would strengthen the war effort by giving the Negro people something to fight for; otherwise there was no reason for a black man to fight overseas for freedom when he did not have it at home.

Before Davis could speak, Ford angrily strode over to Richard and said: "The alternative to support of the war and of Roosevelt is the support of reaction! You're an obstinate, subjective fool!" Anger engulfed Richard; a shade more and he would have smashed Ford in the face. Instead, trembling inside from the effort at control, he looked at Davis and ignored Ford. Davis quieted Ford, who turned away and left the room. But instead of replying to Richard's suggestions concerning Randolph or blood banks, Davis clapped him on the shoulder in a fatherly manner and commanded: "Go back to your writing, Dick, and leave the politics to the Party."

Without a word, Richard left the office and walked down Lenox Avenue. He was still trembling inside and felt sickness wavering in his throat. "Keep cool," he told himself. "Don't let this get out of hand." Davis' reaction and his consistent refusal to deal with Negro psychology was a result of his middle-class upbringing. And Browder's thesis that the American bourgeoisie, in order to win the war, would be forced to abolish segregation in the armed forces and liberate the Negro at home was historically objective nonsense. The truth was, Richard thought, the Communists had decided to abandon the pressure for feedom for the Negro because it might interfere with the war effort.

A few weeks after the episode in Harlem Richard learned that the Party intended to attack A. Philip Randolph and the march on Washington. Such a march would be an embarrassment to President Roosevelt, who was engaged in a war against Fascism. The line was clear—the Party intended to give unconditional support to the war. Randolph's plans were divisive and destructive. From reliable sources Richard learned that the Party intended to refuse legal, moral or financial support to any Negroes seeking through legal means a Supreme Court decision upon the constitutionality of the biracial discriminatory administration of the Selective Service Laws.[1] Still later, Davis, without an iota of apology, urged Negroes to contribute blood to the Jim Crow bloodbanks.

Richard's mind was made up. He was holding a tainted instrument in his hands and he would drop it. The Party had stopped fighting for Negroes and "poor guys in Harlem and emigres from farms . . . they are the backbone of the race and it is through them—when organized and led—that salvation will come."[2]

In Richard's mailbox one morning was a letter from Antonio R. Frasconi, the artist, in Montevideo, Uruguay, asking for his advice. As he read the letter sympathy and concern rose in Richard for an artist whose perplexity had made him appeal to a stranger across such a geographical and psychological distance. Frasconi had prepared an album of woodcuts dealing with the Negro in America along the lines of the Belgian wood-engraver Frans Masserel's *History of a Rebel*. Criticism of American democracy was unavoidable and some of Frasconi's comrades objected to the book's publication because the time was not propitious. Unity had to be maintained on all fronts because of the anti-Fascist war; therefore no attack should be made upon the United States and her racist practices.

As soon as Richard had finished reading Frasconi's letter a first time he went through it again more slowly and then sat at his typewriter to write an immediate answer. He felt that he could not tell Frasconi what to do because he was ignorant of the language and culture of South America and of the political pressures upon him, but he recognized the phraseology and position of the Communists. Richard could answer the questions from his heart:

Your question implies that some of your advisers feel that your artistic representations of the Negro will create disunity; if that is so, then I would question seriously the kind of human unity that some of your advisers are striving to build. I, of course, take it for granted that your art is seeking passionately to render an honest reaction to the problem of the Negro in North and South America; and, if so, then your expression of that reaction in terms of images that kindle feeling will create the deepest sense of unity between the Negro, in North or South America, and other oppressed men, black or white, wherever they are found on earth, a sense of unity that will make men feel that they are brothers!

Paint, draw, engrave, and let all facts that impinge upon your sensibilities be your subject matter, and let your heart strike the hour as to when you should give what you have said to others! And I assure you that in answering your letter I have not looked at the clock in my room to see what hour of the day it is; I have not consulted the calendar to determine the day of the month; I have not examined a map to see where our armies are standing; in short, I have not tried to give you advice conditioned or limited by expediency or fear. Instead, I sat right down and wrote you what was in my heart; and my heart is full of this: There are 13,000,000 black people in the United States who practically have no voice in the government that governs them; who must fight in the United States Army under Jim Crow conditions of racial humiliation; who literally have the blood, which they so generously offer out of their veins to wounded soldiers, segregated in blood (plasma) banks of the American Red Cross, as though their blood were the blood of sub-humans; who, on the whole, live lives that are possessed of but a few rights which others respect; who, daily and hourly, are restricted in their behavior to an orbit branded as inferior; who must, for the most part, live their lives in artificially marked-off, ghetto-like areas of our cities and countryside; and whose manliness and self-assertion generally warrant instant reprisal![3]

Who is qualified to give you the signal to express yourself? Richard asked Frasconi. It might happen when he was in the throes of creation that the line would change. Or that an entirely new line would come into being. Or when the work was done it would be criticized for not expressing enough militancy, for not having been soft enough, subtle or tender enough in the light of a "new" political situation.

Richard knew that one of his comrades, Joseph Freeman, a staunch Communist, had been forced by the Party to suppress one of his books, *An American Testament*. A few months after the book appeared and received good notices in both the Party and regular press,

Freeman was called before Browder and informed that *Testament* had been condemned in Moscow—he had referred to Trotsky as a man instead of referring to him correctly as a class enemy and murderous Fascist. Browder instructed Freeman to kill the book, and he canceled all orders from bookshops and called off a scheduled lecture tour. And Mike Gold had called Leo Cherne a traitor for writing *The Rest of Your Life.* The Party attempted to stop the book's sales through a slander campaign. When his own novel, *Native Son,* had been published Richard had been threatened with expulsion by the Party. All that had saved him was its enormous popularity and public acclaim. The leadership had decided that he was too important to lose and Browder and Davis had disagreed in their interpretation of the novel. Davis, a black man, smelled in the book a fundamental disagreement with the Party in relation to the Negro, and he had caught a whiff once before in "Bright and Morning Star," an earlier novella of Richard's. But Browder had said, "I see nothing wrong with [Native Son]." And reality was what Earl Browder said it was.

Although Richard looked upon writing as his way of seeing, of thinking, of feeling—of working out problems—it was not until he had been out of the Party for several years that he grew aware of the devastating attack he had made in his first two books. It had not been deliberate; he had been thinking and feeling his way. He had joined the Party because he believed in "the essence of Communism," which meant brotherhood, universality, hope of harmony, universal reason and an assumption of natural immutable moral laws. When he discovered Communism he embraced its aims with the freest impulse he had ever known. As his gift—for all that it meant to him—he "wanted to make the lives of these men known through the images already accepted as the common coin of communication . . . wanted to make them know that they had allies, that more people than they knew, and in ways they did not understand, were their friends, and that [he] was their friend. [He] wanted to voice the words in them that they could not say, [he] wanted to be a witness for their living."

But the Communists were fearful of his ideas and could not accept the wide picture of Negro life in America which he was drawing in story after story. Naïvely, Richard assumed that if he told the truth it would be accepted as the truth. In his first series of short stories, *Uncle Tom's Children,* he set himself a conscious problem: what quality of will must the Negro possess to live and die in a country which denies his humanity? If one could not understand this fundamental, then one could not begin to understand any Negro in the

United States. This was the reality of life for a black man in America.

For the first story, "Big Boy Leaves Home," Richard used "a simple, straight, poetic realism"[4] to describe a fourteen-year-old boy, his three friends, and a day in their lives in a rural Southern community.

The boys are as natural and uncomplex as a basket of puppies, innocents not rebels. White folks are mean, white folks have everything but that is the natural order of life and not something over which they brood. It is more fun to roll fighting on the grass or sing slightly smutty songs, half-thrilled by their own daring. But the difference between their lives and those of any other children is that a spirit of adventure leads them to swim in a pond on a white man's property. Curiosity and adventure—natural attributes of man and especially boys—lead to doom as simply and inevitably as the stages of Greek tragedy.

And like one of the Fates, Atropos, smallest in stature but the most terrible, robed in a white skin, a Southern woman appears on the embankment, her hair lit by the sun, and stares transfixed at four naked black boys. They stare, equally transfixed, their only movement an instinctive covering of their groins. The woman screams; her husband comes running and kills two of the children as easily as if they were quail. To prevent a third death, of his friend "BoBo," Big Boy grabs for the rifle and kills the white man.

Naked, the two children clutch their clothing and run home through the woods—BoBo weeping, Big Boy clinging to one thought, to get home to Ma and Pa. When Big Boy's mother hears his story she moans: "Nobody but the good Lawd kin hep us now," but living in a pre-individualist black community,[5] she sends for its members who she knows will rally in defense of her son. And Big Boy's father, a kindly religious old man, gets out his gun and leans it in a corner of the kitchen. Brother Sanders is the first to arrive: "Whut we gonna do?" Black boys in trouble are "we", not "they" or "you."

Arrangements are made for the two youngsters to hide in an old kiln in the hillside overlooking Bullards Road and a trucker en route to Chicago will pick them up the following morning. It was in these kilns that Big Boy and his friends had played so happily a few days before. Big Boy arrives before BoBo and engages in a daydream—he is attacked by a white mob and he kills as many as he can before he dies. Imaginery headlines appear in his mind: "Nigger kills dozen of mob befo lynched." A nightmare occurs—a real-life dog belonging to a member of the lynch mob pokes its head over the edge of the kiln and Big Boy chokes it to death.

Big Boy grows hungry but saves his cornbread to share with BoBo.

But his friend does not reach the kiln. He is caught by a mob. High on the hillside Big Boy looks down upon white men and white women taking souvenirs of ears, penis, fingers, from the tarred, twisting body of his playmate. Early the next morning the truck arrives and Big Boy, ripped from his family and community, leaves home.

What quality of will was required to live in such an environment? Only that of the most elemental level—ability to endure. Survival depended upon the communal nature of the black community which planned, aided, organized an escape. Even then, one child did not escape. When Richard wrote the final sentence to "Big Boy Leaves Home" he felt both immense pleasure and immense dissatisfaction. The pleasure came because it was a story well told and the dissatisfaction came because somewhere in the material or in the character of Big Boy lurked still more vital things to be expressed. Poor Big Boy had not had a chance. Surely he deserved a fate far better than merely saving himself from a mob. Richard was not moved by compassion, nor were the "tear jugs" near. The plot of the story had simply driven poor Big Boy to the wall. There was in him a fine manifestation of will which events had partially buried, or rendered socially ineffective. So, with that tiny germ in mind, with the idea of expressing a more ample and positive idea of will and determination in a Negro character, another plot and another character thrust itself into his mind.[6]

In Richard's imagination was the character and a knowledge of a quality of will which the individual would represent, but the social context which would call it forth in strength and simplicity was difficult to find. One day he sat reading Burrows' *Social Basis of Consciousness* when a footnote caught his eye. It described how a woman had run out into a lake in Switzerland in the foolish hope of saving a man who was drowning. Burrows pointed out that this showed that group or social consciousness was stronger than individual consciousness. That was enough. The two vague ideas—the image of water, a lake in faraway Switzerland, and the image of a woman forgetting her personal safety to save others—simply sprang up at once, in full bloom.

From the moment Richard formed an image of Mann, in "Down by the Riverside," standing in his shack above the rushing waters of the flood, the story wrote itself, carried forward by its own logic and momentum.

Trapped in his cabin by fate—the rising Mississippi—Mann, his pregnant wife Lulu, her mother and Pee Wee, his young son, wait for a boat. A friend finally arrives with a stolen boat because local white people would not sell one for less than forty, fifty or a hundred dollars. But this family and community is not like that of Big Boy; there is disharmony centered around the theft. Even though her daughter has been in labor four days Granny refuses to ride in the stolen boat; her objections are not moral; it is that she is afraid the white people will kill them. A local parson arrives but Mann does not dare reveal their predicament to him—he would refuse help on moral grounds. Eventually, Mann puts his family in the boat and heads for the hospital through heavy currents. Near town they pass a half-submerged house and Heartfield, the owner of the stolen boat, shoots at them. Mann returns his fire and Heartfield falls dead.

Mann rows on against the current, hands burning, head aching, weak from fear, with a choking impulse just to give up because he is lost—he has shot a white man. But the current fights the boat and he fights back with the oars. They arrive too late to save Lulu but the military grab Mann roughly and he is commandeered to save white people. Through Mann's heroism, nurses, doctors and patients are saved and the colonel in charge praises him warmly and promises to see after him when the emergency ends. Despite his heroism he is not permitted to join Granny and Pee Wee but is assigned a boat and sent to rescue Heartfield's wife and son.

Brinkley, a young Negro, is assigned to drive the motor boat to Heartfield's, but Mann is afraid to confess the murder. He thinks to himself that he should be able to confide— "Ahm black like he is. He oughta be willin to hep me fo he would them . . ." but he keeps silent. The rescue is made under great difficulties and when all reach safe high ground Mrs. Heartfield and her son make their accusations against Mann. Sentenced to be shot and surrounded by a lynch spirit emanating from those he has saved, Mann breaks free and runs toward the river. They are going to kill him but he chooses to die, shot in the back, before submitting.

And for a second time, Richard was pleased and dissatisfied when he finished the story. A flood was too fluid, he decided; it had swept Mann not only to a wall like Big Boy but through and beyond it. He had had a chance to make decisions, but not to carry them out or act upon them with any degree of freedom. Mann had been motivated by the Ten Commandments and the idea of trust in God. He had laid down his sword and shield, down by the riverside, and the result had been that fear and helplessness became an undercurrent in his life. Only at the end had he rescued his own personality by refusing to be lynched. Existential in quality, he defined the limits of his personality through a final act, a defiant suicide.

Richard brooded over the two characters. He had brought the second one out into a wider arena but he had been crushed. "After all," he told himself, "Negroes do go on living in America in spite of lynchings, terror, hunger and robbery." And, too, he was dismayed by the bleak endings. Mann had been Big Boy grown up, blunted and dulled by circumstances. So, Sarah, a limited character deliberately conceived, a simple peasant woman who loves her hills of northern Mississippi, who wants only to live and be happy in her own humble way and not bother about jobs, land, houses and issues, grew into the story "Long Black Song."

Sarah lives in a one-room cabin with her husband Silas, and her small baby. In emulation of the white man Silas has saved and purchased his own small farm. Sarah is grateful that she does not have to work in the fields like all other black women in the neighborhood, but a home and a husband who "was as good to her as any black man could be to a black woman" is not fulfilling. Sarah is introspective and poetic. She hates violence and blood and is drawn to the physical beauty of the countryside: ". . . black men and white men, land and houses, green cornfields and gray skies, gladness and dreams, were all a part of that which made life good. Yes, somehow, they were linked, like spokes in a spinning wagon wheel. She felt they were. She knew they were. She felt it when she breathed and knew it when she looked."

While Silas is in town trying to sell his cotton, a red-haired white salesman comes to the farm to sell a combination clock–record player and during his visit he seduces Sarah. Silas returns home joyful over the sale of his cotton because he can purchase more land and hire a helper. "Ain tha the way the white folks do? Ef yuhs gonna git anywheres yuhs gotta do just like they do." But when he begins to make love to his wife he finds the white man's sperm-wet handkerchief in his bed. The fence behind which Silas has tried to live in the Southern no-man's land is shattered and his choices are narrowed: he can accept this violation of his woman and his own sense of manhood or he can die.

Sarah begs her husband to run away after he kills the white man the following day, but he tells her: "The white folks ain never gimme a chance. They ain never give no black man a chance. There ain nothin in yo whole life yuh kin keep from em. They take yo lan. They take yo freedom. They take yo women! N then they take yo life." And then he makes his decision: "When they come fer me Ah'm gonna be here. N when they git me outta here theys gonna know Ahm gone." Silas sends his wife and child away to safety and stays in his house to shoot it out with the lynch mob. Big Boy, in the first story, dreams of such an act—Silas kills as many whites as he can and when the mob sets fire to his home he stays inside and burns to death without a murmur.

Richard looked at the story he had written with an emotion approaching amazement. It was paradoxical. It was the bleakest one of all, and Silas had taken over the story from the original character, Sarah, almost entirely. He was far more pleased than he had been with the first two but still more disgruntled. Somehow, too, he had made Sarah intensely human, as if he himself had doubted the existence of her particular characteristics in a black woman.

Casting about in his mind for a story idea in which he could blend all three of his previous characters into one and for another social context in which that character could live, he was drawn irresistibly toward the "old Negro, the Negro close to the soil, that Negro whose staunch will four centuries of arduous oppression had not broken. And especially was [he] drawn toward the religious expression of the 'old Negro.' And [he] made the startling discovery . . . that the images, symbols, and attitudes of Christianity were the highest crystallizations of the Negro's will to live he had made in this country . . . embodied in a complete system of imagery, symbols, attitudes. . . ."

When Richard made the discovery for himself that Christianity was not sheer escapism but had provided the means through which the black mass fought back by retaining its dignity and sense of itself in a world that denied its humanity his mind made a temporary retreat. Religion *was* the opiate of the people. He had seen its effect upon his own family and had had to preserve his own will against the religion of his mother. Materialism was the answer, the hope of the earth. How easy it would be, his mind insisted, to take his new character—the combination of Big Boy, Mann and Sarah—and simply draw the picture of one of his Communist friends. The idea was alluring. "Do they not hope? Do they not express their will from day to day? Do they not sacrifice, struggle, and suffer? Do they not do these things of their own will, conscious and free? Yes, all that and more. One is almost struck dumb by their courage." But there was a gap—a no-man's-land—between the Negro Richard knew and saw daily and the Negro he saw in the Party. Communists might object to a tale which placed credit for Negro will and strength in the church.

Feeling daring and rash, Richard decided to mix his ideas and try to bridge the chasm between Communism and Christianity.

In "Fire and Cloud," Taylor, a Negro minister, unconsciously identifies his will with that of God under conditions which call for a struggle which is essentially a class one. He is called upon to do class battle with the only spiritual weapon he has, a belief that Negro people have a right to the earth.

Taylor's church is in the heart of the Black Belt in a stricken Southern community where both white and black are starving and unemployed. A demonstration is planned by "Red" organizers to force city officials to take steps to relieve the suffering and Taylor becomes the center of a vicious controversy. Both Mayor and police demand that he use his authority to prevent the meeting; Mrs. Taylor asks him to keep silent and not jeopardize their future; his son Jimmy believes in meeting violence with violence; Deacon Smith, a rival for his position, stirs up the congregation against him; and the Communists ask for his support. Confused and disturbed by the forces vying for his aid, Taylor refuses to act. He will leave it up to his congregation and follow them. Taylor is not a coward—in his past he has staved off a mob of whites to save a black man but that act was directed against a few individuals. Now he is being asked to take a stand against the entire power structure of the community. It would mean civil war and he is not prepared to break with the government. In the past he has been a white man's leader, supported and chosen to keep other Negroes from action. But Taylor has not been aware of his conciliatory role. When he leads his church in prayer it is a social protest and not simply an appeal for spiritual relief: "The white folks say we cant raise nothin on Yo earth! They done put the lans of the worl in their pockets. They done fenced them off n nailed em down. Theys a tryin t take Yo place, Lawd.

"Yuh put us in this worl n said we could live in it. Yuh said this worl wuz Yo own! Now show us the sign like Yuh showed Saul! Show us the sign n well ack!"

Although the congregation votes to march on City Hall Taylor wonders if he should have dissuaded his people—they could be killed. But while he wonders he is kidnapped by white men and forced to pray on his knees while they curse and beat him until he is unconscious. Another black man is killed because he fights against his attackers and the Communists are jailed and beaten.

When Taylor has to face his son, his back bleeding and in ribbons, and answer his questions—are we going to be dogs all the time and not fight back?—he formulates a new philosophy of social unity and action through the church.

"It's the *people!* Theys the ones what mus be real to us! Gawds wid the people! N the peoples gotta be real as Gawd t us! We cant hep ourselves er the people when wes erlone. Ah been wrong erbout a lotta things Ah tol yuh, son. Ah tol yuh them things cause Ah thought they wuz right. Ah tol yuh to work hard n climb to the top. Ah tol yuh folks would lissen to yuh then. But they wont, son! All the will, all the strength, all the power, all the numbahs is in the people."

The demonstration is successful, white and black together march on City Hall to demand food, and the local government is forced to capitulate. The congregation feels a power it has never known before—freedom belongs to the strong.

Taylor had not become a Communist even though the mainstay of the story came from the Communists' slogan—black and white unite and fight. And superficially the idea that the problem of Negro and white is a class question to be overcome by a revolutionary move-ment uniting all the poor against the power structure was main-tained, but Richard refused the Communist pitfall that one class is pure good because poor and the other totally evil.

Richard made another discovery when he completed "Fire and Cloud." He had been seeking, unconsciously, for an efficient way of projecting his will into the manifold context of conditions under which Negroes were forced to live. Each previous story had been a test flight, an experiment. Big Boy, Mann, Sarah, and Taylor had been assumed excuses, pretexts, cloaks, armor he had donned to sally forth to battle. And he had found a temporarily satisfactory answer to the question he had posed when he started the sequence. Will is linked with the forces that thwart it and the least exertion of will on the part of a Negro in America is a spark which explodes into violence.

For the fourth time he had written a story he liked and disliked because Wright's aim was not merely to write a good story but a story that answered a question about Negro life. Dissatisfaction became almost an itch in his mind and within a few days he decided to pose an ultimate question: what must a Negro do if he is to find his freedom, if he is to win a place for himself in American life along with others? Such a question should go to the heart of the problem. It was impersonal, a question that involved what he thought of as the sense of honor of twelve million people. No sooner had he posed the question than he thought of an answer: he must be ready to break with his old life, embrace a new one; he must be ready to break with his outlook and embrace a new one; he must be ready to break with his old allies and find new ones.

Boldly, with four stories behind him, Richard decided to take the most beloved and familiar character he could think of in Negro life to act out his drama. An old Negro woman, Aunt Sue, is placed in a position where, in order to preserve the dignity of her self and her love of what has been newly gained, allegiance to the labor movement, she has to give up her life.

In "Bright and Morning Star," Sue is a religious widow with two grown sons, Johnny-Boy and Sug. All three are members of the Communist Party in a small agrarian Southern community. Sug is jailed for his activities as an organizer and Johnny takes over his tasks with his mother's assistance. A meeting of Communists is to be held and city officials are determined to root out of the community all the Reds. Reva, a white girl whose father is also a member of the group, comes to warn Sue that the meeting place has been discovered. After arguing with his mother that she is wrong to suspect one of the new white members of being the informer—"I can't see white and I can't see black. I see rich men and poor men"—Johnny goes out to warn everyone to stay away from the meeting. He is caught by a mob and Sue is beaten by the sheriff and the mob because she will not reveal the names of the members. Half-unconscious, she tells the white informer the identity of the members, presumably so they can be warned, but when he leaves she realizes he is the traitor.

Sue takes a rifle and a wrapping sheet for her son's body and goes to the field where her son is being tortured. Before the lynchers realize that she is not just an old "auntie" she kills the traitor before he can blurt out the names of the Communists. Then both Sue and Johnny are murdered by the frustrated mob.

Johnny-Boy, the young Communist, is heroic but the story belongs to Sue, the old Christian turned Communist. And her speech becomes false only when informed by the new ideology. When she dies she expresses her identity with all oppressed people—"Yuh didnt git what yuh wanted. N yuh ain gonna nevah git it!"—and she embraces her own religion, not Communism. "Focused and pointed she was, buried in the depths of her star, swallowed in its peace and strength; and not feeling her flesh growing cold, cold as the rain that fell from the invisible sky upon the doomed living and the dead that never dies." Sue's "star" comes from a hymn: "He's the Lily of the Valley, the Bright and Morning Star, He's the fairest of Ten Thousand to my soul. . . ."

Through Sue, Richard showed himself, and tried to show the Party, that there were deep revolutionary urges and resources of power in the Negro which seemed to be in conflict with, and, for the Negro people, stronger than, the practicing revolutionism of the Communists. Sue's folk and religious experience was juxtaposed to Communism.

On the basis of *Uncle Tom's Children* Richard signed a contract with Harper & Brothers, which agreed to pay him approximately $1,300 against royalties on publication day; and royalty payments were to be 15½ percent of the wholesale price of the book. In the midst of critical and public acclaim only one sour voice was raised, that of *Story Magazine*, which had published "Fire and Cloud" in its March issue. Two of its editors insisted that Richard had been their discovery and demanded a glimpse of his contract with Harper, but this was circumvented by his agent.

By May 6, 1938, sales from his writings had been good enough to provide Richard with his living expenses but at the same time he could not lose a sense of caution developed during the starving days in the South and he decided to continue working for the Federal Writers' Project while he completed a new novel, *Native Son*.

XII

Awakening early one morning, in his back room behind the parlor, on the first floor of a big brownstone in Bedford-Stuyvesant, Richard lay quietly in bed trying to recapture a dream whose details were fleeing, leaving behind a haunting melancholy. A feeling of having made a mistake, an irretrievable mistake, because it concerned something published. What was it? He turned on his back and looked at the paint peeling from the high ceiling. This place could stand a good cleaning, Richard thought. Head back on the pillow, his right hand unconsciously rose to his neck and his fingers lightly gripped the muscles just above the Adam's apple. Unseeing, he stared around the room, shifting on the studio couch, until his gaze reached the long library table with his portable typewriter, piled books and stacks of mail, some open, some not. When his eyes reached a manila folder filled with newspaper clippings the faraway expression left his eyes and the cause for his somewhat impersonal unhappiness clicked into focus.

The night before, he and Jane and Herbert Newton, in whose home he was living, had been reading the reviews of *Uncle Tom's Children*. Jane, a tall, very striking white woman with a mass of jet-black hair, a prominent, straight nose, black eyes wide apart, a wide mouth and a high forehead, had given her characteristic bark of laughter, and read aloud from the Jackson, Mississippi, *Daily News*. *Uncle Tom's Children* was "a garbage can book" composed of "slush, slop and drivel."[1] Both Richard and Herb looked up and guffawed, as amused by Jane's voice as they were by the Southern pronouncement. "Whew!"—Richard shifted his voice from its natural range to a

167

thin, high sweet tone—"My hometown paper's in good company! Congressman Starnes and the Dies Committee call me subversive, and our good bourgeois black brothers"—with a nod of his head toward Herb's attentive brown face—"shout that the book exaggerated the hatred Negroes bear whites, it's excessively violent and misrepresents their life." Herb reminded Richard that he had said the Negro middle class was going to take his skin off for the book. What was important was the almost universal acclaim the book had received. Richard had gone to bed mulling over their conversation and parts from the reviews they had been reading flashed into his mind.

Charged with energy as soon as his mood had clarified itself, Richard hopped out of bed, thrust his arms into the sleeves of his bathrobe and walked over to the oak table. His hand reached toward the folder of clippings, paused in midair and almost automatically moved beyond and picked up a heavy white linen envelope marked "White House" and postmarked "Poughkeepsie." Richard removed the hand-written letter from its neatly slit square envelope and stared at the words from Mrs. Franklin Delano Roosevelt. *Uncle Tom's Children* was "beautifully written and so vivid that I had a most unhappy time reading it." Singling out the first story, "Big Boy Leaves Home," Mrs. Roosevelt said, "The thing which struck me is what little things bring such tragic results. A silly woman's fear— really an accident in almost every case that could be so easily understood if every one kept his head. . . ."[2] It was a warm and generous letter from a gracious lady, but the revelation that the book had made the President's wife *unhappy* plagued Richard.

Placing the letter back on his desk, Richard picked up his cigarettes, unseeingly shook one out and then replaced it. It would be easier on his nervous stomach to have coffee before smoking at six in the morning. He walked quietly toward the kitchen so that he would not awaken the Newtons' three children—Michelle, Delores and Carl. When the coffee had perked to a deep blackish brown he poured it into a thick mug, added milk, and carried it back to his room. Most of his gestures were automatic. His mind was still pulling and twisting at the word *unhappy* and the distaste it had engendered in him. He had made an awfully naïve mistake—it was clear from Mrs. Roosevelt's response and from white reviewers—he had written a book "which even bankers' daughters could read and weep over and feel good." And when people could *cry* and feel *sorry* they rid themselves of the necessity for action, for trying to change the conditions under which black people lived. Richard swore to himself silently. Well, the next book was going to be so hot and heavy that no one would weep over it—not over Biggy Thomas.

For a long time, *Native Son* had been germinating in Richard. Unconsciously, from the first Biggy Thomas, with whom he had attended school in Jackson and who had been defiant of Jim Crow laws, whose rebellious spirit made him defy all the taboos, down through hundreds he had met in Chicago, Richard had unconsciously stored away their actions and emotions. He had not kept a notebook record of their sayings and doings. Their actions had simply made impressions upon his sensibilities as he lived from day to day, impressions that crystallized and coagulated into clusters and configurations of memory, attitudes, moods, ideas. Gradually, his school friend "Biggy" coalesced with others and became "Bigger," became white and black, tense, afraid, nervous, hysterical and restless. They were men who could be killed but not beaten, native sons who were "a product of a dislocated society; . . . dispossessed and disinherited . . . living amid the greatest possible plenty on earth and looking and feeling for a way out . . ." "But granting the emotional state, the tensity, the fear, the hate, the impatience, the sense of exclusion, the ache for violent action, the emotional and cultural hunger, Bigger's conditioned organism [would] not become an ardent, or even a lukewarm, supporter of the status quo."[3]

As always with Richard, a character developed, began to take physical form, arriving in his mind like a figure out of the fog, until it stood beneath a hot light in his brain and he could see its mannerisms, its speech. If asked, he could imitate its speech patterns, the tone of its voice. Around his created character he would wrap a story. ". . . Bigger Thomas would loom as a symbolic figure of American life, a figure who would hold within him the prophecy of [the] future. [Richard] felt strongly that he held within him, in a measure which perhaps no other contemporary type did, the outlines of action and feeling which we would encounter on a vast scale in the days to come. Just as one sees when one walks into a medical research laboratory jars of alcohol containing abnormally large or distorted portions of the human body, just so did [he] see and feel that the conditions of life under which Negroes are forced to live in America contain the embryonic emotional prefigurations of how a large part of the body politic would react under stress."

So, with that much knowledge of his central figure and the experience gained from handling the diverse personalities in his previous book, he decided to put Bigger on paper. But still Richard hesitated. A mental censor stood over him. What would white people think of a Bigger Thomas? Would not such a brutal portrait give whites the opportunity to say that all Negroes were like animals and reinforce their prejudices? And what would his own black and white comrades in the Party say? He knew that the Party persisted in looking at all Negroes as heroes and refused to accept the fact that brutal ghetto conditions maimed spirit and personality. How could they accept a real human being like Bigger Thomas?

Another constricting thought arose to keep Richard from beginning his book: "What will Negro doctors, lawyers, dentists, bankers, schoolteachers, social workers and businessmen think of me if I draw such a picture of Bigger?" He knew from painful experience that the black bourgeoisie felt superior to and despised the slum Negro and were afraid that white people—so blind anyway—would assume that all black men were like his prototype. Once he had been invited by William Attaway to speak before a college literary society and had read portions of "Big Boy Leaves Home." Many in the black middle-class audience had walked out of the lecture declaiming that the story was sordid and brutal and that the South had changed; Negroes no longer lived in daily fear of lynching.

But Bigger won over all these claims; he won because I felt that I was hunting on the trail of more exciting and thrilling game. What Bigger meant had claimed me because I felt with all of my being that he was more important than what any white person would say or try to make of him, more important than any political analysis designed to explain or deny him, more important, even, then my own sense of fear, shame, and diffidence.[4]

With the whole theme in mind Richard gave himself to the arduous task of imprinting it on paper. Some phases of Bigger's life would not come readily and Richard would jot down as much of it as he could. Then he read it over and over, adding each time a word, a phrase, a sentence until he felt that he had caught all the shadings of reality he dimly felt were there. With each rereading and rewriting he gathered in facts and facets that tried to run away. The first draft of the novel was written in four months, straight through, and ran to some 576 pages. Just as a man rose in the morning to dig ditches for his bread, so Richard worked daily. He would think of some abstract principle of Bigger's conduct and at once his mind would turn it into some act he had seen Bigger perform, some act which he hoped would be familiar enough to the American reader to gain his credence. But in the writing of scene after scene he was guided by one criterion: to tell the truth as he saw it and felt it. If a scene seemed improbable he would not tear it up but stop and ask himself: Does it reveal enough of what I feel to stand in spite of its unreality? If he felt it did, it stood. If he felt that it did not, he ripped it out.

Bigger Thomas, twenty-two years of age, lives in a one-room slum apartment in Chicago with his mother, brother and sister. His father has been killed in a riot in the South. The family lives on relief and the apartment contains only the simplest rudiments of life—two iron beds, a table and four chairs, one communal dresser, a screen behind which the cooking is done. Mrs. Thomas is in poor health, having worked her life away as a servant, and Bigger's brother and sister are in school. A relief agency offers him a job, and if he does not accept, then the entire family will be cut from the rolls. The Daltons, a wealthy philanthropic family who give millions to Negro charity but have made most of their fortune out of the slum buildings in Bigger's community, offer the job as chauffeur. Mrs. Dalton is blind;[5] Mary, their only child, attends college and is in love with Jan, a member of the Communist Party.

Mr. Dalton orders Bigger to drive his daughter to school but instead, Mary directs him to pick up her boyfriend at Party head-quarters. The young liberals force Bigger to sit in the middle, squeezed between their alien white bodies, while Jan drives the limousine. Earnestly, they explain that they are on Bigger's "side" and demand that he take them to a restaurant on the South Side of Chicago. When they arrive Bigger's embarrassment grows because the couple force him to sit and eat with them. He is deeply mortified because his friends see him with "ofays." Still, the young whites are oblivious as they chat at him in political jargon or shift to become intensely personal. They want to meet some Negroes; they discuss the emotions of the Negro and say that if they could ever get them going there would be a revolution. Encased in the armor of their political theory, they treat Bigger like an animal or a freak. He is not an individual; he represents Negroes in general and is not a man propelled by exclusive emotional contradictions. Bigger is drowning in poverty but he is driven toward revolt by the violence done to his sensibilities as a human being. Later he says that they made him feel like a dog.

Mary prattles on: "Never in my life have I been inside of a Negro home. Yet they *must* live like we live. They're *human*. . . ." Bigger knows they are thinking of his life and the life of his people and he wants to seize a heavy object and with one blow blot them off the face of the earth. Unaware, Jan takes up when Mary stops: "That's what we Communists are fighting. We want to stop people from treating others that way. I'm a member of the Party. Mary sympathizes. Don't you think if we got together we could stop things like that?"[6] And Mary tells him that they would like to be friends of his. Bigger, whom they do not know, a potential murderer, is repelled.

When the evening ends Jan and Mary are drunk and make love in the back seat of the car while Bigger drives through the park. Finally, Jan is dropped off near his streetcar stop and Bigger drives to the Daltons'. Mary is too drunk to walk and Bigger carries her into the house and puts her on her bed. Trembling with fear, dread and a fleeting thrust of sexual excitation, he turns to leave the room but the blind Mrs. Dalton is in the doorway. Mary stirs restlessly, and, afraid that Mrs. Dalton will discover him in her daughter's room, Bigger puts a pillow over her face. In the brief interval that Mrs. Dalton stands in the doorway Mary smothers to death.

Beside the dead white girl, Bigger stands and thinks—he is aware for the first time in his life of a Negro's position in relation to society, which had only appeared before as a "big white fog"[7] against which he dumbly reacted. White people said Negroes raped white women and they would kill him. His mind activates itself on a new plane—he has to act. Unleashed, his brain bounds as if in its natural habitat—he has murdered many times in his heart, has killed in himself emotions which would bring retaliation from whites—and now he will accept Mary's death and hide her body to save himself. He carries her body to the cellar and burns it in the furnace.

Bigger has been a shell of a man. Life has been something happening around him in which he played no role—perhaps tolerated but unrecognized as human with hopes and cravings. There was nothing he could do except hang around the street or lose himself at the movies. But murder makes him discover his own unique personality. In the struggle for self-preservation, Bigger discovers faculties, energy, initiative, strategy, decision, and capacity for action on a grand scale. All the qualities he and his friends have wished to exercise in the normal adventurous ways open to many white American youths have been denied to him because of color.

Bigger has never been able to accustom himself to discrimination: "I know I oughtn't think about it, but I can't help it. Every time I think about it I feel like somebody's poking a red-hot iron down my throat. Goddammit, look! We live here and they live there. We black and they white. They got things and we ain't. They do things and we can't. It's just like living in jail. Half the time I feel like I'm on the outside of the world peeping in through a knot-hole in the fence. . . ."

Bigger and his friends have discussed a plane flying overhead: "I could fly one of them things if I had a chance," said Bigger. "If you wasn't black and if you had some money and if they'd let you go to that aviation school, you *could* fly a plane," his friend responded.

Bigger has lived in fear. In flight from the consequences of the accidental death, he plots and schemes and laughs secretly to himself as he recognizes that no white person would suspect an illiterate Negro of such a crime. Bigger sends a ransom letter for $10,000 to the Daltons. Mind and body are given free play—first the idea, then purchase of paper, pencil, envelopes, gloves and then the creation of phrases for the letter. Then he plots how the money will be delivered, enlists his girl friend, Bessie, to help but tells her only enough to awaken interest but not to implicate him in any murder. Boldly he returns to the Daltons' after slipping the note under the front door and lies on his bed. His mind whirls with a multitude of ideas and choices. A feeling of sheer luxury pervades him as his mind gyrates—"He could run away; he could remain, he could even go down and confess what he had done. The mere thought that these avenues of action were open to him made him feel free, that his life was his, that he held his future in his hands."

Newspaper men discover Mary's bones in the furnace and Bigger hides with Bessie in an abandoned building on the South Side. Eighty thousand men are scouring the district for him and Bessie breaks down, making it clear to Bigger that if caught she will bear witness against him. He has to kill her; he can't take her with him and he can't leave her behind. It is not easy for him to kill his girl friend and only by a mental reenactment of his own perilous position can he bring himself to smash her head with a brick. "He felt that if he should ever see her face again he would be overcome with a sense of guilt so deep as to be unbearable."

After he throws Bessie's body down an airshaft he lies down to sleep, horrified by the act. "And, yet, out of it all, over and above all that had happened, impalpable but real, there remained to him a queer sense of power. *He* had done this. *He* had brought all this about. In all of his life these two murders were the most meaningful things that had ever happened to him. He was living, truly and deeply, no matter what others might think, looking at him with their blind eyes. Never had he had the chance to live out the consequences of his actions; never had his will been so free as in this night and day of fear and murder and flight."

Bigger is captured by the mob after a heroic fight on a snowy rooftop and dragged down the stairs, his head bumping along the steps.[8] A Communist Party lawyer, Max, a finished exponent of Marxism, becomes his attorney. Arrangements for Bigger's defense are made by Jan, the murdered girl's boyfriend. Through Bigger's actions Jan has begun to discard his stereotyped thinking about black people and visits him in jail. Confessing that he had not recognized what Bigger had felt when they forced him to eat with them, Jan claims that, in a sense, he is the guilty one. "Bigger, I've never done anything against you and your people in my life. But I'm a white man and it would be asking too much to ask you not to hate me, when every white man you see hates you. I—I know my . . . my face looks like theirs to you, even though I don't feel like they do. But I didn't know we were so far apart until that night . . . I can understand now why you pulled that gun on me when I waited outside that house to talk to you. It was the only thing you could have done; but I didn't know my white face was making you feel guilty, condemning you. . . ."

Jan is redeemed from his blindness of Party politics through his attempt to recognize Bigger. And Bigger, who at first hates and fears and feels guilty in Jan's presence, is moved by his honesty and courage. Jan tells him, "Let me be on your side, Bigger. I can fight this thing with you, just like you've started it. I can come from all of those white people and stand here with you." Jan does not try to persuade Bigger to another course of action nor does he mouth platitudes or ideologies. He examines himself and discovers his own prejudices, that he has been an unconscious bigot despite Communist principle. A religious simile springs to Bigger's mind when he accepts Jan: "The word had become flesh." And for the first time in his life a white man has become a human being. He sees Jan as if an operation had been performed on his eyes or as if someone had snatched a deforming mask from Jan's face.

Max, the other Communist, a Party leader, is a sympathetic man with "a head of white hair, his long face, the deep-grey soft, sad eyes." But Max, a Marxist, asks Bigger the same racial questions as Buckley, the vicious prosecuting attorney: Did he rape Mary? Why did he hate her? Who helped him? Why wasn't he more understanding of Mary's attempt at friendship? Why didn't he speak up and tell Mrs. Dalton that he was in Mary's room? Why didn't he go to the leaders of his race and tell them how he felt? But Max means well and Bigger does not become hostile. Instead he attempts an explanation: "They [Negro leaders] wouldn't listen to me. They rich, even though the white folks treat them almost like they do me. They almost like white people, when it comes to guys like me. They say guys like me make it hard for them to get along with white folks."

Patiently, Max explains to Bigger that he understands all his feelings because he, too, has been discriminated against as a Jew. In addition, he has a double burden of hate because he fights for trade unions, which "they" hate. But Bigger disagrees: "They don't treat union folks like they do me."

In the courtroom Max explains Bigger sociologically, economically and historically. But when he talks privately with Bigger he cannot understand him at all. Bigger tries to explain that the murder has made him comprehend himself as a man, as a human. All that Max can answer is that there are rich who own everything and there are poor who have to be organized to end prejudice, violence, and all other social inequities. "What I killed for I am!" Bigger insists. But Max turns from him in fright, his ". . . eyes were full of terror," and he gropes for his hat like a blindman. Bigger calls to him, reassures him that he is all right, he is not afraid to die, but the lawyer will not turn his head nor look him in the eyes. Bigger is left alone in his condemned cell, looking at Max's departing back, holding onto the bars with a faint wry bitter smile on his face.

Richard could not fit Bigger's act into the framework of ideas which Max represented. It was an act symbolic of the regenerative force of revolution. But a revelation of the violence of the Negro as typified by Bigger and his insistent justification of his action terrified the Communist. Richard did not mean that individual Negroes should murder white people but he believed that there were forces and depths in the black mass not comprehended by the representative of a supposedly profound revolutionary doctrine. He was examining through Bigger the ultimate nature of man, using him as a kind of anti-hero through which to express the result of centuries of oppression and the type of violent action by which freedom would come. *Native Son* foreshadowed Richard's ultimate break with the Communist Party.

XIII

While at work one day in his back room at the Newtons' Richard heard the ring of the front doorbell. He lifted his head and swiveled part way around in his chair and looked at the closed door, listening intently. There was a low murmur of voices, then Jane Newton's unique short laughter, but Richard could not make out any words or whether the visitor was male or female. Well, he could not sit still unless he knew who was in the front room. Turning back to his typewriter, he glanced at the half-completed page and decided to finish it before going out to investigate, but a gusty female laugh came to his ears and he jumped up from his chair, bounced to the door and went out, closing it behind him. He did not want anyone to walk into his room and look at incomplete work.

All along the hallway to the front of the house at 175 Carlton Avenue, he heard the new voice but could not decide if he recognized it or not. Before reaching the room he decided that he had not heard those tones before and his interest quickened. Good spirits—an effervescence of mood—quickened his steps and he bounded into the front room, smiling in anticipation of the unknown personality. Sitting on the long couch, somewhat on the edge, with a zippered briefcase at her feet and papers on her lap, was a small delicate girl. The girl looked directly into Richard's eyes and smiled and he noticed a small space between her two upper front teeth exactly like his own. Freckles dotted the bridge of a pert nose and the top of her cheeks were rosy red; in fact she seemed to be blushing with energy and excitement.[1] What strange eyes she has, Richard thought. Green? Or amber? Or brownish-hazel? They seemed to change color as he watched, seemed almost to alter shape structurally too as she looked at Jane and then back into his face. Brown shoulder-length hair parted on the left side was pulled back from a wide white brow and held with a barrette. Little wisps escaped and curled forward. Her lips were full and sweet above a rounded childish chin but he shifted his gaze back to her eyes. In their depths was an apparent sweetness, a trusting dependence—she's easily hurt, Richard decided, and then contradicted himself. Whoa, these little women had a wiry toughness.

Vaguely, Richard heard Jane introduce the girl as Ellen Poplar, but his mind really focused when she added that Ellen was organizer of one of the Party branches in Brooklyn. This child an organizer! Richard marveled. How curious—then what was the air of fragility and helplessness he sensed in her eyes? He had to find out! When she looked in his direction or spoke to him he sensed that she was enormously attracted—the space between them bristled with something electric. But suddenly it was gone. Ellen picked up her briefcase, handed some papers to Jane, put the rest from her lap into the case and in a no-nonsense voice gave her a résumé of a previous branch meeting. Then she jumped to her feet and reached for a coat which had been thrown across the back of a chair. Richard took it from her and put it around her shoulders—she smelled of lilac and autumn leaves—what an unusual combination of qualities, he mused as he looked down at her uplifted face. Turning to Jane, Ellen told her that she would return the following week to keep her apprised of branch activities since she could not attend meetings. There was no one with whom she could leave her three children and Herb, her husband, a Party leader, was too busy to care for them. Richard was intrigued and planned to be at home on Ellen's next visit. And when she had gone he decided to have a cup of coffee with Jane and talk about her before going back to work.

Richard learned that Ellen was the youngest daughter of Rose Goldfarb and David Poplovicz, who had emigrated to the United States from Poland before their three children had been born. Ellen, who was born Frieda Poplovicz,[2] had been delivered by a midwife in Manhattan and shortly after her birth her parents became naturalized citizens and took the name Poplar. In her infancy the family moved to Brooklyn, where Ellen and her brother and sister attended school. Although she still lived at home with her family, there was friction because they did not approve of her association with the Communists. Stubbornly, she went her own way, although, at times, the nervous tension between herself and her mother ended in shouting matches.

Jane teased Richard by telling him that Ellen was entirely too busy for any romance; she was "all Party" and along with the job as organizer of a large branch she had to attend the Workers' School for lessons in labor history, political economy, Party organization, China, imperialism, the Negro question, and American history. Besides visits to Jane each week and any other comrades who could not attend regular meetings Ellen had to report to the section office to pick up mail and literature, report to meetings at district headquarters and also go to receive her instructions from Israel Amter (J. Ford), her party "boss," member of the Central Executive Committee in charge of all Brooklyn organizations. Richard knew Amter, a "hard period" Communist whose intentions were to "Bolshevize" the Party into a fighting arm of the working class. Richard knew that Amter, as Ellen's superior, would encourage single-minded devotion to politics with a vengeance. He had been a pianist as a young man but had given up music entirely for the organization and, as a result, had little patience with writers or artists who demanded freedom for experimentation.

Once every week for about the next month Richard waited until he heard Ellen's voice in the front room and then he put down his work and dashed eagerly down the hall to greet her. Sometimes he simply listened quietly while she and Jane discussed politics—there were no secrets; Ellen had not read any of his books but she was aware that he was attached to the upper echelons of the Party so she spoke freely before him. But what piqued his interest was that, although she was always glad to see him, her mind was obviously not on any flirtation and Richard had grown accustomed to attention from women, particularly white women.

During the time of Ellen's visits, his old friend Theodore (Ted) Ward, whom he had known in Chicago, a distinguished playwright, came to New York with the Federal Theatre Company's *The Swing Mikado*. Richard accepted an invitation to see the show as Ted's guest and afterwards invited him to pay a visit the following day—he wanted his opinion of his new book, *Native Son*. On the next day, Ted arrived in Brooklyn in the afternoon and spent the evening, since it was a Monday and there was no performance of the "Mikado" that night. Richard introduced Ted to Jane Newton and was delighted to see how well they got on with each other. Late in the afternoon, he felt festive and went out to buy a huge porterhouse steak and rum and Cokes for his favorite drink, a cuba libre. They ate and drank and talked and laughed until late the following morning. Richard was surprised when it began to grow light outside in the street—the night had passed so fast. Wouldn't it be wonderful, he thought, to have Ted in the same house? In the kitchen, while Jane was making coffee, Richard asked her to see if she could get a room for Ted in the same building, on the top floor. Then he suggested that Ted move into the seven-dollar-a-week room the same afternoon. As soon as Ted was settled in Richard handed him *Native Son,* and until he left for the theater that night he hardly took his eyes from the pages of the book. When he had finished he told Richard he was overwhelmed. "It was to say the least, the most amazing literary experience of [his] life, and [Richard] was very pleased to learn it."[3]

A week or two after Ted Ward had moved in Richard suggested that they attend a party at the home of one of the members of Ellen's branch. When they opened the door of the apartment Richard saw Ellen across the room. She was dressed in a dark skirt with a white peasant blouse which had a small lace edging standing against her slender neck and when she saw him enter, her whole face seemed to grow shiny. Crossing the room, he asked if she would go out with him after the party. For a moment she hesitated and then said that if the party ended early enough she would but that she could not leave before the rest because she was responsible, as organizer, to stay until the end. Richard had to be satisfied with her answer, but for the next few hours he was restless and walked from group to group listening to various conversations but not entering into any. Maybe in that way he could silently will everyone to go home. And he explained to Ted that he probably would not accompany him back—"I think I've got a date," he said.

Before too long the party gave signs of ending early and Richard sighed with relief; he really wanted to get to know that girl. As they left the building Richard was glad to see that she did not take hold of his arm or his hand; it still made him uncomfortable to show affection of any kind in public and particularly with a white girl. They walked for a while and then sat in the park "just talking and having a wonderful time. There seemed an instant understanding between them as if they had known each other for many years." For the first time in his life, he discovered himself talking freely, telling Ellen things he had never confided in anyone before. It felt as if something unlocked and he emptied out of his mind all his reflective and brooding thoughts. He told her of his childhood in Mississippi and the tangled relations with his family, particularly his mother—to whom he was deeply attached but always needed to fight himself free and clear from her hysteria. From then on Richard attended meetings at Ellen's branch or went to hear her speak at street-corner meetings. Each time he waited patiently to take her home afterwards.

But at the same time Richard was spending some evenings with a ballet-trained modern dancer, Rose Dhima Meadman, who had danced in the Soviet Union and whose mother, Utis, had been an actress in a repertory theatre in Russia. "Both she and her mother were very friendly people. Dhima . . . had considerable warmth and strength." And Richard loved to visit Utis' big townhouse on Hamilton Terrace; the comfortable rooms were filled with a tingling, yet warm, excitement. Dhima had been married to an Englishman but was divorced and had custody of her two-year-old son. And there was Utis, about whom an aura of theatre still hung, although she was working in the garment industry as an organizer for Local Twenty of the Industrial Ladies Garment Workers Union. And a pianist, Dhima's accompanist, was always around, often practicing on the large piano. Mrs. Meadman suffered from heart trouble but rarely allowed ill health to destroy her spirited appreciation of music, art, food or politics. Dhima had been all over the world and Richard was impressed by her "knack of picking up lingos like a dog picks up fleas."[4] She parted her black hair in the center and pulled it straight back, ballet-fashion, and her dancer's legs were long and sensually full at the calves. Dark brown eyes were deep set above a long nose and often held an impish look; her mouth was large with shapely strong lips and what excited Richard were her rather large, white, even teeth. When she listened to someone speak her lips parted slightly and he could see the edges of her teeth as if waiting to bite.

Early one evening Richard invited Ted to accompany him to Hamilton Terrace to meet the Meadmans. When they left, hours later, he was eager to know what Ted's impression had been—especially of Dhima. "She was quite chic, and [he] would call her beautiful." And he thought Richard "was completely absorbed in her, and she seemed deeply attached to him, but not as a clinging vine type, but a robust woman who believed herself a match for any man."[5]

A few days later, at the Douglass Hotel in Harlem,[6] Richard and Ted sat around talking about women and recalling their rivalry over three girls in Chicago—Deborah Smith, Fern Gayden, and Alberta Sims—whom they mutually admired. Then they talked about white women versus black and Richard described some experiences with girls from Negro middle-class families. During his first weeks in New York he had gone with a girl who was not only pretty but intelligent and seemed free of the strictures of her family but just when he had gotten sexually aroused she informed him that she was revolted at the idea of going to bed with a man. She was lesbian. Coupled with Richard's irritation at the loss of what seemed to promise excitement in bed was a horror, religious in intensity, a remainder of his moral mother's strictures, at having embraced a lesbian; he felt soiled and angry.[7]

After that experience, he told Ted, there had been a handsome girl in Brooklyn whom he had wanted to marry. Shortly after he received $500 from *Story Magazine* for "Fire and Cloud" he had approached the girl's parents and an ugly scene broke out. "He said the girl stood aside in tears, while the mother, refusing to declare her sympathy one way or another, could only sit and shudder hysterically, 'That little $500' . . . the father thundered, 'ain't going to last. How're you going to support my daughter?—I say No!'" He went on to tell of another experience in Harlem "where it seem [ed] he had been a victim of the same sort of 'brush off,' in his effort to find a Negro woman of the educated class willing to put her faith in his ability to support her as a writer."

A core of resentment and distrust toward middle- or upper-class Negro women remained. When he began to date Jean Blackwell he was attracted by her youth and her slender curved body, as well as her keen intelligence. Educated in Baltimore, Jean had become interested in John Reed and had gone for a visit to the Soviet Union but never joined the Communists and Richard enjoyed her company—she was pretty and he could talk to her. Stupid women bored him. But at some point during the evening whenever they went out together Richard attacked her as a bourgeois Negro woman.[8] Negro "society" was a make-believe world peopled by "pet niggers" interested in mink coats and Cadillacs, baseball, poker, and psychic phenomena who helped the whites keep down the black masses.

Richard looked at Ted's handsome, smooth, brown, soft-featured face and admitted that although black women seemed impossible, at least those he had known with their emphasis on money and status, he had qualms about marriage to a white woman.[9] It was Ted's conviction that a writer, an artist, had to settle down if he was to do anything worthwhile with his craft and he questioned whether or not a black artist should be disturbed by the opinion of others, whether black or white, toward such an intimate matter. He told Richard "that there could be no question but that he could expect resentment from both sides, that his position was like that of Ulysses when he had to steer between Scylla and Charybdis but that [he] felt every man had a right to choose the one he loves."

Lifting his wrist, Richard looked at one of the two watches he had purchased; it was almost morning, he and Ted had talked all night. Suddenly, he felt exhausted and faintly embarrassed that he had revealed his most intimate thoughts to another individual. But Ted was a friend and he had yearned to talk to someone, a confidant to whom he could confess that he was going to marry Dhima. What the hell! Why did he feel an uneasy sense of shame because he had opened up his guts? Yawning, he said good night and went to his room.

Although he had felt tired and sleepy in Ted's room, once he slid between the sheets he grew restless. Parts of the evening's conversation flitted through his mind, garnering unto it faces, memories, situations until he became wide-awake. He twisted on the bed, crumpling the sheets with the movement of his body then straightening them smooth again, puffed up his pillow until it fitted his neck exactly right and for the thousandth time lay still, trying to wash anxiety out of his mind. Slowly his tension eased and he hovered between sleeping and waking. Then, just as he almost plunged into sleep, convulsively, his whole body jerked; his hands grabbed at the bed to end the terror of falling through space. Eyes wide open again, Richard stared at the lowered green windowshade with its minute points of daylight glinting into the room and thought about marriage and desire. "He knew himself too well not to realize the meaning of what he was feeling; yet his self-knowledge, born of a habit of incessant reflection, did not enable him to escape the morass in which his feelings were bogged. His insight merely augmented his emotional conflicts. He was aware, intimately and bitterly, that his dread had been his mother's first fateful gift to him. . . . As her son, he was much too far from her and at the same time much too close, much too warm toward her and much too cold."[10]

What if he found himself married to a hysterical woman! And what of his own sensual desires—could he love one woman—would he not recoil from a continuous intimacy? Could marriage be created from desire? Was that not too tenuous and shifting an emotion upon which to make promises and swear vows?

Richard turned on his back and closed his eyes. He thought of his mother's role in shaping his character. Without knowing it, and because she was always ill and had been disappointed in his father, his mother had created a frigid world, a restrictive world born out of fierce devotion. "His first coherent memories had condensed themselves into an image of a young woman whose hysterically loving presence had made his imagination conscious of an invisible God— Whose secret grace granted him life—hovering oppressively in space above him. His awful face shaped in the form of a huge and crushing NO, a terrifying face which had, for a reason he could never learn, created him, had given him a part of Himself, and yet had threateningly demanded that he vigilantly deny another part of himself which He too had paradoxically given him. This God's NO-face had evoked in his pliable boy's body an aching sense of pleasure by admonishing him to shun pleasure as the tempting doorway opening blackly onto hell; had too early awakened in him a sharp sense of sex by thunderingly denouncing sex as the sin leading to eternal damnation; had posited in him an unbridled hunger for the sensual by branding all sensuality as the monstrous death from which there was no resurrection; had made him instinctively choose to love himself over and against all others because he felt himself menaced by a mysterious God Whose love seemed somehow like hate. Mother love had cleaved him: a wayward sensibility that distrusted itself, a consciousness that was conscious of itself. Despite this, his sensibilities had not been repressed by God's fearful negations as represented by his mother; indeed, his sense of life had been so heightened that desire boiled in him to a degree that made him afraid. Afraid of what? Nothing exactly, precisely . . . And this constituted his sense of dread."

While Richard was making up his mind to get married, Ellen Poplar went away for the summer to Camp Unity, a Communist school and vacation spot in New York State. He had not actually proposed to Ellen but had discussed with her what marriage to a black man required from a white woman. It demanded love, of course, first of all, but unlike love between white and white, or even white men and black women, the union of black man and white woman rasped in the teeth of all bigots. A white woman had to be prepared to make a clean and total break with society—and it expressed itself first in the home, with one's own mother, father, sisters and brothers. It required strength of will and clarity of mind, for in the North it was the white woman who had to withstand the greatest pressure. Few white men could accept such a relationship. Many black women would be angry, and with good reason—another presentable wage earner removed from an already limited circle within the ghetto. Only the black man would be understanding and sympathetic.[11] But if a break was made, "just cut clean away," such an act had an expansive effect on the personality and there was a grim exhilaration in facing the world and creating one's world out of one's self. But after their discussions Richard was not certain that Ellen really understood him. She was so enmeshed with her family the ties would never loosen. "She's a confused child who doesn't know her own mind," Richard told his friend Ralph Ellison.

Just as Richard was leaving his room at the summer's end in 1938 his telephone rang. It was Ellen. She had just returned from Camp Unity; her voice bubbling over with warmth and excitement, she asked when she could see him. Deliberately, Richard spoke coolly, making his voice distant and formal, but Ellen continued to talk. Please, she *had* to see him, where could they meet? She explained that she had moved from home and taken a hotel room in Manhattan. Would he come there? She wanted to talk to him—there were things she had thought about all summer that he should know. At last Richard gave way and said he would meet her in Central Park, near the lake just below 110th Street, but he would not visit Ellen's new room.

Before walking to the park, Richard stopped at a luncheonette for a cup of coffee and a sandwich. When he tried to eat, the food stuck in his throat. The last thing he wanted to do was see Ellen. He knew he was going to hurt her and it made him so uncomfortable and so guilty that he was filled with dread and then anger at her and then at himself. He had a hot impulse not to keep the appointment—he would go to a movie or take a walk or go see friends downtown. His stomach, sagging under the weight of his gloom, felt like lead. Ah God—why did he get himself into such a situation? Ellen had such helpless eyes; she trusted him and he had to hurt her. Well, it had to be done; and as quickly and cleanly as possible. As he walked toward the park he was terrified; he wanted to blot everything out of his mind and not explain that he had decided on a new course of action for his future life.

From a distance, Richard saw Ellen sitting on a bench, practically on its edge. She was looking all around so eagerly. How petite she was! What if she cried? Might she become hysterical? Richard wanted to turn around and flee the park but he forced his feet to keep stepping forward. Ellen caught sight of him when he was a few yards away and jumped to her feet. For a sick moment Richard was afraid she would throw herself into his arms and he glanced around—there were few people in the park at that hour. Besides, Ellen understood how he felt. She would not embarrass him in public. When they were seated on the bench, side by side but not touching, Richard looked into her eyes and then stared out across the small lake, which was darkening as it lost the sun. Keeping all warmth from his voice, almost as if he were speaking to a stranger or discussing some abstract point out of a book they had both read, Richard again explained that in interracial marriage both parties had to know their own minds. Ellen, he said, was torn between her family and the feeling she had for him. She could not cut herself off; she might never be able to cut herself off. Ellen listened intently and looked at him all the time he was speaking. As soon as she saw that he was through she eagerly insisted that she had been "sort of torn between [her] family, not so much that—[she] knew [her] own mind but was trying to figure out a way to get out of [their] influence . . . and just cut short—"[12] Richard interrupted the stream of eager words: "I have met the woman with whom I want to spend the rest of my life."[13] After he spoke, Richard waited for Ellen's protestations with an inner irritation. He had made his intentions as clear as anyone possibly could; now he hoped she would go away quietly without making a scene. Embarrassment was beginning to make him feel guilty and a slow, assuaging anger began to build up to forestall anxiety. But Ellen did not protest, so Richard arose from the bench and without looking directly into her face as they left the park he walked to the subway and left her at its entrance.

After the final meeting with Ellen, Richard married Dhima, with Ralph Ellison as best man, in the minister's office of the Episcopal church on Convent Avenue. Then he moved into the large house on Hamilton Terrace, which almost seemed to engulf him. There was something happening every night. During the daytime Richard worked quietly at home because Dhima was rehearsing long hours—she had won a Liz Whitney scholarship—preparing for a concert. And when there were too many distractions he went to Crompond, New York, where he could be alone to work on a new novel.

Dhima was a whirlwind. The more work she had to do the more she seemed able to do. Vitality and enthusiasm for him, for her son, mother, friends, for work and politics, seemed to rise visibly from each graceful movement of her trained body and her somewhat large, expressive hands. When Richard was preoccupied Dhima answered his letters and telephone calls—problems seemed to fall away if she turned her dark brown eyes in their direction. And everywhere he took his wife, her vivacity and charm stirred interest. *Native Son* was published shortly after his marriage, and more money than he had ever thought about in his life seemed to pour into the office of his agent.

Harper & Brothers took a three-column advertisement to announce that the public had stampeded the bookstores. Three hours after its appearance the book sold out in Manhattan and Wright's name was placed on the World's Fair "Wall of Fame." His editor told him that he was under consideration for the Pulitzer Prize. Book-of-the-Month Club selected *Native Son* for their membership, with a guarantee of $9,380, half of which would go to Richard. In addition, his royalty rate was twenty cents a copy. Critics seemed to have gone wild, Richard thought. He felt both humble and proud when he read proclamations that his work was beyond that of Dreiser, Steinbeck and Farrell in probing the depths of human misery. Almost everywhere he spoke—in churches, universities and clubs—he was interrupted by wild applause as he described the lives of men like Bigger Thomas.

Life magazine vied with *Look* and offered its pages for an extensive review. Time-Life, Incorporated, flew Richard to Chicago for background photographs on March 18, 1940.[14] Then Hollywood wrote and asked him to write a screenplay of Booker T. Washington's *Up From Slavery*, which Richard had never read,[15] and Eddie Cantor and Edward Lasker asked permission to produce *Native Son* on Broadway. *Harper's Bazaar* sandwiched one of Richard's brutal short stories, "Almos' a Man,"[16] between its elegant flat-breasted models and he snorted with laughter. He did not laugh when he picked up a copy of the *Sunday Worker* and read a tentative attack upon his book by Ben Davis. Two weeks earlier, Mike Gold had praised *Native Son* in the *Daily Worker* and three days before that his agent had written that word had been received from the State Publishing House of the USSR that *Uncle Tom's Children* had reached a second edition with a total of 75,000 copies sold.

Toward the end of January, 1940, Richard came in by train from Crompond, New York, where he had been staying so that he could work on a second novel away from all of the excitement, to see Dhima and make a speech, on the problems of fiction writing, at the Dalcroze School of Music. As the train slid into Pennsylvania Station Richard stood up and slipped on a new Harris tweed gray overcoat, picked up his briefcase and hat and stepped from the train when it stopped. Automatically—he had been freezing in Crompond—he turned up the collar around his neck even though he was taking a subway to Times Square.

While standing and waiting for a subway train at Times Square Richard glanced over the titles of magazines on a newsstand near the center of the platform. Suddenly, the word "escapist" caught his eye and then he saw the name of a friend, Lawrence Martin, a writer. Quickly, Richard handed the vendor twenty-five cents, picked up the magazine, and stepped onto his train. While riding along reading Martin's enthusiastic description of life in Mexico, all of Richard's subconscious desires came bubbling to the surface. On his knees, under *Mercury* magazine was the latest issue of the New York *Post;* its headline proclaimed that Americans might fight for Russian-occupied Finland without loss of citizenship. Other "newspapers were yelling it up for war. . . . This, coupled with the gradually descending cold wave of fear which was gripping this nation, made [him] resolve to 'escape.' "[17]

For the first time in his entire life Richard felt secure. He did not have to worry about the price of a trip, or of anything else for that matter. He had received well over $20,000 from sales of *Native Son,* and even though he had purchased a home for his mother in Chicago, had had his teeth fixed, and had bought War Bonds, he felt that money would continue to pour in. The World Publishing Company, under the imprint of Tower Books, was going to bring out *Uncle Tom's Children* for the revolutionary price of forty-nine cents in cloth, hardcover, for mass distribution through chain stores.

As soon as Richard arrived at Hamilton Terrace he thrust Martin's article into Dhima's hands and "she went through the roof. At once she suggested that she, the kid, [Richard], her mother, and her pianist light out for Mexico. [Richard] fell for it." He sat down to his typewriter immediately and wrote Martin, asking him to rent a house for him while Dhima, armed with the article, rushed downtown, phoning Richard later to say that she had booked passage to Mexico for April 5. "The thing is settled," he wrote his friend.

A ten-room house, with a huge swimming pool, spacious grounds, flowers and fruit trees everywhere, was found at Madero 33, Colonia Miraval, Cuernavaca, Morelia, which rented for only $300 for eight months. Richard could not believe in his good fortune; a house in New York without gardens or swimming pool would have cost at least $300 each month, he told Dhima. Cuernavaca was beautiful; the climate was wonderful. If he could not work there then he would be able to work nowhere. Almost as soon as he was settled Richard sent off a 960-page manuscript[18] to New York and assured his agent that it would soon be completed in such surroundings.

But then Irene Lee of Warner Brothers Motion Picture Company flew down to see Richard as emissary for Orson Welles and John Houseman to discuss a Broadway production of *Native Son* preliminary to a film. And Dhima seemed to know everyone in Cuernavaca. She introduced Richard to John Steinbeck, who was filming *Forgotten Village* with Herbert Kline. No immediate rapport developed between the two writers; Steinbeck accused Wright of viewing the world solely through the questions concerning black men and Richard was astounded, then hurt, and then indifferent to him.[19] Dhima also introduced Richard to members of the large Spanish refugee colony and Constancia de la Mora, the author of *In Place of Splendor,* urged that she be permitted to translate *Native Son* into Spanish. But Dhima's principle interest was in the American colony, and Richard disapproved of its members' fruitless and frenetic activities. At the beginning of his stay he was fascinated by a pervasive air of intrigue among the North Americans but after a time they bored him. When he could not settle down to work he grew restive and irritated.

Mexico was a primitive society—"very few people read at all." He could not speak or understand the language and began to believe that the Spanish refugees possessed a higher degree of intelligence than Mexicans. When in May a mail truck from Mexico City collided with another car and burned, destroying the incoming Cuernavaca mail, he was certain that he had lost valuable letters. And the day after that disaster Richard came upon four dead lying on the highway—another accident. Curiosity impelled him to watch until the mangled bodies were removed but afterwards he came to a conclusion that it was a violent country—accident, theft, murder, seemed to be the order of the day in that unbelievable land. "Life here is cheap," he decided. And when he looked at the Indians he saw a sad glint in every eye; life was melancholy and grim to the copper-colored millions and relieved only by religious ritual.

While lying in bed one morning Richard listened to the voices of their servants in the patio below the second-story bedroom. He quietly eased into a sitting position and swung his feet onto the marble-tiled floor, fitting them into leather slippers. Dhima stirred and then turned onto her stomach, stretching her arms and legs over the whole bed. A sensation of emptiness, of waste, followed by revulsion and then irritation, came over Richard with such strength that for a moment he wondered at the futility of life. For some months there had been growing a distaste and anger toward Dhima; she had no conception at all of what made him operate on many involuted and intricate levels. Even her magnificent body was suddenly repellent. Without justification he was convinced that Dhima was indolent, slothful and bourgeois. She loved having servants and she loved most of all ordering them around. They were dumb animals to her—she was a peculiar Communist sympathizer—how quickly she had been able to exploit poor red and brown peasants. What does she think I am? he pondered. This was not the type of life he intended to live. Everything was a mistake—he was living in luxury, surrounded by cooks and maids and gardeners, mixed up with refugees and stupid American expatriates and he simply could not understand his wife's mentality. There was no peace in his home and too many hot, senseless arguments. Well, he had had it! He would cut clean away and forget the whole mess. Ten days later, Richard left for Mexico City, where he stayed a few days at Calle Paris 7 and then left for the United States. Feeling a vague desire to renew himself after his Mexico experiences, Richard went back, for the first time, to Jackson, Mississippi, and Memphis, Tennessee. He would look the South over and reaffirm emotional reactions for still another book which was vaguely circling the outskirts of his thoughts.

After a trip to the South Wright went to Chicago to see his mother and brother in the new house on Vincennes Avenue, and from there he traveled to Chapel Hill, where he spent two weeks with Paul Green. Orson Welles[20] and his Mercury Theatre had taken an option on *Native Son*. Welles would produce and John Houseman would direct the Broadway production with Jack Berry acting as stage manager. Richard chose Paul Green, over whose play *Hymn to the Rising Sun* he had been transferred from a Federal Theatre job years before, to write the stage version.[21]

In August Richard returned to New York and settled into a room at 343 Grand Avenue in Brooklyn. Shortly after he arrived he called Ralph Ellison and learned that Dhima was at the Ellisons'. Dhima had asked Ralph and his wife, Rose, to share expenses of an apartment on Hamilton Terrace near her mother's large house.[22] Her purpose was to place herself in Richard's path and she knew that he would call Ralph as soon as he returned to New York. Dhima loved Richard and hoped for a reconciliation. As far as Richard was concerned the marriage was definitely ended; all that he wanted was to be left alone to master the irritation which ran along his nerves and upset his stomach, but he knew that he would have to face his wife one last time.

Rather than have the pending visit nag at his mind, Richard reluctantly took a subway from Brooklyn up to Harlem and walked to Hamilton Terrace. Dhima and the Ellisons had taken the top floor of the building. At each end of the large apartment were a bedroom and living room with kitchen and bath acting as a division in the middle. When Richard saw the size of the large apartment he wondered how much rent was being paid. How could Ralph and Rose afford such luxury?[23] An answer came immediately into his mind: Hell! It's probably my money paying for this layout—the conclusion stiffened his irritation toward Dhima. As his wife entered the room Richard's face assumed a bland expression but he greeted her coldly. Dhima remained calm in front of Ralph and she led Richard into her part of the apartment and closed the door behind them.

An hour later Richard came out of the room alone, closed the door firmly behind him and left the building. That was that; his nerves felt jagged but relief would soon drive away irritation. Now, he would purge Dhima and the marriage from his mind[24]—he was free again and the first thing he intended to do was to find Ellen Poplar.

Ellen and Julia

XIV

While Richard was in Mexico a letter had arrived from Ralph
Ellison, who had just returned from the third meeting of the National Negro Congress in Washington, D.C. Ralph had been covering the conference as a reporter for the *New Masses*.[1] Among the
1,300 delegates had been Ellen Poplar, as a representative of the
Communist Party, which was taking over the organization whose
founding resolutions stated that it was not and would never be
dominated by any political party or faction. During a speech by
Congress President A. Philip Randolph, "the Communists arranged
a demonstration and walked out, leaving only a third of the audience
when he finished talking. Thereafter nearly all speeches followed the
'party line,' and the Negro protest was skillfully draped in Communist slogans."[2]

Ellen, a staunch Communist, had of course left the hall with her
comrades and when she reached the corridor she saw Ralph in the
distance. Ralph had been surprised when, unexpectedly, Ellen ran
up and put her arms around him, then hugged him enthusiastically.
Almost at once, she had asked about Richard: Was he in New York?
Where was he? What was he doing? When she learned that he was
married and living in Mexico she had been crestfallen and confessed,
to Ralph, that she was still in love with Richard and probably always
would be. And Ralph had written the news to Richard in Mexico.

On his return trip from Mexico Richard discovered that thoughts
of Ellen were persistent. Staring out of the window of the train, an
image of her face had appeared, especially her eyes, which held a
remote, shy, impulsive look. Then he remembered the last time he

had seen her in Central Park. She had had a blank, bleak look, as if stunned, when he told her about Dhima. Sometimes she looked so sweet; there was a plaid suit she wore with a slightly flaring skirt and with it a little hat clinging at the back and to one side of her head. Ellen might be a child but he could always talk to her and she was willing to understand. And, "I never see a woman prettier than she no matter where I go. She looks so much younger than all the others, and so little and so pretty."

Late in the afternoon of the day following his meeting with Dhima at the Ellisons', Richard left his room and headed for Jane Newton's house. If Ellen followed the old schedule she would go to see Jane that evening. The November day had been gray, sunless; the night air brushed his face damply. But Richard did not notice the chill of winter or silently curse the approach of snow and icy winds, which he hated. When he arrived at the Newton's apartment he played with their three children until it was time for them to go to bed. Then he sat talking, but at the same time he waited, emotions concealed behind smiles and laughter. At last he heard the sound of the street door opening and he went out into the hallway. A paneled encasing of the stairway prevented him from seeing who had entered: He called out—Ellen? Ellen! And Ellen ran up, almost stunned: it was so unexpected—she had not known that he was in New York and he had been continuously on her mind. Richard, smiling, laughing, held out his hands and they "fell into each others arms. There was no talking after that; the whole thing was settled." Ellen and Richard moved into the back room at the Newtons' that same night and their marriage began.

Four and a half months later, on March 12, 1941, Richard married Ellen in a civil service, at Coytesville, New Jersey, performed by the Reverend Edward Kelder. Ben Davis and Abraham Aaron, a close friend of Richard's, were witnesses and the two Communists were given a little booklet with roses on the cover entitled: "Our Wedding Day." On the return trip to Manhattan Richard read the Bible references in the small booklet. He knew the Scriptures well and the small white folder was certain to quote one that he knew from memory:

And Ruth said, Intreat me not to leave thee, or to return from following after thee: for whither thou goest, I will go; and where thou lodgest, I will lodge; thy people shall be my people, and thy God my God. . . .[3]

Shortly after their marriage Richard and Ellen moved from 140th Street, a two-room apartment they had taken near the Ellisons[4] across the street from City College, to a three-room and kitchenette apartment at 11 Revere Place in Brooklyn. Richard was tired of eating in luncheonettes and restaurants; he wanted to teach his wife the chemistry of cooking. It was simple, he assured Ellen, as soon as she learned what foods and seasonings scientifically suited each other she would become an expert. Almost as soon as they were settled, Richard went to a bookstore and purchased Fannie Farmer's *Boston Cooking-School Cook Book* and presented it to his wife. After finishing his daily six or seven hours of steady writing, he was too stimulated to sit still and had to calm his overexcited nervous system gradually through another, to him less creative, medium. He cooked, designed furniture for their home, and taught himself photography.[5] Three of the first cooking lessons he gave his wife, demonstrating as he explained, were how to make bread and rolls, chocolate cake, and dry fluffy rice. Richard would happily eat rice three times every day and when his stomach grew tense, or gave pain, he did just that. Ellen mastered cooking easily and soon grew sure enough to improvise a lamb ragout to serve with the inevitable rice; it was so delicious that Richard wanted to eat it every night.

Ellen's parents disapproved of their daughter's marriage to a Negro and were angry and hurt when she simply refused to see them. She agreed with Richard that explanations or arguments were futile. Her family would have to accept Richard and until they understood that primary fact she did not want to see them at all. Peace in his home was vital to Wright's well-being. Arguments or hysterical outbursts made him feel physically ill; he had had as a child all the senseless violence he could endure. He liked to argue and discuss, but about ideas and issues which were more or less impersonal. Ellen told Richard that she always knew when he answered the telephone if it was Mrs. Poplar. She laughed and said that his voice assumed a sweet, purring, neutral tone. It became "slow, toneless, yet charged with a certain false, hearty warmth." "But how else can I speak to her?" Richard asked. "Ours is a mixed marriage, yet I and Ellen never think of it as such until we're reminded that it is. There're no problems in people of different races marrying and living together; the only problems that may arise come from those who look on, and those who look on are usually the ignorant."

If prejudice was not utterly routed, at least it was blunted and brought under control when in August Mrs. Poplar learned that Ellen was pregnant. She wept, she smiled, she became a mother again, she would be a grandmother; and after all the baby was half-Jewish. But she and her son-in-law remained aloof. She could never bring herself to speak to Richard frankly or even admit her prejudice and he, in turn, treated her as courteously as a stranger. Only one time, during one of her visits, Mrs. Poplar "became a little carping about the way [they] ran [their] house . . ." and in private Richard told Ellen to tell her mother to go home and stay there. He put his relations with her family on a simple basis: ". . . either they come to the house and behave themselves or they stay away. They prefer to come and behave; as long as that lasts they are welcome, but the moment they cook up any monkey business they'll get the gate. Ellen and I think of one accord about this. It works; there's peace and love in our home."

Ellen went into labor on April 13, 1942, and Richard took her to the hospital. He stayed by her side, holding her hand when she had pains but she labored on and on and by the end of the twenty-third hour she sent Richard out to eat something. When he returned he beamed at his wife and handed her a present. Under different conditions Ellen might have shrieked with laughter. The book was *Grapes of Wrath* and between Ellen's convulsive pains Richard described the wonderful book. At last it was time to go to the delivery room and Richard, awestruck and nervous but curious of all that went on in the green amphitheater, watched the birth of his big, eight-pound two-ounce, baby girl. They had decided on the name Julia for a girl and Richard chose his own private reference: "Julia-baby." He was so excited it made him feel as if his skin was tight, as if he were filled with air and would float off in space. Compassion, near to affection, swept over him and he laughed and smiled with his mother-in-law, who had waited through the night until the birth on April 14. When Ellen finally fell asleep Richard went downstairs, found change, and at three-thirty in the morning, oblivious of the hour, called all of his friends to give them the news. Life *was* good sometimes; he had wanted a girl all during Ellen's pregnancy—"I wish . . ." he had kept repeating until his wife told him, "Stop saying 'wish,' dear . . ."

A week later Richard went to the hospital with Becky Crawford, a friend of the Wrights', to take his family home. He was consumed by anxiety and Becky had increased his tension by arguing for breast-feeding all the way to Manhattan. It was vital for a baby to get a good start in life and mother's milk was a protection against disease for at least a year. Even more important was the psychological damage that occurred when a child was not nursed; and Richard and Ellen were thoughtless; they were putting their own convenience ahead of the baby's needs; and their doctor could not be a very competent man to urge bottle-feeding. She did not approve of the so-called modern approach to parenthood, and she talked on and on.

As soon as she looked at Richard's face, Ellen knew he was nervous but she did not insist that Becky carry Julia when he asserted that he would carry her home. Julia seemed very small when he picked her up in his arms and beads of perspiration broke out along his forehead. What should he do? He was in terror: "He didn't know whether to hold it tight and to squeeze it or hold it loose and risk letting it fall."

By the time they reached Revere Place and Richard placed Julia in a new crib and got Ellen in bed, he felt nervously ill. And Julia began to cry. Before leaving for the hospital he had made the formula and put it into sterilized bottles. Now he scrubbed his hands with a brush, set the milk in a pan of water to heat, and opened the jar of sterile nipples. Becky stood silently by watching. The nipples were new and stiff and Richard's hands were shaking with tension. Just as he almost fitted the first nipple on the warmed bottle it shot out of his grip, flew into the air and then dropped to the floor. Amused, Becky watched—point one, she had scored. A second nipple bounded onto the floor. Point two for Becky. With almost staccato rapidity nipples flew to the floor until there was only one sterile rubber-thwarting monster left. Julia was screaming so loudly that Richard thought she would burst her lungs. Cautiously, he reached in two fingers and took up the final nipple, holding it by the rim. Becky stood by, silent, waiting for a final vindication which would be proof that the natural way was superior to the scientific. Perspiration was rolling down Richard's face and neck while he eased one side of the nipple into position and then the other snapped down on the bottle.

Visitors came to see the new baby and Richard's work was interrupted by different duties. He stood "like a sentinel" at the door of Ellen's room. Anyone who came within six feet of the bed or crib "had to cover his mouth with a handkerchief."

When he stood beside the crib alone he looked at Julia and came to a conclusion: "I think Ellen and I were a good combination for her. . . . But, what to hell, maybe every mother and father say that about their kids. After all, kids are the most common thing on the face of this earth. Yes, but Julia is different, I know it; I feel it."

An early summer afternoon Richard met George Davis, an editor and friend who had published "Almos' a Man," one of his short stories, in *Harper's Bazaar*. Davis was a bachelor who knew everyone in the whole literary world and Richard had heard that he and Carson McCullers had taken a house together in Brooklyn Heights. But he had not known the preliminary steps which led to the joint undertaking and he would not ask directly. He knew that Carson had separated from Reeves but he knew that any tie between her and

Davis was simply that of kindred spirits. "How's the new house?" Richard asked. Then, as if on cue, Davis captured Richard's imagination. He described a dream he had had one night of a huge clapboard Victorian house in Brooklyn Heights. When he had awakened the dream had lingered with such vivid detail that he could not force it out of his mind. Almost against his conscious wish he had taken a subway to Brooklyn Heights and walked through the picturesque streets. After covering a few blocks Davis had come upon the house he had seen in his dream. It stood at 7 Middagh Street just under the shadow of the Brooklyn Bridge. From the weathered steps leading to the porch trimmed with fretwork in every detail it matched the house he had seen in his sleep the previous night. After such an omen Davis decided that he had to live in the house and he persuaded Carson McCullers and other artists to rent other parts of the big dwelling.

Davis' account of his mysterious dream excited Richard's imagination and when he was asked to join the household he accepted at once. The following month Richard moved his family into the parlor floor and basement of the old mansion which Davis and Carson McCullers had rented on the maple-lined street. Later there were other famous tenants: W. H. Auden, Louis MacNeice, Chester Kallman, Christopher Isherwood, Golo Mann, Paul Bowles and his wife Jane, Oliver Smith, Benjamin Britten, and Peter Pears. "Over the years, dozens of house guests and hundreds of callers, among them some of the most impressive names in literature, art, and music during the War years," came to call or to live temporarily: "composers Virgil Thomson, Aaron Copeland, Marc Blitzstein and Leonard Bernstein; surrealist painters Pavel Tchelitchew, Eugene Berman, and Salvador Dali (accompanied by his wife and model, the fabulous Gala) ; ballet critic and patron of the arts Lincoln Kirstein; and author Denis de Rougemont,"[6] and Anais Nin, who gave it the name which everyone used because so many of its guests had been born during that month—"February House."

Davis' dream was more inspiring to Richard than the reality of the ménage. For a few weeks he enjoyed visiting with George, who had decorated his apartment on the floor above in plushy Victorian splendor; and talking to Oliver Smith on the top floor. When Richard admired the huge semicircular desk bequeathed him by his illustrious ancestor Henry James, Smith promised to give it to him.

But some days the stimulating talk, talk, talk among the writers and poets drifted downstairs to distract him; he had to know what was going on.

One afternoon, Richard sat drinking tea as he watched Carson

McCullers move around the room serving and talking. She was dressed in slacks and a white shirt, her lanky, light brown hair straggling down the sides of her head, and he noticed that her eyes looked slightly bloodshot and puffed. An emotional reaction set in: he was fond of Carson but she never stopped talking about herself. He admired her writing, particularly her deeply sensitive depiction of the Negro doctor in *The Heart Is a Lonely Hunter*. What he thought of as a tortured soul attracted him to Carson as well as her zest for the ordinary moments of life. He shrugged away his mood and smiled at the repetitive remark she made each time she had been out-of-doors on one of her long walks: "Isn't it wonderful to live in a *real* neighborhood and breathe fine salt air!"

As weeks passed and Richard saw that Carson seemed to be drinking more and more, he worried about her health. He was not aware of a stroke she had had during the winter of 1940, but at twenty-five, still a girl, she seemed to be driving herself to destruction. A morbid concern for his own daughter grew as he envisioned a scene with Carson collapsing at Julia's feet. Then he wondered whether the general overstimulation and excitement in the house were good for his child. As soon as these questions formed themselves cogently he made a decision: "We're moving," he told his wife. "This is not a proper environment in which to raise a child."

Thus decided, it did not take long for Richard to find a new home. Near to a building in which he had lived in 1939 he found a large, two-bedroom apartment at 89 Lefferts Place in Brooklyn, and he and Ellen began to furnish their new home.

XV

Putting down a letter he had just read from his agent, Paul R. Reynolds, Jr., in early 1940, Richard was astonished, then alarmed and finally curious. Paul tentatively suggested that sometime in the future he should consider writing an autobiography. The idea had risen from a reading of scraps from Richard's life published in a WPA Writers' Anthology entitled *The Ethics of Living Jim Crow*.

"Hey! Whoa! I'm only thirty-two! I've got a lot of years ahead before I'm ready to sum up the meaning of my existence," was Richard's initial reaction. A second emotion came crowding into his mind with a powerful urge to write and find out what was going on deep down inside but with it a warning that it was dangerous to probe into oneself too intensively. But Paul had proffered the idea and he would have to think about it because he respected his agent's opinions.

Paul Reynolds, Jr., a tall, semi-walrus-moustached, scrupulously honest New Englander, was Richard's second agent. His first representative had been Ann Watkins, to whose agency he sent some short stories the week of his arrival from Chicago. Margot Johnson, a member of the firm, had written of the "mixed emotion and wonder" with which they had read his fiction. It was far and away the most powerful, exciting prose that had come into their office in months.[1] But after only a brief association, Richard decided that Ann Watkins was an eccentric lady who could not possibly understand him or his writing and he complained of his dissatisfaction to two friends, Franklin Folsom, executive secretary of the League of American Writers, and his wife, Mary Eltin.[2] After showing him a

197

list of literary agents—none of whose names had any meaning to Richard—Mary had taken him to Paul R. Reynolds and Son, where she worked, and explained that the firm was one of the oldest and most respected in New York.

At their first meeting Richard's curiosity was aroused by a modesty which appeared extreme to the point of shyness in Paul Reynolds, Jr. "This is a neurotically sensitive man, a descendant of New England stock . . . he is good at heart," Richard thought. More important to Richard than personality was that Paul Reynolds, Sr., the first literary agent in America to handle the works of Frances Hodgson Burnett, Winston Churchill, Richard Harding Davis, Jack London, and Stephen Crane, had also represented a black man, the gifted poet Paul Laurence Dunbar.[3] He hoped the new association would work out but held in reserve a definite opinion until he could find out whether Paul Jr., a white man, would recognize without wearying explanation what he was attempting to say through fiction. That would be the test.

And Paul gave Richard exactly what he had been hoping to find— an honest opinion, which was so difficult for a writer to obtain, along with an acute critical perceptivity. Richard was amazed. Paul had an absolute talent for literary criticism. Carefully and profoundly, he analyzed Richard's novels and each individual character. At the same time he gave reassurance that "Nobody can tell an author success- fully what to write or how to write it. All an author can do is to consider what is thrown at him, make use of anything that seems to ring true to his way of thinking and discard any suggestion that doesn't.[4]

Paul had another talent. He knew what to say, when to say it and how to put the seed of an idea into Richard's mind. Either from a natural reticence, based not on fear of offending, but coming, per- haps, from a sense of his own values and morality, reflected most of all in the manner in which he approached his job, Paul did not impose on the intensely suggestible mind of his client.[5] Thus when Paul suggested an autobiography Richard was compelled to turn it over, back and forth in his mind. Perhaps he would write such a book when he had completed a third work of fiction, on which he was working. An inner distaste toward revealing in first person instead of through a fictitious character the dread and fear and anguished self- questioning of his life was a temporary dam and he preferred not to use the term autobiography. He would give Paul's suggestion some thought, he wrote to his agent; and if he were to do such a book he would have to look at his hometown, which he had not seen in over twelve years. What better time than when he left Mexico—it was actually on his way home and he would have the experience in back of him when he finally sat down to write. Well, he mused quietly, let's see if the South has changed at all.*

In Mexico, John Steinbeck and Herbert Kline drove Richard to the train depot and the three men discussed the South and its prejudices. The moustached, craggily handsome Steinbeck turned his eyes from the road and asked Richard: "Have you got any subversive literature in your baggage?" "Yes," Richard answered. "I've got Lenin's *What Is to Be Done,* Karl Marx's *Das Kapital. . . .*" Steinbeck looked concerned. "Don't take such stuff; they'll grab you at the border for a Red," he warned Richard. "Ship your baggage and travel by air," Kline admonished. But Richard smiled to reassure the two men and said, "I'll risk it." He thought it was possible to enter the South, act as he knew whites wanted Negroes to act, and not have any trouble, even though his baggage contained books which advocated "dangerous thoughts."

Richard took a sleeper from Mexico City and rode with American whites, Mexicans, Germans, English and Spaniards, but when the train reached the Texas border, the races were separated. The white people were put into one coach and the black man, Richard, was put into another coach. A queer kind of segregation occurred in his coach; he sat at one end and the white American conductor motioned the Mexicans to the opposite end.

Soon the customs official came through the train; he examined the baggage of the Mexicans and then approached Richard. When he saw the official start to walk in his direction he washed all expression from his face, widened his eyes slightly and tried to look stupid. He was trying desperately to recall how he had acted when he was a child in the South and resolved to act that way again, for he wanted no trouble. If he gave any offense, there was no one to help him; the only other brown-skinned people were Mexicans and he knew that the state of Texas despised them equally, if not more, than they did a black man.

"What you got here, boy?" the inspector drawled.

"Just baggage."

"Well, open up," he said.

Richard opened a suitcase which contained clothing.

"All right. What's in there?" the man asked, pointing to Richard's typewriter.

* The following account of Richard's trip is from notes prepared for a speech on Negro literature, a portion of which appeared in "How Jim Crow Feels."

"My typewriter."

The air around the two men seemed to change abruptly. It seemed to Richard that soundless bells were clanging like the far-off yet approaching sirens of fire engines as the man stared first at the large standard typewriter in a custom-designed case and then into his face.

"Is it yours, boy?" the official asked.

"Oh, yes, sir," Richard answered.

There was another silence while the man stared at Richard suspiciously. Finally, he made up his mind: "What do you do? Teach school?"

"No, sir; I write," Richard said.

"You're a preacher?" the official half asked and half declared, as if he had not heard Richard's answer.

"No, sir; I'm a writer," Richard told him again.

"What's in there?" the man asked, pointing to the case containing Richard's books.

"Books."

By this time the customs official was genuinely puzzled and he bent over the box to glance at the rows of books.

"What are these books?"

"Just books," Richard told him.

"You teach school, don't you?" the man asked.

"No, sir; I'm a writer."

"You're a preacher," the official insisted.

"I'm a writer," Richard said once again.

He knew that the man had never in his life met any black men who, if they were not laborers, were not schoolteachers or preachers, and he was puzzled because he could not fit Richard into a familiar category.

A sense of chill, of hair lifting slightly out of the pores on the back of his neck entered Richard's body when the man bent over, picked up *Das Kapital,* glanced at the title and asked: "Boy, these books ain't Communistic, are they?"

"Oh, no, sir," Richard lied. "They are books dealing with writing."

"Dealing with writing," the inspector repeated slowly, uncomprehendingly. He had been so conditioned that he could not actually recognize words he had not been conditioned to hear. "All right, you can pack up now," he said uneasily.

Richard quickly locked his baggage with nervous fingers, expecting at any moment to be told to open his cases again and spread out all his books and papers. What would happen if the man saw the new novel he was working on? A thin line of perspiration formed along his upper lip; in the story was a girl who married a white man and then murdered him. Ah, God! the man was still standing by his seat. Now, what? Richard wondered.

"Where were you born, boy?" the man asked.

"Mississippi, sir," Richard said.

At last the official had one familiar fact to which he could cling and his face changed entirely.

"I knew you was a Southern nigger," he said, smiling happily.

"You niggers can travel all over the world, but when I meet a Southern nigger, I know it.

"O.K., boy," the man said, still affable, as he walked away down the aisle.

In San Antonio, Texas, where he was to make connections for the trip to Mississippi, Richard warily stepped off the train. He checked his bags and wandered about the station looking at the signs: FOR WHITE—FOR COLORED. They brought the old, choking feeling into his throat even though they had become hard to believe after twelve years in the North. But they were only too real and he turned to walk away quickly. Some white bastard might read anger on his face. Out on the station platform he stood and looked into the distance. Suddenly he heard a soft whirring sound in back of him and turned. A white man in a wheelchair was slowly propelling himself directly at Wright. When he was about two feet away, he stopped and stared at Richard with that queer, open look that men use when they stare at animals. Richard looked away and then glanced back at the man. He was still staring. Richard was sensitive to the slightest change of expression in a passing face and if he saw that a person had become aware of his glance he immediately looked away to spare him embarrassment. But the white man in the wheelchair continued to stare and Richard grew uncomfortable. Then rage came up in the back of his throat and he could almost taste the acridity of bile. Turning, he walked away, already in control of his anger, cautioning himself to cool off.

The chair whirred again behind him and shamelessly the man propelled himself toward Richard. Then he reached out a hand and caught hold of the edge of his grey tweed suit and fingered the texture of the cloth.

"Where'd you get that suit, boy?" he demanded.

"In New York," Richard murmured, afraid not to answer but irritated by the man's presumptiveness.

"What'd you pay for it?" he asked.

Richard thought quickly. He wanted to be safe so he cut the price in half and told him. The man did not reply but simply shook his head. Richard walked quickly away and reentered the station, anxious to get away from a man who had no regard for his privacy, for his personality, and assumed without question that there was nothing about him that he had to respect.

Wearily, Richard climbed aboard his train when it arrived en route to New Orleans. In the comparatively short distance from Mexico to Texas his emotions had been flogged by white customs until his necessary control had tired him physically. A little while after boarding the train he ran out of cigarettes and asked a Negro porter if it was all right for him to go into the dining car to buy a package.

"Ah, naw," he told Richard, shaking his head. "You can't go through that car where them white folks is sitting unless you got on a suit like I got on," he said. "I'll git your cigarettes."[6]

Richard knew that in some Southern states a Negro could not go into the dining car at all and in others he could only eat, provided there was a thick dark curtain around his table to screen his presence from the eyes of white diners.

During the night it was hot and the Jim Crow coach seemed to steam from the bodies sprawled in sleep in all the seats. Richard could not sleep;[7] he sat staring into the darkened coach, thinking about the South and its people. Suddenly at the far end of the coach a white man appeared; he was fat, he wore a black hat pushed far back on his head. In his mouth was a dead cigar which he rolled slowly in his teeth. As he walked through the coach, Richard saw that he was mumbling. Finally he passed Richard, putting his hands on the edges of the seats to keep himself steady against the rocking of the train. He murmured pleasantly: "Niggers sleeping; niggers sleeping; niggers sleeping . . ." There was no malice in his voice and no hate. Crazy laughter came into the back of Richard's throat but he kept silent. The white man might as well have been walking through a field of wheat or corn and mumbling "nice wheat," or "nice corn."

When the train stopped the next morning in Birmingham a group of white soldiers got on board but Richard simply noted the fact idly and thought nothing more about it. As the morning passed he grew hungry and asked the porter if the waiter would bring him some breakfast since he was not permitted to enter the dining car. An hour later the waiter appeared, took Richard's order and then disappeared. Ten o'clock came and there was still no waiter and no breakfast. Signaling to the porter, he asked him to find out what had happened to the food. He was very hungry.

Eventually, the porter returned but he would not look into Richard's eyes. He mumbled that they were very busy in the dining room and kitchen and that he would have to wait. Richard waited all morning and at noon the train stopped and the soldiers got off; five minutes later the waiter brought breakfast. Nervously, the man tucked a napkin over Richard's knees and put the tray on his lap: "Here you are," he said. His voice was nearly hysterical in pitch and Richard knew that the man did not want him to ask any questions. "What happened?" he asked.

"What you mean?" The waiter smiled.

"Why were you so long?"

"It was them white soldiers in the next coach," he murmured and avoided Richard's eyes. "They was just playing," he assured him.

"Tell me what happened," Richard demanded.

"Now, now, mister, you is in the South," he said. "Don't you know it? Now, here's your breakfast; I'm doing the best I can."

"But tell me what happened?" Richard insisted.

The waiter backed away as if he had been threatened and left the coach without answering.

When he had taken a few sips of his coffee Richard saw the porter and waved to attract his attention. "Tell me what happened?" The porter bent his head low and whispered: "He had some trouble with them white soldiers; he was bringing your breakfast, but them white soldiers wouldn't let him . . . They said they didn't wanna see no tray taken to the nigger coach."

Wright saw fear in the man's eyes when he begged him not to make trouble on the train. He and the waiter had to live in the South and Richard was only passing through.[8]

While still on the train, Richard came to a decision that when he wrote the "autobiography" the experiences between the Texas border and Mississippi would be clues to feeling. Fear was predominant in all black and white relations in the South. "This is how Negroes feel in the South; this is how they feel, with variations ranging from terror to anxiety and tension, all over America."

As soon as Richard stepped off the train in his hometown, the place of his birth, Natchez; he wondered why he had returned at all. Nothing had changed. "True, the tall, moss-hung oaks were still there, but somehow they now reminded [him] of cheap picture post cards. . . . Jim Crow was still Jim Crow and not a single racial practice had altered" during a twelve-year absence. "Fat pigs wallowed in the filthy front yards of Negro laborers. Sparrows flounced in the dust of gutters. People moved and spoke slowly, as if lacking bodily energy, as if their diets, composed mainly of lard and starch, were deficient in vitamins. A sour stench hung in the air—there was still no plumbing—and magnolia scent blended with the sweet, sickening smell of the outdoor privies."

Feeling that only he had changed, Richard looked at the faces of people who were once familiar and saw that many had become old and wrinkled. He was surprised to discover that there had been so many deaths or paralytic strokes and wondered if unremittent tension was the reason or explanation for the prevalence of that disease.

Even his own family seemed strange to Richard. Nathan, his father, had returned from Memphis and was again working as a sharecropper; there was little change in his physical appearance. Only Nathan's hands showed age; they were heavily veined and muscled. When he shook his son's hand Richard felt large rough callouses scrape against his own smooth skin almost like an emery stone. Nathan asked Richard about Alan, his other son, and when he mentioned Ella, the anger Richard had felt toward his father when he was a child again entered his mind but he kept his face bland and replied easily. Then there was very little more to say as the two men walked around the neighborhood. When his father was silent, Richard had a sensation of pain, low at the base of his throat. It was an ache caused by his realization that his father had been trapped in the South and had lived out his days planting and hoeing and picking cotton. What a wasted life, he thought. Everywhere he looked he saw poverty; this was the black peasant, inarticulate, imprisoned "in a Sargasso of racial subjugation."

Inside a wooden house, with its door ajar in the summer heat, Mrs. Maggie J. Hunt, Richard's first cousin, placed a crisp white table-cloth on the table for the family dinner which was being prepared. When they all sat down to eat Richard was not hungry. The heat, a feeling of being alien, a compulsion to make conversation when he had nothing to say, made the muscles of his stomach tense. Dinner finally came to an end and Richard went outside. As soon as he could, he fumbled in his pocket for two antacid tablets and slipped them into his mouth. Then, feeling a little better, he took out a camera and photographed his family, his father standing with friends, and the area around the house. Finally, the visit ended and with an inward sigh of relief Richard said his good-byes and left. Had his father and cousins felt as awkward as he had felt, and were they relieved—as relieved as he was—to see him go, he wondered.

Settled into his seat on the train, Richard felt gloom invade his thoughts. Everything seemed hopeless. The Southern black man was ignorant, and bad housing, malnutrition, and the unremitting pressure of the whites could actually deform the body and soul of a people. Yet, "the burden of the solution of the Negro problem in America lies mainly with the Southern Negro. For a statement of the problem, the burden lies with the Northern Negro and foreign

Negroes." And he would try to make a statement—could he do it? Using portions of his own childhood, stories told him by friends,[9] things he had observed happening to others, he would write an "autobiography."

But it was not until after his marriage to Ellen and the birth of Julia, that Richard could begin work on the story of his own life. Something held him back. Yet, all the while, and interfering with the novel on which he was working, special scenes from his childhood isolated themselves and allowed him to examine them unmasked, yet others seemed simply to fester in his mind, concealed by the imposition of adult experiences. A strange, almost morbid feeling began to possess him, a painful suspense, the welling of an irrepressible curiosity, night dreams and daytime fantasies[10] merged. Sometimes he could not separate what had actually happened to him and what had been told him by others. The word "autobiography" troubled him and interfered with what seemed an orderly fictional progression, and he thrust it to the back of his thoughts. But it would not always be repressed and then he would jot down stray notes on scraps of paper, afraid that simple facts might escape if he were to combine fact with fiction. He wrote: "Dr. Johnson was the music teacher at the Jim Hill School. Stomping feet in school to answer questions. Popping fingers. Freedom turns to responsibility—Lyle Drugstore, Main and Beale. Job in restaurant $10 per week at night. Almost all the sensitive people I was attracted to in my environment were homos. Why did momma send me to a private school in Memphis. In Helena. In Jackson. Read—Postman Rings Twice."[11]

Early one morning, suddenly and abruptly, he put aside the manuscript on which he was working; it had "frozen on him" and gave himself over consciously to ideas rather than images of the new book. It would be autobiographical but it would be more than that; he would use himself as a symbol of all the brutality and cruelty wreaked upon the black man by the Southern environment. And what could be better than to use childhood—symbolic of purity, of beauty, of innocence—through which to reveal the Southern dark so that whites would bear full responsibility for it? No one could be innocent any longer. To expose that dread most nakedly, the child would have to be representative of most Negroes; not those in the middle class who escaped the worst terror through the "pet nigger system."[12] His own experiences had enough harsh similarity to those of the average black man's to make his identification with the poorest truthful. His own family's essentially middle-class status would have to be underplayed; their attitudes had been essentially white middle-class attitudes. But the poor Negro had "black" values—the values of rebels, of all oppressed peoples and he would choose that side, as he always had, for that was symbolic of the future.

When Wright was not quite halfway into the new book he went to Fisk University in April, 1943, to lecture before an interracial audience. In the middle of his speech he sensed, and then observed, that the audience was restive and he received a distinct impression of hostility emanating toward him as if upon waves of air. He was not surprised, because he had been describing some of the more sordid aspects of his childhood and developing the theme of what it felt like to be a black man in America. Such disclosures as he was making were supposed to be hidden or discussed in privacy. Neither Negro or white wanted a description of the shabbiness and emptiness of life lived under white domination as reflected in the personalities and relationships in his own family. No one wanted to hear about the fear and terror and dread inculcated in a Negro unless smoothed over with panaceas. As soon as he finished speaking the people in the audience began to leave quickly. There were no questions and there was no applause—just a quick clutching at pocketbooks, an indignant fumbling with jackets and a scurry for the exits. A brief ironical smile passed over Richard's face and suddenly, a strange surprising sensation, of a sort of bitter hatred for everyone leaving the auditorium, passed through his body:[13] "Nobody is ever expected to speak honestly about the problem. You must wrap it up in myth, legend, morality, folklore, niceties and plain lies. When the truth is plowed up they shake and tremble and don't know what to do." Gazing about him, Richard discovered that not everyone had left the hall. Separately, two men, one white and one black, were approaching to speak with him. The black man shook his hand. "You've got courage," he said. The white man gave praise: "You've really brought the race issue to Nashville."

Seated on the train for his return trip to New York, Richard leaned back, one hand holding his throat above a starched white collar, and absently stared through the window. His mind was on the speech he had made and the audience's reaction: "We're all scared all the time . . ."[14] And his thoughts went to the book he was writing. "I suspect that the Negroes will pick my bones for this book; that they will hover about me like vultures and hack away at me; for I'm convinced that they cannot as yet fathom the motives that made me write this book; they are not emotionally independent enough to want to face the naked experience of their lives."

On December 17, 1943, Richard sent his autobiography to his agent. A title had given him his usual difficulty and after a consideration of *The Empty Box, Days of Famine, The Empty Houses, The*

Assassins, Bread and Water, he had decided upon *American Hunger.* Whether it was of any real value or not he could not say; he was so numbed by fatigue. "Read it and if it is worth showing to Harper's, then let them see it . . . I don't think that there is much that I will ever be able to do to this script," he wrote to Paul Reynolds.

Almost at once a telegram arrived from Paul: "Your autobiography is enthralling. Believe has possibilities of a very large sale. Publication this spring. Will see you Monday. Any suggested work on MS will be of most minor nature."

By March, the manuscript was at Harper & Brothers, where plans for advance publicity were being worked out and technical questions discussed. After the manuscript had been set in type and Richard received the galleys he received a telephone call from his editor who told him that Harper had decided to cut the book by one-third. The story would end at the point where Richard left the South, leaving out his experiences in Chicago and New York. His editor explained that there was an acute paper shortage because of the war and that Harper was afraid it might run out of stock altogether.

After hanging up the telephone, Richard picked up the galley pages of his book and turned the long strips of paper until he reached the end of Chapter Fourteen. When he had read the last paragraph he put the sheets aside, relieved to find that a natural break seemed to occur at that point and he would not have to do any rewriting. He suddenly paused in his reflections and got up from his chair; an expression of profound suspicion gleamed in his face for an instant. Was a paper shortage the real reason why Harper did not want to publish the whole book? Mistrust glinted in his eyes and he tried to recall exactly what his editor had said and each nuance of his voice. Had he been honest? Was that the sole reason? No, by God, there was something strange about the cutting of his book; very mysterious. A thrill of excitement, like a shiver, ran through his mind as he sought for an explanation of the mystery. Something was in back of Harper's request, but what, or who? He sat down again, suddenly feeling in his whole being that his book was being censored in some way. When he reached that conclusion he jumped up from his chair and went to find his wife. As he told Ellen of his conversation with his editor his voice lowered conspiratorially while his eyes shone and a look of glee flickered in his smile. Catching fire from his mood, Ellen asked eager questions: But why! Who? What is behind it? All at once, two possible answers came into Richard's mind. Since the United States and the USSR were allies in the war Harper did not wish to offend the Communists.[15] Or, maybe the Communist Party itself was exerting some sort of influence over the publisher.

Whatever the reason, he decided to find some way for the material to be published. The section was almost too long for any magazine he could think of unless it was serialized; he would think of something. And it would be a secret from both his publisher and his agent.[16]

Something was left dangling, a piece of his own life, with the amputation of his book's last chapters and Richard was left with a vague unrest. Within those chapters were his experiences with the Communist Party and he felt a need for his readers to know what they had been. Richard changed the title from *American Hunger* to *Black Boy* and when the book was chosen by the Book-of-the-Month Club he made a political statement to Joseph Gollomb, hoping for its inclusion in a review for the Club's magazine:

I am as collectivist and proletarian in my outlook as when I belonged to the Communist Party, and the Negroes are my people. But there is a need to think and feel honestly, and that comes first.[17]

By March, 1945, the sales of *Black Boy* had reached over 400,000[18] and the book was listed in every New York newspaper at the top of its best-seller list. White reviewers seemed to have gone mad, Richard thought. "I'm dead tired. One does not get much of a chance to react when reality impinges too hard upon one. One sees, talks, walks, eats, but impressions do not sink in too deep, for there are too many of them." Sometimes he merely glanced at the reviews and then handed them to Ellen, who had purchased a huge black scrapbook and affixed a gold-plated facsimile of his name, given by an admiring reader, across its top. Critics declaimed: "Genius defies explanation; great literary talent; outstanding literary achievement of the last few years," but the words made only visual impressions and when Dorothy Canfield Fisher referred to *Black Boy* in comparison with Rousseau and St. Augustine, Richard told his wife that the writings of Augustine were boring and seemed naïve to him.

There was always too much to do and Richard yearned to start another book. Instead, there were interviews every day and radio programs for which he had to prepare; one after the other, he spoke on Town Hall of the Air, Author Meets the Critic and the Mary Margaret McBride Show before the largest daytime audience in radio. A thousand letters flooded his mailbox discussing and complimenting his book; and one he framed. It was from William Faulkner— undated, marked "Tuesday"—who had just completed reading *Black Boy*:

It needed to be said, and you said it well. Though I am afraid (I am speaking now from the point of view of one who believes that the man who wrote Native Son is potentially an artist) it will accomplish little of what it should accomplish, since only they will be moved and grieved by it who already know and grieve over this situation.

You said it well, as well as it could have been said in this form. Because I think you said it much better in Native Son. I hope you will keep on saying it, but I hope you will say it as an artist, as in Native Son. I think you will agree that the good lasting stuff comes out of one individual's imagination and sensitivity to and comprehension of the suffering of Everyman, Anyman, not out of the memory of his own grief. . . .

There were reactions different from Faulkner's: Mississippi banned the book. Senator Bilbo attacked *Black Boy* and the author in Congress. *Black Boy* should be taken off the shelves of stores; sales should be stopped; it was a damnable lie, from beginning to end; it built fabulous lies about the South. The purpose of the book was to plant seeds of hate and devilment in the minds of every American. It was the dirtiest, filthiest, most obscene, filthy and dirty, and came from a Negro from whom one could not expect better.[19]

Bilbo's tirade amused Richard but he worried for the safety of relatives in Jackson and he hoped they would not be engulfed by wild hate. *Life* magazine sent a photographer south to photograph the scenes of his childhood for a picture story and Richard counted the days until the man returned; he hoped he would leave before the whites caught him and beat him for the pictures he was taking that might insult the South.

How many understand how they make us feel
and live . . .

XVI

On the day before New Year's, December 31, 1944, Richard, Horace
Cayton, and Elmer Carter decided to go to Joe's, the most famous
seafood restaurant in Brooklyn. Horace, a sociologist, and the grandson of Hiram R. Revels, the first Negro Senator ever to be elected to
the national legislature, had come to New York from Chicago to
spend New Year's at the Wrights'. And Richard had invited Carter, a
suave Harvard-educated writer and sociologist who later became
chairman of the New York State Commission against Discrimination,
because he wanted the two men to work with him on a new book for
which he had gotten the approval of his publishers.

Horace, whom Richard had met years before in Chicago, was in
agreement with his conception of a book tentatively entitled *The
Meaning of Negro Experience in America*. Each chapter would be in
the form of an essay—The American Negro Looks at History; History
Looks at the American Negro; America With the Negro; America
Without the Negro; What the Negro Pays to Live in America; The
Folklore of American Race Relations; and Richard planned to write
the title piece. He and Cayton had conceived of the idea after the
publication of Gunnar Myrdal's *An American Dilemma*. If a white
man could go that far in an analysis of race relations in America,
Richard thought that he and his friends could top him. He felt honor
bound to do so and Cayton felt the same. Together they made a list
of writers and subjects and agreed that the book was not to be an
appeal against race prejudice but a series of essays dealing with ideas,
valuations and interpretations about the American Negro and his
place and meaning in the country. The whole tone of the book

would be more radical than Myrdal's and differ greatly from another book that had just appeared called *What the Negro Wants*. Richard knew that a long and bitter argument between Negroes and white liberals had developed over the latter book, and his authors would be Negro scholars only. These were to be Jay Saunders Redding, St. Clair Drake, Lawrence D. Reddick, E. Franklin Frazier, C. L. R. James, Cayton and himself.

Cayton and Carter had only just met and Richard thought that the two men would become friends. Both had so much in common— "college, sociology, newspaper work, and whiskey"—but he saw at once that both were reserved, and slightly antagonistic. Maybe they are really too much alike! Richard thought to himself. Carter had been to Joe's restaurant once before but Richard was apprehensive. "Call up," he asked Carter, "and see if we need reservations, then they won't be able to turn us away with that excuse." Over the telephone the restaurant manager told Carter that no reservations were necessary so the three set out from the apartment on Lefferts Place for a midday meal. It was a dull, cloudy day and the damp December air was chilling. Richard was glad when they reached the warm air of the restaurant and the aroma of seafood and ravioli made his mouth water.

When they stepped in the door of Joe's, Richard felt as if a thousand "white" eyes were stabbing him. Assuming an indifferent, unseeing air, he strolled to a table and sat down. A waiter came for their order and Richard asked for three martinis and appetizers of ravioli. Then he leaned forward to expound his favorite thesis: "Fear is the most dominant emotion in Negro life." Horace agreed; Carter agreed but seemed to shy from the discussion. Richard paused in a sentence to sip his martini, raised his eyes from the glass and looked into the face of a faded, elderly white woman. The woman kept staring at him and he mentioned it to Cayton and Carter. Carter smiled and pulled on his pipe silently but Horace said: "Just ignore it," and Richard saw him stiffen slightly in his seat.

"We're all scared all the time," Richard continued, and when the two men agreed he felt it was an accomplishment. All three knew that it was rare for Negroes to admit the simple fact, "the fact that we are scared all the time of white people." Whenever Richard lifted his eyes the white woman was staring and whenever he stared back she glanced away. He looked about the café. Yes, others were staring and he wondered if the white patrons would complain to the proprietor when they left. To himself he murmured: "But, the hell with them. We are orderly; well dressed; and we have the money to pay for our meal. That damn white bitch is still staring at me; I doubt if she can really enjoy her expensive food. But, oh, this Italian ravioli is good; never have I tasted anything so delicious!"

Then it happened. Wright watched the swarthy waiter walk down the aisle with a tray filled with dirty dishes. He looked hurriedly to left and right, hunting for a place to set them temporarily. Motionless, Richard watched the developing crisis; he saw that the waiter was terribly busy and anxious to serve a new group of white people sitting just in front of their table. The waiter selected Richard's table upon which to place the dirty dishes. All three men became rigid while the same thoughts raced in their minds—"That damn white waiter would not have placed those dishes on any other table but ours. And he chose ours because we are black; somehow in his mind he thinks that we don't care; or that we won't notice; or he emotionally associates dirty dishes with our brown skins."

"I don't like that," Carter said, his face was tense.

"Oh, what the hell," Horrace said. "Ask 'im to take 'em off."

"I'll be goddamn," Carter said.

The three men were silent. Richard looked again at the white woman nearby: "Yes, that white bitch is staring at me again, white people are simply not sensitive when they look at Negroes; she is staring at me as though I were a dog, a cat; and she turns aside only when I stare back at her. If she were young, I'd sicken her by winking; but, hell, she's ugly!"

"I'm going to push these dishes off this table," Carter threatened.

Horace laughed easily, doubting, and watched Carter while he chewed on some fish. "You wouldn't," Richard challenged, hoping to egg Carter on, but not too much.

"I'm going to do it," Carter said.

"What good would that do?" Horace questioned.

"He should not have put them here," Carter said and his right hand slowly reached toward the pile of dirty dishes while he continued to look at Horace and Richard.

Transformed into a lookout, Richard glanced up. "That damn white bitch is looking at Carter's hand!" Softly, he said, "Don't do it now . . . Let me give you the signal." Carter took his hand away and waited, his eyes on Richard's face. "I have compulsions like that too sometimes," he told Carter, seizing as he liked to do upon small details of madness to generalize.

"I'm going to do it, goddamn!" Carter burst out quietly. His hand went out toward the pile of dirty dishes and he kept looking at Richard and pushed at the dishes slowly. They were then balancing on the edge of the table. The white woman was staring at Richard and he stared her pale gray eyes from his face. Then the woman watched Carter's brown hand as it pushed the dishes closer to the edge of the table.

"Not now!" Richard whispered.

"I'm going to do it," Carter said, his voice tense, his face strained, biting his pipe and staring at Richard and Horace.

"CRRRRASSSH! The dishes went and Carter jerked like struck by a .45 bullet. Horace was tense; he stared at Carter, then at the pale, white-faced waiter who came running and stood appalled."

Richard looked back at the white woman and silently registered: "That goddamned woman saw Carter! Her face is a mask of frozen horror. She's not angry: I see that she simply cannot believe what she saw. These goddamn ignorant whites. Yes, I think that that woman will never try to tell anyone what she saw three niggers do at Joe's; I don't think she will ever quite be able to tell if she saw it or not, so far removed from her stinking, peaceful life is the tension and hate we Negroes live and feel at all moments. I think that she will from time to time in the coming years stare at that suddenly present image of that brown hand pushing those dishes from the table to the tile floor and hearing them crash. . . ."

"I had to do it," Carter said.

"What did you really feel?" Richard asked.

"Before or after?" Carter asked, his voice whistling through his mouth.

"Both," Richard answered. The waiter stooped and began to pick up the shards of broken china. He suspected that the dishes had not fallen and, straightening up from the floor, he stood and stared at Carter.

"You were careless," Carter said in an off-hand manner in his flawless English speech. "You balanced them on the edge."

"Oh, no!" the waiter said, growing excited. "I never do that! They could not have fell!"

"They did *fall*," Carter said coolly, his Harvard accent more noticeable than before. The waiter wanted to say more, to argue, but he checked himself; he knew what white and black were facing each other and a fight would come easy. He swallowed and turned away.

"Tell me what you felt, Carter?" Richard persisted.

"Just hate before I pushed them," Carter explained, in a low and tense whisper.

"And after?"

"Pain in my legs, nausea, fear, tension, but I'm all right," Carter told him.

"I wonder how many white people realize how common such

feelings are among Negroes. How many understand how they make us feel and live," Richard pondered.[1]

A few days after New Year's Richard invited a group of men to his apartment to discuss the proposed book for Harper. Horace invited St. Clair Drake, a sociology professor who had joined the Merchant Marine and was stationed in New York, with whom he was collecting material for a book about the South Side of Chicago.[2] Horace assured Richard that Drake would be an excellent addition to their proposed roster of well-known scholars to write essays. Also expected were Lawrence D. Reddick, a young historian and curator of the Schomburg Collection of the New York Public Library; C. L. R. James (J. R. Johnson) a West-Indian scholar and anti-Communist Marxist; Ralph Ellison; and Elmer Carter.

Before the meeting, Ellen took Julia and went to spend the afternoon with friends; and Richard prepared coffee, then filled the ice bucket and got out glasses and liquor to serve when they were finished with the discussion. But nothing worked out as he had planned. Horace was late—he was visiting a young girl named Amy who was "love-struck" by him; then Drake and Reddick arrived, bringing with them a Negro war correspondent named Waters who wanted Richard's advice on how to write a book. Richard had wanted a disciplined business meeting as a basis for launching the proposed book, and was irritated when he met Waters. But, curbing his pique, he explained that if Waters was ready to write a serious book which would expose the mistreatment of black men in the armed services, he would help him find a publisher. Waters listened but did not comment and Richard thought "he seemed a strange, cunning, and kind of scared fellow." Then Drake said cautiously that Waters wanted "to go back" overseas. And Richard was disgusted; his face remained friendly but he knew that Waters was willing to withhold the truth if it offended anybody and he did not want to have anything more to do with the man. Fortunately, Waters had to leave to keep an appointment, and the rest of the men arrived for the meeting. After some milling around and cross-talk they settled into their chairs while Richard explained what he and Horace were attempting to do.

Drake listened awhile then he came out with his criticisms. They were astounding. He wanted to be reassured that James would not make a Marxian analysis but write out of a body of knowledge already gathered about the Negro in the United States, a body of knowledge for which Richard would not give three red cents in hell. Richard pointed out that Gunnar Myrdal had discredited much of that knowledge in his book; but Drake did not answer him. Drake stated that he was against general statements about *the* Negro. Richard said that one could say that generally the English are a naval, a seafaring, people. Drake said that one could not, for the simple reason that not all Englishmen went to sea. Then Richard said that one could say that Americans had a genius for production. Drake countered by asking if there were any Englishmen, and what is an Englishman? Richard stared, utterly aghast and thought to himself: "I seem to be listening to the talk of an insane man. I have never before in my life heard whites carry on in such a manner." Finally, it became impossible to talk to Drake and it slowly dawned on Richard that scientific integrity was not what Drake was trying to protect; he was fighting against a certain view of life that was painful to him as a Negro. For example, Drake did not believe that whites in general, passively and actively, kept Negroes in their place. The whites did not actively hate Negroes. Leaning forward in his chair, as if by stretching physically he could widen Drake's vision, Richard said that whites did not have to actively hate black men; whites had already put them in their "place" and they did not have even to think of Negroes until they tried to get out of their "places" and then violence was used against them.

Drake shook his head. Richard's remarks were making no impression and he glanced toward C. L. R. "Nello" James, whose long body was relaxed in a chair while he pulled contemplatively on a pipe. A slight smile hovered at the corners of his mouth and he looked back at Richard as if to say he was wasting his time and energy.[3] But softly and without belligerence, Richard asked:

"Why are Negroes in a subordinate position in the United States?"

"There are poor people everywhere," Drake answered.

"Are they penalized because of their race?"

Drake replied that they were penalized because of other things, therefore, race prejudice was put on the level of one's disliking a man because of his blue eyes or red hair. What's the point, Richard thought; then aloud, he ended the discussion: "I've never heard of a white man being lynched because his hair was red."

Then Reddick and Horace entered the argument but made no more impression on Drake than Richard had. Exasperated, finally, Reddick told Drake that he was infantile. The first meeting to discuss the proposed book ended in confusion and no decisions were worked out. When everyone else had left the apartment Richard sat with Horace and talked for three hours. His mind was almost made up to stop work on the idea for a Negro symposium.

"Negroes are so, each and all, caught and held in the vise of their fear about race relations, that they cannot meet and talk to each other. They are like a bunch of worms all tied together, each seeking to suck nourishment from the other. . . . It's quite clear that Drake's fierce rejection of art, of intuitive perception, of emotion, is his way of getting away from a hard real world, a world that no Negro can escape. Ideology has little or nothing to do with his attitude. Drake is really afraid of me; when he meets me I set off his deepest complexes, rouse his sense of fear and racial failure. If he believed me, he would either kill some white person or he would leap out of a window. Like Carter, he wants to dodge what a Negro means; if and when he accepts it, he would push dishes off the table. . . . I wonder if whites would believe that there are intelligent, sensitive Negroes who feel this way. And I wonder why I've never felt that way. . . ."

The following morning Richard awoke feeling tired and Ellen let him stay abed for two hours past his usual rising time while she took Julia to nursery school. Clasping his hands behind the back of his neck, Richard listened to hear if Horace was awake, and hearing no sound from the front room, he thought about parts of their conversation the night before: "Why is it that he is about the only Negro in America with whom I can talk and be understood?" Richard wondered. "I like Horace because he is scared and admits it. . . . Horace has more brains and guts in ten minutes than most Negroes have in ten years." When Richard reached that conclusion about his high-strung intellectual friend he felt an urge to continue their talk and got out of bed to cook ham and eggs for their breakfast.

Later in the afternoon Richard and Horace took the subway to Manhattan. He wanted to introduce Horace to his friend Dorothy Norman, publisher and editor of *Twice A Year* and a columnist on the New York *Post*. Richard had met Dorothy at a party of Theodore Dreiser's shortly after the publication of *Uncle Tom's Children*. She had loved the book and found Richard "fond, searching, with an honest simplicity." Through Dorothy, Richard had met Marc Chagall, with whose genius and fey quality he had fallen in love, Paul Tillich, Hannah Arendt, Lillian Smith, John Marin and later Jean-Paul Sartre and Simone de Beauvoir. At their first meeting Richard had known immediately that Dorothy thought of him as a man; she was simply unaware of the color of his skin—it had been registered in the same fashion as she might have noted that Chagall had brown eyes. On the train Richard told Horace about Dorothy; he was eager to share his friends each with the other.

But when they arrived at the large townhouse at 124 East 70th Street, Richard thought there was a stiffening, almost of fright, in Horace as they entered the beautiful home. His impression grew stronger of a feeling of trepidation in his friend when Dorothy entered the room smiling, regal grace in the motion of her large body. "Horace is floored," Richard thought. "Here is beauty and brains." For a while Horace was silent and then he began to talk excitedly. Dorothy suggested that the men help themselves to whatever they cared to drink and Richard had two during the visit but became worried when he could not keep up with the amount Horace was drinking. He watched Horace nervously and thought silently that his fear was an aggressive fear: ". . . he rushes forward to meet danger. Here is symbolized all that Negroes cannot get: white sex and money, lots of it." Suddenly, Richard's skin almost crawled with horror at Horace's conversation.

"He sailed into Dorothy, wanting to know why was she concerned about Negroes, what insecurities did she have that made her take up with Negroes."[4] Richard's horror and tension increased; he simply could not ask such questions of people. "Dorothy replied, laughing; she has poise; she said quietly that she knew that Horace was suspicious, and that she would gladly reveal herself. Rip the zipper down and turn yourself inside out, Horace boomed. [Richard's] foot, which had been mysteriously swelling for some reason for the last four hours, was paining [him]; [he] was dead tired and sleepy, so [he] sat and listened with mounting horror while a Negro asked questions of a rich white woman that no white man would have dared ask. And the white woman, poised and full of wisdom, with a smile and clenched fingers, calmly recited the history of her life. [Richard] wanted to yell, Stop! Dorothy saw that [he] was suffering. Yet, was not this as natural as Carter pushing dishes off the table at Joe's; as natural as Drake denying that the Negro was oppressed? Yes, here again was the same reaction but dressed in a different guise. Here was symbolized all that challenged Horace and he had to attack it. Horace is being now psychoanalyzed and his method of attack is to try to find where others are weak, like he is. He seems to feel that if he can find that, then it equalizes things somewhat. Dorothy knew that; no doubt she knows a lot about psychoanalysis, and she skillfully skirted what she did not want to say, and said what she wanted to say. Horace does not understand where she comes from culturally; he does not understand that Hart Crane, Waldo Frank, Alfred Stieglitz, Lewis Mumford created the dream that she is seeking to realize. Since Horace has a wound from his living, he must find one in Dorothy or then Dorothy seems superior to him. But Horace did not find it. . . ."[5]

En route home, Richard tried to explain to Horace something of the character and personality of a person like Dorothy Norman, but he insisted that she was neurotic; that she was compensating for something; that she was lonely, that she was suffering. "In short," Richard said, stabbing the point home, "something like you! But I do not think you've really convinced yourself of that at all." Horace did not answer and when Richard saw that his words had been painful he kept silent. But he could not stop his thoughts: "What a need he has to strip off the civilized clothes off of whites and see their fears; I think that Horace would really hate a healthy person white or black. Ah, God, what a world. A sick world!"

By the next morning, however, Richard believed that he had gotten Horace "a little sober and straight about Dorothy Norman. He suspects now that he made a mistake. Horace and [Richard] [then talked] about Drake, Carter, and the Negro problem, the problem that never ends, the problem that colors and conditions our thoughts and feelings."[6]

Horace returned to Chicago on January 2, to his job as director of the South Parkway Community Center, promising Richard that he would see him toward the end of the month. The two men had agreed that the ideas for a book on the Negro, consisting of essays from black scholars, would not work out and instead, they would publish a magazine. Richard would draw up a prospectus and the two men had already discussed their plans with C. L. R. James, Ralph Ellison, James T. Farrell and Bernard Wolfe, a young writer. All four men had been enthusiastic and Richard and Horace felt certain that it would be relatively simple to raise money for such a publication.

Tension over race relations was at a height in the country. While white America fought a war against Hitlerian notions of inherent racial inferiority, her own black citizens were rioting for the right to serve in unsegregated Army units, give their blood in unsegregated banks, and threatening marches on Washington for the opportunity to work in defense plants. The war was an ideological war fought in defense of democracy. The totalitarian dictatorships in the enemy countries had even made the ideological issue much sharper than it was in the First World War. Fascism and Nazism came to power by means of racial persecution and oppression and to carry on such a war meant that the United States had to stand before the world as the protector of universal brotherhood and the inalienable human freedoms.[7] Sympathy toward Japan, a "colored" nation, was strong among Negro Americans and the logic of their arguments in articles and newspapers was irrefutable.White Americans were beginning to feel the pressure and there was a widespread interest among publishers and charitable foundations toward "Negro books" and causes.

A few days after Horace's departure, Richard took a subway from Brooklyn up to the Bronx. When he got off at the Freeman Station and walked up the hill toward the home of C. L. R. James, he shivered from the cold wind. A heavy snow had fallen the night before and its undercoating was pure ice. When he had climbed the four flights of stairs to his friend's apartment he greeted him warmly. When he said, "What do you say, Nello?" his voice was high and sweetly clear. On his face was an expression of glee mingled with an element of surprise which widened his large eyes slightly and left an impression that he had not seen a loved friend for months instead of two or three days before. After Richard had warmed up with a cup of hot coffee the two men sat down to work out a prospectus for the new magazine. Both took long yellow, blue-lined pads on which to jot down subjects; "Nello" propped himself on the couch—he had an ulcer of the duodenum which was bothering him—and Richard sat in a big white leather armchair, propping his legs at the end of the couch.

In a few hours, Richard had taken voluminous notes; he and James had agreed that the magazine was to be a popular publication which would appeal to the white middle class in an effort to clarify the personality and cultural problems of minority groups, using the Negro as an abstract and concrete frame of reference to reflect a constructive criticism upon the culture of the nation as a whole.

Such a magazine would be a means of "psychoanalyzing" the American middle-class reader, his culture, value assumptions, habits, experiences, and would attempt, without telling him so, to resolve his conflicts, rendering him conscious of his false illusions about race and "subject peoples," about individual lives, and about America's "happiness and success formula." It was hoped that he would be brought face to face with the simple outlines of his culture as it actually was, with the attempt to forge a knowledge of the emotional cost among majorities and minorities alike of what it was to live in America.

The assumptions were broad and essentially optimistic. It was assumed that the individual life experience in a highly industrialized nation did not emotionally sustain or nourish the average American in a dignified, purposeful or enriching manner. It did not provide a ritual of living that administered to his deepest impulses, did not embrace the whole of him, did not create significant forms of living, thereby leaving large areas of his life uncharted and unused.

Such experientially truncated individuals groped crudely toward antisocial, gratuitous, fortuitous, and violent goals in an effort to satisfy the unrecognized and unconscious portions of their lives.

There would be no "preaching" in the articles or feature stories but an attempt to depict what such a lack of balanced living gave rise to in all Americans: mob violence, casual cruelty, adolescent posturing, crime, race hate, gang life, drunkenness, crazy fads, restlessness, cheap movie adoration, cheap pathos, cheap morals, cheap art, cheap journalism, cheap aspirations and inescapable loneliness.

More specifically, there would be fiction, articles, essays, poetry, cartoons, profiles of individuals who lived the "American way" such as Frank Sinatra, Gene Krupa, Frances Farmer; surveys on race tension's popularly written, exerpts of novels that revealed the American scene, studies of crime and criminals, black and white.

What would be the primary assumption of such a publication? It was to be that the Negro problem was the problem of all minorities, and the problems of antisocial individuals were but phases of one overall national cultural problem, a lag in consciousness, a primitive expression of personalities caught in an industrial society whose demands were far beyond the emotional capacities of the people to contain or resolve them. No pleas or begging for justice or rights was to appear in any of the material, but recognizable life problems shared in a degree by both majorities and minorities.

Both men agreed that Negro self-discovery, the facts of Negro life, constituted a great body of facts of importance about Americans in general. And Richard wound up the meeting—in the Negro people was contained, as in a test tube, in embryo, the emotional prefigurations of how a majority of white Americans would act under stress.[8]

A week after their meeting, Wright had drafted an outline for the magazine which listed a hundred and eleven points. His suggested title was *American Pages* with a subtitle: "A magazine reflecting a minority mood and point of view. Nonpartisan, nonpolitical, espousing no current creed, ideology or organization." Every detail was painstakingly outlined: the magazine would be a monthly of 250 to 300 pages, printed double-column, on cheap paper; payment would be made for contributions from writers and artists; it would sell for fifty cents a copy; operating costs per 5,000 copies, exclusive of manuscript payment, office staff and miscellaneous, would be roughly $1,500 to $1,700 each issue.

In part, subjects to be covered were: series on black and white folklore from the South; sections from books of high caliber pending publication, or reprints of entire novels dealing with minority problems; monthly newsletter with field reports on lessening or rising racial tension in the nation and failures or successes of various minority groups; analyses of attitudes of mobs, lynchers, criminals, interviews with participants (not to criticize or attack per se) to reveal the startling fact that a great pleasure was derived from such antisocial behavior. One section would be called "Gallows Humor," a national collection of jokes which Negroes made concerning their plight, their views of whites and reactions to the world scene. A section would be given to simple, illiterate letters from Negroes, whites, or other individuals, revealing their bafflement before the American scene; interviews with foreigners and their initial reaction to the American characteristics; portraits of prizefighters, what actually happened when black and white fighters met in the ring; sex illusions held by Negroes about whites and sex illusions held by whites about Negroes. Critical estimates of fads, crazes of American people and why; articles on the Black Legion, Ku Klux Klan, Father Divine, Penny a Day Movement, Marcus Garvey. Richard knew that many people he knew would willingly write for the magazine: Nelson Algren, James T. Farrell, Robert Rice, Allison Davis, Jack Conroy.

Enthusiasm grew to such a height among the men involved that Richard could not wait until Horace returned at the end of the month. He read him the prospectus by telephone and they discussed the question of raising enough money for the first year's publication. As they compared names it suddenly occurred to Richard that he should go to Chicago, spend a day with Horace, and together they would solve the financial difficulties.

Almost as soon as Richard reached Chicago they went to see Mrs. Clara Florsheim, widow of the shoe manufacturer, outlined their idea and asked for $16,000. Mrs. Florsheim agreed to provide part of that sum but she suggested that they also talk to Marshall Field. If Mr. Field would put up a portion of the amount needed, she would put up the balance. Horace made an appointment with Field, an urbane man, who was interested in their scheme; he had been actively trying to form some type of interracial committee which would seek ways of lessening the nation's racial tensions during the war. He told Richard that his eagerness and enthusiasm were reminiscent of Ralph Ingersoll when he first came to Field for financial backing for the newspaper *P.M.* "Well, fine—I'm like Ingersoll— where's the money?" Richard thought silently to himself as he smiled and veiled his eyes with his lashes. Field promised that he would speak to Richard again when he was in his New York home and the men left hoping for a positive answer soon.

On January 12, Richard was invited to have luncheon at Field's home on Park Avenue. He went, tired and cold, though clear weather had driven away clouds which had hung murkily over the city for a week. Field had not mentioned either money or the magazine over the telephone, and Richard was already certain of a refusal. Well, he was going anyway; he would never give up trying or hoping until hope was dead; and it would be curious to see how the inside of one of the world's richest men's houses looked.

A butler took Richard's coat and hat and a uniformed maid led him toward the drawing room of the baronial house. A discreet hum of voices reached his ears and he knew that it was not to discuss his own project that he had been invited. A fleeting wish that his wife were with him passed through his mind when he observed the decor—was it Victorian? Ellen knew about such things and she had a passion for antiques.

Field had invited a group of Negroes and whites to discuss the formation of a committee which would work toward easing racial friction in the nation. At the table Richard sat next to Marshall Field's lawyer, whose first question was—had the South changed very much since his childhood as described in *Black Boy*. Richard replied that there had been little improvement, that when he had visited his home in 1940 he thought some black men, in certain sections, had a meaningful standard of judgment. To his surprise, the lawyer agreed and from that the discussion ranged wide and long, with everyone at the table eager to hear what Richard had to say.

Secretly amused by the fact that he was sitting at the table of a man who, it had been said, had received five hundred million dollars as his share of the family estate, Richard assumed a slightly diffident manner as coating—to make the pill more palatable—for his words. He began by saying that he, personally, preferred to say that the Negro had succeeded or failed in relation to his assimilation of the highest consciousness that America and the West had to offer. He quoted Gunnar Myrdal, who had written in *An American Dilemma* that making what Negroes experienced known to the American people was one of the most powerful things that could be done to help solve the race question.

Immediately, Field's lawyer interrupted to say that he agreed but then he tried to move the discussion to a more personal plane and asked: "How do Negroes *feel?* I have the feeling that this being a Negro must do something to their gizzards. Living as I live, as a Jew, is hard enough; what must a Negro feel?" A familiar nausea and feeling of disgust came over Richard as he thought—Gosh, how these whites pick and pry and want to know what a black man is feeling. While his emotions burrowed and hid in a recess beneath a bland smile Richard answered noncommittally. He knew that the lawyer and every white person at the table would take away from the luncheon an impression and conviction that he was simply grand! Simple, straightforward and uncomplex!

Looking toward Field, Richard noticed the intensity of his gaze and the smoothness with which he directed the talk back to an impersonal level. The man is keen! thought Richard. Field said that in reports of crime the word Negro should not be deleted; instead, a motive ought to be given—why a black man did this and did that. But the middle-class Negroes at the table argued against him and Richard mused that it seemed that some whites were more willing to admit that black men reacted to their position as black men, with violence and force, than educated Negroes. And he leaped into the argument on the side of Field, attempting to show how adverse crime stories could be turned to the black man's advantage. He was argued down and retreated thinking that they were willing to surrender their most potent psychological weapon—"Oh, God help us black people to be strong and brave; give us courage and knowledge!" It was a silent prayer to himself for strength and will. There was nothing to be gained in continuing a black-versus-black argument and he turned the discussion against the white man. Deliberately, though sweetly, fully cognizant that Field represented the men he would single out as illustrative of the falsity and failure of American democracy, he spoke to the millionaire.

"America had a creed of equality, something which Americans were growing progressively afraid and ashamed of, and national life had grown into opposition to that creed. The essence of Americanism, in distinction to all other lands of the earth, was a concept of human freedom. Other nations conceived of freedom in terms of wages, politics—only America stated it in terms of the individual, the personality, dignity and rights of man. Such a conception was revolutionary: one could not be for human freedom unless you were for freedom not only of peoples from oppression but freedom between and among people. America exported the most glorious things in history, revolutionary ideas, ideas that swept the earth and affected human life everywhere. But those ideas were being quoted by rich people against those who sought to free man. The ideals of the nation had become progressively cheapened but so slowly cheapened that most people were not aware of it. What had been thought of once as personality development, character, and freedom were replaced by ideas and words of commodities. All the emphasis was on comfort.

"And the poor men who came to America's shores to make their own free way were Protestants and they felt that if they made their way it was proof of God's blessing upon them. Wealth in America had no sense of guilt; Henry Ford really thought that his auto plant was a finger of God; Rockefeller thought that God showed him where the oil was; hence when Ford entered politics it was in league with fascists like Lindberg who he thought could help him keep his gold and reinforce his notion that it came from God. If all Americans were rich there would be no trouble with what had become a split vision; but the rich felt that God gave them their riches and the poor kept believing in the pristine ideals out of which the nation was born; those millions in a life-and-death struggle took their sanction from the most valued ideals in the history of the world. One compulsion in the nation was to spread the ideals of democracy everywhere, but secretly the rich felt that the poor were not deserving, were not God-blessed, because they had nothing. Hull, the ex-Secretary of State, was an example of one view: spread the word of democracy everywhere. That was the old Baptist view. Stettinius' view was 'we got it, and we're going to keep it and by keeping it we are obeying the will of God Almighty himself.' Across this fog the voice of the Negro cuts, crying out for freedom in its original sense—for he never had a chance to get it; freedom for growth, for personality, for a chance at life."*

After lunch, Field led the way back to the drawing room and June Blythe opened the meeting with a speech which described what the committee could do to help better race relations. Idly, with one ear tuned toward the speech, Richard looked around at the urbane and sophisticated group. Well-dressed, well-mannered, their voices never rose above the accepted level. They called people together to see what could be done; they formed councils, committees, and organizations, they honestly want to do something, their hearts are in the right place; they say it must be hell to be a Negro; this and that should be done; and then they wind up with nothing changed. The main problem of shunting Negroes into a separate life was not really touched, it was skirted always in thought and feeling. Death meted out to black men between sips from a delicate glass.

Richard was surprised to find that June Blythe had omitted all mention of churches or religion from her presentation. It seemed impossible that it could happen so he spoke again, although he had not wanted to: such a committee should contact bishops, priests, ministers, and then Richard slipped while looking directly at Marshall Field. He said, "Yes, let's get in touch with these, these [he could not find the right word to designate the power of the men of

---

* The preceding account of Richard's discussion with Field is from conversations with the author and his Diaries.

the cloth] and [he] said, 'These Tycoons of Mysticism!' And the room rocked [with laughter]."

After four hours of discussion the meeting ended and Richard walked down Park Avenue toward Grand Central Station, where he would catch a train to Brooklyn. He was exhausted and drained by a sense of futility: Americans had evolved a subtle magic, a folklore of race relations; his sitting through four hours of "race talk" by both white and blacks was ample proof. What evasion; what fear; what lies; what meaningful silences. Could those have been the sons of the men who built the nation? Never had he seen so many gilded, polite, smooth lies and evasions! He became convinced that the problem would be met only when the liberal and kind whites were out of the way, when their fear reached the point where no Negro could meet a white in his drawing room. Whites were afraid! They were willing to be told something, to feel something, and it was all going to waste. "Oh, speed the day when . . . the black people, together with millions of outraged whites will be willing and ready to settle scores!"

XVII

"What a hell of a thing it is to ask a man to die a Jim Crow death, to give his blood only to have it segregated. I wonder how and why Negroes stand for it?," Richard said to his wife while he was dressing to appear with Red Barber and Bessie Beaty on WOR-Radio in March, 1945. He had accepted the invitation from the station because he was curious to learn what Barber was going to say about the war.

At the station, Richard sat quietly and watched a crew of workmen make preparations for the program; a red light was burning and the men had been cautioned not to speak. Barber had come in hurriedly, red hair ruffled, with the faint air of a man's world, baseball games and stadiums about him, a frank, nonchalant consciousness that he was an important person. All Richard's appreciation of Barber disappeared when he began to make his radio speech and in a Southern drawl spoke glowingly of the great Red Cross, its fairness and justice as an organization. There was no mention that the same just Red Cross was refusing to accept "black" blood. When a man in the control booth pointed a precise finger, his eyes on a clock, at Wright he spoke briefly of black and white relations in the South and avoided mention of the war. But after the program he turned to Barber and reminded him that when Charles R. Drew, a black man, who had perfected the blood-bank technique, had offered his services to the Red Cross he was refused. He then organized a blood-bank service for the British government, early during the war, while the Red Cross continued to turn away black would-be donors. Barber answered evasively and Richard felt disgust; above everyone, a newspaper man should know the facts; it was his job.

A few months earlier, in January, Richard had gone up to see L. D. Reddick, curator of the Schomburg Collection in Harlem. Swearing Richard to secrecy and a promise not to use the material in an article, Reddick had shown Richard a massive collection of letters received from Negro servicemen. All of an entire afternoon in the library gloom Richard sat hunched under a reading light going through the anguished letters:

"Reading the letters was horrible, a sea of despair to swim in. A wail, a cry . . . for not in one letter was a ghost of an idea as to how they could get out of their situation." One man wrote, "I feel deeply and sincerely that the most important roles Negroes are playing in this war are that of hostages to prevent Hitler, Goebbels and company from using our omission from the war effort as propaganda. The longer I stay in the service, I wonder why in hell we criticize Hitler and his Jew-eliminating technique. . . ." Another young man explained his feelings: "I'm not a coward, I never was one. I'm not afraid to fight when I find something worth fighting for. But this much I know: If the so-called democracies win this war they do not intend to do the right thing any more than the Axis. Right now, the English are exploiting more colored people than Hitler is exploiting white people. Even if England wins the war how willing are they to give democracy to colored people? How willing is America to give full measure of democracy to the millions of poor people, white and black, in this country?" A bitter young man wrote to his mother: "I've finally ended up in the South, and I suppose you've guessed the answer. I don't like it. We arrived here Saturday; and I had my first experience of what the South was like when two of my friends and I went to the Post Theatre yesterday afternoon. They have about 10 rows of seats reserved in the rear of the theatre for Negroes. And some of the people look at you as if they'd never seen a Negro before. At the main PX and cafeteria they don't want to serve you. If what I've already experienced is any example of southern ways, I think I'd just as soon be overseas, or dead, than to stay down here."[1]

A few days after he had read the letters from black servicemen Richard described their contents to Ralph Ellison, who was serving as a cook in the Merchant Marine. Ralph had sought to enlist in the Navy Band in 1942 but enlistments had been temporarily suspended —at least for trumpet players who would serve in Negro bands. And Ralph—who often felt as if he were ten years older than Richard rather than the other way around, because of his permanent sense of outrage at each new example of injustice—listened avidly while Richard told him of a group of seventy-one Negroes who had been indicted for treason for mutiny by the Army and each sentenced twenty or thirty years. Another story which worried Richard was that there were instances where Negro and white crew members had fought one another on the high seas; ". . . in some instances the naval gun crews [had] threatened the whites and blacks with their guns to keep them from rioting while carrying cargoes to the war zones." Richard was furious: "Why does not the country call off the war with Germany and concentrate singlemindedly on Japan, a nation whom they can hate without reservation for they are colored? I think that the average white man would fight Japan for fun."

On January 22, Richard felt gloomy and somewhat restless, even though the afternoon was sunlit, so when Ralph telephoned, in a highly nervous state and said that he had received induction papers for the Army despite Merchant Marine affiliation, he asked him to come over in the evening. Gloom and restlessness vanished—this was a crisis, something would have to be done, Ralph could not serve in a Jim Crow Army. But at the same time Richard felt that it was Ralph's fault that he was in a mess; he should not have waited so long to let people know of his nervous stomach and low blood pressure. He was trapped; if he left the merchant ship because of tension, the Army would take him and he would be segregated! Richard completely forgot that Ralph had tried to enlist in the Navy Band; all that he could think of was that his friend's life was once again being decided and coerced because of racial identity.[2] He kept thinking and worrying until he came up with a solution. If there were justifiable cause, he might be able to get him a "psychiatric out" through his friend Dr. Fredric Wertham. Wertham would not be compromising his medical integrity because of the state of Ralph's health.

At about seven o'clock, Ralph arrived; a pallor lay under the natural light tan of his face, and his large eyes appeared sunken. To Richard, he seemed faintly bent, the merest curve in his body, as if protecting himself from pain. His own stomach contracted in sympathy and, feeling a real flash of pain, he took up the bottle of tablets on his desk and chewed Amphojel, washing it down with sips of water. Ralph was explaining what had happened: he had actually received induction papers but he was not going into a Jim Crow Army—he would get a ship and go to sea before they came for him.[3] Richard told him of his plan for a psychiatric excuse and Ralph "was fascinated with the idea . . ." Although Richard doubted that he would try for it. "He's too scared." But Ralph agreed to let him call his friend and Richard picked up the telephone and dialed the number of Dr. Wertham.

Wertham agreed to talk with Ralph but cautioned Richard that it would be unethical if he was already consulting another psychiatrist. If that were the case he would not see him at all. While Richard listened, a vague memory stirred—one of his friends was consulting a woman psychiatrist; was it Ralph? Horace? Ellison had never been under psychiatric care and a tentative appointment with Dr. Wertham was arranged for later in the week. After Ralph's departure Richard sank exhaustedly into a chair. He was worried and upset; would there be reasons strong enough to keep Ralph out of the Army? An anger toward his friend arose momentarily. It was Ralph's fault. He should not have waited so long without doing anything for himself. Then Richard wondered whether he was asking anything unethical from his friend Dr. Wertham. Ah well, he reassured himself, Wertham would simply examine Ralph and tell the truth about his condition.

Richard later helped Dr. Wertham to found the Lafargue Clinic* in Harlem in 1945 with the aid of Earl Brown, a *Life* magazine writer; Marion Hernandez, district secretary of the Hannah Stone Center of the Planned Parenthood Foundation; and pastor Shelton Hale Bishop of St. Philips Episcopal Church. Ralph had brought Reverend Bishop into the project and secured two basement rooms of the parish house for the clinic. Prior to the establishment of the clinic there was no available psychiatric service for Harlem's mentally ill except at Bellevue Hospital.

The thin, long-headed and long-faced Wertham named the treatment he wanted to give "Social Psychiatry."[4] He was convinced that a psychiatrist had to understand a patient's economic and community life before he could treat him with any degree of success. Richard had been drawn into friendship with Wertham because they both believed that a Negro was an exaggerated American—his problems were the problems of all other people only more naked and obvious because of oppression. There was not a breath of "charity" in Wertham's approach to Harlem nor did he want to "study" Negroes; he merely wanted to be a physician to those who needed his care. Born in Bavaria, Wertham attended schools in Europe and then taught psychiatry for seven years at Johns Hopkins in Baltimore. That had been his first experience with the Southern mentality, but when he came to New York he told Richard that the psychiatric problems of Negroes were more serious in the North than in the South. "The exploitation of Negroes in the South is a very direct and

* Named for the French Negro M.D.

brutal one. In the North, it is very insidious—half concealed—and in the long run really much more ruthless and deadly."[5]

Richard had still not made up his mind whether or not it had been "ethical" to draw Wertham into Ralph's problem, but as he prepared for bed he decided that it had been the only step to take. During the night he tossed and turned, arose the next morning still troubled. Before sitting down to breakfast he telephoned Ralph and asked him to call as soon as he had been examined.[6] Four days later, on January 26, Richard was still worried that Ralph might have to enter a Jim Crow Army. He went to his desk and sat down at the typewriter to write in his diary:

Again I say that each and every Negro, during the last 300 years, possesses from that heritage a greater burden of hate for America than they themselves know. . . . Perhaps it is well that Negroes try to be as unintellectual as possible, for if they ever started really thinking about what happened to them they'd go wild. And perhaps that is the secret of whites who want to believe that Negroes really have no memory; for if they thought that Negroes remembered, they would start out to shoot them all in sheer self-defense. So I say that when a white man kills a Negro he is acting right and when a Negro kills a white man that it is not killing at all. Yes, there must be a lot of blood shed in this nation between whites and blacks before it is over. Perhaps the killing may not be directly between whites and blacks, but that will play a part, a motor part in whatever happens. The Negro will be so spurred that some whites will welcome him into their ranks for encouragement in what they are trying to do. Who will tap this pit of red-hot lava?

Within a month or so Ralph sailed again on a Merchant Marine ship and when he returned in a short while he was released from service. He had received a Rosenwald Fellowship the previous winter and left for Vermont, where he began work on *Invisible Man*.

On January 30, the telephone rang and when Richard picked it up a voice which sounded like that of a Negro or a Southern male identified itself as "Coleman of the War Department Military Intelligence." It was urgent that he speak to Richard about a confidential matter and it would have to be that day. An appointment was made for "within an hour" and while he waited Richard wondered whether the visit had anything to do with Ralph and the Army, but decided no. It was probably connected to his association with Paul Robeson and the recordings they had been making for broadcast to the Southwest Pacific. He and Robeson and Carlton Moss wanted to build a Negro broadcasting unit for the Office of War Information and eventually produce a film which would give a true picture of Negro life in the Army.

Coleman, a white man, arrived promptly and Richard asked to see his credentials before taking his coat and hat. When they sat down, Richard heard the wind howl outside in a cold fury, and Coleman clasped his hands as if to warm them. A fleeting impulse to give the gray-eyed man some hot coffee for warmth, as he would have offered to anyone else, checked itself abruptly: No! Let the sonofabitch freeze; he was nothing but a cop; worse than a cop, he was a spy! Snooping in people's lives. . . . Outwardly at ease, calmly smiling, Richard waited to hear what the man had to say.

Coleman glanced at Richard shrewdly behind a casual smile, his pale eyes grave, and asked if he knew Ralph Waldo Emerson Ellison, and what was his association with the Communists. Wheeew! Richard thought to himself, that's easy; there was nothing to hide in that direction. Ellison was not, and never had been, a member of the Party, he told Coleman. It appeared to Richard that Coleman received the information somewhat indifferently and he was suddenly on guard again. "What about Carlton Moss?" the man shot at Richard. "Now, we know that he is a Communist and we know that you are working on some project with him right now." Whatever he was occupied with at the moment, Richard told Coleman, had nothing at all to do with Communists; he had dissociated himself from the Party years before, in a public statement.[7] He knew nothing of what they were doing and he would not answer any questions about people who had once been friends. He was not a stool pigeon and under no conditions could he be forced to become one. Then Richard launched into his own ideas about the Negro in the United States and referred to his own writings; he "was afraid Coleman might ask him questions about real and important Communists whom he knew were in confidential government positions."

That same evening Richard was startled to hear loud voices in the hallway and, going to the door, he stuck his head out to see what was happening. Just outside his door were two Negro men in uniform. They appeared drunk and as soon as they caught sight of Richard they told him that they were Military Police and demanded entrance to his apartment. When Richard asked why, and barred their way, they shouted that they were looking for a girl who had stolen some money and intended to search for her in every apartment in the building. When he was unable to quiet the men by talking to them reasonably, and they wanted to fight, he escaped into his apartment and called the police. Looking at his watch and waiting nervously, he noted that the police car arrived just four and one-half minutes after his call.

After the soldiers were put into the police car, one of the officers came to Richard's door and explained that one of the men did not have a draft card and that both were drunk; they would take them to the station house and then notify the Army.

As soon as the car pulled away from the curb Richard had a feeling of guilt. He hated to report the men but asked himself, "What can one do? These men, inflamed with a sense of outrage and injustice and lit with alcohol, what will they not do? Of course, they'll only resent life more by being taken away, I don't know. . . ."

By the following morning Richard was wondering whether or not the visit of Coleman in the afternoon and two Negro Military Police in the evening were related. It was very mysterious and oddly exciting. Abruptly, his mood changed from tingling excitement at the thought of government intrigue to disgust, verging on despair, at how much time and energy and money were spent in meaningless directions. He was almost convinced that an elaborate drama had been played at his doorstep the day before. And for what? Anything he had to say *they* could read in his books or hear in his lectures. Why was not the same power and single-minded concentration toward the pursuit of "Reds" utilized toward making America the land of her professed ideals; and to spring the black man, and all other men, from the pitiless steel trap of their lives.

Why were his countrymen so blind? Why could they not see life as it *was?* "The very conditions of life that bred Hitler were not acknowledged for what they were: Seed-beds of revolution. And it [was] doubtful if a war—costing 55,000,000 casualties, war with all of its terrible and bloody immediacy, [had] made what the *real* reality [was] real for them . . . Hitler saw and cynically exploited the weak spots in . . . society perhaps more skillfully than any politician of modern times."

"Why!" Richard thought, history would "no doubt dub the Hitlerites the most devastating critics of our disorganized industrial order, not even excepting the Bolsheviks of 1917!

"Hitler knew his industrial slums, knew the brutalized millions trapped in them, knew their hungers, knew their humiliations, knew the feverish longing of their hearts.

"Capitalists hated Hitler for his wholesale, gratuitous murders; but they hated him for another and subtler reason: They hated him for revealing the shaky, class foundations of their society, for reminding them of their sundered consciousness, for flaunting their hypocrisy, for sneering at their hesitations, for manipulating their racial hatreds to a degree that they had never dared."[8]

Only the American South dared; only it had manipulated its white citizenry with the hope-symbols man could not forever live without; made it feel a chosen people; gave it the black man for a victim; all the while it kept it ignorant and poor for easy exploitation by the Southern rulers.

And all over America Hitler was tied in a neat psychological package: "Well, they say, you know, the Germans are a people who just love and crave order. They want a master. They want somebody to tell them what to do. They are natural born sadists. That's why they had fascism in Germany. . . . When you try to tell them that what happened in Germany is but the stage of crisis of a certain degree in the development of the process of industrialization, and that every country must face that crisis when it comes and that the old basis for living is gone, and the fascism and communism and all other isms are clumsy attempts to find a new basis and principle for living, for reorganizing human relations, they become terribly scared and feel that you are against God and home and country."[9]

Richard told his friends over and over that "there was a danger of America collapsing in a panic when she faced the problem of the Negro—as she really had to some day—just as Europe collapsed when she faced the problem of the Jew."

In the heart of industrial America was a surviving remnant, perchance a saving remnant of a passion for freedom, a passion fanned by a national humiliation, for "American Negroes, with but minor exceptions, still believe in the hope of economic rewards; still believe in justice, liberty, the integrity of the individual."[10]

One afternoon, Richard went into Manhattan to see the documentary film *Triumph des Willens*, which showed the rise of Fascism and "the 'joy' that Hitler gave (while Himmler burned the dissenters!) millions of his duped followers. What vital images flickered across the screen! What limpid faith, what completeness of living! But, as [he] watched the tragedy of men being cynically betrayed unto death, [he] wondered if men who love life would lead the next 'wave of the future,' or would haters like Hitler? [He] could not answer with certainty."

A week or so later, Richard's mind was preoccupied with an introduction to *Black Metropolis*, which he had promised to write for his friend Horace. As a theme, the film *Triumph des Willens* arrived in his mind as buoyed on a wave, with drossing off of everything extraneous. The idea came with such force and clarity that he half considered sitting down at his typewriter at once, although it was late in the day. But he felt tired; the paragraphs would germinate and begin to shape themselves in his mind during the evening; then, in the early morning, when he was fresh, he could hammer out five or six pages.

Walking to the window, he looked out at the street; spring leaves— so lightly green against New York's steel and concrete—were beginning to open on the still bare tree limbs. After a moment he grew restless: where were Ellen and Julia? Gosh! In three days his daughter would be having a birthday party; how she had grown and so lithe, so gay! So full of life! A faint smile, utterly different from his public expression, came to his lips. Idly, he flicked on the radio. It was April 12. President Franklin Delano Roosevelt had died suddenly at Warm Springs, Georgia, and Harry S Truman had been sworn into office.

Until the announcer repeated the news, Richard sat without moving; he was stunned. He could not believe it! Only the past month he had talked with Mrs. Roosevelt at tea with Dorothy Norman, Mrs. Joseph Lash, and Mrs. Adele Levy, about how to raise funds to keep Wiltwyck, a home for wayward boys, in operation. Poor woman. She must be numbed by shock. And Truman as President! A Southerner!

During the night Richard could not sleep. He felt as if a relative had died and he worried about the changes which would ensue under a Southern-born President.

*To live in this land is to breathe poison
each day . . .*

XVIII

Leaning over his daughter's bed, Richard anxiously felt of her
forehead for the hundredth time. She was so hot; heat rose from her
body, like the aridity of a desert. Slipping his hand under the soft
curls of her neck, he touched moisture and nervously covered Julia
with still another blanket, tucking the pink wool high under her
chin and pressing it down all across her thin shoulders.

Julia laughed and struggled to free her arms. "Lie still, Julia-baby,
you'll feel better soon. Then you can play," Richard murmured. A
frantic thought entered his mind: "My little daughter, my poor Julia-
baby. Oh, I wish we could move out of New York for Julia's sake; or
I wish she could develop a body strong enough to toss off these
infections without our dosing her with sulfa."

Was tonsillitis ever fatal? There was only one bright spot, Richard
thought, ". . . she keeps laughing and talking and singing all the
time. She's so damn well-adjusted that she just won't and can't feel
that anything's seriously wrong." But she was too thin and had one
sore throat after another. What was the cause? Richard worried.
Maybe the long subway journey from Brooklyn to Greenwich Village was a strain on her system. But the Bank Street Nursery School
was the best in the city, he had been told, and Julia was going to have
a good education. Then they would have to move to the Village, near
the school; Julia would gain weight. Such a move would be good for
Ellen as well. She had too many colds too; and she did not know how
to take care of herself.

A few weeks before, she had complained of "feeling a little fluish"
one morning and then the very next day had waited in the snow for

235

an hour for a bus. "Her feet were so cold that they ached her. She waited an hour just one block from a subway station, but she would not tell [Richard] why she did not go to the subway! She [was] lovely and strange and helpless sometimes."[1] Richard could not understand a woman's psychology; if he had been freezing he would have crossed the street and gone into a drugstore or something. When he asked Ellen why she did not do that she would not answer. "Why do women resist doing things that are good for them?" he wondered. Ah well, it was his job to look after these most prized possessions; they belonged to him and he would take good care of his family.

"Ellen!" Richard called enthusiastically. "Let's pack. We're going to move!" After he had explained how much healthier it would be for Julia to live near her nursery, his wife laughed and protested: "But Richard, there's a housing shortage! How are we going to find an apartment?" He would take care of it, leave it to him, Richard assured Ellen. And as soon as Julia's temperature became normal he went to see his editor at Harper and asked him if he knew of an apartment in Greenwich Village. A few calls were made and an apartment of four rooms, just off Washington Square, at 82 Washington Place, was found for the Wrights. Their new landlord, a Jew, defied the racial prejudice in the Village and gave Richard a large four-room apartment on the third floor of his building.[2] By November 1, 1945, Richard had settled his family into the apartment just off 6th Avenue.

After living for a month in the Village Richard and Ellen decided to look for a house to buy; it was a convenient area; after Bank Street they would enter Julia in the Little Red Schoolhouse; black faces were tolerated on all except a few Italian-populated blocks; and Richard felt safe; he could go into most places to eat or drink. Except for the usual tension in his stomach when entering a new restaurant, he felt fairly certain that he would not be insulted or that they would not put salt in his coffee to indicate that no Negroes were served. And on Sullivan Street, down a few stairs in a basement, was a good restaurant run by a large friendly West Indian woman named "Connie." The food was delicious and Richard could meet black friends and white radicals in the dark little room, lighted by candles. There, no one stared; if they did, Connie would diplomatically indicate that they were not welcome. She would not stand any nonsense from ill-mannered bigots. It was true that one problem, an aggravating one, remained: Richard still had to travel either to Brooklyn or to Harlem for a haircut. No barber in the Village would cut "Negro" hair.[3]

In the West Village, on Charles Street, just off Greenwich Avenue, Richard found a large red brownstone house which was for sale at a cash price of $17,500. He walked joyfully home and darted up the stairs to the third floor on Washington Place to get Ellen. He led her at a rapid walk to the corner of Greenwich and Charles, turned left, then slowed to a stroll like any couple out for an afternoon in the Village. They paused for a minute in front of El Charro, a Spanish nightclub and restaurant that was almost directly across from the big brownstone. Afraid then that someone would look out the window and wonder why a black man was staring at the house, Richard moved on slowly up the short block until they reached 7th Avenue. He would risk one more glance at the house so he crossed the street and sauntered slowly past the red building again. As Ellen's enthusiasm for the brownstone grew, Richard felt topful of excitement. Let's buy it, he told his wife.

But buying a house was not easy for a black man—even one as famous as Richard Wright. First, Salzmann, his attorney, examined the building in the company of a construction expert and found that it was in good condition and worth the asking price. Then he sounded out the owners without revealing his client's name and discovered that they would not sell to Negroes. So Salzmann suggested to Richard that he draw up papers for a corporation which would make the purchase and then neither owners nor tenants in the building could attack him when he moved into one floor of the house.

Reluctantly at first, and then defiantly, Richard decided to play "the dirty tricks of the American game." There was no other choice and he remembered that the owner of the building in which he was then living had hidden behind a corporate identity.

"So will I hide and then let the white neighbors howl, and I'll say . . . the corporation says that I could have this house and you try and pry me out of it. Of course, we'll own the corporation. Hot Dog! American life is a game of lie and steal and graft and racketeering. . . . I'm an American Negro; I feel that I want to live like other people live; I respond to life as others do; I do not know how to do otherwise. But I'm forbidden to act on my own best impulses; so, in order to act upon them, I must practice the tricks which American businessmen practice. To live in this land is to breathe poison each day and hour of the day. God, I hate this, but I'm going to do it and all hell cannot stop me! Such is the divided soul that rules the American Negro. Such is the war that sets up in our souls when we react honestly to American life. Why should I live in a black belt area and be cheated like all other Negroes are cheated;

why cannot I live where there are good schools for Julia and stores that carry good food at reasonable prices; why should I live in a black belt and pay a premium for being born black! I'll be damned if I'll do it!"[4]

Still another problem arose; Salzman called Richard one morning to say that not one bank in the Village would give a Negro a mortgage for that area. For a few weeks it seemed as if everything would fall through and Richard worried; he was afraid that someone else would purchase the house before he could surmount all the racial obstacles. Through a private individual, and without revealing Richard's identity, Salzman got him a partial first mortgage of $8,000, which left a sum of $3,500 to be raised.

Finally, through his agent, Paul Reynolds, Jr., Richard was able to get a bank loan with his Harper contracts as security. The arrangements took most of the day but by five o'clock Richard had signed the last paper and hurried home. Julia was playing in the snow in front of the house, busy digging at a mound with a new shovel; she smiled abstractedly when her father greeted her with the news—"We're going to have our own house, Julia-baby!" Richard called from the street:

"Ellen! Ellen!"

Ellen came running down the stairs and Richard kissed her: "I got it!"

"The whole amount?"

"Yes, darling!"

Arms entwined, they went upstairs to their apartment to prepare dinner and while they worked together in the kitchen Richard looked at his wife:

"She is so happy! Yet she gets terribly tense, too . . . poor little Ellen darling is so happy and tense that she is developing a headache." Richard made his wife take two aspirins: "I, too, am tense," he thought to himself.

Two weeks after contracts were signed for the new house a fire engulfed the building next door, at 11 Charles Street; and when Richard heard the news over the radio he jumped from a chair, seized his coat and almost ran to his new house. Anxiously, he paced back and forth on the block until he was satisfied that there had been no damage to the building he owned. Sometimes a sense of estrangement from himself and his environment overcame him when he looked at the building: it was hard to believe that he was really going to own a building and live in Greenwich Village. And so far, neither he nor Ellen had put one foot inside the door of their brownstone.

They had to wait and pore over floorplans until the title search was completed so that they could move in.

On March 8, Salzman and his wife stopped by to tell the Wrights that everything had been completed: they could move into their new home. He gave Richard a list of the people to whom he would be landlord and among them was listed Franklin Folsom on the top floor of the building. Richard was floored: Folsom was a staunch Communist, executive secretary of the League of American Writers and an ex-friend. What would be his reaction when he learned that Richard was his new landlord? A day or so later, Salzman told Richard that Folsom had threatened a rent strike when he learned that he was moving into the building. Two of the tenants had paid their rent but three had not in support of Folsom. But Salzman served a dispossess notice and the furore ended.

At the end of March, a letter arrived addressed to Ellen; it was an offer of $20,000 for the brownstone—$2,500 more than they had paid a few weeks before. A low dirty throat-laugh escaped Richard's lips but it really was not funny, he thought: "Fate, look here at this and do your worst! Goddammit, we're going to live at 13 Charles Street. We ain't smiling at you Fate, we're grinning through tightly shut teeth. . . ."

While negotiating for the house on Charles Street Richard was involved in a different, though complicated, manuever to purchase a 241-acre farm in northern Vermont. The property was only $1,800 and would serve as a summer home and winter hideaway for Richard while writing fiction. A down payment was made on the farm in addition to fees for a title search but the latter was torturously entwined in the life of an ex-Broadway actress, Mrs. Watkins. "Why do I meet so many weird people?" Richard wondered, when he learned the actress' problems with the Vermont property.

Mrs. Watkins' husband, a New Jersey policeman, owned a 241 acre farm in northern Vermont; he fell behind in taxes, and she paid the taxes and it was transferred to her. Her policeman husband died, and right off Mrs. Watkins . . . up and marries a young—what she thought was—socialist —who, as soon as he was married to her asked her for some property in his name. She gave him the Vermont farm and had the title registered in his name. He was much younger than she was and was said to have leanings toward spiritualism. Anyway, it [was then] said that he was an undercover Communist. What he was, nobody will perhaps ever know. But when the war in Spain broke out, he joined the Abraham Lincoln Brigade and went off, but first he transferred the title of the Vermont farm back to Mrs. Watkins. Mrs. Watkins got word from the Abraham

Lincoln Brigade that he had gone into action, had been taken prisoner, and was presumably dead. Then Mrs. Watkins wanted to sell her Vermont property, but was told that it was not hers completely unless she could prove that her husband was dead. No court would accept the word of the Abraham Lincoln Brigade, and the Brigade went to fight in Spain against the laws of our country, hence there's no official proof that her husband was dead, no legal proof.[5]

So the sale of the farm to Richard was not consummated and he often wondered whether or not it was ever agreed that Mr. Watkins was dead or alive.

Temporarily, Richard gave up his plans for a country home but the desire persisted, overcame him to a degree that again he longed for quiet, rolling landscapes. He was "fed up" with asphalt; ". . . though city living, by draping about the Negro a cloak of semi-anonymity, offers him his best haven from the grosser forms of race prejudice, affords him a somewhat negative protection. But, when an American Negro harbors a yearning for a landscape, it wisely behooves him to choose with care, for, for him, most American landscapes have been robbed of the innocence of their sylvan beauty by the fact that almost every lynching in American history has taken place in such an arcadian setting. To go South, then, was unthinkable. The West Coast, with its 'fruits' and 'nuts,' held no appeal . . . Where, then, could a Negro go? New England! That was it! Had not the dauntless Abolitionists risen in that transcendentalistic atmosphere? Had not Hawthorne, Emerson, and Thoreau sprung from that stubborn but free Yankee soil?"[6]

By chance, Richard discussed his desire to buy a home in New England with two white friends who lived in Hanover, New Hampshire. They were delighted at the prospect of having him for a neighbor and placed their home at his disposal as a base from which to look for a piece of property. Gratefully, Richard accepted.

New Hampshire greeted him magnificently. A lemon-colored sun made the snow-carpeted, plunging hills gleam. When he stepped off the train into the pure, bracing air Richard took a deep breath, almost dizzied by the unlimited visibility. A deep silence permeated the valley in which he stood and all around were tall green pines. This was what he needed, an immense indifference of nature, a neutrality.

Two days later, Richard had found a "dream house" just across the New Hampshire state line. It was a study, roomy, wooden house; and it was empty. The nearest neighbor was at least half a mile distant. At first glance Richard wanted the house. It was simply perfect; and he stood on its front porch already imagining his daughter playing in the yard or running under the trees to watch whatever wildlife might appear. Ellen could search the area for antiques and they would make it into a real home. He'd buy it—cash.

Richard drove to the real estate office and spoke to the agent in charge. At first glance the man appeared friendly but when Richard explained what he wanted the man scratched his chin, smiled, and said:

"All right, . . . I'll communicate with the owner and let you know."

"But I thought the house was for sale," [Richard] said. [He] sensed an air of disquiet in him.

"Oh, it's simply routine," the man answered.

"When will you let me know?" Richard pressed. He fought against a familiar dread and tried not to leap to conclusions.

"In a couple of days, . . . I'll phone you."

In the home of his host, Richard waited in front of a blazing fire, reading and waiting to hear from the agent. Four days passed. When he called the man he was told, "No word yet."

Richard ". . . became fairly certain that the dreadful issue of 'race' was lurking somewhere amidst those lovely, snow-clad New England hills."

[Finally Richard asked his host to visit the real estate agent and find the truth. When he returned to the house Richard knew what had happened before he spoke. The man's face held a look of shock as if there had been a cessation of all emotion.] "A curious, sensitive scene followed, a scene which has haunted American history for 300 years. . . . A white man was wrestling with his conscience because he had to tell a Negro something which he knew would cause that Negro pain."[7]

His host's agony made Richard speak quickly, keeping his voice casual as if it were not important. He assured him that he knew the white owner did not want to sell to a Negro, but that he should not be too upset by the episode. This was "normal" in the life of a Negro American.

Next day on the train for New York Richard mentally reviewed all the complications of a black man's life; the simplest, most ordinary tasks were always thrown out of proportion. One's energy was always being drained away in meaningless preoccupation with routine procedures that a white man never had to think about at all. Ah, God, he was tired of democracy and the "will of the people."

Dear Richard,

It is obvious that you and I are the only two geniuses of this era . . .

—Gertrude Stein

XIX

At seven, one freezing morning the very end of December, 1945, the telephone rang and Richard, who had been at his desk working since six, swore to himself as he snatched up the instrument. It would awaken Ellen and Julia. Dammit! Some day he would live without a telephone! It never ceased to ring—but 7 A.M. was too much!

Richard said hello but all he heard in return was a crackling static sound. After a moment or two he heard the voices of two operators and realized that it was a long-distance call. Finally, a voice, speaking in an accent he could not immediately recognize, asked him to hold the phone; a member of the French government wished to speak with him. Richard was too startled to react or even wonder why he was being honored by a foreign official so early in the morning.

Numbly, and hardly breathing, Richard waited until a Frenchman spoke to him, identified himself as a member of the government, and then invited him to visit France as a guest of that country. It was weird! He and Ellen had been studying French in private lessons for the past month hoping one day to visit—it was as if they had read his mind! Bursting with excitement he said to the French official: "It's not possible!" which meant that the invitation was accepted and that it was one of the most unexpected and wonderful of surprises in his life. A few perfunctory sentences were spoken by the Frenchman but Richard was half listening, the connection was poor, and the man's accent was difficult to understand.

As soon as he hung up the telephone Richard bounced from the chair and hurried into the bedroom. Ellen was awake, sitting up against the pillows, and Richard sat on the edge of the bed, put his arms around her in a hard squeeze: "We're leaving for France! Let's pack! We're invited as guests of the French government!"

Richard and Ellen packed their suitcases, made arrangements to take Julia out of nursery school, applied for passports and made reservations on the S.S. *Brazil,* an unconverted troopship. And they waited for an official invitation from the French government. Weeks went by. Each day Richard watched out of the third-floor window for the postman and was waiting at the mailbox by the time he reached their building. But still no invitation came from France.

A cold spring engulfed New York and Richard continued to wait; the first weeks he had riffled through his voluminous mail, watching eagerly for a French stamp or a heavy seal-embossed envelope. Gradually tension began to build and he alternated between optimism and despair. By nature and conditioning he always lived at the edge of his nerves, and waiting was something which made him feel unsteady.

In the mail one morning was a notice from the Passport Division of the State Department. Richard was stunned. His application for a passport had been rejected on the grounds that conditions in postwar Europe were so bad that the government feared that United States citizens would become stranded. Fighting off a feeling that more was involved in the rejection, Richard promptly sent a letter to Washington indicating that since his earnings had been in excess of $30,000 the previous year and would be still higher in 1946, there was no danger that he would be stranded in Europe. A week later the State Department sent a reply; the answer was still no.

When Richard consulted his lawyer he was told that as an American citizen he had no legal right to a passport, that a passport was a privilege given or withheld at the discretion of the Secretary of State or his agents, that the real grounds of that discretion needed not to be divulged, and there was nothing he could do about it. But Richard was determined to go to France. It had been a dream since 1939 and he would not be thwarted. First, Richard went to see his friend Dorothy Norman and asked if he could represent her publication, *Twice a Year,* in France.[1] Mrs. Norman agreed and in addition offered to get in touch with influential friends in Washington who might intervene with the State Department for his passport. Next Richard talked with a French friend, Michel Gorday, the journalist, and his father-in-law, Marc Chagall. They, in turn, made representations to the French government through its cultural attaché, Claude Levi-Strauss. From Paris, Gertrude Stein, to whom Richard had written, promised to use her influence with both American and

French officials. And last, Richard telephoned the man who had tendered an invitation in the name of the government. The Frenchman was astonished. He explained that an invitation had not been sent because Richard had told him: "It's not possible!"

On April 15, the French government sent the invitation to Richard and he was "bowled over" when he saw that they were paying his passage, hotel, and all expenses for three months. Four days before the invitation's arrival the State Department had asked Richard to submit proof that the French would give him a visa before issuing a passport. He had rushed to the office of the French Consulate but the man he wanted to see was away on a honeymoon trip and would not return for another week. So the French invitation arrived just in time and Richard sent it off to Washington, hopeful that at last all problems had been overcome. He did not want to take any chances so he sent it registered airmail, but in his haste and general anxiety he did not keep a copy of the document.

Again Richard waited through long days for a response to his letter: none came. He phoned the Passport Division and after a long delay while they transferred the long-distance call from one official to another Richard was dismayed to learn that his invitation had been "lost." He was baffled. But he telephoned Paris and requested a duplicate invitation be sent. The duplicate was airmailed to Washington and Richard waited. There was no reply. Once more he phoned Washington and was informed that no such invitation had been received. "Take it easy," he said to himself. "You are dealing with the most powerful government on earth. . . ." Dammit, he'd go to Washington and see about the matter. Richard telephoned the Passport Division and said that he was flying down; a suave-voiced man tried to dissuade him but he quietly told him that he was on his way.

Early in the morning on April 29, having lost confidence and most of his optimism, and fully convinced that the government was doing its utmost to keep him from leaving the country, Richard realized that he would have to use whatever influence he could find; he did not believe that the State Department had held up his passport because he had been a Communist. It was because he had written extremely critical books concerning Negro life in America. "After all," he told a friend,[2] "they had just fought a second war to bring democracy to other parts of the world. They did not want anyone to raise questions of freedom for black American citizens."

A few phone calls were made in New York by influential friends and at 9:30 Richard called to see a famous American surgeon who gave him the name of a "contact," a member of a group reputedly sympathetic toward the Fascists, friends of Evelyn Walsh McLean. He wanted a passport and he was, by then, ready to use any means. He was directed to see a "certain man" in Washington. At 11 o'clock the same morning he flew to the capital, met with the friend of McLean's, recited his difficulties, and received his passport one hour later. No questions were asked.

Later the same day, back in New York, Richard received a visa, paid his passage on the ship, which was sailing two days later, and went home exhausted but victorious. Before sinking into a restless sleep that night he smiled to himself at the irony: in Washington the National Gallery had entrusted him with pictures to take to France.

Racial conditioning went deep in Richard; ". . . but, one-half hour after debarking upon French soil, [he] shed it all without a moment's trouble or regret, glad to be shut of a vicious burden of feeling that [he'd] never wanted." "For the first time in my life," Richard said, "I stepped on free soil. If you are not black you will never know how heavy weights seem to fall off your body. . . ."

Richard stood in the corridor looking through the windows of the boat train; he was sorry the weather was cold. He felt a desire to thrust his head into the air of France so that nothing would pass unobserved and he could not wait for a first glimpse of Paris at Gare St. Lazare. How beautiful the countryside was! It was so tidy and cultivated into squares and oblongs and rectangles. Not an inch of land was wasted. An April green was beginning to overlay the winter-dead grass, and in the distance he could see clumps of spiky yellow flowers. As they neared Paris he looked into village streets and here and there, behind an old wall, were the tops of blooming trees—pink or white and sometimes pinkish-white shading to red. Am I really here? . . . this minute, on this spot, here in France where I've always wanted to be? It was hard to believe.

When Richard descended from the boat train, at Gare St. Lazare, he had a moment of complete stupefaction which he concealed by a wide smile. Not only was Gertrude Stein waiting but the American Embassy in Paris had sent a public relations officer, Douglas H. Schneider, with two long sleek limousines to meet him. Also in the group was Maurice Nadeau, writer and editor of *Les Lettres Nouvelles*, an important French publication.

The customs formalities had been taken care of at Le Havre and on the train; and now Schneider directed that the luggage be packed into one of the giant American cars while Richard, Ellen, Julia, Miss Stein, Nadeau, and the cultural attaché went in the other.

Gertrude Stein, dressed in a tweedy brown coat and a hat shaped like a bowler on top of her short gray hair, reminded Richard of an American pioneer, a frontier woman. She had made hotel reservations, for a two-room suite at the Hotel Trianon, for the Wrights, but first, she suggested a drive across the Tuileries Gardens, up the Champs Elysées and back along the quais.

Spring was cold in Paris in 1946, but the chestnut trees along the boulevards drooped red and white blooms, and roses and lilies of the valley scented the pure air. Richard had never imagined such a sky; he had read of the famous Paris light, which the Impressionists struggled to capture, but he gazed in amazement: it was bright and yet not bright; there was a radiance which softly shimmered. "The beauty of Paris and its springtime in blossom amazed him. And Gertrude Stein said to [Schneider], 'Don't you feel the privilege we have in revealing all this to a tender heart?' "[3]

Arriving at Gertrude Stein's, at 5 Rue Christine, for lunch, Richard had seated himself when Julia, catching sight of a childsize Louis XV armchair, darted toward it. A blood-curdling shriek tore the air, stopping Julia and frightening both Richard and Ellen. Alice B. Toklas had darted at Julia, screaming wildly, to prevent her from touching the small chair. It seemed that it was covered in gros-point, embroidered by Alice on an original design by Picasso. Ellen soothed Julia, wondering to herself why they did not loop a rope across the chair, museum-fashion.

After luncheon when the Wrights left Miss Stein's a voluble swarm of newspaper reporters and photographers surrounded the limousine when it stopped in front of Richard's hotel, the Trianon, on Rue Vaugirard just off the Boul' Mich near the Sorbonne Chapel. The reporters greeted him in French and English, almost tumbling over one another for a position beside or in front of him. Wow! Hot Dog!, Richard thought. I feel like a damn movie star! He answered their questions, which were mainly concerned with racism in America, truthfully but without much elaboration.[4] Julia and Ellen were tired and not feeling well and Richard wanted to unpack their bags and get his family settled in their rooms. And he wanted an hour or two in which to examine his impressions of Paris and the exhilaration and sense of freedom coursing in his mind.

The following day, Richard slipped out of the hotel alone; he wanted to walk and he was afraid that there would not be much time left to him in the weeks ahead. Already arranged were receptions, dinners, cocktail parties, interviews, and engagements with Miss Stein as well as with publishers and translators interested in French editions of his books. And as soon as possible Richard wanted to move into an apartment promised by Dr. Sidney Pilage, a Sorbonne professor, who was leaving for a visit to the South Pacific. "Whenever [he] went to a foreign country [he tried] to live like and with the natives. That [was] the only way to learn to know the country. And too [he found] that [he was] more at ease without certain Americans than with them."[5]

Press coverage of his visit was so extensive Richard noticed that people on the street seemed to recognize him. There was an emotional warmth from the French people he had not expected. Everywhere he went, men and women smiled, nodded or sometimes greeted him by name. Feeling a little foolish at first, Richard smiled and murmured: *"Bon jour,"* grateful that he had studied a little French.

Consulting his Michelin, Richard headed in the direction of the Bastille; he wanted to look at Notre Dame. As he strolled alongside the Seine he marveled at a new feeling in his brain which seemed to transmit itself into his legs. They swung along from his hips differently than he could remember ever having happened in his lifetime; there was an effortlessness about their motion. Strictures, no, weights—that was a better word—had lifted from his entire being. Walking in the United States made a black man feel like a puppet, a marionette, as if jerked by invisible white strings—even when he was alone; his nerves were always bunched up by the need to ignore or defend or attack in defense of his personality. French people stared at him when he passed by but it, too, was different than in the United States. Their stares were open, a friendly curiosity; he saw no hint of hostility and he sensed a profound self-confidence which was expressed through an indifference which overlay every expression. He did not bother them! They were not eaten up inside by the fact that he was black and was strolling alongside the Seine. They really did not give a damn about him! What a wonderful country! "I'm at last in Paris, city of my dreams! . . . will I ever be myself again after all this?"

He reached Notre Dame "rising nobly in the warm summer night like a floodlit dream . . ." and sat down on a bench. "Lines, space, harmony softened by dark mists . . ." the church rose above him, its gargoyles rearing less in attack than as if defending the giant, uneven structure. There was more freedom in one square block of Paris than there was in the entire United States. Why was it, Richard wondered, that "some people need more freedom than others, and I'm one of them. Unless I'm uninhibited in letting my instincts range, unhampered in my comings and goings, free to question and probe my environment, I languish, I wither . . . to me, freedom is equated directly to reality, to life; it's not an abstract dream to be realized, an ideal to be worshipped from afar—but life itself, each moment. . . ."[6]

Richard's first months in Paris flowed by smoothly. The Parisian public politeness embued him with a sense of social confidence. The city was all that he had always hoped it would be and there was such an absence of race hate that it seemed unreal. Paris was "truly a gentle city, with gentle manners." When at last he moved into an apartment at 38 Boulevard St. Michel, near the Sorbonne, he began to feel comfortably settled. With the exception of two worried weeks—when Ellen developed appendicitis and was operated on by Army doctors in the American Hospital and Julia developed sudden giant hives and entered the same hospital for observation—Richard was happily in "a state of constant stimulation; every day seemed like the night before Christmas."

In July, at one of the many receptions held in his honor, Richard stopped in the middle of a sentence: a thin man with heavy brows, high cheekbones and burning, hollowed eyes had entered the room. He glanced around and with a flutter of his long cape made his way straight to Richard. "It's Gide!" Richard's mind registered as he stepped forward to meet the great writer. He had a moment before Gide reached him to marvel at the fact that no introductions were needed on either side and he felt humble and a little proud. "Gide was an honest man and a superb craftsman." The two writers fell into conversation as if they had been continuing a conversation on a previous day. Gide was eager to hear of Richard's experiences in the Communist Party and then to discuss the "white assassins of the dignity of black men in America."[7] Toward the end of their discussion Richard described the sense of freedom he had felt since he had been in France. And with a Frenchman's pride in his nation Gide smiled and said that "The more uncivilized the white man, the more he fears and hates all those who differ from him."

During July Richard had long talks with Gertrude Stein. They had become friends by mail. After she had read *Black Boy* she had written him a short letter: "Dear Richard, It is obvious that you and I are the only two geniuses of this era." And Richard had roared with delighted laughter, nearly as loud as when he first read *Melanctha*.[8] In Chicago, when the Communists had attacked Miss Stein, saying that she lolled on a silken cushion in Paris, writing unintelligible prose which no worker could understand and was thus throttling the revolution, Richard had gathered together a group of stockyard workers who were semiliterate. He read *Melanctha* aloud; the men understood every word and kept interrupting enthusiastically to comment and substantiate the ideas with examples from their own lives.

After lunch one day, Richard sat in Miss Stein's old house, on the

Left Bank, in an armchair facing the door. He felt so at home, he mused. How strange that this strong-faced, gray-haired woman made him feel as comfortable as a relative; just as he had reacted when first reading her prose. The room was flooded by sunlight which illuminated some of the Picassos, the Matisses and Grises which lined the walls. Behind Richard's chair, just over his head, was the famous portrait of Stein painted by Picasso and across from him, reclining on a horsehair sofa, her bare feet in leather sandals stretched out before her, wearing a brown skirt of some homespun material with a light tan blouse, was Miss Stein. "How she can talk!" Richard thought. "What absolute genius this pioneer-looking American has. . . ." A controlled nervous energy flooded her voice and her hands were ceaselessly moving. Behind Miss Stein was a wood table, over six feet long; its surface was scarred by wormholes and blotches of ink could be seen where it was not covered by layers of books. Her laugh was almost as vigorous as his own, he thought, and shifted comfortably down in the chair.

They had leaped from topic to topic in the manner of very old friends; "she was as eager to hear as to speak" and the immediate emotional harmony had been cemented early in the conversation. "William James taught me all that I know," Miss Stein told Richard, and he quoted the philosopher from memory ". . . a man has as many social selves as there are individuals who recognize him and carry an image of him in their minds."[9] Then he picked up a book, one of a stack he had brought to Miss Stein, and showed her the introduction he had written for *Black Metropolis*. "This is the shimmering nightmare in which the black man lives in America." "No more fiendish punishment could be devised, were such a thing physically possible, than that one should be turned loose in society and remain absolutely unnoticed by all the members thereof. If no one turned round when we entered, answered when we spoke, or minded what we did, but every person we met 'cut us dead,' and acted as if we were non-existent things, a kind of rage and impotent despair would ere long well up in us, from which the cruelest bodily tortures would be a relief; for these would make us feel that, however bad might be our plight, we had not sunk to such a depth as to be unworthy of attention at all."

America could not completely reject the Negro, Richard told Miss Stein, but he had come as near being the victim of a complete rejection as the country could work out; "for the dehumanized image of the Negro which white Americans carry in their minds, the anti-Negro epithets continuously on their lips, exclude the contemporary

Negro as truly as though he were kept in a steel prison, and doom even those Negroes who are as yet unborn."

"Rose is a rose—a Richard is a poet, is a poet," Stein said, smiling when Richard guffawed.

Then Miss Stein told Richard that in her visits to Army camps she had been aware of a terrible fear in the white soldier toward the black soldier. They seemed drawn together only in battle or through jazz and swing; only when fighting (and she explained that she had not personally witnessed that unity, naturally) or when young white soldiers and black literally put their heads together to talk about "hot" music. At such times music was similar to a secret code and racism was forgotten. In what way was this a reflection from the United States and how worried were white people about racism? she wanted to know.

"So much has happened in America since you were [there] and it has influenced us all, Negroes included," Richard explained. "But I feel that fear is the greatest thing that Negroes feel in America; it influences them all, from the black Ph.D.'s to the janitors. The gap between blacks and whites is so wide that honest communication is almost impossible. Whites guiltily shun blacks and blacks fearfully shun whites. Blacks, locked in their dream of fear, and whites, locked in their dream of guilt, look at each other and wonder what will happen to them. . . . Everybody just waits. No doubt the Negroes you saw were just waiting, waiting and wondering what was going to happen to them."[10]

What about the riots? Stein asked.

"In a riot the Negroes get rid of their fear and the whites get rid of their guilt. Then they live in an uneasy peace until the next outburst comes."

Stein then asked what type of letters he had received from white people after *Black Boy* was published. Were there many letters?

"On that book alone," Richard answered slowly, "there were more than a thousand letters; but in all the letters, there was one thing missing. The American mind finds it hard to ally itself with my vision. The French refugees embrace my work instinctively. How strange it seems. And no review linked me with writing being done in the world. They looked upon it in a moral light." He paused for an aside—"Why is it that all Americans, even Jews, are Methodist preachers at heart?"—and both writers laughed.

Richard paused to light another cigarette, his eyes were quiet when he continued: "Most people approached my book in this moral framework; how bad this life was; how did I learn to write? we must do something. No one said, yes, this is life how it is lived and here we have a sort of meaning in it; here the Negro states the theme of modern living."

Stein remarked that she had read his book and written to him that her impression had been that he wrote as a man, not as a Negro; just as a creative human being. Richard felt something flinch internally but he kept his face still and pleasant. He hated that phrase! There was a lot he could say about that question, things he was feeling his way toward but it would take too much time; although he felt Stein would understand.

Quivering on the rim of his mind was the idea that "When the feeling and fact of being a Negro is accepted fully into the consciousness of a Negro, there's something universal about it, something saving and informing, something that lifts it above being a Negro in America. Oh, will I ever have the strength and courage to tell what I feel and think; and do I know it well enough to tell it."

Only a second had passed and Miss Stein asked if people felt impelled to change their own behavior toward Negroes after reading his books. Had any of his mail touched on acting or action?

Richard's voice rasped faintly: "They all ask me—tell me what to do. And I cannot tell them what to do, for I know that they know what to do about Negroes. They know what to do and they would rather die than do it. So what can you say to people like that? The people come to me. They want to talk; they want to hear what Negroes *feel*. Sometimes I tell them and when I do they are unhappy, sad, depressed . . . They say, if I felt like that, I'd kill myself. To some people, I've answered—using your Melanctha—'If I ever killed myself, it would be by accident, and if I ever killed myself by accident I'd be awfully sorry.' Then I expect them to laugh, but they don't. No one has laughed so far."

He smiled. "Strange country I live in, huh? I've been working toward an idea—and hope, somehow to reveal it in my next book, taking off, only as far as style, from the middle section, "Flight," of *Native Son;* that Negro self-discovery, the facts of Negro life, constitute a great body of facts of importance about mankind in general. But white Americans probably won't accept it. I think Europeans will accept and understand what I'm saying and then it will filter back to America from Paris and London and Rome. And then the Negro may be better known. Maybe the Negro must present his case to the world, to Europe."

Gertrude Stein listened quietly. Then she got up from the sofa and walked behind it to the long table. Under some books, which she moved aside, were what looked from where Richard was sitting like various sizes of paper. She found what she was looking for; it was a letter he had written to her a month or so before he left the United States. "I was very interested," she told him, "in what you had to say about our similarity in the manner in which we criticize America."

Richard remembered exactly what he had said. He had just finished reading Henry Miller's book *The Air-Conditioned Nightmare*,[11] which attacked America. At the same time he read Philip Wylie's *Generation of Vipers*, which he thought was the stronger of the two books. Every sentence dripped with gall, yet it was a book written by a man committed to being an American. And he had brought the book for Miss Stein.

Miller's book was very violent, he had written Miss Stein, but Wylie's was still more violent. "I'm very interested in this matter of how one regards one's country. It is very easy to damn America by rejecting America and it is very hard to damn America while accepting America. Most of the new generation of writers have no illusions about America, yet they feel themselves above all as Americans. I criticize America as an American and you do too, which I think is the only real way to do the job."[12]

The bright sun which had streamed into the room when Richard arrived had been gone for hours. He had not noticed; he could go on talking forever. Miss Stein could too, he thought: she has such fervor; her judgments are vigorous. But they would have to continue another day because Ellen would wonder what had happened to him. He had not called all day. Alice Toklas, silent, dark-skinned, with a long prominent nose and large brown eyes, took Richard to the small foyer, where he put on his coat. She told him good-bye in a low, rather harsh voice but did not smile. Slyly, Richard wondered if she was shy; maybe she was jealous? He chuckled to himself. No, that could not be so—Stein's home was always swamped with writers and painters. As he bounced down the exposed outside stairway he felt exceptionally cheerful.

A few yards from the apartment on Boulevard St. Michel, Richard looked up at the Paris rooftops and the rows of small chimney pots: they look like rows of teeth opened at the sky, he thought; then unaccountably he felt depressed, his spirits drooped. What did he have to do tomorrow? And how many more appointments had Ellen made for him while he had been gone that afternoon? I wish I did not have to attend the reception for me by the Société des Gens de Lettres, he thought. Miss Stein had told him it was highbrow, like the Académie, and they probably would not know his work. It would be boring. Well, he would go and smile and be gracious. But he wished that some of the official functions would ease up. He was tired and felt "rushed from all sides." But he did want to remain in Paris until he saw *Uncle Tom's Children, Native Son* and *Black Boy* off the press in their French editions; and he still had to make a trip to Switzerland, to Zurich, to meet with his German publisher, who had slated *Black Boy* for 1947. French publishers were strange. "Things [were] done in such queer manners; one [did] not attend to business unless one [ate] at the same time. Somebody told [him] that French publishers would spend a 100,000 francs to get an author drunk in order to buy cheaply a story for 10,000 francs." "Sounds kind of screwy," Richard thought, "but I think it is partly true."

In October, Richard booked passage for home on the *Queen Elizabeth,* sailing from Southampton on January 11, 1947. And Ellen and Julia went to the south of France while Richard went to see his publisher in Zurich. When he returned to France, at the end of November, he decided to leave Paris on December 29 and spend two weeks in London. All his new French friends had difficulty understanding why he was returning to the United States. Patiently, and somewhat dramatically, he reassured them that someday he would return to France but that his mind's tether was in America; he had been fashioned in that peculiar kind of hell.

As soon as Richard had made reservations to return home he became restless; he "had liked it awfully [in France], but the things [he] wanted to get done [were] not done. *Native Son* [was] still being translated. Everything over [in France took] a long, long time." The French people simply had no sense of time as he knew it. And he could not accustom himself to electric power which was shut off two days a week; stores that closed Sundays and Mondays and half-days on Saturdays. Privately, without mentioning his attitude to the French people he knew, he wondered: How can this country manage to keep going with so little work going on?

One thing drew him home above all others: his house on Charles Street was at last ready. He owned a home in which he had never lived and he was anxious to put it in order—perhaps, he thought, it will be an anchorage for me and my family. An even stronger reason to return to his own country nagged at his mind. It was his conviction that the next quarter of a century, just beginning, would see a tremendous struggle *among* Negroes "for self-expression, self-possession, self-consciousness and individuality." He had to be in the center of what would happen and he wanted to be settled, to work, and to help in whatever was going to occur. "The next great area of discovery in the Negro will be the dark landscape of his own mind, what living in white America has done to him. Boy, what that search will reveal! Richard mused. There's enough there to find to use in transforming the basis of human life on earth!"

I feel certain that she knows already
much more than she knows she knows . . .

XX

Long before the tugboats met the *Queen Elizabeth* to take her into a slip in the Hudson River, Richard went on deck. It was icy cold and flakes of snow were blowing in straight lines held horizontal on the wind. For a moment, he contemplated walking toward the open deck because the windows were so misted he could not see all that was going on. But when he turned in that direction the force of the frozen wind struck wildly against his body as if it would rip the buttons from his heavy tweed coat and tear the muffler from around his throat. Richard put up his gloved hand to fix the hat, tilted above his high forehead, more securely in place, and walked within the enclosure to the windows nearest the approaching city. Using his sleeve he wiped the mist from the inside of the glass and strained to look out. He hated snow, and the cold; but strangely, it did not bother him. It's the excitement, he thought, and leaned closer to the window.

Very shortly, the tugs jockeyed into position below the steep sides of the *Queen* and soon Richard saw New York above him, smudgily defined in the murky air. How the city soared light and free above the river. Home! He was almost home! How strange that I should be so happy to return, he marveled. Suddenly Richard was impatient; the ship's progress was shudderingly slow. But, no; there was bustle on board, and workmen and sailors passed behind him, darting up stairways and down companionways, ignoring passengers for the first time on the long journey from England. Richard turned from the rail and walked back inside the ship to wait with Ellen and Julia.

254

Quite early the next morning, Wright went out, alone, to walk in the Village. He wanted to savor the strange impressions striking at him from his familiar town, which he had not seen for such a long time. What was so astonishing to him was that everything had such clarity; every building and street looked as new as if he had never seen it before, or only dimly. And the abundance of food and books and various objects was startling. At 8th Street and Greenwich, the streets angled toward a meeting with 6th Avenue and Richard walked slowly past a giant fruit and vegetable store. Its wares were piled lavishly, so different from postwar France. When he reached 6th Avenue he continued down to Bleeker and turned right onto the picturesque street which was lined with food stores, fish markets, vegetables on pushcarts, fruit mounded high in baskets and every cheese, fresh and spiced meat in the world. The scent of Italian fresh-baked bread made Richard hungry.

Citrus fruits had been scarce in France but on Bleeker "oranges were piled high—gold balls bursting with juice and everywhere a profusion of food, an abundance." An exultant emotion filled him and silently a sentence formed and became a gleeful chant under his breath: "It's like Christmas! Just like Christmas!" Like a child, he wanted everything: he would take home to his family some oranges, some lemons, some grapefruit, some tangerines—some bread, a round one and a long one . . . With his eyes fixed on the fruit stalls, Richard went on farther, thinking only of the food. He paused in front of a store to choose the fruit he would buy.

A swarthy man darted out of the doorway, a soiled white apron tied over a sweater, scarf, and coat; a woolen cap was pulled down over his ears. He looked cold and impatient; his breath steamed in a small eddy around his face when he rasped out: "Whudda yuh want, boy?"

Richard's mind seemed to come suddenly to a stop. For a second he looked into the man's eyes—why, he's as dark as many Negroes, Richard thought. A goddamn Italian, a Sicilian; can't even speak English and he's calling me Boy! But he was silent and turned away. No, it was not Christmas. It was not Christmas for a black man. Would it ever be?

Stubbornly, and forcing himself without enthusiasm, Richard purchased a bag of oranges and tangerines farther down the street and started back to Charles. Anger had been replaced by a calm melancholy which heightened his senses and without their being aware of it he observed white Americans as they observed him. How they stare, he thought. "Americans were so new, so raw, so crude a people. They were so lacking in human feeling and sensitivity. And the dopey white Village girls, all acting like Lauren Bacall in a Hemingway movie, they stared most of all. . . ."

Next door to his house a group of four or five women were standing, two on the lowest step of the brownstone entryway. Neighbors! Richard thought as he crossed in front of El Charro to reach his house. Watching from the corner of his eye, he saw the women stop talking when they observed his approach. There were scowls on their faces and one woman turned her body in his direction as if for an angry confrontation; then, as Richard continued to ignore them, the women began to mutter and chatter. He reached his own stoop and as he placed his foot upon the stairway a word floated clearly in the air. "Nigger!" It was not snapped in his direction; the word had simply detached itself from a general cacophony of other sounds and hisses and reached his ears. Richard did not think he was meant to hear; or maybe he was, but his feet continued their steady upward climb, neither faster nor slower, and an expression of bland indifference masked his face.

Several weeks later, Richard met a young white friend at Walter Goldwater's University Place Book Store, a few blocks above the Square. They browsed through the extensive collection of books on Africa for a while and then decided to take a walk. Richard was having a fine time describing France and England, the people he had met, assuming various identities as easily as a professional actor. His voice changed from high to low, sometimes mysterious, at others querulous or rough, and laughing softly but always aware that he was in public and covering his open face smoothly when people passed by.

Only the cold reminded Richard that they had walked a long distance, in and out of streets, paying little attention, and he saw that they had almost reached 23rd Street and 9th Avenue. Suddenly he felt chilled and wondered how girls could go about in silk stockings and skirts and not freeze to death. He decided to warm up with coffee and took his friend into a tiny short-countered luncheonette on the corner of 22nd Street and 9th Avenue. Richard did not look first to see if there were other black faces or Puerto Rican, or Chinese—all signals that a place was "safe" to enter. After all, it was only a small lunch counter and it was just above the Village. Usually, and automatically, his eyes or senses flashed a message: Safe. Unsafe. Maybe . . . But this time he was not paying attention; he was teasing his companion, chortling because she grew so serious and defensive. She never knew when she was being teased and she said angry things in reply. He had just called her a "WASP" and she retaliated, after lecturing him as to why, that he was a "BASP." It was like having a kid sister.

Seated at the counter, he stifled his laughter, although his eyes were still gleeful. A white waitress brought two cups of coffee and set them steaming before them. Whew! He was really chilled. Coffee would taste good! He took a sip; it tasted terrible! Just bad coffee? But every pore was alert, poised, already aware that it was something more than poorly made coffee. At the next sip, a very small taste, he knew and turned his eyes toward his "kid sister." She had pushed the cup away from in front of her, two fingers still on the saucer; all the red in her face from the wind outside was gone. Rage was widening her eyes; her mouth opened but Richard spoke first: "Salt! There's salt in the coffee!" "The dirty bastards," the girl said. "Wait," he answered and looked at the waitress who had been watching for his reaction. "There's salt in our coffee," he spoke quietly, but there was a steel sound beneath the soft words. In a vicious voice and with a twitch of her lumpy hips the waitress spat out: "That's how we serve it. If you don't like it here, then go somewheres else." Her speech was crude and thinly defiant but she stepped back toward an opening in the wall leading to the kitchen. A dirty white man stood there: in his hand was a heavy skillet, his arms were heavy and powerful-looking. He glared at Richard and waited. Silently, he and his companion walked back into the street—she was swearing. He had never heard her swear and, automatically, he reproved her: "Don't say that—it isn't nice. What would your mother say?" trying to make her laugh.[1]

Around four o'clock one afternoon, Richard put down Clement Wood's *Complete Rhyming Dictionary*, which he had been reading off and on ever since he had finished work at one-thirty. He stretched and yawned, his mind was still on the book he had been reading: language was magical. Maybe a poet was a man who was always psychoanalyzing himself? For how could anyone try to write poetry without hauling out of himself strange forms of inner life from the dark deeps? Rising from the couch, he walked to the front of the living room and looked out into the street. Gosh, how quiet the house is when Julia is away, he thought. They have been gone for hours. I hope Julia-baby won't be too tired. Her excessive activity worries me, Richard worried. "My little daughter is so tense, so eager; it stabs me to see her."

Richard leaned against the side of the window, watching down the street for his child, seeing in his mind a picture of how she had looked that morning. How wonderful she was! "She plays about the house like mad, thinking up one game after another. She made me lie upon the floor this morning while she put me to sleep. She was taking over the image of Ellen and acting it out. Already there is lodged in her mind images of both me and Ellen; they are very real to her, and they'll no doubt remain there for her lifetime, influencing her actions and lack of them. But if they influence her in any way, it will be toward action, for she's surrounded by that in both me and Ellen." Richard smiled to himself when he thought of Julia's favorite game: "She also assumes my identity sometimes; she'll sit quietly, cross her legs and lower her voice and ask me questions, looking around in a wise sort of way. Now and again I asked her: 'Julia, what's my name?' 'Richard Wright,' she says promptly and seriously. 'What do I do?' I'll ask. 'You write books for me,' she says. 'What books?' I'll ask. *Native Son* and *Black Boy*' she'll answer. Then we'll both laugh. She has identified me with books and she's never really happy unless she has one in her hands. She sleeps with them. She seems to picture me always in the office at my desk, pounding the typewriter, which she likes to try to do. As soon as she's a little older, I'll get her a toy typewriter," he decided.[2]

Richard looked again at his watch; his restlessness just beginning to lap over to anxiety, when he saw Julia with a friend entering the house. He opened the door with a wide smile on his face, laughing as he picked up his daughter. Julia had an ice cream cone and she was fussing, laughing, and demanding to eat it. She did not want to wait until Ellen sat her at her own small table. Richard fussed, laughed, and demanded that Julia wait until she was seated and a napkin put around her neck. "Gosh, how she's growing!" he said to the friend, who had been out to Central Park with Julia. But when he glanced in her direction he felt uneasy; something had happened! A feeling of dread crept faintly across his skin and he glanced quickly at his child—she was all right; nothing had happened to her! Or had it? What was it? His friend was talking and laughing with Julia and Ellen, but he knew her very well; she was angry and tense. When Julia finished her cone and went into her room Richard asked:

"Something happened? I feel it; I know it. What is it?"

Richard listened in silence. His face was impassive but he took long, frequent drags on his cigarette and occasionally narrowed his large eyes when the smoke rose near his lashes. After a few hours in the park, the girl took Julia along Fifth Avenue to wait for a bus. Suddenly, the child needed to go to the toilet. It was urgent and she was too young to wait very long. The nearest store was Bergdorf Goodman so they hurried through its doors. An elegant blond saleswoman at the jewelry counter said yes, there was a ladies' room, and she lifted her hand to point the direction. Just as she pointed her eyes dropped and she saw Julia, who had been too small and too near the counter to be seen but had stepped back. The woman's face became rigid. She dropped her arm, stared right at the little girl and spat out: "There are no restrooms for *you!*" The friend could not stay to argue because Julia would hear so she turned abruptly, after putting all the contempt for the saleswoman that she could into her face, and left the store. Julia pulled at the hand holding hers and asked, "Why did the lady say that? She was pointing to the bathroom. I have to go to the bathroom!"[3]

Richard's eyes flashed murderously. It was the only change in his face; the muscles were well-trained to hide anguish. But he could not sit still; he walked back and forth across the room quietly, then stopped to light another cigarette. "That is why you bought her an ice cream cone so late in the day," he stated quietly. It was not a question. "Yes," the girl answered. "It changed the subject for Julia immediately!" Richard laughed sardonically.

A pain so sharp that it hurt his throat burgeoned; it made his skin feel as if every pore was overloaded with grief or rage. There was hate alternating with pain. "Sometimes I look at my sweet child and I wonder just how much does she know—I feel certain that she knows already much more than she knows she knows. Yes, my baby is getting quite old enough to understand it all." Waves of anger rushed into his mind and displaced every other emotion. He wanted to stand up and wipe that saleswoman from the earth, just blot her out of existence. If he could lift his hand and erase every bigot from the earth's surface, he would do it without a qualm. An image of his daughter's tender, helpless face formed in his mind, and his heart beat wildly, trying to force its way out of his chest. No! Not this! Not Julia! Poor little innocent Julia-baby! Dimly, he heard his friend's voice. She was talking and talking. God! I wish she would go home now! Then he took a deep breath, imposing his will over his body. His right hand hurt and he glanced down; he had gripped the back of a chair so hard that his muscles pained him. Deliberately, he relaxed and forced his mind into objective channels, to link the personal to a generalization. How else could it be borne?

"Oh, God! If a man is to be loyal, to love, to show pity, sympathy, mercy; if he is to refuse cruelty; to care for the rights of others, to live and let live, to believe in civilization, culture, glory, progress, then they will have to demonstrate how it can be done so that the carrying out of these ideals and the practicing of virtues in the modern world will not reduce a man to a creature of nervous dread and give him a sense of the meaninglessness of life. . . ."

For weeks, Richard was filled with disgust, uneasiness, and a sense of dread. Whenever he looked at his daughter he worried: would her mind and emotions be crippled in such an atmosphere? Parents were responsible for what happened to the children they brought into the world. He had survived; he would continue to fight and survive. Could Julia? And if she did, then at what cost?

Richard became increasingly aware of the attitude of his Italian-American neighbors. They were always making anti-Negro remarks within his hearing and every time Julia and Ellen went outside he worried about their safety. Fitfully, sometimes in the midst of his work, he was drawn toward the front window as if by the solid substance of his body he could protect them from wounding epithets or physical harm.

Richard had reason for his growing alarm. In April or May roving gangs of armed Italian youths were terrorizing Village residents. A cab driver, stopped for a light at the corner of 8th Street and 6th Avenue, was pulled from his taxi and beaten for carrying an inter-racial couple. The passengers, a Negro girl and a white man, were knocked to the ground and kicked by teenagers. On two different occasions gangs entered the Howard Johnson's on 6th Avenue and the Humpty-Dumpty on 4th Street, dragged two Negro men who were eating with white women into the street and beat them. One of the black men had his jaw smashed. The young man had just returned from overseas where he had served four years in the Army of the United States. While out walking one evening with friends, Richard was warned that an armed gang had gathered at the intersection of 7th Avenue and 11th Street and was threatening to "get the niggers." Reluctantly, he returned home because his friends were frightened; he wanted to "go and take a peek."

At the end of April, Richard finished work late. It was two in the afternoon and he had been at his typewriter since six that morning. Ellen was out and Julia was at nursery school. He went into the small kitchen at the back of the house and took some lettuce and tomatoes from the refrigerator. It was late, and he did not want to spoil his dinner. Putting together a sandwich, he paused for a minute to look at the bowl of cream on the second shelf of the box. It would taste good with the strawberries Ellen had sugared and left in the fridge. No, he was putting on weight. He'd wait until dinner. Feeling virtuous because he had resisted temptation, and fully aware that he had, he took his sandwich into the dining room, which adjoined the narrow kitchen. When he had finished eating he drank a cup of coffee, taking heavy cream from the chemist's bowl—one of several—they had brought back from France. He then wandered into the front of the apartment and burst into song. Ir—eeene, goood—

niiiite, he sang, following with precision Leadbelly's famous rendition of the tune. How these songs soothe me, he thought to himself, and put on the Ledbetter record. Idly, he waited until "Irene" was sung, singing along with the famous singer, and then he picked up all the newspapers from the morning. It had been a good day! Twenty-five pages of a new novel. He had reached a passage that seemed almost to write itself; it came rarely, but when it did, how good it felt. Really, writing was "the one decent thing in his life. . . . It is the one area of one's life where one can be one's self. . . . Would not the strength of writing come from the fact that it is the one place where a person could throw the whole of what's good in him?" Oh! he felt so good! Still humming along with the record, Richard picked up the New York *Times* and sat down in an armchair to read.

An article caught his attention. It concerned a report by the National Opinion Research Center in Denver, Colorado, and stated that after long and intensive questioning of many white people in the United States, it had been found that 66 percent of the white people of America did not feel that Negroes were unfairly treated, did not think that the Negro resented his debased role in American life, did not think that Negroes thought that they were oppressed.

Richard's first reaction was that in some way the whole report was fraudulent. Somehow it must have been rigged. But as he read further along his spirits plummeted. Ah, God, what a crazy world! he thought. "This means that most of the white people in America, really, honestly believe that Negroes are merely inventing a case, conjuring up complaints, and that there [did] not exist a material basis for their eternal bleating about their condition."

"Well," Richard thought, "the reactions of those whites as given to the Denver poll were not charged with hostility; they were merely expressing what they had been taught at home, in church, at school, in the press, through the radio, and in the movies.

"Imagine a white child of six being taught by its mother that there is a God, being taught—in words that are wordless—that it must observe the incest taboo; and on the same level with these two powerful ideas—God and incest—being taught that Negroes are inferior and must not receive treatment such as is accorded other people!

"Perhaps someday someone will explain how it [is] possible for us to construct the atom bomb and at the same time entertain myths, legends, and downright folk superstitions about race!"[4]

By the time Richard finished reading the *Times, Herald Tribune* and *Daily News* he felt will-less, aimless. "We are barely out of one war and the papers and the radio are beating it up for another—

against Russia," he decided. "There's no hope for this country. It is sliding right into Fascism.[5] Congress has been taken over by Southern Democrats and Northern conservatives, most of them Republicans—they're chopping away at whatever was good in the New Deal. Fear! A climate of fear is moving over America. And with the atom bomb hanging over us the problem of human unity is terribly important."

He felt sluggish; he put down the papers and decided to take a walk. He went out the front door, listening to hear the harsh voices of his neighbors. But nothing happened. "What a way to live," he thought. Whether epithets were hurled or there was outright violence, anticipation drained off valuable energy. How could he write under such conditions? He had entirely forgotten the twenty-five pages he had written that morning. "A black man is living always in expectation of viciousness or an attack and unfortunately he is seldom disappointed." Richard ambled to Washington Square and stood looking at the pigeons fluttering around the trees, alighting on patches of bread or corn that someone had put on the ground. He went past the bookshops on Fourth Avenue, browsing here and there. It was late; he would go home.

A resolution welled up from his depths. Why continue this pointless grappling with racial muck? "The hell with it! [He'd] get out of it! [He'd] go to France. [He'd] leave the land of [his] birth, [his] home, [his] relatives, [his] friends . . . [He'd] defeat the culture that shaped [him]. [He] was tired of democracy and the 'will of the people.' "[6] If white Americans could not understand educated Negroes who spoke a language they understood, then it was all but hopeless to expect whites to understand and sympathize with the millions of inarticulate Negroes trapped in ghettos.

He would go to Europe and present the case of the black man to the world; then, perhaps, it would filter back. The question of race had to be caught up and found in a larger and more generally human context. This is no American, Russian, Italian, or French matter; it is man's matter. But, oh! How he would be attacked. Everyone would say that he was deserting his people; deserting the struggle. Well, let them![7]

But I am filled with the details of living . . .

XXI

Three times on August 7, 1947, Richard lost his way between the port of Boulogne and Paris; carefully and nervously he guided the big black Oldsmobile along the narrow French by-ways until he found the correct route. A keen sensation of vitality invaded every pore while the car's tires hummed smoothly beneath him. Only at the approach of oncoming Peugeots, Citroëns, Renaults, and other small automobiles, like toys beside the heavy American machine, did Richard's nerves coil and tense. He was still unnerved by his experience in England, driving on the left side of the road; it frightened him. Each time he saw a car approach in the distance even though in France it was the same as in America, he was still unnerved and wondered if it would veer to his side of the road and smash head-on! "There was something morally wrong about driving on the wrong side of the road!"

After a champagne party in his first-class stateroom aboard the S. S. *United States* with Ralph Ellison, Mrs. Daniel Guerin, C. L. R. James, Bernard Wolfe and other friends, which he had not enjoyed,[1] Richard had sailed for France on July 30, a hot sultry day. The house on Charles Street had been sold for twice the amount he had paid just one year before, and furniture and dishes had been put in storage. On the ship were trunks and crates of food and clothing totaling seventeen, his car was in the hold and Knobby, a Siamese cat, prowled in a small cage in the ship's kennel. Richard hated the S.S. *United States,* whose speed and general construction made the ship vibrate, pitch, and roll as it assaulted the dark sea. It had been so hot on board that he had slept with his stateroom door open and he had hated the long narrow corridors joined with strips of metal which made the ship seem to switch in every direction in the night; it had been almost like riding a subway and standing where the cars coupled.

And there had been no feeling of elegance; "Americans did not know how to render service; the ship was democratically shoddy, and the passengers, mostly American, had stared and stared, internationally wet behind the ears." But at night, when he had gone on deck to stare at the Atlantic, he thought it inhuman; "One may hate the people around one but how kind they are, how good, compared to the wild sweep of black sea water that heaves tamelessly in the night; the hot darkness beyond the porthole! Man is something apart in this world, the life of man is different from that of nature. No matter how much we may hate one another, we still cling to each other because there is nothing else in this world to cling to. No matter how much we may hate men, we are still men and we are not really nature, though we are a mysterious part of it."

At last, a little after seven o'clock in the evening, Richard reached Paris. Night descended beautifully; a pale light illuminated the age of the buildings as the sky became a mysterious blue and then darkened into black. It was a great moment for Richard; "like a dream to be riding one's own car into those beautiful Paris streets," and he "arrived breathlessly at Rue de Lille" and stopped the car before the small private hotel[2] of Madame Odette Lieutier where an apartment waited. It had been a long drive and Richard was so tired that he trembled, looking about him down the ancient street, and his eyes smoldered with excitement. He was glad to find that his hostess-landlady was not at home. A maid showed them to their rooms and Ellen was able to put Julia to bed quickly. She was fretful; giant hives similar to the ones she had developed on their last trip had erupted all over her body. Richard and Ellen sat with their daughter until she fell asleep in the strange bed and then Madame Lieutier arrived with friends who wanted to meet him. For about an hour, Richard sat drinking brandy and growing more and more sleepy. Suddenly, he grew impatient—if he went to bed then morning would soon come and he could start his new life—besides, his body was aching with fatigue. He waited, finished the last sip of his drink, looked toward his wife, signaling her secretly, and she rose from her chair, made their excuses, said good night and at last they were in their own room. "Paris!" Richard sighed, and fell into a troubled sleep.

Two days after his arrival, Richard awoke and lay for a minute in bed—he had been dreaming that he stood on a rooftop looking at a strange city, not Paris, it had been somewhere else, minarets thrusting strangely among skyscrapers similar to those in New York. He tried to recall what it had been about by forming an image of the scene behind his eyelids and then tracing it back step by step, but it was elusive; it was gone. Quietly, so that he would not awaken Ellen, he slipped out of bed and went into the next room to his typewriter. He listened for a moment and then pulled out some sheets of paper he had hidden between the pages of a novel he had been working on. Ellen had looked at him strangely the day before; he wondered if she knew he kept a diary. He would hide it in a different place today. Into the typewriter he inserted a small three-holed sheet of white paper, adjusted the margin to match what he had written the day before, and typed: "August 9: No work today and no work yesterday." He started when he heard a door open and his hand flew up automatically to roll the sheet from the typewriter, but it was somewhere else in the building. Richard sighed; the phrase he had typed made him feel depressed and the sound to which he had reacted irritated his nervous system. Sighing again, he conquered the twin emotions and faced their turbulence, staring at the wall before the desk, until a paragraph formed whole and complete in his mind. Again he typed: "I live alone. My deepest thoughts are communicated to no one. No one around me. I just think them and try to write them. How can I live free, freely? That is the question of my life. . . . But I am filled with the details of living and no free time to act free. What can one do?"

When he finished writing in his diary Richard sat on at the typewriter, hoping that the act of recording his thoughts would propel him into work on the novel.[3] But he could not concentrate; an interminable, unending list of tasks kept thrusting itself to the front of his brain. Ah, it was no use to sit and stare in front of him; he would not work again today. Milk had to be found for Julia. Knobby, the cat, had to be picked up at the station. Trunks should be unpacked. A maid had to be found—he would try to get Alice back, the maid they had on their first visit to Paris. A garage was needed for the Oldsmobile. Dollars had to be changed into francs at the best possible rate so he would have to find someone who knew how it could be done. He was out of cigarettes. Would he have to buy American brands on the black market?

Covering the typewriter, he left the room and went into the bathroom. Damn! There was no hot water! He went into the kitchen and filled a teakettle with water so that he could shave. How impractical Odette Lieutier was! She did not seem troubled because there was no hot water. When the water was barely warm the flame went out and Richard could not light it again. The stove was broken! He took the barely warmed water into the bathroom, shaved and washed, feeling irritability rising steadily in his stomach. Just to be on the safe side he opened the medicine cabinet and dosed himself with pills to forestall stomach pains. Suddenly, he felt a slight lightening of his spirits; the pills were good for him. He was glad that he had brought several large bottles with him from America. When he finished a sponge bath in the water, which had grown cool, he dressed quickly. But he did not feel thoroughly clean. Damn the impractical French anyway!

As soon as he left the bathroom Ellen, her hair tousled but her eyes bright, darted into the hallway. "There's no hot water again," Richard told his wife. His tone of voice blended with a faintly exasperated and helpless appeal for her to take charge. "I'll speak to Odette when I'm dressed," Ellen reassured her husband briskly. Then, sticking her head back out of the bathroom, she called to him: "Don't forget that both your wristwatches are broken. And Dick? We have to register with the police today." Richard called back that he would pick Ellen up after he had gotten Knobby at the station and left the house quickly. Out in the street a rush of pure joy removed every annoyance. Odette lived in the same neighborhood in which Proust had lived, and it pleased Richard to see the scenes he had read of in *Remembrance of Things Past*. Whistling, he walked to his car.

Two hours later Richard drove back to Rue de Lille, deposited the cat, and took Ellen to a store on the Champs Elysées. Waiting in the car for his wife, Richard felt his mood begin to change again; it shifted between shame and pride. Uneasily, he watched the French people who passed along the sidewalk. Everyone stared at the large American car which towered like a ship over tugboats in contrast to the small French models. No one passed him by without reacting; "eyes bugged and tongues clicked." He loved his shiny new car—he had never owned a car in his life! But, then, what is it I am feeling? he wondered. Pride? Or am I ashamed? It seemed important to decide which emotion was uppermost and material advantage over others made him uncomfortable. His uneasiness left when he thought to himself: "I'm ashamed most of the time."

Driving home in a dreamlike state, Richard grew alarmed when sparks began sputtering forth from the steering mechanism. At the General Motors French garage, mechanics examined the Oldsmobile and began to list a whole series of troubles, one of which involved an expensive removal of the gas tank. Richard could understand only some of what they were telling him and he grew suspicious. It was a new car, only a few months old; they were trying to cheat him! Unable to decide what to do, Richard stood and looked at the car for a few minutes. An American walked over and introduced himself: he was co-owner with a Frenchman of a new garage in Paris and would be glad to help. In about five minutes the car was repaired. A wire had in some way become stuck to another and merely needed realigning. When Richard asked the mechanic for a bill he replied there was no charge; but he insisted that the man take a few dollars. As he steered his black car out of the garage a feeling of relief filled him: thank God he had found an American! He could always tell when an American was cheating him but not a Frenchman.

Near Odette's Richard found a garage in which to park the car at night; the idea of leaving the Oldsmobile parked on the street worried him. But he began to suspect that someone was using the car when he was not around. It was already warmed up some days when he called for it and he sensed that it felt different in other ways as well. For a few days he watched and waited; suspicion became certainty, irritation became anger; the car had almost had to have its whole motor removed! God only knew what would go wrong next if a stranger was taking the car; he might be French and unfamiliar with automatic transmission; there could even be an accident which would smash up the car entirely. Around midnight on August 16, Richard returned to the garage with two white American friends;[4] that morning he had complained to the owner, telling him of his suspicions against a young night attendant. As soon as Richard and his friends climbed from the car the young man dashed up and began to shout at him in rapid French. Helplessly, Richard turned to his friends, both of whom spoke French fluently. "What is he saying?" There was no answer. It was as if both had been struck dumb. They acted as if nothing was happening at all while the Frenchman grew more excited and voluble. "Tell me what he's saying," Richard asked again. "It's nothing; let's go," his friends answered, starting to walk away. "They're scared!" Richard thought in amazement. And without another word he opened the door of the car for them, got into the driver's seat and left the garage. "Why do all white people, even your friends, act like that?" he wondered on the way to Odette's. At the building he awakened the concierge, who opened the wooden doors, and parked the car inside the courtyard.

Often, unless it meant leaving the cat alone too long, Richard took Knobby in the car with him. Even though Richard teased the beautiful Siamese and attempted to teach it tricks, sometimes persisting until the cat ran under a chair or the bed, it was attached to him. On the boat en route to France he had visited it in its kennel every day; and the moment the animal had heard his voice, while he was still out of its sight, it had given a pathetic and "plaintive meow." He had sneaked it to his stateroom before debarking to give it reassurance during a two-day separation.

In Paris, the Siamese did not want Richard to leave the house without him, and when he did Knobby followed him to the door and looked into his face with "wide blue eyes and stare[d] with a hurt, wondering look. . . ." Each time Richard returned and called the cat's name it came running, rolled on its back with joy, and then gave a particular meow which meant "Pick me up." But one afternoon Richard opened the door expectantly and called out: "Knobby!" There was no response. Richard was alarmed. Maybe the cat had run away? Or been stolen? Was it lying somewhere injured? No, probably it felt guilty and was hiding. He had scolded the cat that morning because it had defecated in his room. It did not adjust to France immediately and Richard believed that its forgetfulness of toilet training was a form of revolt. Then he remembered that he had locked Knobby in the kitchen with a pan of sawdust that morning: "A cat is indeed a strange animal . . . Wonder if there is a way of making them behave. I don't think so. They are so utterly independent."

How happy Knobby would be to see him and to be released from prison, Richard thought, and he hurried to the kitchen. Smiling in anticipation of the cat's joy, he called its name as the door opened. But the cat merely lifted its head and gave a pitiful, slightly raucous sound. The lithe tan body was curled tightly, its dark brown feet hidden by the long tail. After a first sound of recognition, Knobby put his head down on his paws and looked up at Richard with staring aquamarine eyes. The cat was sick! What should he do? Ellen wasn't home! Tenderly, he picked up the animal and felt of its nose. It was hot! And dry! He murmered soothingly, keeping his voice soft, but beads of perspiration covered the upper part of his forehead. Still holding Knobby, he went to the telephone directory and looked for a veterinarian; it took a few seconds because all he could remember in the midst of panic was the word for cat, *le chat.*

When Richard arrived with Knobby at the clinic of an animal doctor he carried the cat into the examining room and laid it on a metal table. Then he watched closely while the doctor felt the cat's body. Putting on a rubber glove, the veterinarian put his fingers into the animal's rectum and began to remove splintered bones and hair. Knobby did not fight or cry; he just looked up wildly into Richard's face. After the ordeal ended the doctor cautioned that a cat must not be fed chicken unless it was removed from the bone and charged only one dollar for the visit.

During the ride home; Knobby nestled against Richard's thigh and he reached down to smooth the soft fur; relief was superseded by annoyance. Dammit! He had told Ellen and Alice, the maid, not to give the cat chicken bones! Why didn't women listen to what they were told! Knobby's pain could have been avoided! How could he work when he was forced to take care of such details? Well, he would insist, this time, that the two women listen to him! No more chicken bones! He was exasperated: "It is not enough that I spend my damn time worrying about the human race, but goddammit, I must worry about the animal kingdom too!"

Around the middle of August, Richard received a telephone call from Carson McCullers and he took a taxi to the apartment she was sharing with Reeves, her husband, with whom she had reconciled. It was a hot, sultry day. When Richard bounded out of the cab he glanced at his wristwatch: 3 P.M., he noted. Wonder when it will cool off this evening. The door opened almost before he had removed his hand from the bell. Carson was alone; she seemed feverishly happy to see him. He hid his shock under a wide smile which widened his eyes and raised his eyebrows slightly. God! She looked ill. Carson was dressed in trousers, a white shirt open at the throat, and her lank brown hair straggled limply. She could not see out of one eye, and the whole right side of her face was numb, while the left side of her body seemed paralyzed.

Within five minutes of his arrival Carson brought out several bottles of chilled beer with two glasses. Smiling wryly, her face twisting from the numbness, she told Richard that her doctors had said she must not drink at all. She's "pathetic—all from too much drinking," Richard thought sadly. "She was seized with absolute tension, afraid that something [had] gone wrong with her brain."

When Carson had drunk four bottles of beer, she pulled herself up from the chair and brought out a bottle of cognac. Taking a small glass, she poured it half full of the gold colored liquid and offered it to Richard, but he shook his head. Tilting her chin, Carson paused, then repeated the doctors' warning, and swallowed half the brandy. "It is because I am so glad to see you," she told Richard. "I haven't been anywhere in two months."

Carson described a second stroke[5] that had bludgeoned her body in June. Reeves had been in the American Hospital, in Neuilly, suffering from an infected leg, and Carson had been at home alone. In the middle of the night she had awakened with a parched mouth feeling terribly thirsty. She had taken only a step or two from her bed, intending to get a glass of water, when suddenly she fell to the floor, conscious but unable to move at all. For eight hours she lay on the floor alone and paralyzed.

Richard's mind ached from the description; it brought back his own fear—as if he were reliving it—on the day his mother had had her first stroke. Her face, with its staring eyes, seemed to superimpose itself on Carson's. He watched her hands tremble when she picked up the bottle of cognac and poured another drink, a few wet drops shook over the rim of the glass. Hoping to ease her tension, Richard told her of his mother's experience, and without actually lying, simply omitting the fact of Ella's life-long invalidism, he assured Carson that she would recover and that nothing at all was wrong with her brain.

For the first time in an hour Carson smiled; then, leaning forward and staring out of the window where the streetlights were beginning to glow, she confessed that something else was troubling her in addition to her own physical condition. It was Reeves. He was not well. People were staring at him all the time, he believed; watching him. It was getting worse and worse and he was drinking heavily. Sometimes she even suspected that he might be taking drugs.[6] Richard was fascinated. To conceal his avidity toward the story which Carson's genius made so lucid, he glanced at his watch. Eight o'clock! He had been there since three! Please, don't go, Carson pleaded. Reeves had left home early that morning and she had not heard from him since; she was afraid something had happened.

When Carson begged Richard to have dinner with her he agreed; he wanted to hear the rest of the story and he was curious to look at Reeves—if and when he came home—and find out if he was taking drugs. After he called Ellen and explained only obliquely that he was remaining at Carson's, lowering his voice mysteriously, they sat down to dine. During dinner they both drank wine and ended the meal with cognac and coffee. "Nobody can worry like a Southern woman," Richard thought to himself. He was growing restless; it was late and he wanted to leave, but Reeves had not returned. How could he leave the poor woman? he thought. He had lost count of the number of drinks she had taken but wished that she would stop prefacing each one with the doctors' instructions. Her face seemed to have grown pasty white. "Why does she repel me so? The more I talk with her the more I feel that there is something in her that I cannot like; and she is one person whom I want to like."

At last Richard heard a key turn in the door; but it was only a neighbor who had come to stay with Carson. Good! He could leave.

As soon as he had said good night and reached the street exhaustion made it difficult to walk. He was drained—limp emotionally. "She will die soon . . ." he thought. A sly, malicious idea made him smile: "Maybe she has other visions of what has happened to [Reeves] visions which she will not tell us about."

Early the next morning Richard was awakened by a shrilling telephone bell and, still sleepy, he got out of bed, thrust his feet hurriedly into his slippers and picked up the receiver. It was Carson and she was nearly hysterical. Reeves had not been home at all; she was convinced that he was dead, injured or in jail. As well as he could, Richard calmed her slightly, promising that he would try to find Reeves himself. All morning, Richard and Ellen made telephone calls to the police, to various hospitals and to all their mutual friends. No one had seen Reeves. Late in the day Carson called again. Reeves was at home; he had been wandering around all night and day, going from café to bistro, drinking.

A few days later Richard drove Carson and Reeves to a party. Ellen sat in the front with him and Reeves and Carson climbed into the back. Curious to see if the handsome blond Irishman was taking drugs, Richard peered at him in the rear-view mirror when they stopped in traffic. He saw no evidence of drugs. When they arrived at the party Richard was surprised to see that Reeves was only about as tall as Carson; seated he had appeared taller. When he spoke or laughed his voice was pleasantly modulated, but Richard thought there was something about him that reminded him of public relations men. He was too charming!

During the evening Carson talked to Richard about her husband. Chain-smoking, Carson squinted slightly through the haze; she blamed most of Reeves' despair on herself. Reeves had also wanted to be a writer and when they had married they agreed that they would take turns: she would work for a year and support him while he wrote, and then the arrangement would be reversed. But somehow, partially through Carson's outstanding success with fiction, Reeves could not write. If only he could find some interesting creative work in Paris, she told Richard. And, unasked, he volunteered to introduce Reeves to Claudet-Edmonde Magny and one or two other writers to see if a job could be found.

An hour or so later Ellen, who had been talking to Reeves, told Richard that she had to leave. Alice, who was looking after Julia, had to go home before twelve. She would take a cab so that he could stay. And Reeves, who stood at her elbow gallantly, though somewhat drunkenly, insisted that he put Ellen into a taxi. When she demurred he continued to insist so, making a small moue to Richard,

Ellen left with Reeves. In about ten or fifteen minutes he was back at the party taking another drink.

Ellen was still awake, reading in bed, when Richard tiptoed lightly into the apartment. Idly, as he took off his suit jacket Richard glanced at his wife. She looks so pretty; and her cheeks are all pink, he thought. Ellen smiled at Richard and then laughed: "Reeves made a drunken pass at me. He tried to climb into the cab but he was so drunk I just pushed him away." Richard was momentarily numbed by shock: many men had flirted or stared at his wife but no one had ever dared make a pass at her! His cheeks felt hot! Absolute outrage seemed to shake his mind from side to side like a dog tearing and pulling at a rag. For a second he could not see at all; then he grew aware of Ellen's figure on the bed, the rounding of her hip under the covers, the small breasts curving under the folds of her nightgown. She was staring at him, waiting for him to laugh with her; her eyes had deepened from amber to a deeper shade. Something about Ellen was so vulnerable, he thought. She depended on him, belonged to him. It was his job to look after her and see that nothing ever hurt her. A flash of revulsion toward Reeves came and then disappeared. There was something disgusting about a man who would make a pass at his wife. Then he felt the pressure of her fingers on his hand and, turning, he put his arms around his wife.

At six o'clock the next morning Richard took out his diary and sat down at the typewriter. Reeves and his effrontery toward Ellen the night before was still in the front part of his mind. It's true he was drunk, Richard thought, but then, putting a sheet of paper in the typewriter, he described his anger. "I've been trying to find a job for Reeves, but can you help a man to find a job when he molests your wife? I'll not help him anymore and I'll keep away from both Carson and Reeves."

The following week Carson called to remind Richard that they wanted to meet Claudet-Edmonde Magny so he took them to meet the writer. And early in November Carson telephoned to tell Richard that blood had been found in her urine. She was sure that she would die soon and then her pain would be ended. That afternoon Carson entered the American Hospital; she had had another stroke. Ellen and Richard picked up Reeves in their car and drove him to Neuilly. Carson lay in a high hospital bed; "as usual she was pasty white, puffy cheeks, watery eyes—all from drinking" was Richard's diagnosis. Her kidneys were infected; Carson was seriously ill. He sat down at her bedside and tried to alleviate some of her terror by telling her of medical case histories describing recovery from stroke and paralysis.[7] When he saw that she was a little cheered and had stopped saying that she was going to die, Richard got up to leave; he did not want to exhaust Carson and he hated the hospital atmosphere.

Reeves jumped to his feet and followed Richard from the room; he was not staying with his wife, he wanted to leave too. As he walked rapidly to his car Richard brooded about Reeves. What a peculiar man! It was still early in the evening! Carson was seriously ill and frightened! Why didn't he stay with his wife? Richard glanced at Ellen's face and knew that the same thoughts were going through her mind. Then he glanced at the face of Reeves, whose virile facial contours were softened from excessive drinking; he was striding along quite cheerfully. A sharp distaste for the man made Richard anxious to leave his presence. A self-destructive man, he thought: "There was something cruel about him."

On August 17 Richard refused an invitation for dinner and a sense of contentment and virtue pervaded him when he was at last alone. For almost half an hour he stood in the doorway of the room he shared with Ellen and looked out at the garden. A waning sun fell sharp and clear across buildings whose age seemed to absorb and soften the light. Far off were faint street noises that seemed held on a periphery around the oasis of his solitude, and a love of France entered his thoughts: "How calm I've felt in Paris! No more of that tension which grips so hard that it almost makes you dizzy. I walk down a street and I feel my legs swinging free. I'm much more at home this time in Paris; the last time I had to adjust myself. But this time I accept Paris and its quiet charm."

When he contemplated the small hotel room he had just rented across from Odette's, his pleasure increased; it was all set up for work the next day. It was a dirty little place but cost only 100 old francs a day, fifty cents—where in the United States could one get such a bargain? His Underwood was in place on an old table; paper was arranged in boxes; books were stacked nearby; bottles of vitamins C, B, D and three types of antacid pills were lined up on the desk. Tomorrow he would start to work again. Satisfaction grew stronger as he thought to himself: it's the first time I've refused to go out to dinner, "the first conscious gesture I've made to get out of losing so much time since I've been here." The weather was so hot he decided to rise earlier than ever so that he would have a few quiet hours to work. All three of his books were being published in French editions in September. "Gosh," he thought, "everyone wants to see me. There have been four and five column spreads in several newspapers already!" His mood began to change. "How can I get any work done when reporters and photographers call me all the time." His mind shifted to the hotel room across the street: "Wonder if my typewriter is safe there?" Suddenly, he was certain that it had been stolen and, taking the key to the room, he hurried across the street. When he switched on the light he saw that everything was exactly as he had left it that morning.

Back in his own apartment he prowled into the back bedroom which Julia shared with the cook, then back to the front room and into the garden. Finally, he went to the kitchen for a glass of mineral water. His stomach felt tight; he hoped it was not a signal that it would soon start to churn and grind again. He pulled two cellophane-wrapped pills out of his pocket and chewed them thoroughly. He was restless and, glancing at his wristwatch, he saw that it was still quite early. Ah! He would make some dough for bread and rolls. That would help him to relax. Feeling happy, he hummed while he took out flour, crumbled yeast into a cup of warm water and set it to one side while he mixed the other ingredients. After he put sugar into the bowl of flour—he wanted sweet rolls—a few grains adhered to his fingers and he licked them clean. Dammit! Ellen had let Julia play with the salt and sugar again. They were mixed together. Anger rose when he wondered if the combination would spoil the dough for the rolls. Ellen let her daughter play with salt, sugar, butter and tomatoes; and "all this in front of people who are almost starving. [He] had to have an end to it, as it is rather shameful."[8]

Early the following morning, before it had grown light outside, Richard went across the quiet street to his new workroom and stayed until nearly twelve o'clock. When he crossed the street to return home he looked up at the sky: it was a beautiful day, hot again, a little sultry, but a lovely Paris summer day! He had written 2,000 words on the novel; at last he was starting to work again. Life was good! What a city! "I have to remind myself that I'm a Negro when I live in Paris. There are whole days when I forget it. How lucky!" Whistling, he entered the apartment.

Going into the kitchen, Richard looked for his daughter, but she was upstairs with Lila de Nobeli, the niece of Vertès, who wanted to paint her portrait. Alice was preparing the midday meal and the aroma made his mouth water. He took a potholder and lifted the lid on one of the casseroles. It smelled good he told Alice and turned to smile at her. Her face did not look as bright as usual—was something troubling her? Richard asked if she was feeling well and at his concern a spigot seemed to open. It was Odette. Odette and Julia. Alice said that every time he and Ellen left the house Odette complained to her about the child: she said it was no longer her own home; Julia touched her possessions; her voice was too penetrating; she was walking on the flowers in her garden. Richard's face remained calm but abstracted as he listened to the long list of complaints. He reassured Alice, telling her not to worry, that he would take care of the problem. But as he went in search of Ellen he seethed with anger. Odette just did not like Julia; she did not like any child; as a matter of fact, "The French people really [did] not like children. They hate them! [He'd] seen it in every adult Frenchman [he'd] yet met. Yet they like[d] to say that they like children."[9]

Odette's criticism of Julia jogged Richard's memory and brought to the surface a house mystery. From the first days in the apartment he had noticed a mysterious little man, carrying a doctor's satchel, enter the house early each morning. He had asked Ellen a few times if someone was ill but she had not thought so and Richard put the incident out of his mind. Now, as he thought back over the months at Odette's he remembered that the mysterious man came every day. That was strange and exciting. What was going on? Did the dark-suited man always enter Odette's apartment? There was something eerie about the whole business and with that thought a thrill went through Richard. What kind of secrets were hidden in the house? Curiosity flared insistently and he felt such pleasure that he smiled, wanting to laugh. A gleeful expression covered his face and within ten minutes more than half a dozen possible answers, as detailed in plot and minor characters as a short story, went through his mind. He was entering secret ground. When a decision was made to find out all he could about Odette his face assumed an expression of innocence.

When the "doctor" arrived early the following morning Richard was secretly watching. Dressed all in shabby but neat black and wearing a starched white shirt, carrying a satchel, the man appeared furtive. Richard was convinced that the little man was involved in something that made him feel guilty. Later in the day he looked at Odette more closely than usual. She was very talkative; but then she was always talking, talking, about art. But wasn't she too vivacious? Her eyes glittered and she moved her hands restlessly when she spoke. There was a feverishness about her that could mean only one thing—dope! The "doctor" came every morning to give her a shot of dope! Suddenly, Richard was convinced; there was every symptom. Glee and relish of the mystery died abruptly. Worry crowded in on him as he thought of his daughter and Ellen. What a terrible environment for his family; he would have to move out as soon as possible.

Securing an apartment in France had to be approached scientifically, Parisian friends told Richard. Secretly, Richard believed that the best way to find a place was to inquire in barbershops or brasseries in the neighborhood of one's choice. "Then you give a little something to the small man or woman who needs it," he thought. And the "French people were peculiar. Legally they [did] the illegal things, but if you [went] to them as a friend they [would] not gyp you too badly."

An apartment was found at 16 Avenue de Neuilly, Neuilly-sur-Seine in October. Richard signed a year's lease for 194,000 old francs, which included a security of 50,000 to be returned when they moved out. And Odette offered to return the money she had been paid and willingly canceled the year's lease Richard had made with her. They parted on good terms with Madame Lieutier.

As the packing progressed Richard felt that he had to oversee everything. He collected large wooden boxes in which to pack the food they had brought from America. After the packages and tins were safely stored inside he covered the crates with paper and sealed the boxes shut: the movers must not see how much food they had. They would steal some of it, no matter what, if they saw it. "And could you really blame them if they saw food and stole some and were hungry?" Salaries were low and commodities were high: two movers received only eight dollars for taking Richard and Ellen's possessions from Rue de Lille way over to Neuilly. Before the trunks and boxes were unpacked in the new five-room flat Richard left and walked to the Métro where he caught a train for Porte de Clignancourt and the Flea Market. Gosh! How Ellen loves this place, he thought, as he searched along the open-air corridors for a large worktable. He poked about systematically among the furniture stalls, not allowing himself to be distracted. Pressure was building steadily: he had to get settled so that he could work. At last he found a large, sturdy oak table for the study he was arranging; it would hold his typewriter, boxes of paper, carbon, books, and miscellaneous pill containers with ease.

On the way back to the apartment Richard stopped to buy wooden planks and bricks with which to construct a bookcase. He felt too impatient to wait and search for one that was suitable; that would mean more delay. In the midst of his activities for his own study he gave instructions to Ellen. She was to go to the Flea Market to buy a large wardrobe in which their food could be stored. A few hours later she returned happy and excited: a beautiful antique wardrobe had been found in the Latin Quarter. While he completed his bookshelves Richard listened to his wife's bubbling description without comment. He was exceedingly skeptical: an antique! Women were impractical creatures. It would be too fragile or weak to hold all the cans of food. And it was huge, the way Ellen described it. "How will we get it up the stairs?" he asked. He was not to worry about it at all; when it was delivered the next day she and Alice would carry it up to the kitchen.

Around noon, on the following day, two men brought the beautiful, but mammoth mahogany wardrobe. But they could not carry it up the stairs alone and Richard had to help. Even then it was too large for the areaway, so the three laboriously took the entire thing apart and got it into the house. "Another day lost," he muttered to himself. "Women are strange and how peculiarly feminine of Ellen. She thought she could carry it up the stairs herself when she could not even lift it up one step."

Twice on September 2 Richard went to the ice house and returned home the last time in a well-concealed rage. He went into his study, closed the door part-way only, so that he could hear what was happening in the rest of the apartment, and typed in his diary:

Now, I ask you, is not that the reason that France is so damned poor today? I don't understand it. I left word with the ice man to say yes or no to me about the ice. Imagine a man refusing money! But he did. I love this French mentality sometimes, but not always. Not when practical matters are concerned. I see that most French stores are closed not only for two hours during lunch, but for longer periods. No wonder the men do not have suits to wear; the women are shoddy. I love leisure, but not the kind of leisure that leaves a nation of beggars and cheats. Leisure should come after you have made yourself secure. Leisure that comes before security is pathetic. Now at five o'clock I must go for ice myself. There must be somewhere a blending of the tolerant way of life of the French and the love of comfort of the American. Each would enrich the other; I've found that most Americans are quicker to take what France has to offer than the French are to take what America has to give. Mostly when the French do take what we have to offer, they take the wrong things, like race hate. . . .[10]

Richard hid away his diary and then walked over to look out the window. It was an airy, clean, fine apartment and he liked the neighborhood. Well, he was all set for a year at least. He was going to live in Paris! Feeling cheerful, he left his study to find Ellen and see what else needed to be organized.

When Richard opened his eyes on September 4 he lay still for a minute trying to fasten his mind on the reason for a feeling of anticipation. It was his birthday. "I'm thirty-nine years old . . . And not much work done. I don't feel old, just tired from too much worry about petty things." Later in the morning when Ellen awakened they baked a chocolate birthday cake together. Richard was feeling sentimental. In the afternoon he decided to walk to the public market and toward the Etoile on Avenue de Neuilly. A crystal blue sky covered Paris and Richard looked at everything in the food market: "He had six eyes." "What a riot of rich life," Richard thought, "what people are these French; how unashamed they are to sell and buy; how frank and dirty and fat and wobbly are the French housewives; how the women went with their breasts trembling and with not a thought of a brassiere. [He] wandered slowly through [the market] and came out with a keen sense of having been fed at the pap of life itself. What smells! What sights of vegetables, wares, bottles!"

Just two weeks after Richard's birthday Ellen took Julia to the country and in the evening he went to the Tabu with a group of friends. As soon as he walked into the club photographers began to take his picture. He did not like it but concealed his irritation, smiling until his face felt stiff. Restlessness made him drink too much cognac and the music was imitation New Orleans jazz. The atmosphere was hot and people seemed to shout in his ears. "[He] hated that place; it made [him] feel like [he] was living again those horrible days in Chicago when he was lonely and hungry and scared. He could not tell his friends what he was feeling, but simply said that he had gone off the track somewhere and wanted to go home. He did not really want to go home, but he wanted something that would nourish him. That was what he was missing, nourishing experiences. Driving home, he felt that he wanted to blot out the sight and sense of reality that was "stale and crumby." But the evening had not been a complete waste, he thought; there was a sharp pressure to put down in his diary a paragraph that hung clear in his mind as if on a sheet of paper. He would lie in bed in a few moments and again late in the morning to "think and dream some so that my own DEEP REST-LESS AND HURT SELF CAN COME ONCE MORE TO THE FORE, SO THAT ONCE AGAIN I CAN STOP FEELING LIKE A HUNTED BEING AND FEEL LIKE A BEING HUNTED. THERE IS A SUBTLE BUT PROFOUND DIFFERENCE, YOU KNOW."

I choose exile . . .

XXII

How rare a man is this Sartre, Richard thought, looking across his living room at the short, rather homely man with thick eyeglasses. Sartre was speaking with the enthusiasm of a youngster and Richard heard every word, but his mind pondered the Frenchman's quality. "His ideas must be good for they lead him into the areas of life where man sees what is true." And he was the only person in France who had voluntarily made an identification of the French suffering, under the Fascists, with that of the rest of mankind.

When he had met Jean-Paul Sartre in the United States at the home of Dorothy Norman in 1946 Richard had found him interesting but felt that he was holding back what he really thought and felt about America. At the time all of New York's intellectuals had been "buzzing over existentialism, trying to understand it. It frighten[ed] most folks. . . ."[1] And the fright and excitement Richard sensed in white writers sent him straight to Brentano's to buy the Christian existentialists, Kierkegaard, Heidegger and Husserl. Then he had read Sartre and Camus; he had been astonished. "Why!" he told a friend, "they are writing of things that I have been thinking, writing and feeling all of my life!"

Man as an alone, anguished being in an unintelligible world which led him into areas of cold dread, fear, anxiety, and psychic pain was the everyday world of the American black man. Excitedly, Richard went to the bookshelf, ran his eyes quickly along the copies of his bound volumes and pulled out *Black Boy*. "Look," he said, "this is existentialist," and read from his book.

From the accidental pain of southern years, from anxiety that I had sought to avoid, from fear that had been too painful to bear, I had

learned to like my unintermittent burden of feeling, had become habitu-
ated to acting with all of my being, had learned to seek those areas of life,
those situations, where I knew that events would complement my own
inner mood. I was conscious of what was happening to me; I knew that
my attitude of watchful wonder had usurped all other feelings, had
become the meaning of my life, an integral part of my personality; that I
was striving to live and measure all things by it.

It was a dangerous way to live, far more dangerous than violating laws or
ethical codes of conduct; but the danger was for me and me alone. Had I
not been conscious of what I was doing, I could have easily lost my way
in the fogbound regions of compelling fantasy.[2]

Richard differed from the existentialists in that they understood
modern life through philosophical contemplation. In the black
American fear led to dread, then anger, then self-hatred and ended in
a sense of emptiness and meaninglessness—the ennui and malaise of
Sartre's characters. But it was more than philosophy to the black
man; it was life itself. He knew that his own unbearable times of
futility arose when he was confronted by the abysmal ignorance and
stupidity of the white man who could not understand what a Negro
was saying. And his preoccupation with self-hate and anguish was an
examination of a reality, not philosophy. "What does a Negro do,
emotionally and mentally, when he reaches the American-Chinese
wall in his aspirations?" For the black man in America there was
always an actual wall; that was the reality of his existence and it was a
reality that he could not accept. Sartre's heroes accepted that life was
an unvarying torture, it was the condition of man and all that
remained was to accommodate himself to anguish and seek freedom
within the realm of a total act. Anguish drove Richard to the side of
the rebel, and total involvement meant a collective involvement; he
was indissolubly linked with his people. Sometimes, he felt that the
French existentialists were naïve. At the core of the personality with
extremes of character reaction lay fear and hatred of the white man
who had humiliated and frustrated the black man. That was an
objective fact. And on his return from Paris in 1947 Richard's reply
to those who asked his opinion about existentialists was simple:
". . . existentialism is a manifestation of a lack of effectiveness for
political action among the intellectuals and the petty-bourgeoisie of
the Western World. They feel the failure of the bourgeois world and
the inability of the proletariat to express their conceptions. They are
therefore restricted to the personal expression of what they want.
How can I blame Man? Something intrinsic and unchanging in his

nature? When they lynch a black man in Mississippi, I am lynched. And that is fact not philosophy!"[3]

Richard was feeling "very close to Sartre and Simone de Beauvoir" the evening of September 7; he and Ellen had gone to a little restaurant with Simone on Boulevard St. Germain, while the French philosopher had dined with his mother and then joined them later in Neuilly. While he listened to Sartre he glanced at the handsome, blue-eyed Simone. Frenchwomen are the strangest in the world, he thought. They like men and they know what to do with them. And they're not ashamed of being women. . . . This combination of womanness and sharp thought is something almost unknown in America.

They discussed Richard's favorite topic: freedom. "Freedom for you is not freedom for another," Richard suggested to Sartre. "Perhaps it has to be defined negatively because when you define it concretely you lose it?"

Sartre felt that it was "his right rather than his duty to defend, on purely humanistic grounds, the interests of workers, to castigate anti-semites, racism, and imperialism." And Simone, too, shared the same humanistic passion to defend the dignity of man, to advocate an equality of respect among peoples—a passion they felt compelled to weave into their artistic productions. That was part of their freedom.

Richard marveled that the French did not argue about *personal* freedom; they just *lived* it. It was in America, where so much freedom was lacking, that one heard loud and passionate argument about it. It was like listening to a starving man tell of his need for bread, Richard thought.[4]

And the French intellectual was being confronted with almost as sharp a loss of freedom as the black man had always known in America. To be anti-Fascist or anti-Communist in France was a totally different thing from being anti-Communist or anti-Fascist in America. American anti-Communism was vague, highly emotional, somewhat hysterical; French anti-Communism was concrete, definite, specific. The issue there was not whether you wanted to be a Communist or not, but what concretely could one do under a Communist regime? How much freedom, if any, would be left?

Richard discovered that the ideological divisions in French public opinion deepened daily. De Gaulle waited in the wings. What was referred to cynically as the Schuman Intermezzo seemed to be turning into an independent work of its own; the drama between de Gaulle and the Communists had been temporarily stalled. Schuman acted quickly to keep the Gaullists and the Communists from tearing at each other's throats, a battle which would have meant civil war in

France. But he battled daily to hold his own. His fight to save the franc had not succeeded, and almost every move he made, no matter how drastic, actually weakened it. Technical manipulations could not solve problems rooted deeply in people's hearts.

Before the formation of the Cominform, hundreds of thousands of honest French intellectuals had, in relation to Communism, become, in the language of the Communist Party, "neutralized"; that is, they would not have actively opposed an attempt to seize power on the part of the Communists. But the formation of the Cominform shook them badly. One of the stock arguments of the French Communists was that their revolution would be a *French* revolution, that their Communist Party was a *French* Communist Party. But such illusions were forever gone. Many of the "neutral" intellectuals fled to de Gaulle, not because they loved de Gaulle but because they feared the power and might of Moscow.

Two French families asked Richard if he would take their children to America if Russia moved in France's direction. Another friend told him that the suffering under German occupation had been so terrible that if Russia advanced on Paris he would kill his wife and children rather than submit them to torture again.

The two countries most on the lips of Frenchmen were America and Russia. The Left wanted to side with the USSR, but they had been weakened and did not have enough support; the Right sided with America, not because it wanted to but from fear of the Left and in light of the terrible need for aid to rebuild the country.

Sartre was groping for a "third way" out, a way that admitted the inevitability of industrialization but would keep individual freedom intact. Gaullists sneered at him and called such thinking *la troisième farce*.

"The great danger," Richard told Sartre, "in the world today is that the very feeling and conception of what is a human being might well be lost." During their long talk, the two men agreed that it was "up to the individual to do what he [could] to uphold the concept of what it means to be human."

The ideological divisions in French public opinion deepened daily. Journalists and literary critics found it increasingly difficult to make a living by writing what they wanted to, what they felt. The Paris press was sharply Right and Left with hardly anything in between. Not only was all serious journalism political, but violently partisan. Many journalists and critics were thinking of turning to other professions, less dangerous ones. A crack French journalist, a friend of Richard's, confessed to him that he was thinking of taking up law; another, a critic, an ex-schoolteacher, was seriously making plans to resume her teaching career. Certain kinds of activity, feelings, thoughts were no longer possible, acceptable, or wanted.

When French newspapers reported the questioning of actors by the House Un-American Activities Committee it was incomprehensible. People kept asking Richard: "How many Communists have you in America?" And when he answered: "Not more than a hundred thousand,"[5] they did not know what to say. Frenchmen were used to dealing with Communists by the million, not by the thousand.

Richard went to meetings at the Quai d'Orsay which shocked him. Wild cries of hate and revenge resounded; there were fistfights and senseless singing to drown out opponents from both sides—Right and Left. "When a Rightist would try to speak, the Communists would yell: 'Where is your chewing gum?' . . . And when a Communist tried to speak, the Right would yell: 'Go back to Moscow!' " French national pride kept the scenes from the airways of the world although the daily press touched on them gingerly.

He had seen strange things between August, 1947, and February, 1948: Mobile Guardsmen protecting workers as they strove to remove piles of reeking garbage from the city's streets; troops guarding subways, post offices, and power plants; men and women meekly surrendering their voided 5,000-franc notes to the banks when they did not know where their next meal was coming from; angry Frenchmen trying to wreck a sleek American car with a TT license; 60-octane gasoline selling for 130 francs a litre; a real estate man baldly asking 2,500,000 francs for an apartment; trucks hauling people like cattle during the Métro strike; cooking pots that cost 2,550 francs; people staring at the rubbers he wore when it rained as though they were staring at the feet of a man from Mars.

Well, Richard thought, the situation was bleak; there was no use pretending otherwise. His friend, C. L. R. James, in New York, had advised him to have at all times tickets for his return to the United States. If the Russians entered Paris, it was James' belief, that they would execute Richard forthwith.[6] So he went to Cook's and purchased three plane tickets which he secreted in his passport folder. The act held a touch of intrigue and cloak-and-dagger behavior which he relished, but Richard made up his mind that he would not leave France until the last possible minute. Too much was happening. In extreme situations, such as that confronting the French, men had leaped out and created themselves and the world anew. Would this happen in France? He did not know. But he believed that the battle of the Left and the Right, of the individual versus the mass, of industrialism versus freedom was being fought out in their hearts.

The kind of agony rending the hearts of Frenchmen was unknown in America. And, win or lose, what happened in France would say something important about human life on the earth.

On February 10, 1948, Richard took Ellen to Italy for a five-day combined vacation business trip. He had to talk with his Italian publisher, Einaudi, in Rome. When Richard stepped off the train in the *cave* of the Stazione Termini and walked to the upper level he looked around eagerly at the famous white marble building which Nervi had designed. It was so light! A glittering sunshine struck through what appeared to be walls of plate glass and was absorbed into the pure creamy marble. How clean everything is, he marveled. As Richard stepped outside he looked back at the terminal; normally he hated most modern architecture, but Nervi had created a stream-lined edifice which blended easily and naturally with the old lime-stone buildings around it. A few blocks away he paused in the Piazza dell' Esedra to stare at the largest working fountain in Europe. Water sprayed toward a blue sky, softening still more a view of beautiful baroque buildings.

Rome was wonderful! Richard looked at the shops filled with goods at what Americans would call reasonable prices. Too high, of course, for poor Italians. At night the streets were drenched in light, which contrasted sharply with the dark streets of Paris. There was an odd and vibrant spirit in Italy; it was more alive than France. Richard had never realized how handsome a people were the Italians when seen en masse in their own country. And the Italians seemed even to be able to make something dashing out of chronic poverty. There was none of that sodden hopelessness which seemed to be bogging down the French. Even an Italian begger made a joke about his plight.

Carlo Levi arrived at Richard's hotel and in exuberant European fashion hugged him warmly. Short and fat, Levi was jolly and laughing; his keen eyes glinted sharply at Richard through his glasses and he began at once to talk about a United States of Europe, his face saddening momentarily when he spoke of the "relentless march of the Cominform." But he was gay again when Richard asked about his painting and said that he was working hard at it and doing very little writing at the moment.

Levi arranged a luncheon for Richard the following day so that he could meet Italian artists and intellectuals. Richard asked about Italian sovereignty—"would they be willing to surrender it for the sake of European unity?" To a man, they declared yes. "They were aware of a deep bond with all the peoples of Europe and said that it was stronger than the factors which divided them."

There was really no government in Italy to speak of, Levi told Richard, just an uneasy coalition of many center parties, a coalition which changed constantly. Like in France, the Communists were out of the government and set upon a program to wreck the Marshall Plan. Two of the men at the luncheon questioned Richard about the "march of American imperialism as exemplified by the Marshall Plan." It seemed a curious question; he was no supporter of imperialism but he kept his voice soft and his face impenetrable and serene and replied by asking: "What would you do in Italy without the Marshall Plan?" There was no answer; one man drew up his shoulders; another looked out at the cobblestone street. "Would you consent to America withdrawing entirely from Europe?" Richard persisted. Several of the men began to speak at once—No! If that were done then Stalin would march to the English Channel. Sadly, Richard looked at the group of artists and intellectuals who represented some of the finest minds in Italy: how strange it was to see such sensitive, intelligent men in such a dilemma. They knew what they did not want but they could not really explain what they did want.

Later in the afternoon a friend drove Richard around Rome and finally took him to the Colosseum. The Italian told Richard proudly: "When your GIs raced into Rome in their jeeps, they stopped here and gasped and exclaimed: 'Gosh, look what our planes did there!'" How they have learned to protect their egos from the might of America, Richard thought to himself. But he laughed obligingly at the story and made no defense of the historical ignorance of his countrymen. A little later in their conversation, innocence in his voice, Richard asked why Italy had no price controls; the very necessities of life were skyrocketing in cost—even bread and pasta—the poor across the Tiber in Trastevere were starving. There were beggars everywhere; children with faces covered by sores and dirt, their skinny arms jutting out from ragged clothes, some hobbling on sticks—"What relationship do you intellectuals who dream of a strong and United Europe have with these child beggars and the poor?"

For a moment the Italian did not answer; then he shrugged, raised his fine black eyebrows and began to tell Richard, in an amused voice, that Lenin's prophecy about the withering away of the state after the dictatorship of the working class was coming true in Italy. Only, there had been no revolution in Italy. Lenin's theory that the people would become "good" when the class struggle was resolved, and that the state would no longer be needed as a repressive force had been turned upside down. There was so much corruption that the functions of the state had been replaced by an unbridled and ungovernable individualism. Hence, the state was "withering away" because everybody was so corrupt. Richard laughed lightly but he did not think corruption was something to joke about.

Levi had told Richard that the government had decided to issue a new currency a few months previously and had new plates engraved but then someone in government had stolen the plates, made duplicates, and had been ready to issue the same currency simultaneously. Italians seemed to find it an amusing story. Richard shook his head: it was immoral. And he wondered if Italians were related strongly to one another in a social sense. No, he did not think so. They were related through the church to eternity. They let social relations take care of themselves as best they could. And he did not believe Italians as a people were very honest. No, he had never met an honest Italian, he mused. But, no—that was wrong! There was Levi and there was Fabio Coen, his Italian representative; and his friend Alberto Mondadori.

Before returning to Paris Richard stopped in England and Belgium. He was eager to contrast the political situation in Italy with that in other countries. "England [was] grim, but the English possess[ed] a community spirit which enable[d] them to play the old ritual. After twelve hours on English soil [he was] aware of a vague sense of physical discomfort, and it [was] with shame that [he came] to the conclusion that [he was] simply plain hungry. The food [was] badly cooked." Disgust drove Richard from restaurant to restaurant, and finally he went to a Chinese restaurant, feeling that they could not destroy the taste of food with the same consistency as did the English but he found that even the Chinese could not cook well under the English system of rationing. Slowly, the English morale was cracking; the government was demanding too much. It was not much satisfaction to an Englishman who had lived seven drab years to know that his country had at long last begun to export coal. Instead of qualitative pleasures and joys, the Labor government was feeding the masses on abstract slogans dealing with quantities of exports. And when an Englishman grumbled, he was told through his press that the nation's dollar balances were dwindling in the USA . . . Taxi drivers voluntarily told Richard that they were sick and tired, that they wanted to go to a land where the sun shone and people laughed and where there was some food. He suspected that many Englishmen would be willing to exchange places with some of their colonial subjects.[7]

In Belgium Richard found a difference in the atmosphere that repelled him. The United States was using certain ports and its payments to the Belgian government were helping to keep the country on its feet. More important were the rich uranium mines in the Congo and the sale of that highly prized ore had brought about a fantastic prosperity. Sleek and gleaming American cars roamed the streets of Brussels. He could purchase anything he wanted, but Richard wondered at the high prices. How could poor people afford them? The stores were filled with American products, from chewing gum to Wheaties. The most innocent-looking product was stamped "Made in the USA." Ugh, Richard thought. The Belgians were fat, dull, and their minds as narrow and devious as their winding streets. Without the Congo, Belgium would be nothing but a slag heap. A struggle in Africa would soon burst out, a fight over the uranium, and the Belgians would do all in their power to deceive and confuse the issues. But it will be the blacks who will define the kind of relationship that would take place ultimately, Richard thought.[8]

Seated on the train en route to Paris, Richard stared out at the countryside. In each of the countries he had visited he discerned a lack of a keen sense of direction among the people. They were in favor of some of the ideas of both Left and Right but their daily worries absorbed all of their emotions and intellectual energies. No one had any confidence in the money of his country; in the future of his country; in the literature of his country. American novels and movies were the most popular everywhere. And when an Italian or a Frenchman made a few thousand lire or francs, he rushed to buy American dollars or gold. They were afraid to invest in the business enterprises of their nations. And perhaps never in 2,000 years had the reality of the state been so dim in men's minds. Poor sick world. He shook his head, leaned his head back against the seat, unconsciously raising his hand to grasp his throat above his collar. The intellectuals everywhere were talking about a United States of Europe while the masses worried about bread and wine and coal. There was a brooding and fateful stillness and quiet; people were waiting. On the Left and the Right secret armies were arming for power. Neither side was appealing to the people and whichever side won they would lose.

It was no longer a struggle between the Right and the Left: each day the two extremes possessed more and more in common. Russia had her cultural purges and so did the United States; only in Russia it was official, and in America it was the force and so-called moral power of the community. But the results were the same in the end—a suppression of the individual, the devaluation of personality, and preachments against what they called "subjectivity." Common to both countries was an unbridled industrialism, an industrialism which was the yardstick of all value. "As things stand now," Richard thought, "the only difference is that Russia has taken our industrial methods and applied them with a ruthlessness which we cannot use because of our traditions of individual freedom. What is needed is something which is not of either of these two schools. . . . What is happening here in Europe is not only a contest between Left and Right, but a total extinction of the very conceptions of what it has meant to be a human being for 2,000 years. . . . Indeed, from the way the future looks, one can well ask if freedom is possible in the coming world? . . . What is happening now calls into question the very conception of man as man, and perhaps at no time since the decline of the Catholic Church in the Middle Ages can one ask with more pointedness: What is Man? For upon that answer will depend the kind of world we will build or allow to be built."[9] Man was not an animal whose needs could be met by making more and more articles for him to consume. Man could not be contained within such a definition.

Well, whatever happens in this struggle for freedom, Richard thought to himself, I'm going to be here to see it. Thank God he had married a woman who had the same propensity for rootlessness that he himself had! He and his family would remain in Europe, "in exile." There was nothing in America, its drugstores, skyscrapers, television, movies, baseball, Dick Tracy, Black Belt, Jew Town, Irish Section, Bohunks, Wetbacks, dust storms, floods, that he would miss or yearn for. He would maintain his American citizenship, pay his Federal income taxes, guard his American passport, keep his Social Security, serve in no foreign armies, subscribe to no alien ideologies, but he preferred to live out his daily life among alien peoples.

"Yes!" he seemed to hear raucous voices demanding: "What do you mean? *Freedom?*" He knew he ran the risk of being branded as un-American and to that he would plead guilty. What was more important was that he did not feel that he was anti-American. His un-American sentiments added up in his mind to a fundamental right: the right to live free of mob violence, whether that violence assumed the guise of an anonymous blacklisting or of pressure exerted through character assassination. His attitude was predicated upon an adherence to a democratic ideal which granted to all men the right to develop and exercise their natural and acquired powers of personality, so long as that development and exercise did not limit others to do the same. He was a democrat but he saw no democracy in America.

Ellen told Richard that during Julia's first days in school she had been given paper and crayons and had drawn a picture of some fruit.

His daughter had colored cherries blue and the teacher had corrected her; cherries were always green, red or yellow. A variation within that natural range was permitted but not self-expression which resulted in blue. And the lines for the cherries had to be followed precisely; Julia had colored free-spiritedly within the circle for the fruit and outside of it. It was self-indulgent to express oneself until one had learned the rules governing art.

"How strangely interesting," Richard thought. "In America they began in nursery school stimulating self-expression. Julia was given finger paints and encouraged to smear as she would like. Crayons were the same; every color, every design, every scribble was acceptable. How different was education in France."

"Education, that all-powerful instrument that shapes us to be more or less what we are. America romantically assumes that each man is born an embryonic genius and that equality of opportunity is all that is necessary to make him a wise, free, rich, and powerful individual. On the other hand, the French assume, with a supporting accumulation of sober wisdom which is the fruit of bitter experience, that we are born antisocial savages who must needs be molded into human beings and taught to curb our crude instincts so as not to wreak harm upon our neighbors." A world-famous French physiologist told Richard: "I'm an animal. But, through reflection, I *know* that I'm an animal, and it's my knowing this that makes me human. . . . Like Goethe, I feel within me the possibility of committing any crime. That's why I prefer to be civilized. And being civilized is a problem." As Richard listened, he felt a pathos of distance as he recalled having seen white mobs confidently running amok in American cities to chastize some hapless Negro.[10]

And at an Anglo-American Press luncheon held in honor of Richard and Senate Chairman Gaston Monnerville, one of the two chief representatives of the colonies and adviser to de Gaulle of the sentiments of the peoples of the French Union, he realized a further differentiation from his country's attitude. Looking at the distinguished black Monnerville, he decided that there were no insuperable barriers to those who declared their allegiance. The phrase *la famille française* was not a biological concept: though black and alien, he *could* become a Frenchman. But born in America he could never, with his black skin, hope to meet America's prime racial requirements of first-class citizenship as long as the atmosphere of Anglo-Saxon racial jealousy prevailed.

France was not a paradise and what freedom she had might not survive in a world bent upon stamping it out; and she had a brutal colonial system. But she gathered the most intelligent of young men from the black tribes, transported them to Paris, processed them through her universities, and later these educated blacks represented their lands in the Chamber of Deputies and the Senate. When Richard had criticized French colonization it had not been a Frenchman who rose to denounce him. Instead, these educated black men would buzz like hornets about his head. "It may not be justice," Richard thought, "but at least there's some logic in it."

At home I had spent half my life advocating the rights of the Negro, and I knew that if my fight was not right, then nothing was right. Yet I always felt a sneaking sense of futility because I knew that there was something basically wrong in a nation that could so cynically violate its own Constitution and democratic pretensions by meting out physical and psychological cruelties upon a defenseless minority. From the distance of a freer culture, my feelings somewhat changed. Anger turned into a sort of amazed pity, for I felt that America's barbaric treatment of the Negro was not one-half so bad as the destructive war which she waged, in striking at the Negro, against the concept of the free person, against freedom of conscience, against the Rights of Man, and against herself! I was disconcerted when I realized the vast dislocation of human values which the mere presence of the Negro in America had brought about.[11]

On May 15, 1948, Richard moved his family from Neuilly to 14 Rue Monsieur le Prince, on the Left Bank, near the American Community School of Paris at 261 Boulevard Raspail, which six-year-old Julia attended. Richard liked the large five-room flat on the third floor of an old building in the heart of the Latin Quarter. Just a block or two away were the beautiful Luxembourg Gardens and a little farther away, the Sorbonne. It was an old building with an inner courtyard, a stained glass window lighting the stairway, solid walls and heavy carved doors. Now, Richard thought with satisfaction, I am truly settled in France. He looked at Julia and laughed: she spoke French as if it were her native tongue but she would not let him or Ellen speak anything except English to her. "Children are funny," he mused. "It must be some form of security that she finds, something unchanging in her little world to have her mommy and daddy speak to her in the first language she ever knew." At least now I won't have to worry about going back to the States with a child who knows nothing about racial matters. It would make her ill! Her education would be brought to a standstill. One cannot really study and learn under racial conditions of life. That much I know. And she was going to have a sister; he and Ellen had made that decision while they were on the Continent. It would be a girl, another wonderful girl; he had made that decision too! He always preferred girls to boys and how happy Julia-baby would be to have a younger sister.

In June, and one month pregnant, Ellen sailed for the United States alone while Richard remained in Paris with Julia. Since all their belongings in storage in America—furniture, linens, dishes, silver, books, records, bedding—had to be divided into what was needed in France and what they would sell, Ellen, who could make such decisions, made the trip. And on January 17, 1949, in the American Hospital at Neuilly a small, seven-and-one-quarter-pound, baby was born. It was a girl. They named her Rachel.

I must make this film . . .

XXIII

During the summer of 1948 Richard received a telephone call from a
stranger who introduced himself as Pierre Chenal,[1] a motion picture
director. A meeting was arranged at a café, the Royal St. Germain,
and Richard donned a French beret, his dark glasses, and bounced
lightly down the stairs to the street. A mood of high excitement
gripped him; a new adventure might be in the making.

Chenal, a well-known European film maker, had just returned
from Argentina, where he had seen a production of the play Paul
Green had adapted from *Native Son*. "The story made so deep an
impression that it will not leave my mind," Chenal, his expressive
hands moving and his alert eyes glinting with enthusiasm, explained.
"I must make this film," he told Richard. Above all, there would be
no attempt to dodge any of the values or implications of the original
book.

Richard was impressed by Chenal's avowal of integrity. For many
years he had secretly believed that his novel held all the ingredients
for a dramatic murder film that would so engross an audience that
his "message," and attack against America's structured society would
slide easily into their minds and influence their actions. And there
had been many offers—one for $500,000—from American film
makers. But each one had his own notions as to the changes that
would be required to make *Native Son* palatable to a market which
included the Southern states. Richard had received an almost classic
letter from Harold Hecht Company, in Hollywood, which proposed
Joseph Fields, a screenwriter, for a working script. When he read the
letter Richard laughed until tears streamed down his cheeks and he

was finally overcome with a fit of coughing. Then, still gasping and emitting high thin laughs, he read the letter again:

The plans are to change the leading Negro character to an oppressed minority white man, but rest assured that we have every desire to preserve the integrity of the original work. Mr. Fields has a tentative idea which calls for the picture to start with a Negro, a Jew, and a Pole or Italian, all applying for the same job. The Negro and Jew step aside for the other man. He needs the job more than they because of some personal reason, perhaps because he is married. At the end of the picture we will tie this together by a scene with the Jew and the Negro who realize that it could have happened to them, or to anyone who does not have the opportunity of living in equality with other people; that when one group is disenfranchised the meaning and the basis of what we live for is destroyed.

. . . It will have a relationship to life as it is lived in this country and not be a glamorized, fictional Hollywood report.[2]

If a black man and a Jew were such damn fools as to step aside and give up a job they needed, they deserved anything they got; and no Jew or Negro needed experiences to prove or educate them that there was inequality. And he hooted in laughter again when he imagined Bigger Thomas as a white man. Ah, God! That's rich! Richard sighed.

Canada Lee, who played Bigger Thomas at the St. James Theatre for 116 performances in New York, before taking it on the road, and Mark Marvin, who worked with John Steinbeck on *Forgotten Village,* wanted to form a company to produce *Native Son* but it had fallen through for financial reasons.[3] A Canadian musician asked to do an opera based on the book and students, housewives and businessmen[4] wrote from all over the country asking if they might do adaptations. Still another film maker offered to produce the play as a musical. With a straight face, as if he were considering the offer, Richard told a friend: "Can you see Bigger Thomas being dragged down the steps to the tune of the 'Surrey With the Fringe on Top?' Or, maybe, the classics would be better?" and he hummed the opening notes of Beethoven's Fifth Symphony—"Dum-Dum-Dum-Dummmm, Dum-Dum-Dum-Dummm. . . ."[5]

While vacationing in Canada in 1945 he had become friends with John Grierson, Canada's Film Commissioner, and had told him that he would like to make films: "Or engage in some sort of government work. I know that as long as I live in the United States, I can never change my profession, for I'm regarded fatally as a Negro writer, that is, as a writer whose ancestors were Negroes and therefore the Negro is my special field." Grierson was shocked. He exclaimed: "Your lips are touched with fire . . ." and brushed aside Richard's suggestion that he had "set his heart on trying to work for the Canadian Film Board." Grierson refused to take him with seriousness: "It would be a terrible loss to the world if you stopped writing fiction," he said.

In April, 1944, Richard wrote a motion picture script about the adventures of the Jubilee Singers, who toured the U.S. and England during the 1870's to raise money for the building of Negro schools in the South. It was entitled *Melody Limited* but was never accepted by a motion picture company. And he collaborated with George Crosby, a novelist, on a movie idea, *The Last Flight,* for Columbia Pictures, at the request of Eve Ettinger, story editor for the company. It dealt with an American Nazi, à la Ezra Pound, who worked for the Germans as a radio broadcaster; seeing Germany begin to crumble, he sneaked back to the United States. But Miss Ettinger had not liked the final script and the project was forgotten.

It was Richard's conviction that the motion pictures of Charles Chaplin explored to the depths the social needs of the country and that the best fiction, for some years ahead, would celebrate the man whose arm is caught and crushed in the meshes, cogs and pulleys of a machine. "The theme is still Charlie Chaplin's *Modern Times,*" he told his friends. Chaplin was the universal man of the modern age, appealing to everyone, intellectuals and mass alike. Like Don Quixote, wearing a rose and a sweet smile, he fought the windmills of automation in defense of individual liberty.

As an aid to writing dialogue Richard purchased an Ediphone,[6] even though he had practically total recall of voices he had heard. He spoke the lines of each of his characters, assuming their guise and mannerisms, his voice slipping easily from high to low to in-between. Then he would play the cylinder and listen for any single false note which might be inconsistent to a character, a paragraph or an entire page. The motion picture had "sensitized the ear" of millions of Americans and a novelist of the twentieth century had to be cognizant of that advancement.

Chenal's proposal that he and an Uruguayan named James Prades make a film of *Native Son* pleased Richard. He was startled and intrigued when they told him that their offer rested in part on his agreement to play the role of Bigger Thomas. It was to be a three-way partnership: Prades would organize the venture, raise money, see to transportation, actors, scenery; Chenal would write the film-script and direct; Richard would act, supervise dialogue, guide the general meaning and color of the film and surrender the rights of the play to the corporation. But Richard could not surrender the rights, which were worth about $6,000, because they were held in conjunction with Wellman, Incorporated, in New York and Paul Green in Chapel Hill. Prades and Chenal offered to pay the necessary $6,000 to Richard in francs but he told them: "Oh, no. Under no circumstances will I accept that amount of money in a country where its value is in such doubt. If you can't come up with American dollars, then the whole deal is off." The two men agreed, and pre-option papers were drawn on *Native Son* for a one-month period after which the details of the partnership and the necessary contracts would be arranged. By that time, presumably, Prades and Chenal would have paid the $6,000 to secure the rights. Richard also insisted that if, after a screen test, he was not suitable for the role of Bigger Thomas, then the company would hire Canada Lee. It was agreed.

A few days later, early in the evening, Richard got in the car and decided to drive over to Montmartre. It had been many months since he had been at LeRoy Haynes restaurant and an age since he had talked to Haynes, his French wife and small son. Richard laughed down in his throat; the little boy was brown-skinned, with "good" hair, a typical French nose, and the sense of superiority hidden by the aplomb typical of his countrymen. Richard would sit at the bar with big, black, barrel-chested LeRoy, an ex-noncommissioned officer in the Army, and listen to his raucous stories. At some time during the evening Richard would ask the question he always asked, and LeRoy would answer with the same phrase as he let out guffaws and slapped him on the back. "LeRoy," he would say, "when are you going home?" And LeRoy would fake a serious soul-brother expression and answer: "Have they built a bridge?"

When Richard stepped through the door of LeRoy's, just a few blocks from a busy thoroughfare, up a winding hill, a blast of jazz struck his ears; and LeRoy, who was talking with some customers, barreled toward him with a shiny face and his arms stretched apart for an embrace. It would not have mattered whether he had been talking to the Premier of France. There was no one like Richard and Haynes loved him as one fighter loves another. There was nothing that he would not do for Richard Wright![7]

After he was seated LeRoy draped his huge white-apronclad figure onto a chair and leaned forward: "Why don't you eat something, brother?" he asked. "You want some of them good ole greens with pig tail, or shall I fry you up a nice young chicken?" And he laughed evilly at the double entendre. LeRoy had even let Richard in on the secret of his "greens." The French did not grow the greens of the Southern United States and LeRoy had experimented until the dish was perfectly approximated. He went down to the market at Les

Halles and bought up the youngest broccoli he could find. It had to be untrimmed because he stripped off the deep green leaves and prepared them Southern-style—then they were served with a slice of tomato and a thin sliver of onion on top. No one ever knew the difference, and LeRoy and Richard laughed at the oooohs and aaaahs of white customers when they ate the "real greens!"

While listening to LeRoy it occurred to him once again that he was a type of Bigger Thomas—better educated, a college-trained man, wider experience, but containing violent energy and brooding frustrations which he kept in check through success in France, laughter when they grew too painful, and too much liquor.

The proposed film flashed into his mind. Funny! Though he had become Bigger while writing his novel, as he did with each principal character, he himself had not gone in the direction of violence. Whoah! His violence was contained and directed—sometimes against himself—through writing. No, that was not all of it. He had never become utterly estranged from the religion and folk culture of his race; and he had reacted to the glitter of the dominant civilization by taking from it what he could. He'd been lucky! His mother and Granny, Aunt Maggie—yes, even Addie and Uncle Thomas—had in some way fortified him with their Horatio Algerisms and their Calvinism. And so, though he shared the moods of Bigger—the intense elations and depression, the melancholy when brooding over the plight of his people—he had been fortified; they had given him something which made him feel that he had to wrest from the world what he needed, a need to redeem his life with some meaning.

Could he play the part of Bigger Thomas? Gosh! He'd sure look funny with his 160 pounds playing a starving boy of twenty! Well, he could diet! It would be an entirely new experience; exciting and strange. And after all, did he not act every day of his life, hiding his deepest emotions from everyone except Ellen? Everyone always said he was so sweet! So uncomplicated! Such simplicity!

"LeRoy," Richard smiled over the top of his glass. "I'm going to become an actor. What do you think of that?" And with the decision, an excited thrill curled and unleashed itself in his stomach. He would try it! What the hell!

Many years earlier Richard had visited Chicago to gather information for *Black Boy*. An old friend, Dorothy Farrell, had given a party for him at the home of her mother, Mrs. Butler. In semi-seriousness, during the evening he had insisted that they all perform *Native Son*. He had played Bigger that time. Thora Nixon played Mary Dalton; Nelson Algren was Jan; and Jack Conroy played the big white cat.[8]

Richard was not entirely inexperienced; and there had been Arthur Leaner's minstrel shows in Jackson.

As enthusiasm for the film and the role increased, he worried that Chenal and Prades might not act quickly enough to buy out Orson Welles, John Houseman and Paul Green (Wellman, Incorporated). He had persuaded the principals involved to sell. What if they changed their minds? Or wanted much more money? Green had already taken more money than he deserved! Well, he "would just go ahead and put up the money to do the buying."[9] He cabled his agent to buy the rights for $6,000, pay the Theatre Guild approximately eighty dollars, and keep the entire transaction a deep secret from his partners whom he did not quite trust to return the money if they knew it had come from his own pocket. A letter of explanation would be sent immediately. Then Richard sent off a letter to Reynolds in which he described his fear that if Chenal and Prades discovered that he had already paid the money then they might take their time to repay him. He was sorry if these arrangements complicated the life of Reynolds, who confessed that he knew very little about film matters, and Richard insisted that he take his usual commission plus the cost of the lengthy cables that flew back and forth across the sea.

Prades and Chenal in the meantime had received a promise from a French company that it would back the venture in return for 50 percent of the net profits. The other 50 percent would be divided three ways—among Chenal, Prades and Richard. During production, the company would pay the living expenses of the cast while those of the three partners would be written into the contract for repayment out of their share of the profits. Richard looked at the project as a "communal idea and undertaking."

Before many months the arrangement with the French company collapsed but Atilio Mentasti, head of Argentina Sono Film, S.A., took its place. And on Saturday, August 20, 1949, Richard, Chenal, and Prades sailed for New York, where contracts were to be drawn up and signed. Richard had not received the $6,000 and he paid for his passage and that of his secretary, Jacqueline Clark, a small dark-haired New Yorker who was living in Paris.

A feeling of high adventure not yet tinged with doubt gripped Richard as the taxi drew up in front of the Hotel Albert on University Place. He looked fondly at the old building as he entered, walked up a few steps, checked their reservations at the desk and strode toward the elevators. On either side of the long corridor were paintings by unknown artists—an openhearted gesture by the management which sometimes resulted in sales for young men and women too poor and little known to have gallerys or exhibitions. He was fond of the funny half-antique, half-modern building; it had been the first integrated hotel in all of New York. And he knew that a stand against racism was a principle of its owners.

While in New York Richard and Chenal continued their work on a shooting script and Prades lined up the actors and actresses. The very blond Jean Wallace, ex-wife of Franchot Tone, whom Richard had met on the periphery of the Communist Party; beautiful Gloria Madison of Chicago, an actress and archaeology student, whose aunt, Mrs. Lillian Charles, was to write a song, "The Dreaming Kind," for the film; and Willa Pearl Curtiss, a maturely handsome woman, were signed. While waiting for a working script they were asked to read the novel to gain understanding of their roles.

By November 3 all exterior shots had been made in Chicago and the cast and directors were assembled in Buenos Aires. But Richard, settled in his room at the Golden Home, Posadas Numero 1557, was beginning to have doubts; everything was too fluid. Prades had drawn up a new contract in Spanish, ambiguous in nature and devoid of many of the agreements they had reached in Paris. Richard could not read Spanish, and Jackie, his secretary, knew only Italian and English. He refused point-blank to sign, returning it to Prades with the suggestion that a new one be drawn to include the original points. Prades gave him another and Richard took it to a Spanish-speaking lawyer for translation: it was improved only slightly. Again he refused to sign. He would hold off and check it against the French contract, which was in his hotel room.

In the evening, alone in his room, Richard pushed open the long French doors on to a balcony and gazed for a few minutes at the scene below. Then he went to his briefcase to take out the French contract and compare it with the new one Prades had given him. He could not find it. That was strange! And there had been three copies. Richard tried to stifle an uneasiness, like a voice humming within him. He had just put it somewhere else. There was no reason to be suspicious of his partners. Methodically he searched for the papers in all of his luggage. The contract was gone. He knew it! His bags had been rifled. Richard stood in the middle of his room abstracted, and stared at his luggage. He should have heeded the warnings his emotions had been thrusting upon him and examined everything before he had gone through it: now he could not tell if someone had searched his room—he had destroyed any evidence that might have remained. Goddamn! Then relief flooded his mind: Paul, in New York, had the original. He would simply eliminate Prades, hire someone to draw up a new contract based on the one in New York, compare them and ask the two men for their signatures. It was not a pretty picture. Well, if it become necessary he would call in a lawyer. But that should not be necessary; "Prades was a nice guy." And after all, it was Prades who had gotten Mentasti to put up the huge amounts of money to make the film and he had power of attorney for Sono Film; he was a substantial person. There was nothing to worry about.

Feeling lighthearted, and with a sense of relief that his suspicions might have been wrong, Richard undressed, stepped into the shower and, whistling, soaped his thin body. He had lost thirty pounds and almost resembled his earlier photographs except that his face was not so gaunt and starved-looking. Still whistling, he put on a light tropical suit: it would be an enjoyable evening. He had a dinner engagement with Jean Wallace, one of his leading ladies. He chuckled at the expression "leading ladies"—he was an actor! A self-derisive smile turned up his mouth at the thought. Jean, with her turned-under bangs and short white-gold pageboy hairstyle and her blue blue eyes, was a lovely girl. He could not stand stupid women even when they were beautiful, and Jean was intelligent and bold. She had risked her reputation to make the film; already the Hollywood racists were blasting her in not-so-private conversation. Undoubtedly they would blacklist her, and the boys in Chicago would see that she did not find work in nightclubs.[10] But the beautiful actress had a stubborn, independent attitude about everything. True, she had extraordinary sexual charm but Jean had piqued his interest first because to her he was not a cause, he was just a man. And then when they had talked together an intense physical awareness hit them simultaneously and continued to flow from one to the other whenever they were in the same room. Walking down the corridor, Richard was already smiling and his eyes were gleeful: he would make her angry tonight; her blue eyes would darken and she would turn up her nose when he teased her and called her another Jean Harlow. Oh boy, how she hated that! She did not want to be anybody but herself.

Jean Wallace was one of the few pleasant episodes in the making of the film. By the middle of 1950 Richard was caught in one of the most searing experiences in his life. He hated Juan Perón's Argentine dictatorship. All the beauty of the Latin country was wiped out by the fear that overlay every relationship and affected the gestures of its citizens from the lowest to the highest. There was corruption everywhere he looked and it seemed to Richard that the country was structurally a stool with three legs: the Catholic Church, the army, and Perón—he despised all three. He was told by Argentinians that if one got in trouble with the government it was no light matter and that there were "many dead men to prove it. They [did not] try you; they just [shot] you or put you away in some cold jungle to rot."

At Mentasti's suggestion and reassurances, Richard did not take out a work permit because the producer explained that he would be liable for extremely high taxes and that with a small degree of palm-greasing no one would pay any attention. But by degrees he discovered many unsettling factors: his mail, outgoing and incoming, was opened and read; a cable from Ellen was never delivered, and when he inquired of friends he learned that there existed an organized system of espionage at all cable offices. A pilot in Montevideo had to be approached secretly and bribed to take his mail out of the country and once he went to Uruguay to send a message to his wife through his cable address, Nativeson, in Paris. On the set one day a contingent of soldiers, all wearing guns slung around their waists, surrounded the performers and asked for a private word with Richard. He walked out with the soldiers feeling that he was going to be shot—far from home—and no one would know what had happened to him. One of the officers merely asked if he could watch the shooting of the film, and Richard wiped his perspiring brow, and answered a shaky yes, although he hoped never to see the men again at all.

In the negotiations over the contract Richard discovered that Prades had involved Mentasti in the film without informing him of its enormous costs. He had lied about the length of time required, about contracts, the pay of the actors, and "Everybody connected with the production was caught in . . . a whirl of misunderstandings and cross-purposes. Naturally, there came a day when all this had to be faced, when everybody, including Mentasti had to know the truth. Prades was scared that he would go to jail for what he had done; he had not stolen anything; he had just lied to everybody and got them launched into a vast production which they did not have the money or the technical means to finish."

As soon as Richard discovered what Prades had done he went immediately to see Mentasti to make his position clear. Mentasti, a shrewd businessman, sized up Richard with cold eyes and came to a decision. Richard was the mainspring in the production and since it could not be made without him Mentasti demanded a contract directly with Richard offering one-fifth of the gross profits. It would have to be a confidential arrangement and exclude Chenal and Prades from all knowledge of their "partnership." And Mentasti made it clear, watching Richard carefully, that he did not intend to lose all that he had paid out in the past months. The film would be completed on his terms.

After Richard signed with Mentasti he left the big man's office feeling weak in the legs; he was so vulnerable without a work permit, in a government filled with police and spies, in a country whose language he could not understand very well; and Prades and Chenal would be "wildly mad and God help him if they discovered that one-fifth of the gross went to him." Wheew! Richard thought; this is a mess and he went to the telephone to place a long-distance call to Ellen. Waiting for his call to get through to Paris, Richard paced the floor in thought. That Mentasti was "a real tough cookie. He is going to cheat Chenal's and Prades' eyes out as only he can."

The film was finally finished by July, 1950; it had taken a year to complete. No one, except perhaps Mentasti, was certain that the investment of so much money and time would bring back a fair cash return. Rumors flew that all was well when Paramount Pictures sent representatives to the Argentine to talk to Sono Films; they were followed by Columbia Pictures, Twentieth Century-Fox and Universal International, who all bid for distribution in the United States. Ambassador Stanton Griffiths, who held an interest in Paramount Pictures, visited the set during the shooting and indicated to Richard that his firm would like to have the rights for American viewing.

Selling the film was not Richard's main concern, nor Mentasti's, although he as an Argentinian was in a better position. How to get money out of a police state was the essential problem which confronted Richard when he began preparations to leave Buenos Aires. He signed a letter with Sono Films stating that no offer for distribution of the film in the United States would be accepted under the sum of $150,000. Such a statement could not be included in his contract because Argentine "Perón's Law" required that the major portion of any sum of money mentioned in legal documents went to the state. Some arrangements had to be made so that any cash monies would be paid into Richard's account at the Reynolds' office in New York without Argentina's knowledge. An honest man had to be found; one whom he could trust not to get "sticky fingers."

Richard selected Erwin Wallfisch, an old film maker and writer from Germany. Balding, with a little fuzz at the front of his head, shrewd-eyed Wallfisch, squinting through clouds of cigar smoke, impressed Richard as an extremely intelligent man. Richard offered him 5 percent of all monies collected and deposited to his account in New York.[11] Wallfisch accepted with such alacrity that a momentary doubt struck Richard. He shrugged it aside: I'd rather deal with a smart man that I have to watch for crooked behavior than a dumb one who is honest and bothersome, he decided.

Together the two men worked out a code by which they would be able to communicate financial matters when Richard left Argentina. All monies would be referred to as numbers of copies sold of Richard's books; there would be no use of real names: Wallfisch would be "George"; Richard was "Adolphus" and Paul Reynolds, Jr. became "Alexander." A third man, Jacobsen, who lived in Argentina and had introduced Richard to Wallfisch, was referred to as "Charles." The code was sent to Reynolds in an elaborately sealed letter and taken to Uruguay for mailing. With it was enclosed instructions from Richard to his agent:

Paul, I know that this might sound like little boys playing to you, but please let me assure you that all of this is deadly serious. Now, about the code. Pages 1 and 2 may be used at once in communicating with Wallfisch. The code relating to figures is a complicated combination of figures which I shall explain to you when I see you personally in New York. In all letters, phone calls, or cables to Wallfisch there must under no circumstances *be any mention of* dollars! Such would get him into serious and instant trouble with the government, and to be in trouble with the government of Argentina is no light matter.

Wearing his mildest expression, Richard sailed from Argentina on the S.S. *Argentine* and after a stop in Trinidad to see Dr. Eric Williams, who later became Premier of that country and Tobago, and another stop in Haiti to see Dr. Giles Hubert of the United States Embassy, he arrived in New York in the middle of August. On August 22 he sailed for Le Havre and home.

On November 4 the first premiere of *Native Son* was held on board a Pan American strato clipper between Buenos Aires and Nice, and on March 30, 1951, the film previewed in Argentina. Reviews were good and Richard waited eagerly in Paris to see his film, which Mentasti had placed in the hands of Walter Gould of Classic Pictures, Incorporated, in New York City.

Gould made drastic cuts in the version which would appear in France and the rest of Europe. The film's opening scene, showing Bigger killing a rat in his mother's slum apartment, was slashed out; the making of a zip-gun and plans for a robbery, a dialogue between newspapermen using racial epithets, all were removed. Max's and Buckley's dialogue in the trial scene remained but the sound was removed so that it became senseless.

When Richard saw the film at a private showing in Paris a wave of sickness was his first reaction, followed by anger. He became convinced that Gould, who was a naturalized citizen, was afraid that he would be termed un-American and would not risk his security by revealing the truth about racist America. In America in the early 1950's Senator Joseph McCarthy had begun his work which eventually led to a threat to "wreck the army."[12]

And there was difficulty with Chenal in Paris. Chenal, a man of integrity, had directed his first film in 1933 and with that single effort had been recognized as an artist. He had been a writer as a young man, on the fringe of the French motion picture industry, and his initial opportunity had come with *La Rue Sans Nom*. His second effort was Dostoevski's *Crime and Punishment,* which was acclaimed as one of the most important films of two decades. At the beginning of World War II he had joined the army and when the Germans occupied France he had a choice of collaboration or fleeing the country. He went to South America, where he directed four pictures, and when France was liberated he returned to the film industry in Paris.

Chenal, a member of respectable standing in the powerful French film unions, knew that he would be attacked by the Communists, who dominated those organizations, if *Native Son* was shown in its cut version in France. He immediately consulted his attorneys with a proposal to safeguard his future: they should urge the unions to bar the film from every theatre in France. When Richard learned of Chenal's action, whatever had been his disagreements with him in Argentina disappeared, and he wrote his agent for a copy of a letter which proved that he had been forced to sign with Mentasti. He agreed with Chenal that the film was dishonest. And he would never have made the film at all without the assurance that it was to be a faithful representation of his novel.

French Communists disliked Richard because he would not have anything to do with them and because he had attacked the Party publicly in *The God That Failed,* a collection of essays gathered by Richard Crossman from Gide, Silone, Spender, Koestler, Fischer and Wright. But they were more sophisticated than their American counterparts. They left Richard alone because they recognized that he was an honest man. He did not lie in his books, articles, lectures or interviews, and an unspoken pact existed: they would leave him alone if he left them alone. If Chenal pressed his determination to influence the trade unions it would result in picket lines in front of every theatre in Paris. Richard shuddered. Ah, God . . . what to do? Well, he thought, I shall just be passive. I will try to influence Chenal to drop the whole matter and then I will not help promote the film in any way at all.

Strangely, the majority of European reviews of the film were laudatory: "Triumph for Richard Wright." "Gives a strong and convincing performance." Critics in his own country attacked the film almost uniformly and it was banned in Ohio. Reviewers wrote as if the film were a personal affront: it was a grisly, meaningless drama; unreal and vicious; distorted the truth; was amateurish and clumsy. Personal friends did not spare him in America: he had made the film only so that he could play the role of Bigger. A man "normally 'tight' with money had lost a fortune for his ego's sake."

And financially it was a fiasco. Richard received only approximately $3,000 for an investment of himself of nearly three years. A final indignity was his request for a copy of the integral version of the film, which he wanted to distribute to film houses rather than the cut and mutilated copy which so amazed and disgusted him. But, despite all his efforts, he was refused by evasion, and when he placed a long-distance call to Classic Films in New York he was informed bluntly that there were no available copies.[13] A few years later Richard learned that both Sono Films in Argentina and Classic Films in America went bankrupt.

The black existentialist and the
white Freudian . . .

XXIV

Early in 1951 Richard was overcome by a mood which preceded the writing of all his fictional work. It was a vague sense of estrangement from his surroundings, a baffled unrest, a slow stirring of myriad emotions which gradually possessed him. Sometimes he was baffled at his total ignorance of what set these moods in motion.

Such a state of mind did not follow any apparent logic: it did not require silence or solitude, and he had no power to order or time the condition, but when it came he could not dislodge it until writing had drained it from his consciousness.

It often seemed to him that in the swelling out of the moods they took on flesh and blood, sucked unto themselves events, long past and forgotten, telescoped alien and disparate images into organic wholes. A random phrase might recall a story told by a friend years before; a face seen through smoke in a bistro, or a mannerism, a gesture, revealed meanings and submeanings of episodes in his youth. Two unrelated events might occur and fuse into still another pattern entirely. A newspaper story evoked excitement far beyond the meaning of the banal crime described, a meaning which in turn conjured up its emotional equivalent in a different setting and possessed of a contrary meaning.

His own psyche would become so enmeshed with a fictional character that when he completed a sequence he had lived the same experience: if the person had killed then Richard had killed. He abhorred the very intimation of anything mystic, and yet in trying to understand the writing process—when the reality encountered receded and hid itself in another reality and when hunted openly altered its whole aspect, thereby escaping introspective observation —there were elements of magic in the whole thing.

For a long time he had not felt like writing at all. The act of tearing up roots in one country and planting them in another was not easy. At first, Richard felt that he was looking at the world as innocently as a child, as if his eyes had just opened, and he went through an overhaul of his values. Living in Europe gave him the distance and objectivity needed to view the pains that living in his own country had caused.

As fill-ins during the long incubation period he read more than he had ever read in his life; there were always press interviews, book signings, honorary luncheons and dinners, the launchings of magazines, and articles for the French newspapers.

Once or twice he had picked up the two novels[1] which he had been working on when he moved from America and put them aside. "Writing froze on me," he told a friend. He sighed; he shrugged; he forced himself not to worry. When he had been younger and in between books a fear had come into his mind, gripping with such force that it could not be dislodged, that perhaps he would not find in himself the impulse or resources to write again. Then he would be filled with an impersonal unhappiness and friends would ask: "What do you have to be gloomy about? You've written a book, sold it, and you have money and fame." They could not understand a hunger that went deeper than a desire for food. But in France he had learned to be quiet, to fret less and trust himself, knowing that there was a logic at work. He learned to gather book after book to read, to cull over reports on trials, murders, suicides, medicine, scientific discoveries, social studies, conscious that answers or questions would form that would force him to examine them on paper. With maturity, earlier fears had disappeared, but what still remained was an amazement and quiet joy when the shadowy outlines of a book broke through his unconscious and shaped in his mind.

Wearing an impenetrable and serene face, Richard one morning wrote to his agent, who had been patiently asking for a novel for several years: the manuscript of a new novel had run to 639 pages or more, and, good or bad, he was full of it, had it in his blood clamoring to be gotten rid of—he would rest for three weeks and then put in three months of hard work—and it would soon be finished.

Within a year *The Outsider* was completed. It told the tale of a mail sorter, Cross Damon, who worked on the night shift in the post office.

Consumed by fear, which in turn produces self-hatred and shame, Damon attempts to tranquilize his dread with alcohol. Asked by a friend why he drinks so much, he replies:

"My soul needs it."

"Makes you feel better, hunh?"

"No, makes me feel *less*."

A subway accident in which another passenger, a victim, is wrongly identified as him frees Damon from an obsessively religious mother, a wife from whom he was separated, a pregnant underage girl friend. The physical outsider coalesces with his spiritual alienation and Damon becomes a whole man at last as he views with objectivity the rituals of his own funeral. A friend who recognizes him momentarily stands in the way of the new wholeness and Damon kills him without hesitation or remorse.

On a train plunging its way toward New York Damon meets another outsider, District Attorney Ely Houston, whose own estrangement from the world is a result of physical deformity. Houston is a hunchback. A New York "crime-buster" and possible state senator, he resembles a giant white spider whose mental processes grind fast and exceedingly fine. Houston represents a threat to Damon because his deformity has given him a vantage point from which he can understand black Americans.

In New York, Damon meets and is invited to live with a Communist leader in a seven-room apartment on the second floor of a red brick building on Charles Street. For the Communists it is a test case: the landlord of the building is an outspoken Fascist and the Party is launching a campaign against realtors who discriminate against Negroes in Greenwich Village. But Damon accepts their interest merely as a matter of convenience and self-preservation. An intellectual, highly introspective and knowledgeable about literature, politics and philosophy, particularly the works of Nietzsche, Kierkegaard, Heidegger and Husserl, Damon sees Communism and Fascism as sharing the same motive force—power.

Communist and Fascist become embroiled in a bloody physical battle and stun each other: Damon then kills them both. "I have killed two little Gods," he thinks in satisfaction as he stands over their crushed bodies.

The chase then begins with both police and Communists following the trail. It is the Communists who eventually shoot him to death on the street. Houston is with him at the end and it is to him, the other outsider, that Damon explains how he has felt: it is horrible because in his heart he has felt innocent. That is what creates the horror.

Though choosing a background of Negro life and Communist life, Richard had not meant the book to be a political work at all. Neither was it intended to be either pro or anti Communist. The book was a study dealing mainly with character and destiny and, according to American scholarly publications, the first existentialist novel by an American writer.

Through the spiderlike, misshapen Ely Houston, Richard interpreted Damon as a social type becoming ever more prevalent in the Cold War atmosphere of the United States. Black men were going to be free; but free for what?[2] They were going to inherit the problems of the Western world but with a difference. They were outsiders and they were going to know that they have had problems. They were going to be self-conscious, gifted with a double vision, for, being Negroes, they were both inside and outside of the culture at the same time.

Every emotional and cultural convulsion that ever shook the heart and soul of Western man will shake them. Negroes will develop unique and specially defined psychological types. They will become psychological men, like the Jews . . . They will not only be Americans or Negroes; they will be centers of *knowing,* so to speak.

A priest in *The Outsider* demurs: all that is needed by colored people is a right to jobs and living space. But Houston will not have such panaceas. Father, he tells the priest, their getting those elementary things is so long and drawn out that they had to, while they waited, adjust themselves to living in a kind of No Man's Land. . . . And any intelligent black man would, quite naturally, brood and probe and question. "A dreadful objectivity would be forced upon him."

The problem started only when the black man got his so-called rights. Would he be able to settle down to live the day-to-day life of quiet desperation of the average American? Or would not his objectivity, learned in agony through three hundred years of slavery, fling him beyond the level of development of his countrymen.

As early as 1941 Richard had been convinced that unless the West could solve the cleavage between its indissoluble parts—the white man and the black man—then both would die. A favorite story which illustrated his conception was told him by Dr. Carl Roberts, whom Horace Cayton had introduced to him during one of his visits to Chicago.

. . . once a white girl in New York, rich and proud, but of the conviction that she could have an orgasm only with a Negro, went down to Atlantic City and picked up the biggest, blackest Negro she could find; she went to bed with him . . . and being modern and wise, she had a pessary in her vagina. Now, said the good doctor . . . the big black buck had such a huge penis that when he inserted it and had had intercourse with the white girl, he found that he could not pull it out. They tussled for hours; the girl became hysterical; the Negro knew that if he did not get it out, he could be killed. It seems, said the good doctor, that the nigger's penis, the head, had become wrapped in some way around the pessary and was held fast. Hours passed; the girl grew exhausted. Finally her screams brought rescue, that is the kind that they needed, a white doctor. He ordered them to a hospital; locked, black body into white body, they were upon a single bed, cursing and clawing at each other. Well, they had to think hard and fast; the doctors said that they had to summon the girl's family, for they saw no way out but to cut off the nigger's penis. The girl's folks came and the decision was made; the doctors cut off the nigger's penis. He died. But, holy smokes, the black amputated penis could not be dug from the body of the white gal; she lingered and died, too.[3]

And he articulated these ideas in a piece entitled "I Choose Exile," written at the request of Ben Burns, editor of *Ebony* magazine.[4] While living in America Richard had often been angry and filled with a sneaking sense of futility because he knew that there was something basically wrong in a nation that could so cynically violate its own Constitution and democratic pretensions by meting out physical and psychological cruelties to a defenseless minority. But in France his feelings somewhat changed. Anger turned into an amazed pity, for he felt that America's barbaric treatment of the Negro was not half so bad as the destructive war that she waged, in striking at the Negro, against the concept of the free person, against freedom of conscience, against the Rights of Man, and against herself. He was disconcerted when he realized the vast dislocation of human values which the mere presence of the Negro in America had brought about.

In a setting of a Cold War of global dimensions, the white American's sense of superiority turned into a kind of queasy dread. White Americans abroad became inarticulate with embarrassment when called upon, as spokesmen for freedom, to justify their racism. At a cocktail party in Richard's honor, a sensitive white American woman living in Paris burst out to him: "What the Negro has *done* to us! Our forefathers brought them to our shores, and we've let our racial fears make us trample our ideas and hopes in the dust!" When Richard observed white American officials abroad he found most of them incapable of regarding other black people of the world with an attitude free of their conditioned feeling of racial superiority. They had a tremendous psychological handicap to take into a struggle against a Communism whose basic slogan called for the liberation of Asia and Africa.

The Outsider despaired that white Americans could liberate themselves from their fears, panic and terror when they confronted black men striving for liberation from irrational ties. Cross Damon, an intellectual black man, awakened in a society which could not contain such a giant. In an immoral society, a man conditioned, shaped and molded by that society attempted to form his own morality and failed.

Perhaps we should define freedom negatively, by showing what it is not, Richard had told Jean-Paul Sartre. And the anti-hero of *Outsider,* a rebel without a set of values, finds an uncreative freedom because it is in a vacuum. Richard used elements from existentialist thought, picked up the philosophy as if it were a dark coat, plucked out the threads he needed and then threw it aside. Just like the French existentialists Richard knew, Damon was driven by an emotional compulsion, religious in its intensity, to feel and weigh the worth of himself. He longed for an experience deeply felt enough to remove or transform his eternal sense of dread. But at the edge of doom Damon drew back and repudiated a dead-end philosophy. Struggling to still an exploding ball of fire that leaped white-hot in his chest, he warned: the search cannot be done alone; never alone; alone a man was nothing. A bridge between man and man had to be made. Tell others not to come down this road, he forced through dying lips.

"Don't think I'm so odd and strange . . . I'm not . . . I'm legion . . . The real men, the last men are coming . . . Tell the world what they are like . . . We are here already, if others but had the courage to see us. . . ."[5]

When the last of the 220,000 words was written Richard leaned back in his desk chair and removed his round steel-framed, somewhat old-fashioned glasses and rubbed his eyes gently. They felt strained and it had taken over a month to fill a prescription for new glasses. He hoped they would soon be delivered, for he had to compress and compress the manuscript until he had squeezed out every excess word that he possibly could. What about a title? These things always bother me, he thought, and he went to find Ellen. The only idea that came to him was *Colored Man;* that might be nicely ironic. Not many Negroes objected to the word; the intellectuals did to some extent but not enough to matter. But he should be able to find something more appropriate. Ellen, who was in the kitchen, had just finished making a special apple pie, lapping thin slivers of the fruit into a geometric design; and she wiped her hands and followed her husband into his study. Taking down from a shelf a complete Shakespeare and the Holy Bible, Richard handed one to Ellen, kept the other for himself, and both sat down to pore over the pages in search of a title. For some reason, they could not find anything suitable for the very hard document he had completed.

Two weeks later a letter arrived from his publisher with a number of suggestions: *A Man Called Damon; The Man with Two Names; The Victim; The Man of Violence; Second Chance; A Name from a Grave; Man in Trouble.* Richard disliked all of them; he would prefer *Last Man* or *Colored Man* if nothing better was suggested. But a day or two later his agent suggested *The Outsider* and explained that a two-word title was keeping a continuity with his previous novels; and Richard was happy. "I think it fits perfectly," he told his wife.

By September, 1952, Richard had finished the last of the revisions on *The Outsider* and after mailing it off to his agent he strayed into the Monaco, just off the Carrefour de l'Odéon. The patron's wife, smiling but reserved, greeted him by name and Richard ordered a brandy. He was finished now, for a while, and he could break the rule of drinking nothing stronger than coffee while at work on a novel.

Relaxed, and somewhat drained, he adjusted his dark glasses and then took them off so that he could look at the people around him without the obfuscating smoked lens. At the other end from where he sat, near the windows, was a crowd of Americans, Swedes, Dutch, Canadians and a few young Africans with tribal marks on their cheeks. They were all speaking English in a dozen accents and they all appeared young and fun-loving. But their heads were bent over their tables or toward each other and all seemed to speak at once. Several times he heard the name McCarthy.

Psychologically he was transported back to his own country, and the book he had just finished entered his mind once more. He was not optimistic about its reception in America. He had dredged from his brain, with a memory ordered to faithfulness, a conception of the world that would not be palatable.

Ah, well, he thought, I tend to be pessimistic, especially when I have just finished a work and no longer have it around to bother me. What a strange thing writing is—as soon as it is over you start looking around for something else to do even though you are glad that you are free of the last job. He reached into his pocket and took out a letter he had received that morning from Paul Reynolds. At least he was enthusiastic about *The Outsider.* Advance sales were 13,500 and Paul was convinced that it would have a considerable success.

Toward the end of March, 1953, *Outsider* appeared in the book-shops. It was not a good year. Every morning, month after month, Richard read all the Paris editions of American newspapers and several French publications. The Wisconsin-born Senator Joseph McCarthy, for whom a whole era of shame would be named, domi-nated the headlines. Anxiously, Richard watched for opposition from liberal intellectuals. There was none. Instead, people bowed their heads in silence or gave their support while slander, invective and terror oozed in what seemed an unstoppable flood. The American Legion attacked as Communist plotters anyone who dared disagree, however mildly, with national policy; every type of blacklist un-rolled; like tulips in springtime investigative committees erupted in Congress; quasi trials were held; the Fifth Amendment became a filthy phrase and people were, in some cases, hounded to death. While the Senator's gross, monotonous voice droned on in Washing-ton, his assistant, Roy Cohn, was lauded by Walter Winchell, George Sokolsky and Lee Mortimer, while the semiliterate, spoiled, rich boy David Schine was seeking out Communists in Europe in between bacchanals.[6] And John Foster Dulles, Secretary of State, revealed to *Life* magazine that the world was on the brink of atomic war.

In the minds of some American critics *The Outsider* was the glove slapped across the cheek. "*Time* magazine certainly ripped into me," Richard wrote to his agent. "But I was expecting it. One does not write a book like *The Outsider* without getting brickbats." And he braced himself for some more. Almost without exception reviewers pointed out that it was Richard's first published book in eight years, as if this, in itself, were suspect. Another affront to many critics were its existentialist overtones.[7] He had been seduced. "Sartre and de Beauvoir have taken him over," they cried. Black critics were the most severe: they appeared to hate *The Outsider* even more than they had resented *Native Son* and *Black Boy*. Accusations that he had abandoned his people were hurled with force, and one reviewer ended with a plea: "Come back to us, Richard."

A sane judgment was rendered by Orville Prescott, for whom Richard was the leading American Negro writer of his generation. *The Outsider* shook Prescott, for if a man as brilliant as Richard Wright could write a book so pessimistic about the plight of man in the twentieth century, it was one of the symptoms of the intellectual and moral crises of the times.[8] And an obscure black intellectual, Henry F. Winslow, looked upon Cross Damon as America's full-sized tragic hero, deeply realized, in great measure Byronic, in greater measure symbolic of the prime force of contemporary civilization, fear.

European critics acclaimed *The Outsider* for posing some of the major problems which seemed to confront the entire world. In Denmark the novel was translated and named *The Witness;* Cross Damon was "The Black Raskolnikov," and its reception was greater than Camus' *The Stranger.* Richard was looked upon as the American Negro's greatest defender. It was a novel of capital importance for the understanding of the picture of the universe being drawn for everyone's eyes by life itself; a literary masterpiece; the most important book received from America in years. The condensed dialogues, especially the shocking examination scenes toward the end of the book, were similar to the sublime dialogues in Dostoevski's *The Obsessed.* Under a surface of rawness and cynicism, as in the Russian's great novels, was a unique honesty, a desire for pure and unpolluted life. Desperately Damon looked for truth, demoniacal in his unlimited desire for freedom. Cross Damon—the demon on the cross. Any man in those frightening times.

If to European critics Cross Damon was any man, to Richard he was a black American, born in Mississippi to a schoolteacher mother whose husband deserted her; a woman who became excessively religious; a man who worked in a post office; had a roomful of books; a girl friend who lived on Indiana Avenue; and when he went to New York lived on Charles Street in Greenwich Village. Fiction was interlaced with autobiography throughout the book.[9] In that part of his mind that was deliberate and conscious Richard hoped to demonstrate that Damon's crimes were part and parcel of the everyday life of man, most particularly black men, and that a few people living outside society, like Houston, the hunchback representative of the law, recognized these types.

For many years the theme of the outsider was one of Richard's favorites. If the government were wise, it would not seek out Communists or those who actively fought its policies, for these were affirmative acts. Instead, for self-protection, spies should be posted in all neighborhoods of the nation, not to break strikes or disrupt student unions, or search out radicals, but to ferret out the outsiders. These were the men dangerous to the status quo, for the outsider was one who no longer responded to the values of the system in which he lived. Communists and Fascists sought to share in the wealth and power of the nation by substituting themselves but without essentially changing its structure for governing. The greatest danger to the government stemmed from those millions of individuals who held no dreams of the prizes the nation held forth; in them, whether they knew it or not, a revolution had already occurred and was biding its time until it could translate itself into a new way of life.

An accident—the death of a white girl—awakened Bigger Thomas. An accident—a subway wreck—awakened Cross Damon. And if the Damons were legion, already at large in society, what were the values and morality with which to bribe them or keep them in check?

Toward the end of his work on *The Outsider,* a second, contrapuntal, novel kept thrusting itself to the front of Richard's brain. The outline had rushed fully formed into his thoughts when he read a short piece in the Paris edition of the *Herald-Tribune.* A New York businessman had been trapped nude in the corridor of his elegant apartment building. In the man's predicament Richard saw hints of terror and fear similar to the daily state of mind of black men.

Savage Holiday was started on Christmas Eve day, 1952, and completed by March 3, 1953. All of the characters are white, and while Richard's emphasis in writing of Negroes was always "existential," for the new book it was deliberately Freudian.

Erskine Fowler, an executive in Longevity Life Insurance Company, is forced to resign from a thirty-year position, to make room for the president's young son. Only the bullying of the president and the other executives make him agree to a pretense of voluntary retirement, and shamed by his own weak collaboration in the fraud, he leaves a testimonial dinner, in tears, carrying his gold gift watch, before the ceremonies are ended.

There is a retirement fund to ensure generous monthly payments and Fowler's cash assets are $40,000. But insurance has been life itself; human nature in the raw trying to hide; insurance is a religion, instinctively and intuitively knowing that man is essentially a venal, deluded, and greedy animal. Fowler has reveled in his talent in ferreting out false claims or lies and defeating those who tried to defraud his company. The job provided him with an identity, and his Calvinist ethic gave him a view that there were good people and bad people, nothing in between. All those who did not fit his particular frame of reference were bad.

Insurance had taken the place of emotions, which Fowler has firmly clamped under the steel lid of his work and fastened and tightened with the inviolate bolts of religious devotion. With the loss of his Madison Avenue job Fowler finds himself adrift in a sea of anxiety. "He was trapped in freedom." Clad in his gray flannel suit from Brooks Brothers, in a neat Ivy League tie and shirt, Fowler has lived an orderly life: if something went wrong, he called in a lawyer, an accountant, or a policeman, and matters were righted at once. But who could one summon when one's emotions went into a state of rebellion?

On the morning after the shabby testimonial dinner Fowler is awakened by Tony Blake, a five-year-old neighbor, who is playing on the balcony. Arising, he turns on the shower, removes his robe and pajamas and then hears the ring of his doorbell. It is the newspaper boy on a collection round, but Fowler sends him away because he has not bothered to put on his robe. The boy leaves and Fowler opens the door a crack to take in the paper; it is out of his reach so he steps quickly into the hall. A gust of wind catches the door and slams it closed behind him. He is trapped, naked and cowering, on a Sunday morning in his apartment building in New York's East Seventies.

Fowler takes the self-service elevator, hoping to reach the superintendent's office on the first floor unseen, but when it arrives two young girls are waiting; wild with fright, he pushes the stop button and then the button for his own floor. A wild ride up and down begins as more and more tenants leave their apartments bound for church services. At last, Fowler gets out on the floor above his own and sneaks down, barely eluding a neighbor lady; he remembers that a balcony below his bathroom window would give him access to his own apartment.

Fowler dashes out precipitously, frightens the child playing on the balcony atop a hobby horse and he falls ten flights to the street. Fowler crawls through the window to safety. Then he wrestles with his conscience: should he tell the police what has happened? But would not people think he was queer to have been in bushy nakedness on the balcony with a child? What of the publicity? And, after all, Tony is dead and can not be brought back to life. He did not harm the boy deliberately. Besides, is not the child's mother the real culprit; she often left Tony alone. He should not have been on the balcony ten floors above the street. Fowler makes a decision to keep silent. Somewhat relieved, he binds a cut on his hand suffered when climbing through the window, puts on his silk robe and goes into the hallway to help other neighbors comfort the child's distrait mother.

To appear innocent, Fowler dresses carefully and attends church at his usual time; and during the service inspiration blooms. Tony's death is retribution for the loose morals of his mother. He, Fowler, has only been God's agent. It is a sign—he now has to justify the death by bringing the luscious Mrs. Blake to the paths of righteousness. At this thought, Fowler unconsciously fingers the tips of a row of colored pencils in his pocket.

During lucid moments Fowler thinks of sex as filthy; but placed in the position of a judge, he is sexually aroused. He returns home from church and is told by the superintendent's wife that Mrs. Blake saw a pair of naked feet dangling in the air, over her balcony, a short time after her son's scream. Fowler is petrified and grows even more frightened by a mysterious telephone call from a woman who declares: I've seen everything.

Judge and criminal coalesce in his personality: he will marry the voluptuous woman, thus reforming and silencing her at the same time. But Mrs. Blake tells him it is strange to receive a proposal—she hardly knows him—she will give him an answer at a later date. When she goes out with her men friends for solace Fowler accuses her of wrongdoing; they quarrel; she becomes suspicious that he has killed her son and threatens to go to the police. Fowler kills her with a butcher knife, plunging the blade into her stomach again and again. Then he gives himself up to the police.

Fowler, white Protestant middle-class American businessman does not know that he has inherited all of the problems of his society until murder makes him a partial outsider. His freedom has lain within the context of a job, a church, Ivy League clothes, money in the bank and an East Side address. These give his soul structure and when they disappear, or threaten to disappear, he samples the terror of the outsider. Unlike the true outsiders, in whom creativity is born along with cognition, Erskine turns into a wild beast pawing the earth to cover its deposits of fecal matter.

Cross Damon is more or less nondescript in physical appearance: he is tall but slightly built with a smooth brown and yellow skin, and his body moves as though it has more nervous energy than it can contain.

Erskine Fowler is a "man of distinction," a man from a television commercial: "A six-foot, hulking, heavy, muscular man with a Lincoln-like, quiet, stolid face, deep-set brown eyes, a jutting lower lip, a shock of jet-black bushy hair. . . . His facial features seemed hewn firm and whole from some endurable substance; his eyes were steady; he was the kind of man to whom one intuitively and readily rendered a certain degree of instant deference, not because there was anything challenging, threatening, or even strikingly intelligent in those carelessly molded and somewhat blunted features; but because one immediately felt that he was superbly alive, real, just *there,* with no hint in his attitude of apology for himself or his existence, confident of his inalienable right to confront you and demand his modest due of respect."[10]

Fowler had $40,000, a pension, a large wardrobe, a luxury apartment; Damon, drowned in debt, amused himself by throwing his change into the street from an eleventh-floor window to watch people go wild as they scrambled for money. When it was gone white folks stood looking up, mouths agape like fish, praying for more coins to fall. Damon and his friends laughed: America was a money-worshipping society.

Damon came to believe that man had to like himself and that was predicated upon self-knowledge—self-confrontation. Fowler avoided himself by seeking a scapegoat.

Fowler was owned by a business firm; Damon belonged to a people gifted with double vision; he was inside and outside his society at the same time.

Damon was a demon—a fallen angel.

Fowler was what he called all men—a venal, deluded animal.

Richard was enthusiastic about his little 60,000 word crime novel, but he worried that white readers might not accept such a book from a black author. It was so different from anything he had written and there were only white characters. Perhaps it should be published under a pseudonym.

For a few months it did not appear to Richard that *The Wish and the Deed*—the book's original title—would be published at all. His new editor[11] did not like it: the novel was dated and it was too psychological. But Richard did not argue, or even protest, because he recognized that the liking or disliking of fiction is highly subjective and personal. Instead, he suggested to his agent that the book be submitted to World Publishing Company. World also turned it down. Two years later the novel was purchased by Avon Publications, Inc., for a $2,000 advance against royalties. *Savage Holiday* was not a financial success. The public did not know of its existence and since it was published in paperback, it did not receive any reviews even though its author was a world-famous writer. But, as with *The Outsider,* there was excitement in Europe and it was translated into French, Italian, German and Dutch. *Les Temps Modernes,* the magazine published by Jean-Paul Sartre, asked for serialization rights.

XXV

Over Easter in 1953 Dorothy Padmore came from London to spend a few days with Richard and Ellen and the children. George Padmore had been unable to accompany his wife on this visit because he was working in England for Kwame Nkrumah of the Gold Coast, who was preparing his Independence Motion for presentation in July.

Richard, Ellen, Dorothy and George had become friends when they met in England in January, 1947. George Padmore, "Father of African Emancipation," had been through an experience similar to Richard's with the Communists but on an international level.

In 1930 Padmore had been a functionary of the Kremlin in charge of a worldwide organization of intellectuals who worked for the independence of Africa. At the Seventh Congress of the Communist International, it was decided by the Kremlin that Japan and Germany were the main enemies, and Britain and France were "democratic imperialists" who had to be courted. This decision reduced Padmore's efforts to a farce: neither Germany nor Japan had colonies in Africa.

Padmore would not compromise. He broke with the Kremlin at once, went to London and continued his work for the freedom of Africa. The International instituted a campaign of vilification, but Padmore did not lose any of his influence among Africans. When he reached London he joined the International African Friends of Ethiopia, an organization headed by another West Indian, C. L. R. James, whom Wright had known in New York. Out of that organization was formed the African Bureau, whose aim was a united states of Africa, or Pan-Africanism. It was the only grouping of its kind in the world, and the founding members were Padmore, C. L. R. James, Jomo Kenyatta, T. R. Mackonnen, Fitz Braithwaite and W. E. F. Ward.

En route to the United States in 1947, Richard had found his way to George's small apartment near Mornington Crescent, in London, and Dorothy Pizer, his English wife, opened the door. Dorothy, a short, stocky, vivid-faced woman, with keen blue-gray eyes and a florid complexion, hugged Richard, kissed him on the cheek and at the same time called to her husband:

"Richard is here! Richard Wright is here!"

George darted out of a room, smiling as widely as his wife, and grasped Richard's hand and arm; a current of electrical energy seemed transmitted. Richard liked him immediately, which was the way George affected almost everyone. George, who was Trinidadian, wore his unstraightened hair clipped African style above a high rounding forehead. He was dressed in a gray English suit of a smooth-textured fabric with white pinstripes, a vest, tie, white shirt, and the edge of a handkerchief protruded from the rim of his coat sleeve, where he had tucked it. Richard wondered briefly if George were dressed to make a speech; there was a sartorial completion and the hint of a dandy in his attire; but he was led into the kitchen-office and saw that George had been writing something. A sheet of paper was still in the typewriter, which sat on top of a wooden kitchen table beside books, papers, a teapot and two cups.

On subsequent visits Richard discovered that through George's kitchen trooped all of the eventual leaders of Africa. "They came seeking information, encouragement, and help, and George gave of his days and hours to expounding the intricacies of politics to nationalists like Wallace Johnson, Nkrumah, Kenyatta, Azikiwe, Joe Appiah, Musazi, Mayanja, and the Sudanese leaders, Abdulla Khalil, Mahgoub, Osman. . . ."[1]

Three months before Richard's visit, in October, the Fifth Pan-African Congress, held in Manchester, had been attended by 200 African delegates who had been brought to London by the Colonial Office for a "very different type of indoctrination."[2] Dr. W. E. B. DuBois, the distinguished American historian and the father of the idea of Pan-Africanism, was co-chairman with Dr. Peter Milliard, a physician from British Guiana who practiced medicine in Manchester.

The Congress had been an enormous success and represented a turning point in George's thinking and in the approach the organization would take toward liberation of Africa. Prior to the Congress, George held the Marxist position that Africa would gain its independence only in the process of a world revolution which would occur during or toward the end of World War II. No such revolution took place and George reevaluated the political situation in Africa. A decision was made for a Gandhian approach—positive action without violence. Marxist ideology was an instrument to George, not a religion. If he had a religion, it was the achievement of freedom for Africa.

However, there was no acceptance of pacifism as an ideology, and the Congress declared that if Gandhi's methods failed then African fighters would return to the policy of revolution. It had also endorsed a Declaration of Human Rights "and advised those of African descent, wherever they might be, to organize themselves into political parties, trade unions, cooperative societies and farmers' organizations in support of their struggle to political freedom and economic advancement."[3]

During his long talks with George, Wright expressed doubts that pacifism, even as a tactic, would work. If a black man turned the other cheek it was then that a Southern white man crashed a two-by-four down upon his head and splattered his brains on the pavement. It would certainly never work in America, Richard told George, for the white man's heritage had been self-defense—and defense of family, friends, the community and even of strangers—which easily translated into meeting violence with violence. The phrase "I'm as good a man as he is" quite literally represented a sense of freedom, an evaluation of his own worth, that was unique in the world and came from a new nation which had never had to overcome the mental fetters of feudalism. A white man began to respect a black man only when he stood and fought for his rights, to the death if need be.

And Richard told George of an argument he had had with Vijaya Lakshmi Pandit, the sister of Jawaharlal Nehru, whom he had met at the home of Dorothy Norman. He had gone to Dorothy's townhouse with a sense of foreboding that he would not like Madame Pandit because temperamentally he had never been drawn toward Asians. They possessed, on the whole, no tension, he thought. Richard admitted that it might well be that it was the Easterners who were healthy and that Westerners, with their tension, excitement and neuroses, were sick. But even so, he preferred the American personality.

Dorothy's large drawing room, crammed with paintings, spilling with books, was full of people when Richard arrived. As he walked toward a group gathered at the back of the room which overlooked a garden he saw that the Indians present were beautiful, with tinted skins, flowing black hair and indescribable eyes. To himself, he had muttered: beauty does not free people from British rule, and never will. Indeed, the more beautiful they are the more the English can point to that odd fact as proof of their childlike state and condition of life; their beauty is flaccid, with no passion and no drive. Richard knew he was being unreasonable but a terrible distaste for the Hindus swept him.

Madame Pandit, gray- and black-haired, brown-olive skinned, was answering the questions of journalists, columnists, novelists, critics and book editors. After introductions Richard sat down and sipped his drink. He noticed that Madame Pandit was sipping tea from a fragile tea cup, and he suddenly recalled T. S. Eliot's lines about lilacs in bloom—she has a bowl of lilacs in her room—and then felt a wave of disgust for all the New York intellectuals in the room. Not one of them, he thought, would be willing to lift a finger to help India get the English off her back.

Richard was silent for so long that he drew Madame Pandit's attention and she asked his opinion of the pacifist ideology of her country. "I would prefer to see some of the spirit that is in the Westerner introduced by Indian leaders . . ." he began moderately, but before he could finish the sentence several people began to speak at once. "Do you want us to kill?" someone railed. "Engage in senseless competition?" Everyone began to revile the West without any understanding of its motive springs, the impulses that actuated Americans. Madame Pandit had retained her poise in the midst of the loud babble: she smiled at Richard, gazed at him with deep dark eyes and waited for him to speak. Gradually the hubbub quieted.

"Can't you see that feudal states, tribal states, are lost in the world today? Can't you see that the great powerful industrial states set the tone and conditions of living in this world? Why not borrow instrumentalities, techniques from the West? We rebels here do not understand this business of nonviolence. Such concepts were not invented by men with iron in their blood and dreams in their hearts."

"I take it that you are not for nonviolence," Madame Pandit said softly.

"No, definitely I'm not. . . . Each and every Indian ought to learn how to make gunpowder in his kitchen just like a girl learning to cook; keep your powder dry; keep it in your compot, your cookie jar; under your pillow; if you are ever free, it will be because you butcher enough Englishmen to get them off of you!" Richard stopped for a minute to wait for an answer, but none came. "No one," he continued, "will ever give you a voluntary certificate saying that you are free; such has never happened in the world and never will; no exploiting power ever out of a goodness of its heart let a captive people go free."

Afterwards, on his way home, he mulled over the people he had met. "These Indians have a long way to go. It's not racial; it's something more subtle than that. They simply do not feel that sharp, urgent degree of personal worth that would make them formulate their programs like a Lenin; they do not feel their sense of individuality hard enough to make them weigh the moment when they'll toss all they have into the scales of struggle. . . . The American Negro is much tougher than these people. We are like white men in that there is a limit to what we'll take; a limit when we'll say that we've had enough; that life is not worth it under certain conditions."[4]

George listened to Richard's story intently, laughing once or twice when he changed his voice to match the tones of Madame Pandit, the angry and shouting intellectuals, and himself. But when he had finished George argued—somewhat pedantically, Richard thought— that he was wrong about the Asians. They were far from placid and there had been plenty of violence in India. And what about the Japanese kamikazes and the jungle foot soldiers? Everyone was agreed that they had displayed the highest degree of energy and tension in the war just ended. And Richard had to agree.

Tenaciously and still pursuing their original discussion, Richard told George that he still did not think that pacifism would be useful to Africans in getting rid of their colonialists. Then George explained that alongside an active nonviolent resistance there was being formed an underground organization among West Africans composed of revolutionaries. This was to be called "The Circle." It was already in its formation stage in London and Kwame Nkrumah would return to Accra to organize Circles throughout his country.

The Circle would admit to membership only those known to be genuinely working for West Africa's unity and the total destruction of colonialism. Members would train themselves "in order to begin revolutionary work in any part of the African continent. It would be a movement consisting essentially of students and young people who would organize the nationalist spirit already in existence throughout the continent."

A motto had been coined: Service, Sacrifice, Suffering. The aims of the Circle, George explained to Richard, were simple:

1. To maintain ourselves and the Circle as the Revolutionary Vanguard of the struggle for West African Unity and National Independence.

2. To support the idea and claims of the All West African National Congress in its struggle to create and maintain a Union of African Socialist Republics.

George asked Richard not to write about the Circle. The essential ideas of the group would be published in a small book on which he was working with Kwame Nkrumah,[5] but a secret document was being drawn up solely for the membership and its leaders. Certainly, George calmly explained, "the CID and the British Colonial Office are well aware of what we are doing—but don't you give us any publicity until I give the word." Richard had solemnly promised, even though the prospect of an independent Africa and the entire secret operation excited him so that he had difficulty sleeping for several nights.[6]

As soon as Richard and Ellen had gotten themselves settled in Paris in August, 1947, George and Dorothy had come to visit and from then on both men visited back and forth across the Channel regularly. George often told Richard that he wanted him to visit Africa and write a book about his impressions, but it was far from his mind on Easter Sunday, 1953.

The table had been cleared and Ellen was pouring coffee. A quiet lay over Paris and Richard could hear the footsteps of people walking on the street below. He sipped his coffee tranquilly and looked out at the gray walls of the University of Paris rising beyond his window. He was at peace; the meal had been delicious and for once they had not discussed politics. If George had been there, it would have been different. Sometimes Richard grew sick of politics—nothing to lift the mind or the emotions—A stab of disloyalty toward his friend disturbed his easy mood. Well, it was true. George tended to be pedantic. But I love him because he is a pure person, Richard thought, and having excused the pleasure he felt at his friend's absence, his mind slid back into the easy somnolence of a holiday.

But suddenly, Dorothy's round face took on its expression of enthusiasm for a new idea and she leaned forward across the table:

"Now that your desk is clear, why don't you go to Africa?" Before he answered Richard glanced at his wife and saw a flare of bright light in her eyes: "Why not?" she asked him.

The idea was not wholly new; Richard had written to his agent several months earlier to sound him out on George's suggestion that he visit the country and write a book about the men who were running the Gold Coast government. Uncertain whether a publisher would welcome such a book, Richard suggested that Reynolds approach the *Atlantic Monthly* to sound out its interest in a series of articles.

For some reason he could not immediately explain Richard felt strangely disturbed, on the defensive, as if poised upon the verge of the unknown. Dorothy's pressure and his wife's enthusiasm made the trip more of a reality than it had been until then. Like a battering ram, Dorothy pursued him: "Francis"—which was what Nkrumah's close friends called him— "is going to table his motion for self-government in July." It would be a great experience, his wife encouraged him. And he knew that it would be thrilling to be present when the first black Prime Minister in history asked the British for freedom for his people.

Dorothy told Richard that George would make all of the necessary arrangements and that Nkrumah would send a personal invitation to him if it was needed. His curiosity had been completely alerted by this vital woman who assisted her husband in all of his work and had helped particularly by her knowledge of foreign languages and by earning money at various jobs to help support the African Bureau and her husband.

Even more important than what Dorothy said to him were the emotions charging through his body. Would he feel African? I'm of African descent . . . But, am I African? True, he had helped his friend Alioune Diop launch the organization Présence Africaine, which Richard had considered a regrouping of forces, among intellectual Africans, to rediscover the old culture which had been shredded and torn by the colonialists, who had almost succeeded in paralyzing the black man for centuries. It was important to discover what was uniquely the black man's culture. And it signified to him that the African was beginning to reorganize his life in accordance with his own basic feelings. Drawn into the orbit of the magazine and its organization were poets and novelists Aimé Cesaire, from Martinique; Jacques Alexis, from Haiti; Leopold Senghor, from Senegal; M. Lasebikan, from Nigeria; Cheik Anta Diop; George Lamming, of Trinidad; and many others. But when some of his friends told him passionately that the African had a *special* gift for music, dancing, rhythm and movement, a genius of their own, and that they had been civilized in Africa when white men were still living in caves in Europe, he had been uneasy.[7] Talk of that kind always seemed to bear tones of apology for blackness. He had always taken for granted the humanity of Africans as well as that of other people. Richard's mind became impotent when it came to explaining life in "racial terms." Habitually, his thinking had been unconcerned with "race"; he had grown up believing that human beings were molded and reacted to a specific social environment. Why, then, he wondered, should he feel so frightened by the idea of a trip to Africa? What was he afraid of discovering? Maybe he was afraid to confront the proof of his own ideas—that he was truly of the West—and wanted some small vestige of doubt to remain so that he could feel that maybe somewhere there was a homeland. Well, he would go and confront Africa. It would be a confrontation of himself.

Later on the same afternoon Richard left Dorothy to Ellen and the children and went into his study. He had not intended to write a single line that day but he needed his agent's support and opinion on such a trip. Going to Africa was expensive and Paul might have some suggestions on where the money would come from.

Richard uncovered his standard Underwood, which he had bought many years before, and slipped paper beneath its roller. Quickly he began to type the letter; he had no doubt about the approach he wanted to take. It would be "an intimate book about the people of the Gold Coast. A kind of close-up, detailed, non-academic, popularly written study of the lives of the people and what they are doing." The Gold Coast, alone among all the subject people in African colonies, was about ready for self-government. The Africans were already running the country and a close-up, day-to-day study of how they were breaking from their tribal life and learning to live the new life of self-government in the modern world was important to learn. He did not want to do a book about a colony that had organized itself against England and won, but a book about individuals—what they thought, felt, planned, and lived each day. Perhaps the best form would be a diary, writing down every day what he saw, thought and reacted to in such a turbulent atmosphere.

In only a few days Richard received an airmail reply: his agent was enthusiastic, and was going to discuss the plan with Harper, but cautioned Richard not to settle on a diary form until he was actually on the spot and had begun to collect material. He asked Richard to include to what extent there was crime, how prevalent it was, to tell about the courts and justice, medical care; and to see the rich and the poor, the educated and the uneducated, the intelligent and the stupid.

Harper sent Richard a substantial advance for a book on Africa; George Padmore arranged that he receive a personal invitation from Nkrumah, and the British government issued him an entry permit. His finances were in good shape: Mondadori in Italy had offered $2,000 for *The Outsider* and there was still enough money in his account with his agent to send Ellen and the children $500 a month while he was away.

On June 4, 1953, Richard sailed from Liverpool aboard the *Accra,* a British ship, the only American on board. The sun was bright but he shivered in a macintosh and wished he had not packed away his heavy coat in his trunk down in the belly of the ship. To help fill the twelve days the sea trip would take Richard had brought stacks of books about Africa, including *The Akan Doctrine of God,* Dr. J. B. Danquah; *The Position of the Chief in the Modern Political System of Ashanti,* R. S. Rattray; *Capitalism and Slavery,* Eric Williams; *A History of the Gold Coast,* W. E. F. Ward; *The Black Jacobins,* C. L. R. James; *The Marginal Man,* Everett V. Stonequist; and a book he carried everywhere he went, *Ideas* by Edmund Husserl. George Padmore had suggested the list and Richard had already read many of Padmore's own books on the Gold Coast revolution. He had also read O. Mannoni's *La Psychologie de Colonialisme.*

At five o'clock Richard heard a mournful blast and felt the ship's vibrations increase as she shuddered her way out to sea. He could not keep from his mind other such voyages; the thousands of English ships which headed toward Africa. An image of the slavers so sharp that he could almost hear the moans and cries of manacled men, women, and children, packed layer upon layer in the fetid hold, swam in his head. Seeking to lose the image, he walked down the stairs to his cabin telling himself that it was a different world. The old Africa was gone. New Africa was learning how to run hydro-electric plants and to make aluminum; the art of manufacture was no longer a secret and machines did not care what color were the hands operating them.

Richard enjoyed the voyage; the feeling of being utterly cut off from the world seemed to disengage fetters from his mind. Since he was never seasick he liked to walk on deck and watch the ship lurch forward, its prow dipping, churning the sea, throwing up spray and foam as it plunged forward. In his berth at night he pictured the ship rolling and then tilting while the weight of the water resisted and forced it back into an upright position.

After four days aboard the *Accra* he had a large collection of notes about the people he had met on board. It was the first time he had been on so purely English a vessel. Aside from one or two Syrians, a German, some Africans, and a few vague Mediterranean nationalities, the ship's passengers were men and women going to Africa to assume civil service positions or returning after a few months' leave in England. Dull, repressed, stolidly English, they spent most of each day playing cards, ping-pong or drinking. What a mediocre lot they were to administer the destinies of millions of blacks, Richard thought to himself. He appreciated their sense of privacy, however, for after one cheerful "Good Morning" they remained taciturn the rest of the day and ignored him.

A tall, balding African shared Richard's table in the dining room. He introduced himself as Justice Thomas of the Nigerian Supreme Court and as soon as he had established that Richard was an American he announced that he was pro-British, pro-African, and pro-United States. Before Richard had quite recovered from that statement Thomas announced: "My ideas are Left." It was all he could do not to laugh but he caught himself, smiled, and remained silent. He wanted to hear what Thomas had to say.

Thomas, who professed to be pro-African, had recently tried and found guilty nineteen nationalists who had committed violent acts against the British government. But, in almost the same breath, he praised Kwame Nkrumah: he had embraced the masses and one neglected the masses at one's peril. "What do you think?" Choosing his words carefully, Richard answered that embracing the masses seemed to be a habit with politicians today.

For some reason that Richard could not quite connect with his own noncommittal answer, Justice Thomas was encouraged to say that no tribal rabble would drive them—linking himself with the British—out of Sierra Leone. Africans were not ready for freedom. Laughingly, Richard remarked that if he did not have a black skin he would swear that Thomas was an Englishman.

After breakfast each morning Thomas hauled from his jacket pockets bottles of yeast tablets, garlic pills, vitamins, and swallowed them down before leaving the table. Health and Episcopalianism seemed the two poles which steadied Thomas' life. And when Wright did not attend the Sunday church services in the lounge Thomas sought him out afterwards. He was appalled to learn that Richard neither accepted nor rejected God.

At last they were in tropic waters and a hot sun blazed upon the blue sea. The ship seemed to rustle and whisper through the calm southern waters. When it reached the port of Las Palmas, in the Canary Islands, Justice Thomas who knew the island, suggested that he guide Richard on shore. They were joined by another male passenger and they walked down the gangway and climbed into a taxi. Almost at once, the driver turned in his seat, drew the outline of a woman in the air and asked, in Spanish, if they wanted to see some girls. Richard was amused when the staid, religious Thomas almost shouted: Let's go! Then he caught himself, looked at Richard uneasily to see how he was taking his change of role, and placed his

hand in a fatherly manner on his shoulder. The taxi bumped along
in the bright sunlight until it drew up before a pale green cement
house. Before he climbed out of the car Richard told his two
companions that he was only looking. He had not come thousands of
miles to pick up diseases from women in the Canary Islands.

Richard felt queasy and yet his curiosity thrust him forward. He
wanted to look, to peek into the lives of these Spanish whores. One
could not pick up a disease by just looking, he reassured himself. A
slight disgust filled him and he remembered a "girly-show" he had
seen in Jackson, Mississippi, when he was about fifteen. All of his
friends had asked him how he had enjoyed it—giggling and drooling
in anticipation of a description. He had felt sickened and turned
away. When pressed for an answer he told them curtly: it was a
wasted afternoon. He had not wanted them to know that it had
shocked his puritanical soul nor confess the avidity with which he
watched a girl rotate her pelvis. Some of the same disgust and dread
returned as they stepped into the whorehouse.

Worn linoleum covered the floor of the front room and its design
was almost obliterated by a litter of cigarette butts. A stale odor of
flesh, liquor, tobacco and the acrid smell of sperm struck Richard's
nostrils and he tried to breathe without admitting the myriad scents
into his body. God! Would his clothing smell when he left? Twenty
or so girls clad in transparent pajamas filed into the room and leaned
against the wall obligingly. Thank God he had made his position
clear before he entered the house: there was white matter at the
edges of the girls' eyelids and their faces needed a good washing.
Some were quite pretty, he noticed, and one or two had lovely firm
high breasts with erected nipples which pushed at the sheer pajamas.

Richard leaned back in his chair and sipped the beer the proprietor had placed before them. He wanted to keep his gaze on
Justice Thomas, whose eyes were roving greedily over the breasts of
the prostitutes. Feeling Wright's eyes on him, Thomas looked away,
leaned back in his chair and then gazed up at the ceiling. Well, that
stodgy, self-righteous, religious old bastard is dying to go down the
hall with one of these babies, Richard thought. He felt perverse. One
word would release the Judge's sense of guilt. He would not utter the
word. Each time Richard caught Thomas staring at a girl he looked
at him reprovingly, silently reminding him that he had an august
position as a defender of Christian values. Then Thomas would fling
himself back on the couch, slap his thighs, and roar with embarrassed
laughter. Ha—this is rich, Richard thought. If the old Christian
wanted a girl bad enough he would have to show a staunch individualism because he would be his conscience as long as they re-

mained in the house. Finally, the Justice sighed and said: "I guess we'd better leave."

Quite early in the morning on June 16 Richard arrived in the coast port city of Takoradi, where he was met by a friend of Prime Minister Nkrumah and taken by government bus to the capital of Accra. The temperature was so high that he felt as if the flesh was melting from his bones. The distance from Takoradi to Accra was only 170 miles but the road was so poor that it took eight hours to make the journey. When he reached Accra Richard was met by Nkrumah's secretary, Erica Powell, who explained that the Prime Minister was in the Northern Territories on an urgent political mission. She drove him in her English car across Accra to the top of some low hills where there were modern bungalows which had recently been built by the British for the new African Ministers, many of whom had only recently been released from prison. The Ministers, however, refused to live in the new houses and chose to stay in the neighborhoods of their constituents. They suspected the British of a desire to separate them from their people and make them a part of the ruling colonialists. But Nkrumah's politicians knew that the most dangerous thing that they could do was to draw a class line between themselves and the tribal voters who had given them power.

Atop the low hills the air was slightly less humid, and the rich black and red soil reminded Richard of Mississippi. The sun was killing and he was grateful that the bungalow screens kept out the flying insects.

Early the next morning before the sun became too high and hot Richard walked down the hill into Accra to look at the city. "There were no sidewalks; one walked at the edge of a drainage ditch made of concrete in which urine ran. A stench pervaded the sunlit air. Barefoot men dressed in cloths whose colors were a mixture of red, green, yellow, blue, brown, and purple stood idling about. Most of the women not only carried the inevitable baby strapped to their backs, but also a burden on top of their heads and a bundle in each hand. [Richard] reached a street corner and paused; coming toward [him] was a woman nursing a baby that was still strapped to her back; the baby's head was thrust under the woman's arm and the woman had given the child the long, fleshy, tubelike teat and it was suckling.

"The women's carriage was remarkably graceful; they walked as straight as ramrods, with a slow, slinging motion, moving their legs from their hips, their feet just managing to skim over the earth. When they glanced about they never jarred or jolted the huge burdens they had on their heads, and their eyes held a calm, proud look. In the physical behavior of both men and women there were no wasted motions; they seem[ed] to move in a manner that conserved their energies in the awful heat."

Men, women and children were clustered around water hydrants filling gasoline tins, old tubs, buckets, pans, anything that held water. Some children were washing the family clothing, others were standing nude, bathing their brown or black bodies in full sight. Another small child had squatted over a drainage ditch and was urinating. Beggars seemed to be everywhere he looked. Some of them were so deformed with swollen legs, running sores, and jutting, once-broken limbs which had not been properly set that Richard was repelled. Poverty and disease did not fill him with compassion; he felt sick to his stomach.

Even through dark glasses which wrapped around at the sides to prevent the entrance of light, the sun burned him and he was forced to return to his bungalow after only an hour or two. Finally night fell and a velvet blackness covered Accra; it was a soft dense darkness he had never seen anywhere and out of the night came the sound of crickets and tree frogs.

A phone call the next morning informed Richard that Nkrumah would send a car for him that day at four o'clock. And promptly at four a long sleek car pulled into Richard's driveway and stopped. A uniformed black chauffeur stepped out, saluted Richard and ushered him into the back of the limousine. When they arrived at the residence of the Prime Minister he was led into a red, two-story brick building which reminded him of a colonial mansion in Georgia or Mississippi. Richard followed his guide upstairs, down a hall and into a living room.

Nkrumah, of medium height, had intense eyes under level brows which curved gently downward, a high, high forehead, a beautiful smile revealing perfectly even white teeth, two of which had porcelain jackets. Wearing a kenti, he stood in the middle of the room to welcome Richard.

Nkrumah was a year younger than Richard and had been born in the Western Province of the Gold Coast to a father who was a goldsmith and a mother who traced her ancestry back to Chief Aduku Addaie. He had been educated in a village school and later attended the Prince of Wales' College at Achimota and then Lincoln University, in Pennsylvania. In 1947 he had returned to the Gold Coast as secretary of the United Gold Coast Convention and two years later broke away to form the revolutionary Convention Peoples' Party. He had been imprisoned by the British in 1950 for political agitation—"self-government now." While in jail Nkrumah had smuggled out messages and a party manifesto written on toilet paper which helped his CPP to win the elections by an overwhelming majority of the country. He was released from prison by the British and instructed to form the new government.

Nkrumah told Richard that he wanted to take him on a tour so that he could see everything for himself. Nothing had been prearranged. He would show him the best and the worst of Accra. The Prime Minister led the way and the motions of his erect body seemed deliberate as if he had disciplined the extreme tension of his personality. A brace of motorcycles preceded the limousine and when their noise was heard people rushed into the street to salute Nkrumah. "Free—doom! Free—dooooom" they shouted. And "Kwame! Kwa—mee!" Then, over and over, "Akwaba! Akwaba!" which was "Welcome! Welcome!"

The Prime Minister smiled and laughed and raised his right hand to salute the people. His usual brooding look left him, and as the sun slanted into the automobile his jet black skin gleamed as if it were onyx. Richard had never seen such crowds of smiling, shouting people and his mind flew back over his long years of argument and discussion about freedom.

Here it was, Richard marveled. At a time that the West was growing embarrassed by the very word, these people knew that it meant the right to shape their own destiny as they wished. Freedom in Africa was more than a word and an African had no doubt about its meaning. Richard turned impetuously to Nkrumah: "They believe in you," he said.

Nkrumah turned his rather long face toward Richard and his full soft lips turned up in a smile. "Would you believe that four years ago such a joyful demonstration was impossible?" the Prime Minister asked. The people were cowed and frightened under British rule. When Nkrumah had returned to his country the mood was bitter. The people trusted nothing and nobody. They had been beaten down to a point where they were afraid to act.

"Who were the first in the Gold Coast to offer opposition to the Convention Peoples' Party," Richard asked.

"Missionaries," the Prime Minister answered softly.

Richard went several times with the Prime Minister to political meetings and rallies and once spoke on the same platform with the leader at a rally in the Westend Arena.

Within a few days after his arrival Richard moved to the Seaview Hotel, which stood at the edge of the beach and fronted James Town, the slum area. Screened bungalows were pleasant to live in but he was too isolated. He wanted to be in the center of where things were happening. The Seaview was a squalid hotel with spat-tered walls, dirty wooden floors, and the stench of old cooking oil pervaded the hallway. Richard looked at the mattress on his bed; it was damp and stained by use. Above the bed hung a grayish-white mosquito netting which appeared unclean. Walking to the basin on one side of the room, he tested the plumbing. There was no hot water but the cold water was as heated by the sun as it would have been by electricity or gas. Flies and mosquitoes hummed and buzzed or settled on walls, bed, and floor. Richard shuddered.

By the next day all the metal in his toilet kit had turned a reddish color from rust and to shave he had to wipe the humidity from the mirror above his sink several times. Soon his clothing begun to spot with mildew and his shoes turn yellow. But in a few days he had grown accustomed to the early morning stench of homemade soap, cooking odors and vapors from excrement which drifted into the hotel from the open ditches.

Using the Seaview as his base, Richard took long excursions into every area of the city. He left the hotel early each morning, wearing dark glasses and a pith helmet as protection from the sun. With two cameras he took hundreds and hundreds of photographs and talked to everyone he met. Before going to sleep at night he typed out conversations, descriptions, impressions and other bits of information gathered during the day. In a deeply thoughtful mood one evening, he wrote a short letter to his agent. "You asked for something on the uplift in the African book, but I'm afraid that it cannot be. I was afraid at what I found here; and yet I'm told that the Gold Coast is by far the best part of Africa. If that is so, I don't want to see the worst."[8] Life seemed incredible and he could not accustom himself to the poverty, nakedness and the illness of many people. At first it appeared to him that one of the few redeeming features in a country where its white occupiers had encouraged corruption was the vigor-ous Convention Peoples' Party which Western-educated Nkrumah had forged into a unit which encompassed tribalism, Christianity, paganism, sex, nationalism, socialism, housing, health, and industrial schemes and thus united all the people. But illiteracy was about 90 percent and Richard believed that self-government would bring hard problems to the CPP. What was sad was that if the experiment should blow up, then the world would say that Africans were incapable of ruling themselves. But he tried to push the future from his mind and concentrated on studying the life of the common people as much as he could. Everyone talked to him wherever he went: and each political group he met was angry at the other groups and each would tell him facts about the others. In that way he got to know a great deal about the society.

After a month in Accra he discovered that his money was melting as fast as it would have in Paris. Everything was expensive and he still wanted to get out into the kraals. But without an automobile he was almost immobilized. Who ever heard of seeing Africa by taxicab? He was convinced that none of the services controlled by the British would be placed at his service because they suspected what he would say about their dirty colonialism. Well, I must rely on myself for everything, he thought. And that is hard. First, he would buy a car, a used one that he could sell at the end of his trip. There was only one railroad and it took an entire day to cover 150 miles, so he wrote to Reynolds and asked for another $750.

While he waited for an answer Richard prepared for the trip. He bought a half-gallon thermos jug for water; eighty or ninety dollars' worth of tinned food; bottles of germicide; a box of DDT; cigarettes; and a five-yard length of cotton cloth to use as a sheet. The last item filled him with a sense of accomplishment. It was a beautiful deep-rose color and wherever he had to sleep he would be protected by the clean cloth.

Expecting difficulties, he presented a request to the Gold Coast Information Service for information. The Prime Minister had over-come his suspicions and persuaded him to ask the British for help. In a few days the British had planned an itinerary which would take him into the high rain forest, to Kumasi, Kumawu, Bibiani, and he was given a list of people to see—doctors, lawyers, chiefs, politicians—and permission to sleep in the government rest houses dotted throughout the jungle area.

By August 6 he was in the bush and had caught on to the way to travel where there were no hotels and no water. Richard's chauffeur, Kojo, was an ex-middleweight champion of the Gold Coast, whom he had been advised to hire for his strength and pugnacity. He visited Kumasi, the capital of the Ashanti, for twelve days then headed south to the forest area. As they drove more deeply into the jungle the vegetation became an intense green and as the car churned up steep hills the trees grew taller. Wawa, mahogany, palm and cocoa trees lined each side of the road with a fringed green curtain. Occasionally, they passed men or women or children and when some waved at him Richard tremored the palm of his hand in a native salute.

In each village he talked to tribal chiefs as well as to their people and even to civilians serving the back country. He had collected books, reports and other material. He looked into timber industries and the large gold mines and talked to the workers. For three months Wright spent every waking hour investigating, looking at, and reacting to Africa; but he was not satisfied. He could not seem to get as close to the life of the ordinary African as he would have liked.

Some of Richard's experiences were puzzling to him. In Accra he witnessed a queer shuffling dance which expressed joy in a quiet physical manner. At first, the movements astonished him; some thread out of the past trailed in his mind. What was it? He could not remember. Suddenly, he knew what it was. He had seen the same snakelike, veering dances before in America in store-front churches, in Holy Roller tabernacles, and in wooden prayer houses in the South. The dancers he watched were African nationalists but the movements were the same as those of black Americans he had seen at worship. A feeling of alienation gripped him as it had when he had watched dancers in the United States. "Never in my life have I been able to dance more than a few elementary steps, and the carrying of even the simplest tune has always been beyond me."

What is this? he wondered. It was a riddle that nagged in his mind and sent him out to watch for other similarities. He did not believe in African holdovers. The American black man had been basically altered by what he had gone through in the United States. His mind had been filled with a new content. "Racial" qualities were myths spun in prejudiced minds. There was a oneness of impulse and singleness of aim in both black and white Americans. He refused to accept the set of theories, quaintly termed "African survivals," expounded by a group of American anthropologists who, he thought, merely clamored for attention. Such arguments touched upon some mystic influence of "race" which Richard's mind refused utterly. And Africans were more alien to him than white Americans. Kinship, for him, resided in the Western world.

He became more bewildered when he began to search for other items of similarity: there was a laughter that bent the knee and turned the head as if in embarrassment; there was an inexplicable, almost sullen silence that came from disagreement or opposition; and there was "African" laughter. That was the strangest thing of all. It was often his own way of avoiding intimacy and pain. The laughter which he had noticed apart from simple everyday humor was not caused by mirth; it was a way of indicating that, though they were not going to take you into their confidence, their attitude was not hostile. Ah, God, how many times had he smiled and smiled, sometimes until his cheeks hurt, to keep hurtful things or people from penetrating his heart to its core.

Even while he began to admit similarities he could not accept these as unbreakable "racial" ties. He was so uncomfortable at times. The assumption on the part of many Africans he met that he would and should feel at home in their country because of the color of his skin often brought him to a defense of his own country—of America. And when asked what part of Africa his ancestors had come from, he could not answer. It made him feel uneasy, and when the questioner was too persistent he responded by pointing out that many Africans had sold their own people into slavery and that neither they nor the white purchasers kept any records. Assumptions of what he was, who he was, and that he naturally would wish to live in Africa made him bristle. Sea, jungle, dirt, nakedness and the crowded marketplaces set up a conflict in his mind and he replaced those scenes by the ordered, routinized streets of Paris. A protest against what he saw sometimes seized him:

My protest was not against Africa or its people; it was directed against the unsettled feeling engendered by the strangeness of a completely different order of life. I was gazing upon a world whose laws I did not know: upon faces whose reactions were riddles to me. There was nothing here that I could predict, anticipate, or rely upon and, in spite of myself, a mild sense of anxiety began to fill me.[9]

One evening at a formal gathering Richard met and talked with Dr. J. B. Danquah. Short, slow-moving, Danquah, a British-educated lawyer, philosopher, politician, dramatist and one of the older nationalist leaders, was part of Nkrumah's opposition. Danquah was a traditionalist who believed that Nkrumah was proceeding too rapidly toward self-government. He was an aristocrat who had little faith in the masses of Africans. Richard had read Danquah's book *The Akan Doctrine of God* and decided to question the man about some of the emotions his stay in Africa had aroused. Even Danquah insisted that if Richard would remain in Africa he would *feel* his race, that a knowledge of race would come back to him. No, Richard insisted quietly, we American Negroes are no longer Negroes, and the world does not realize this. Just what we are, I don't quite know. We are black but in a strange sense we are more Western than the West. Yet, our country rejects us on the basis of skin color.

Carrying a trunk of material—a three-foot pile of books, reports and other material; over 250,000 words in notes; almost 2,000 photographs—and wearing his sun helmet and dark glasses, Richard sailed for Liverpool September 2 on the *Apapa*. He felt limp and damp, as if the humidity in Accra had seeped into his body and mind, and he worried about the book he was writing.

There would have to be omissions in what he would say about Africa, but he would have to tell the truth as he saw it. A delicate balance would be required. Why do I always seem to get myself into these situations? he wondered. For a few hours he debated dropping the project entirely. Ah, but he could not do that whatever pain it would cause him. He had a moral obligation to complete the job. Somehow, he resolved, he would make clear that the continent of Africa was awake and nothing could ever send it back to sleep again. The image of Africa, so long degraded, would now be redeemed. One could be thankful that Africa was in the hands of Africans. If Europe tried to resubjugate her, it would mean that they would leave themselves exposed to Communism. And to try to meet Communism would mean that Europe would have to work out another relationship with Africa. They would not want to do it. White pride was taking a licking; but it was false pride. In the end Europe and Africa would have to work together, but much would change, on both sides of the fence, before that would happen.

By January 1, 1954, the book was completed. He worried about its 600 page-length because photographs had to be included or no one would believe some of what he had to say. That would make it impossibly long for a publisher. And he worried still more about a proper title; each one that came to his mind and was written to his agent was rejected before an answer arrived from Reynolds: *O My People; The Queen Mother; What Is Africa to Me?* The three titles seemed to carry a defeatist ring; what about *Stranger in a Strange Land; Stranger in Africa; The White Man's Grave; This Heritage; Black Brothers; Africa Turns Black; Ancestral Home?* Not one seemed to convey the meaning of the book. At last, in April, a feeling of calm settled over him followed by a feeling of elation. He had a title. It was simple, strong, and it described what the book was really about: *Black Power*.[10]

But almost at once other problems arose to worry Richard. Would Jack Fischer, his editor, an Oxford-educated man, think he was too harsh to the British?[11] Then, one morning, an airmail letter arrived from Reynolds. It was his opinion that Richard should remove most of his criticism about America inasmuch as that country was not directly involved in West Africa. And still another letter of criticism arrived from Frank McGregor, president of Harper: the essential integrity of the book would be maintained; however, it was necessary to make a number of points clear. Richard must state strongly, and near the beginning of the book, that he was opposed to the Communists. McGregor realized that this had been stated several times throughout the work but it should be stated with greater vigor. The reader should be in no doubt that, although Richard was anti-Western in certain respects, he was not pro-Russian. Further, he must be clear about Marxism and the value he attached to it. Page one of the manuscript appeared to him to be political analysis based on Marxism. It would be helpful to the general reader if he indicated how much his own thinking was predicated on Marx. In a letter addressed to Kwame Nkrumah at the end of the manuscript he should make clear that he did not advocate that African leaders adopt the weapons of their enemies and abandon all notions of fair play and decency. Reviewers in the United States might misunderstand and believe that he was using the arguments of Senator McCarthy.[12] And, finally, the manuscript had to be cut one hundred pages. The last point was upsetting to Richard. How could he cut that many pages without distorting the whole?

He sat down to his typewriter to explain his difficulties to his agent:

The trouble with writing a book like this is that the reality of a given phase of the life does not come upon one all at once; for instance, the religion of the people came to me in bits, each bit extending my comprehension of the reality a little more. . . . Now, if I had been writing a straight, factual description of the mores of the people, I'd have treated religion once in one section and then dropped it. But by going from spot to spot, talking to this person and that one, I had to gather this reality as it seeped into me through the personalities of others. There might be some merit in that kind of getting and giving a reality, but it might bore the reader. Conrad wrote all of his novels in that roundabout way. It involves going back to some extent over ground already covered, but each going back reveals more and more of the things described.

One additional problem arose with S. G. van Looy, Richard's Dutch publisher, who wanted to make severe cuts because of his own country's history of colonial domination. It was too anti-British. Seething with anger, but leashing his emotion when he answered van Looy's letter, Richard refused point-blank to make further changes in *Black Power*.

"While I have sympathy for your position," he typed away rapidly, "I must tell you quite frankly that Black Power is a political book and it simply cannot be cut at this stage. . . . As you know, the book deals with both the British and the Africans. Now, for once, I've written frankly about the Africans and their religions. Also I spoke frankly about the role of the British in West Africa. At this moment to try to delete this book would upset a very delicately balanced argument and seemingly make my book favor one side or the other."

It was necessary, Richard told van Looy, for him to take such a stand because he had to defend himself before a critical and often hostile public.

Black Power was received in the United States in September by silence from most critics. Richard was not prepared for the violence of the attack made by the New York *Times.* The newspaper even took the liberty of altering the captions under the photographs in the book. *Newsweek* and *Time* magazines simply ignored it, but a Southern newspaper, the *Observer,* Charlotte, North Carolina, marveled that in such a short time Richard had developed such keen insight into African concepts of life and described the letter to Nkrumah as a masterpiece.

From Accra came the most violent attack, with criticism focusing upon Richard's personality rather than the book itself. Richard was a thoroughly Westernized man who came to Africa in the old-fashioned style of the good old colonials of a century before; he was a pessimist about human life, its motivations, its destiny and was uniformly negative on Ghana. "We fare pretty badly," cried one reviewer. The book was nine-tenths pessimism and the rest all generalization and exaggeration. He had attacked Africa but futilely.

Angus & Robertson Ltd., a British publisher, refused the book and attacked the author:

I, personally, was interested to read *Black Power* because of the author's high reputation. If you will forgive me saying so, I cannot imagine any British publisher offering this to a British community. I do not think British peoples object to the fiercest criticism, even to abuse when it is not entirely deserved; but Wright's opening sentences admit complete ignorance of his subject and that ignorance could not be reversed in the short time at his disposal. He seems to sink to slum backyard intelligence as he flings his crudely poisoned spears at the British. However, this is, of course, only my opinion and perhaps unfairly based on considerable experience of dark peoples under colonial regimes where a few British rats do indeed mix themselves up with a much larger number of very fine British men.[13]

Richard was hurt by what seemed a never-ending stream of abuse, but he forgot his grief when he read that reference to himself which used "crudely poisoned spears" instead of "darts," a more customary British expression, or any number of other phrases. Why, the man's colonialist mentality stood out from the page in almost every sentence. *Dark peoples.* Hah! Richard thought.

Two French publishers refused the book and a storm of confusion broke out in Paris as to its meaning. Everyone appeared afraid of it because it was both anti-Communist and at the same time pro-Nationalist. That was too much even for the logical French. They, too, did not wish to lose their colonies. In disgust, Richard wrote to his Dutch translator that French intellectuals were accusing him of advocating American interference in Africa. If such confusion could arise from a clear, full text, what confusion would have resulted from the cut and mangled book many publishers had requested? Eventually *Black Power* was published in France, and George Padmore, through his influence, entered the argument and succeeded in having it accepted by Dobson, Ltd. Germany found it a fascinating and honest account when it was published in that country. But although it was accepted by the Book Find Club in America, *Black Power* had limited sales and Richard's share of the profits was only $1,250.

Enormous sums of money had been expended for his trip to Africa and, faced with the failure of *Black Power*, Richard was forced, once again, into lecture engagements in order to replenish his Swiss bank account. A new series was scheduled, starting in October, which gave him an opportunity to speak about his experiences in the Gold Coast more forcibly than he had been able to do in his book.

During the fall Richard lectured in Belgium, Switzerland and Holland and returned for two engagements in France. His audiences were held by his melodious voice and the beauty of his hands in an occasional graceful motion. Richard's accent had changed and his speech was permeated by a cosmopolitan flavor gained through spasmodic struggles with the French language and his association with people from every part of the Continent. In a gentle voice he described white and black, East and West, relations explosively and blatantly unacademic. He admitted that his approach was frankly subjective but that anyone who listened would see that his value assumptions were plainly stated.

In the white man's bloody campaign against black and brown peoples it was not simply energy or superior strength that prevailed but that within plundered countries existed a type of fifth column in the form of indigenous cultures. These "collaborators" were the mental habits of the people. Steeped in dependence systems of family life and anchored in ancestor-worshipping religions, the black man was prone to identify those powerful white faces with the potency of a dead father who had sustained him in the past. Loyalty to the Great Father was temporarily transferred to the white-faced invaders. Was the temporary acquiescence due to some "native" inferiority? No, for if a flying saucer landed in a Swiss Village from which emerged dangerous blue men with red eyes flashing lightning bolts which dealt instant death against which resistance would be futile, then a rationalization would be engendered. The religious myths of the Western world of a second coming of Christ and the Last Judgment had conditioned Europeans for just such an improbable event. The little men with blue skins and red eyes would be accepted and obeyed and served as Fathers of the people.

But, to continue to rule the invader had to train and educate a group of the conquered peoples. In the colonies, an intelligent young man was sent to school in London, France, or America. Great works of Western civilization were mastered and those ideas and ideals replaced the tribal culture of his own land. There was more involved than just ideals; if he returned to his own land, he was no longer comfortable sitting on a dirt floor of a swish hut or eating from a communal bowl with his fingers. The West made him ashamed of his own body and he was not comfortable with nudity. Painting his body with bright colors or scarring his skin in tribal symbols became meaningless. The chanting of the chiefs sounded barbaric to his ears. In the West he had developed a sense of his own individuality as being different and unique and he came to believe that he had a destiny and a personality that must not be violated by others. An outsider was created. Such a man could return to his country and serve the masters of his people; he could live in a foreign land the rest of his life; or he could weld his Western knowledge and his own inheritance into a tool with which to destroy those who had usurped Africa. His voice was finally raised in a cry of black nationalism.

Richard discovered a term by which to describe the new leaders and their future: the tragic elite.[14] And the African and Asian elite were in a state of "postmortem terror," compelled to interfere quickly, drastically, decisively, and break the old ways of their people in order to create new secular and rational societies. Often they were attacked by their countrymen as they attempted to bury the fetish-ridden past and abolish the mystical family relations that froze them in static degradation. And from the West came secret armies of CID, CIA, and various government officials who supported the most re-actionary elements of the population and sometimes intervened to bring down democratic leaders who were felt to be too revolutionary.

There would be much marching to and fro, many sundry fusions and meltings of peoples before the redemption of Africa came and the fate of the white West was being decided. The fight would be long and bloody, with hopes rising and falling. And it would con-tinue until the last naked black man had been drawn into the heart of the fight. It would be the blacks who would define the kind of relationship that would take place.

Even the liberal Western mind had been prepared to think that once freedom was taken by Africa, then states with democratic governments would automatically arise. It was not that simple. Already, in some of the countries, the heads of governments were lawyers, poets and writers. The West had had five hundred years to educate or protect the tribal man. It had failed. The people would decide upon their own form of government. Let the tragic elite try for a bit.

"Tragic and lonely and all too often misunderstood are these men of the Asian-African elite. The West hates and fears that elite. . . . For this elite in Asia and Africa constitutes islands of free men, the FREEST MEN IN ALL THE WORLD TODAY."[15]

XXVI

On a scorching hot day, August 16, 1954, Richard stopped his secondhand Citroën, with which he had replaced the Oldsmobile, at the side of the road just a few hours from the Spanish border. To his right were the neat green lands of France and to his left a sandy beach and the sparkling blue Mediterranean. Seated in his car, and as alone as on a ship's deck, he fingered a road map and gazed at the landscape. A compulsion to stop had been with him for a few miles until he had finally given in to an emotion finally recognized as a reluctance toward entering Spain.

What held him back? His health, since the operation for a hernia that had developed while he had been in Accra, was excellent. The attacks against two previous books were almost forgotten. As a matter of fact, Richard thought in amazement, I seem to thrive on adversity. His family was well and Ellen was looking for a country place in Normandy to use as a retreat from the supercharged air of Paris. Harper had raised the advance for a book on Spain from $2,500 to $3,000, and it was something he wanted to do. He *felt* Spain. It was right up his alley.

At first, after visiting Africa, he had wanted to return, either to the French colonies or the Belgian Congo. Especially to the Congo because it was an area that was deliberately kept out of touch with the rest of the world. Belgium had the hardest racial policy of any European nation. He had looked and looked in Paris and in London for an African from the Congo. He had never met a single one and had been told that if a Congolese left his home he was never allowed to return.

Jewish friends in Paris had urged him to take a trip to Israel and do a book, but the subject sprawled back over two thousand years and he felt it would be impossible to write about Jews and not give the Catholics a working over. Then he had not been entirely certain what his attitude was toward a Jewish homeland. He knew of the suffering in Europe and so far could not bring himself to lecture in Germany. What if he had shaken hands unknowingly with someone who had worked in one of the concentration camps destroying his wife's people? But, still, would not the Jews' claim of Israel, even though special, be as wrong as a claiming of Africa for American Negroes. He could not believe in that sort of a claim. There was the problem of the Arabs, toward whom the Jews in Israel were heartless. He had not wanted to approach any subject with a divided heart.

Alva and Gunnar Myrdal, his two good friends in Sweden, had suggested an odd idea. They said he should write about a country such as theirs because it was overcivilized, quiet, with no class or racial problems, with an extremely high rate of neuroses, insanity, alcoholism and suicide. It was too great a contrast to Africa, which was still on his mind, and it had not been appealing.

He had not felt ready to write fiction and he did not, for the time being, wish to say anything more about the Negro in the United States. The problem was much too static. If and when things changed, he might be drawn toward it again. But only time would settle that. His agent had suggested a possible book on the Civil War period but that ground had been chopped over so much that he doubted whether he could wrest anything new out of it.

But some compulsion had leaped in him the moment that his mind centered on Spain. He had resisted that country for a long time. He remembered his last visit with Gertrude Stein, just before her death. She had seemed slightly shrunken inside her sturdy body and torn by pain but her mind was as quick as ever. Leaning against the pillows, she had pulled and twisted a short lock of gray hair above her forehead and almost commanded: "Dick, you ought to go to Spain." Why? he had asked her. "You'll see the past there. You'll see what the Western world is made of. Spain is primitive, but lovely. And the people! There are no people such as the Spanish anywhere. I've spent days in Spain that I'll never forget. See those bullfights, see that wonderful landscape. . . ." But he had not wanted to go; now he was sorry that she did not know that he was on his way to examine a country she had loved.

But on the border of Spain his mind was indecisive and he did not wish to drive on until the problem was solved. It was not Franco that worried him; he had spent a year of his life under the regime of another dictator in Argentina. He had once written articles in support of the loyalists during the Spanish Civil War even though—he had to confess—there had been times when he silently judged his comrades who had found it easier to fight and die in Spain than to fight and die for the black man inside their own country.

Pagan Spain, he mused, and raised his glasses for a moment to gaze at the vivid blue sky. Ah, he had it; and it was the reason that for the first time that he could remember he had so little difficulty finding a title for the as yet unwritten book. Pagan. It was a Western country but it was more pagan than Africa. In some way his mind had made a correlation between those two lands. He knew he was right but he had to track down and prove an instinctive, emotional conviction. Africa had been on the verge of freedom when he had visited Accra. Now he was facing a country in which freedom was dead. How did ordinary people live after the death of all their hopes?

Toward evening Richard crossed the frontier with its intimidating Civil Guard officers wearing dark green uniforms, black patent-leather hats, casually holding their machine guns, and entered his first Spanish town. It was a quiet, dreary town even with the conglomerate pink, pale green or blue houses and to Richard, who was fatigued, it appeared marooned and forgotten. After putting the Citroën in a garage he found a pleasant hotel with beautiful Moorish tiles on the floor and washed up for dinner. A pleasant surprise was the prices: a hotel room with bath cost one dollar and a quarter and a seven-course meal, with wine, was one dollar and a half. A slight feeling of guilt dampened his mood when he discovered that the waiter who served him was paid only about two dollars and fifteen cents a month.

Richard arose early the next morning and after a breakfast of what seemed to be a sort of sweetened gruel, with a cup of coffee with milk, he drove his car into a gasoline station to fill up the tank. Just as he released the hand brake to pull out of the station a Civil Guard officer walked up to the car, reached through the window and placed his hand on Richard's shoulder. A cold sensation gripped his stomach and he thought he was under arrest. This is it! How long did one rot in Franco's prisons? Or did they just shoot you right away? With a trembling hand he reached into his inner coat pocket and pulled out his passport. But the officer waved it aside, shaking his head, and speaking in rapid Spanish, leaned closer to the Citroën. Ah, God, why had he not learned to speak a little Spanish? But, then he had never been able to master French either despite the spasmodic courses he had taken at the Sorbonne to unscramble his verbs. He loved his own language too much.

Relief flooded in him when the gas station attendant, who could speak French, explained that the Civil Guardsman simply wanted a ride. Richard was not under arrest. The officer clambered into the car, bumping his machine gun on the window, while Richard watched nervously. As they drove along relief made him voluble and he did his best to communicate with the Spaniard in French, English and one or two Spanish words. After a short distance the officer touched his arm and motioned to Richard's foot, at the same time pumping his own on the floor of the car. Thinking that the man wanted more speed, Richard thrust his foot down on the accelerator and the car shot ahead. The officer seemed to have gone crazy; his dark skin grew red, his eyes distended, showing white all around the irises, he clenched his fists and again motioned toward Richard's foot on the accelerator. Sweat broke out along Richard's hairline: the road was not too good and he was already speeding along faster than he thought was wise and he had a madman beside him. Fearfully, he stole a look at the officer's face. The man was shaking his head and still gesticulating. Richard suddenly realized that he was motioning him to stop and he drew over to the side of the road. He offered to drive the officer back to where he had seemed to lose his mind—which was obviously his destination—but the man would not let him. He shook hands vigorously, saying *gracias, gracias, gracias,* laughed loudly and nervously and stepped from the car. Richard drove on through the countryside until the officer was well out of sight and then pulled off the road. He took out a bottle of Amphojel tablets, put two in his mouth, and chewed them while he started off again.

From time to time, particularly when Richard crossed bridges on his way toward Barcelona, he passed more Civil Guards, all holding machine guns on their forearms. They stared at him without expression and he stared back, but each time after he had passed, the skin on the back of his neck prickled with a sense of vulnerability. Finally, unable to bear the tension, as he approached still another arching bridge, and the armed soldiers, he lifted his right hand timidly and waved. At once two soldiers straightened to attention, smiled and waved back. It was a simple human gesture that made him feel slightly more confident.

Late in the afternoon Richard arrived in Barcelona and drove in and out of narrow streets and along ornate boulevards studying each neighborhood of the modernistic city. He found a place to stay in a pension just three blocks from the broad tree-lined Ramblas, which began at Plaza de Cataluña and ended at Puerta la Paz. The atmosphere along the boulevard with its cafés, bars, restaurants, motion picture theatres, nightclubs, hotels and travel agencies was as cosmo-

politan as New York, Paris or London. But at the bank fronting the
Plaza de Cataluña the spacious doorway was blocked by a soldier with
the familiar machine gun and more armed guards stood in its dim
interior. Before the teller would cash any travelers' checks Richard
had to show his passport, sign five different documents and wait
while three different officials studied and then stamped the papers.

Out of the window of his room he could see the sweep of modern
skyscrapers standing against the darkening sky, while below him, on
the street, donkeys brayed and throughout the pension the odor of
rancid olive oil sent him to his suitcase for bicarbonate of soda to
quiet his stomach. A mood of unrest had made Richard's stomach
begin to churn, and the odor of oil, combined with the incredible
noise of the city, increased his tension. He planned to stay only about
three weeks on his first visit to Spain and would need to guard
against illness. Before going to bed he took from his briefcase a vial
of eyewash—a solution of Novocain and adrenalin suspended in
distilled water—and doctored his tired eyes. Then with a sigh of
satisfaction that he was physically prepared for his investigations of
Spain, he climbed into bed. He lay in the darkness gradually accus-
toming his mind to the sounds of a strange city. It had been only a
day and a night since he had crossed Spanish borders and he knew
that the assumptions with which he had arrived would have to be
discarded. His attitude had been mainly political: Fascism versus the
people, but no neat dialectics of Marxism with a simple diagnosis of
class relations would clarify the experiences that were flooding in
upon him. This was a journey into the past. It was strange: he
already felt more at home than he had in Africa. And he had not
been aware of any racial reaction to him at all. Only once when a
woman had smiled and waved, a few miles outside of Barcelona.
Maybe she thought I was a Moor, he mused, and fell asleep.

Richard spent about two and a half months in Spain, breaking his
stay into three separate visits. He traveled in his car to Guadalajara,
Madrid, Granada, Málaga, Seville, Córdoba, Alcalá, and Morata de
Tajuña, choosing a route which would give him a picture of life in
the cities and in the countryside. Using the same method as in Africa,
he took hundreds of photographs, spoke to people in every walk of
life, poked his nose into monasteries, cathedrals, peasant huts, city
apartments and official buildings, hidden-away bars and cafés, the
bullring and private homes. And every night before retiring he typed
up his impressions of the land and its people. Through American
and British acquaintances he received permission from the Spanish
government to come and go as he pleased. When the long drives over

high and dangerous mountains prevented him from seeing anything except the road he hired a chauffeur for fifty dollars a month and continued his journey. Sometimes he took tourist buses and followed a guide through moss-covered ruins, and everywhere he let the richness of the country flood his senses.

After a few weeks, a haunting, ever elusive emotion began to fill Richard—the hint of ideas that stood on the fringe of his mind. Even his notes were taking on a very different style than those from Africa. When he looked over the pages of typed rough manuscript he felt that it would take time to digest the material. He would have to ponder the structure of the book. His habit of political observation brought him obvious discoveries. These were a delight. But he knew that often when experience uncovered a reality he had already known it could obfuscate a deeper truth.

Under Fascism, almost everyone he met, at least the ordinary citizen in whom he was most interested, spoke to him of freedom when he had gained their confidence. Lisa, a girl whom he met on a train between Granada and Madrid, had been representative of so many other Spaniards in her pain and solemn passion. She had stood in her tiny cramped living-dining room, under a bare, weakly glowing electric bulb, and placed her palms together pointed toward the ceiling. While her girl friends translated, she asked him: "You love freedom?" "I do, with all of my heart," Richard answered. "You will tell the people in America about us?" "I'll try; I'll do my best." "What will you tell them?" she wanted to know. "I shall tell them that the people of Spain are suffering." There had been a long silence; Lisa stared at him through her black-rimmed glasses and then suddenly covered her face and hurried from the room, weeping. He had met Lisa only twice but after that one evening with her and her friends he felt that they had been life-long friends.

He saw the official Spain and the human Spain and a chasm gaping in between. A chaotic sort of order was kept by the tight bridge of the Catholic Church. Franco and the Church and a revolution that failed had succeeded in banishing the concept of a free, sovereign, responsible, self-motivated citizen. Charity replaced self-respect, and side by side with maudlin sentimentality over children was the prostitution of masses of women.

Gleefully, Richard discovered a white-slave ring in Seville run by a tall blond American with a hard, bullet-shaped head and face. The ring supplied white women, who vied with one another, to be taken to brothels in Africa. "Well, given the conditions, the moral attitude of the Church toward sex, the poverty, the ignorance, this was bound to be. It was all socially determined. The Church could call it sin, but it was something far more awful than that. Crush, inhibit, deny the impulses of man, thwart his instincts, and those instincts would find a devious way out, a way to freedom, and the instincts of women too would find a way."[1]

Spain was moored in the past by a Church which managed to control everything and through rites more primitive than those he had witnessed in Africa. He was startled. Traditions and rituals in Africa were fragile and unwritten. They had been jolted by their impact with the Western world. Africans were free to create a future, but the pagan traditions of Spain were officially revered and honored; they were the political aims of the state. "This was a fact that made [him] feel that the naked African in the bush would make greater progress during the next fifty years than the proud, tradition-bound Spaniard."

Carmen, a short, dark girl with large, shining eyes, gave Richard a thin green book entitled *Formación Política: Lecciónes para las Flechas*. It was a volume which dealt with the aims and principles of the Franco regime in a simple question-and-answer form. Its study was compulsory. And it was while leafing through the book one evening that a clue to the reason he felt so at home in Spain arrived. He had stopped at a section concerning Protestantism. The propagators of Protestantism in Spain were trying to spread the ideas of Socialism and Communism.

That is the sole reason for all their painstaking efforts. Protestantism is nothing but a vague voice, a negation of the true religion; this is why it suits them best for the purpose of covering up their designs whose aim is nothing else but the destruction of society.[2]

Toward six o'clock the following evening Richard waited for two young men who had promised to introduce him to some Protestants. When they finally arrived it was nearly dusk and they directed him to drive toward a small town about a hundred miles from Madrid. Upon arrival they made a telephone call and were instructed to go to a small park near the river and sit at one of the tables under the trees. The rendezvous stimulated Richard's imagination and while he waited he thought of revolutionists plotting the downfall of a government; and the tension in the bodies of his two friends increased the mood. He learned that night that Protestantism was sedition against the state and that its believers were in constant danger of arrest.

Richard, who had no religion and no race except that which was forced upon him, felt an immediate identity and profound sympathy for the Spanish Protestant. What riveted his attention to the Protestants' suffering and emotional torture was "the undeniable and uncanny psychological affinities that they held in common with American Negroes, Jews, and other oppressed minorities." It was another proof to him that the main and decisive aspects of human reactions were conditioned and not inborn. It was like living in Mississippi: that was what had haunted him and why he had felt at home in Spain. He had grown up in a "police state." And the psychological problems and emotional pain of the Protestants had made them into a group of "white Negroes." Negroes were Negroes because they were treated as Negroes. But even Mississippi was more "Western" than Spain, and he believed that this was the result of Protestantism. Black youths in the state of his birth had far more initiative and vigor than the young Spaniards he had met.

As he headed back toward Paris he wondered whether or not he could handle the mass of material he had collected and pound it into a credible book. Could he explain Spain in terms believable to his readers when he could not accept what that country had done and was still doing? It would be like walking a tightrope.

For a long time my own Westernness proved a veritable stumbling block to my seeing the truth that stared me in the face. The cold fact was: *Spain was not yet even Christian!* It had never been converted, not to Protestantism, not even to *Catholicism* itself! Somehow the pagan streams of influence flowing from the Goths, the Greeks, the Jews, the Romans, the Iberians, and the Moors lingered strongly and vitally on, flourishing under the draperies of the twentieth century. . . .[3]

The first thing that he had to be aware of was his own intensely Protestant background, his deep antagonism toward Catholicism, his unchangeably secular outlook. Then he had to consider his own temperament: he had never been able to accept any mystic or, to him, childlike, explanations of a universe represented by a kind of cosmic family whose members quarreled among themselves. On top of Seventh-Day Adventism—the teachings of his grandmother—had come the Communist theory that religion was an opiate. That was not a true description either. The Spaniards ruled in the name of their religion and they would kill in that name and then write a book to justify it. As difficult as it might be, he would have to stand outside, unaccepting, and write as honestly about what he had seen as he could. It had been a journey into the past and Spain in her paganism was stuck in a muddy residue: one Will, one God, one Race, one Aim. How Southern United States an attitude it was:

Convinced beyond all counterpersuasion that he possesses a metaphysical mandate to chastise all of those whom he considers the "morally moribund," the "spiritually inept," the "biologically botched," the Spaniard would scorn the rich infinities of possibility looming before the eyes of men, he would stifle hearts responding to the call of a high courage, and he would thwart the will's desire for a new wisdom. . . . He would turn back the clock of history and play the role of God to man.

How poor indeed he is. . . .[4]

I want to assume an attitude that places me
wholly on the side of feeling in life . . .

XXVII

All of August and most of September, 1955, Richard stayed near the village of Ailly in Normandy. Between trips to Spain he and Ellen had found an old farm with extensive acreage, for only $5,000, near enough to Paris so that he could escape the city's distractions whenever he wished. Lately, he had begun to feel that nothing was ever accomplished when he was at the apartment at Rue Monsieur le Prince; he just ran around aimlessly.

As an escape, he had gone to Moulin d'Ande, to stay at the country place of the manufacturer of "Verigoud," a popular French orange drink. Arriving off-season, Richard's overconscientiousness toward his hosts slashed into his work time. He took on the responsibility of seeing to the connection of electricity, telephones, gas, and the hiring of a local girl as maid. The estate covered miles of forest area along the Seine and was a haven for poets, novelists, painters, movie stars, directors, theatre people, and African diplomats. When the place filled up, his own curiosity brought Richard out of the room which was always held for him and kept him from writing.

And he had stayed with his friends Maurice and Hélène Boka-nowski in their country place at Croisilles, at Nogent-le-Roi, Loire. Maurice, a big sensuously handsome man, who seemed always over-come by extreme lethargy, became Minister of Communications in the de Gaulle cabinet. His petite blond wife had translated two of Richard's books. Richard always believed that it was through the influence of the Bokanowskis that a special permit, *Carte de Séjour de Résident Privilégié,* had been arranged which allowed the Wrights a ten-year residence in France.[1] Hélène was Ellen's partner, for a brief period, in her literacy agency.

Richard had grown to love the green fields in Normandy which seemed to shimmer under the bright sun and the farm at Ailly was not too distant from the Bokanowski estate. Living quarters on the farm were inadequate, but in French peasant style the stables for horses, pigs and other animals had formed a main portion of the house. By breaking through walls these were incorporated and turned into a giant living room. The fine original beams of the hayloft gave it a cathedral ceiling. At one end of the room Ellen designed and had built a large brick fireplace and for the flooring she copied the old tiles in another part of the house. A large brick patio was constructed across the front of the house and Ellen searched for wooden tables and chairs to blend with the rusticity of the countryside.

At the very top of the house, up a narrowing staircase, and under the eaves, was a large room. Two windows looked over the side garden enclosed by a high wall with espaliers of pear and peach trees trained against the brick. On the opposite side of the house from the downstairs living room, the area provided the isolation Richard wanted for his study. He and Ellen papered the walls of the room with maps of Europe; bookcases were built; the broad-beamed floor stained and waxed; and the room furnished sparsely with a large worktable, its chair facing away from the distracting view from the window, a narrow couch, two chairs and a smaller table for magazines, placed in the center under a bright overhanging light.

Richard and Ellen's bedroom adjoined the new study and across a a hallway was a room for Julia. Rachel and a maid slept in a big downstairs bedroom. Down a cold cement corridor, past kitchen, pantry and bathrooms, was a huge storage room for produce. Its dim interior was as icy as a refrigerator and Richard worked on a garden to keep it stocked with fruits and vegetables. Every day after lunch, while Ellen and the girls napped, Richard went into his garden, where he planted potatoes, peas, corn and green beans. Plum, peach, pear and apple trees spread over a large pasture which was covered by the thick green and tufted Normandy grass.

Richard attacked the rich soil as vigorously as he pounded his typewriter all morning—it was his way of coming down from the tense plateau engendered by writing—and the garden flourished. After he filled his own cold-storage cellar he packed the back of the Citroën and delivered vegetables to all of his friends in Paris. Many were dismayed by the largesse: those who lived in small rooms in the Latin Quarter had only small oil stoves or one-burner electric plates. The maids of other friends usually purchased washed and pared vegetables in the French markets. But everyone concealed his irritation when Richard dumped huge piles of gritty fruits and vegetables on tables, chairs and even the floor. He was so proud and happy to share the food he had produced with his own hands with his friends.

When Richard finished his gardening he often walked to the local post office, stopping on the way to talk to the French farmers dressed in vivid blue workclothes who were his neighbors. He was dependent upon them for their advice and help in farming matters. On their part, the peasants "loved him very naturally . . . he always left a feeling of warmth. They were completely disarmed by him and by his smile. He was so gentle, they said."[2]

In October the major renovations on the farmhouse were completed and two wells had been dug after water problems developed. With workmen coming and going, Richard's work was dragging. Voices from below wafted up the stairwell or came floating through his study windows and he darted down the hall to see what was happening. But eventually the days became quiet, although he still had to ask Ellen to keep his daughters away from his side of the house. He could not concentrate. Julia, who at thirteen strongly resembled her father, was a leading student in her class in the French lycée. She was usually quieter than her younger sister; her nose was always in a book and sometimes it worried Richard. She won't do anything but study, he complained to his wife. But Rachel, who was six, a vivacious, beautiful child, had inherited her father's ability to tease. She defied Richard, dancing about on her toes, posturing, singing and shouting, until he helplessly appealed to Ellen to make her behave. When he wanted quiet hours in the house or the garden a demonic energy possessed her. She would escape from her mother or the maid and dart around the corner of the house, down a path in the side garden, to stand under Richard's windows. There she would sing songs or trace patterns in the dirt, talking loudly while she played. Her face would assume an utter innocence when she was discovered, but if her father stuck his head out of the window she became flirtatiously defiant. One day in October she was feverishly active and Richard stopped work and listened; he was prepared to go downstairs and tell his wife once again, "Ellen, please! I am working!" A note in Rachel's voice made him pause. Something was wrong; he was certain of it. He hurried down the stairs, into the tiled foyer, entered a door to his left, and went into his daughter's bedroom. Ellen and the maid were trying to hold Rachel quiet while they took her temperature. Greatly agitated, Richard approached the bed and placed his hands on his daughter's forehead. She felt as if she were burning with fever. And when Ellen removed the thermometer, wiped it off, and held it to the light he waited impatiently. Her temperature was well over a hundred degrees, but Ellen explained that all children have fevers even with minor colds or stomach upsets. But Richard would not listen; he wanted to take Rachel back to the city and to the family physician. In Paris the child's illness was diagnosed as scarlatina, a form of scarlet fever, and she was ill for almost forty days.

By November 31 Rachel had recovered and Richard left for the farm. It had been almost impossible to work in Paris: the phone had never ceased to ring; doctors came and went; Rachel cried; Ellen and the maid called back and forth; something had been happening all the time. If he could have brought himself to close his study doors, Richard would have had complete privacy but he could not do it. He had to hear what was happening all through the house, and it never entered his mind that his nervous curiosity and sense of possession created an atmosphere of absolute horror for his family. Ellen lived in dread when the children were not at school. All through the hours that her husband worked she was forced to restrict the children's play and see that they did not speak in normal tones which might disturb their father. Otherwise, Richard would stride from his room, and in the same exasperated voice speak the same phrase: "Ellen! Please! I am working!" Then the ringing of the telephone drove him wild some days; he very seldom answered it because he could not refuse an invitation, an interview, or aid to anyone. Then, it would be Ellen's task to call the individual back and explain that Richard had other plans which he had forgotten and cancel whatever arrangements he had made.

In Ailly the weather was bitter cold, but Richard heated one downstairs bedroom, which was just off the kitchen, and wrote, slept, ate and rested near a giant fireplace which he kept burning day and night. Peasant families nearby kept watch over the house. They were certain that it would go up in flames, for occasionally fire could be seen within the billows of black smoke rising from the chimney. A rigid rule not to drink anything stronger than coffee when he was writing was broken because of the cold and Richard took sips of cognac throughout the day. He lengthened his hours of work double and three times the six-hour schedule that was his normal minimum. There was so much to be done. The book on Spain required final cutting and it had been interrupted by a month's trip to Jakarta to attend an Asian-African conference and the writing of his report of the Bandung meeting, *The Color Curtain*.

As soon as some two hundred pages were cut from *Pagan Spain,* at the request of his publisher, he had to write a projection of his future work. The time had come to change publishers. From the time he had lost Edward C. Aswell as his editor at Harper he had been restive and had come to believe in a lack of harmony between himself and the publisher. John Fischer, Aswell's replacement, did not understand him or his personality. He had refused two books, *Savage Holiday* and *The Color Curtain,* and Richard believed that Fischer did not appreciate the forthcoming *Pagan Spain* because of its attacks upon an ally of the United States. If Harper gagged on the book he was plotting to repossess the manuscript.

Negotiations had been opened by Ed Aswell, who was at McGraw-Hill, to become Richard's editor again, and he had asked for an outline of proposed fictional work. "Hurrah!" Richard wrote to his agent: "It's Eddie again and McGraw Hill!" Richard never forgot the day he first met Ed Aswell in 1938. Seated at his desk in a book-lined office at Harper, the bullet-headed man, who might have been a violinist or a banker as far as his appearance, looked at Richard in curiosity. Aswell, a Southerner from Nashville, had leaned across the desk and Richard had stiffened. A Southern black faced a Southern white. A traditional enemy faced a traditional enemy. Those were the thoughts that made Richard sit tensely in his chair. Aswell had just read his article entitled "The Ethics of Living Jim Crow," and Richard was waiting to hear his work castigated. The damn cracker would claim that it was a product of Negro imagination. Suddenly, Aswell smiled and said: "Never has anybody spoken of this as you have."

Richard clamped his teeth. What was that? Praise? No, it could not be. Doubt assailed him. What had he done that was wrong in the article? What slip had he made? Never in his young life had he dreamed that a Southern white man would admit that the reality of life for Negroes in the Deep South was a horror. And when he heard it and saw Aswell's smile he suspected a trick. He thought back over the article: had he said something that was detrimental to his people? This editor had a keen mind; he could see it in his eyes. What had he discovered to use against the black man? Even after the editor told him that Harper had accepted his novel *Native Son* he had walked from the office in an emotional state almost dreamlike. Later, as Aswell and Richard worked together they became close friends. So little had to be explained to his editor; as a Southerner who had broken with "white" attitudes, he always seemed to know exactly what Richard was trying to depict. Sometime later in their friendship, Richard felt drawn to explain:

We Negroes fight for our rights, almost disbelieving that we will ever succeed, so great are the odds against us; and when we do make a break-through, we are so startled that we think that some highly complicated game of deception is being played with us. Our life has conditioned us more to opposition than to cooperation. We know how to double our fists better than to stretch forth our hands in the simple gesture of friendship. We can cringe and deceive better than we can stand up and face our adversaries and tell the truth. The traditional image of the white man is deep in us, a part of mental functioning.[3]

Around noon one Thursday Richard poked at the fire, added another log and watched until it began to char at its base, then turned away to sit at his typewriter. It was necessary to write a letter to Aswell. An entire outline with sample stories was worked out in his mind. But first he wanted to explain what it meant to him to have Aswell as an editor again. He said that he had really had no editor since Aswell left Harper—there were editors there, of course, and they were good men in general, but they were not really editors. He had been spoiled and had taken editors for granted until Aswell left—then he knew what a loss he had suffered.

Forty-four pages poured from the battered Underwood typewriter outlining a fictional voyage which had been a dream since 1945. The novels would cut across racial, class, sexual, religious and political questions. But race, which had always claimed his attention, was to be caught up in a larger human context. It was no American, Russian, French, Spanish, black or white matter. It was man's matter. Society and man formed one organic whole yet both, by the very nature of their relationship, were in sharp conflict. Society made and broke man, and too much authority, tradition, custom, government— all of which made him human—inhibited his impulses and robbed him of his humanity. Modern society and its claims were swelling each day and the area of freedom of action was growing narrow. Impulse, fancy, imagination were growing restricted and, although he recognized that without social restriction man would be a beast, he personally was biased toward the claims of the human heart. He would attempt through a whole series of books to pose this conflict in as many ways as possible. The mood of the whole as a conceptual scaffolding was to be *Celebration*.

Each novel would stand on its own and yet its highest significance would be found in the context of an evocative, impersonal mood which would be sustained throughout several volumes. Hopefully, he would combine poetry and prose, using the two, at times merging, to cement the books together. If he could achieve the "mood" it would enable the reader to "overhear" ordinarily abstract considerations.

The poetry/prose would champion and celebrate any experience having as its object a release of the powers of the organism, and reject and turn aside from all that which bogged the organism down.

A prose poem would describe an eagle killing a lamb and then a lion mating in a zoo. Originally, he meant to insert at that point in the poem the story of the moral downfall of a New York businessman already published in *Savage Holiday*. In a natural sequence of plants and animals criticism would be shed—without a "message"—on how repressed men such as Erskine Fowler, lived their lives.

Another novel would follow *Savage Holiday* which he named *A Strange Daughter*. A repressed white girl whose Episcopalian parents had destroyed a normal attitude toward sexual relations would find it possible to have orgasm only with an African. His treatment of her as a slave would bring love and fulfillment. But her pregnancy would result in her death because the African believed that the newborn were reincarnations of the past ancestors of his tribe and he could not allow his dead kin to return through alien white blood. Thus the girl, on the verge of victory over the social taboos of her own world, violated those of another and would have to die.

When the World Was Red would be the story of the king of the Aztecs. Montezuma's intellect would embrace the God of the Spaniards but their wanton murders would force his emotions and spirit to reject Christianity.

Endowing a plant with conscious physical "awareness" of birth and death as still another story would be a Whitmanesque poem as the basis for another volume.

> Restlessly, I come and go, timing myself by my time,
>   judging by my own harshly loving standards,
> Indifferently regarding life and death, joy and sorrow,
> Entering all things, reshaping, spreading, scattering,
>   dissolving, coming forth again in new guises,
>   forever moving, creating and dying, being born at will.
> Jealous I am of myself and my own,
> Avoiding that which does not have the capacity to reap
>   the forms I crave.
> I seek,— I seek myself,
> Trampling as quickly as I build, unmoved between that which
>   breathes and that which endures,—
> Holding fire and water and ice and blood in my mouth.

Aswell did not answer Richard's letter for some time and when a response came he saw that his editor had read, reread, pondered and then read again. It was unlikely that McGraw-Hill would be interested in Wright's proposed theme. He, himself, was not certain that Richard should take on such a work at that time of his life. Why was it, Aswell questioned, that the sources of Richard's creativeness seemed to have dwindled after the move to France? He was only guessing, but could it be that he had found greater peace as a human being and that the human gain had been offset by a creative loss? He hoped to visit Richard the following year to discuss these matters.

Wright had more or less expected a negative reaction from Aswell because Paul, his agent, had written that it was doubtful that the series had commercial value. Interest in poetry was at a low ebb in the United States and most Americans did not care at all about what Indians, such as Montezuma, thought about religion. His future novels should be based upon his life in Paris. Ah, well, Richard thought to himself, I know what my two good friends mean: the American reader wants me to write about Negroes. Three weeks after he had received Aswell's letter Richard sent off an outline for the novel which eventually was titled *The Long Dream*. Aswell was enthusiastic, but before a start could be made on the book he left McGraw-Hill for Doubleday and the project had to be put aside until his own working relationship was clarified.

What to do? Richard wondered. He simply did not want to work with Harper, especially since he had reestablished the old comforting association with Aswell. But money was a problem. In March, 1957, the $500-a-month payments for *Black Boy* would end. Well, there was nothing else to do but accept another lecture trip. He had been invited to speak in Germany because of the immense popularity of his work but he always had refused. He was afraid that he'd have to shake the hands that had helped to burn up people in the murder factories. But this trip was based upon an opening speech on October 10, 1956, in Hamburg. From there he would go to Switzerland, Stockholm, Oslo, Göteborg and Copenhagen. There was no way out. He had to go and as soon as he made the decision he argued down an emotional queasiness that kept thrusting itself upon him: what the hell, they are human and though I don't like them, I must see and try to understand them. Anyway, his topic would be thrust right at their teeth. He would lecture on the "Psychology of Oppressed People." Everywhere he spoke, including Hamburg, his audiences were extravagantly pleased. During a four-day stay in Stockholm 35,000 copies of his recently translated *The Outsider* were sold.

On December 5, Richard left Copenhagen by train for Paris. His spirits were buoyant and as the train sped along he found that he could not rest. Opening his briefcase, he took out paper and pen and began to write quickly, forming the letters slightly to the right and larger than medium size. And before the train reached the outskirts of Paris he had written a short story, "Good Big Black Man."[4]

When the train slowed and stopped in Paris Richard stood in the aisle which ran alongside the windows and peered out into the crowd searching for Ellen. He caught sight of his wife before she found him. How French she looks, he thought. A ray of light touched her hair, which she had reddened, and the curls made a soft halo effect above her tense eager face. How pretty she is, he thought. But she is always tense. She is as tense as I am, as tense as Julia. Well, we are a tense family, that is all. But when Ellen discovered her husband as he stepped from the train he saw something else in her face that was more strained. She laughed but she was sad and the combination made his heart feel squeezed. Had anything happened to the children? It was his Aunt Maggie. She was seriously ill with cancer in Mississippi. The doctors did not have hope for her recovery. Before leaving the station Richard went to an office and cabled his mother, who had moved back to Mississippi, an additional $425, which was his monthly payment toward maintaining the two women. Two weeks later Maggie died and his mother, who was still a semi-invalid, fell and broke her hip.

Aunt Maggie left an uncomplicated will: Richard's two daughters and a grandniece were to inherit 50 percent of whatever sum would be left after burial expenses were subtracted. A Southern bank made all the arrangements and its letters followed Southern tradition. When writing to Ellen they addressed her as "Mrs. Wright" but when directed to Wright he was simply "Richard." He knew that they were determined not to call a black man "Mr." But his principle concern was to safeguard his aunt's small sum of money and property. He damn well did not want white Mississippi to receive one penny. "The whites of Mississippi are about the most primitive whites this side of Siberia and God knows what they will or will not do." And he asked Paul Reynolds to stand by with an attorney who would take up a case in Mississippi if it became necessary. By cable he made hospital arrangements for his mother and care during recuperation with a cousin, Mrs. Maggie Hunt, in Gloster, Mississippi. When she recovered she would go to live again with his brother Alan in Chicago.

A feeling of sadness for Maggie, who had been a second mother, was lost within the details of the will, the arrangements for his mother, and Richard's own need to wipe unpleasantness or pain from his mind. But the death had crowded him once again with memories of the South and what it meant to a black man or woman trapped in unending days slowly turning around the temper or mood of the white man. As soon as he could Richard left his family in Paris and went out to the farm alone. A new book had to be written and he wanted to mull in his mind the memories which had arrived, seeping into him after his aunt's death.

Aswell had settled into his new position at Doubleday and negotiations were under way to sign Richard to a new contract. He would be paid an advance of $6,000 ($1,000 down and $500 a month) on the novel he had outlined to Aswell about the life of a Negro Southerner who goes to Paris and whose problems revolve around his adjustment to Parisian life.

With him in Ailly, placed near his typewriter, was a letter from Aswell, whose arrangements allowed him to contract for novels or trade books independently at Doubleday.

You made me very happy, Dick, and proud when you wrote, "Your letter was like a window opening out upon the world after being closed for many years. It was a great life." I shall return the compliment by saying honestly that no part of my publishing career and experience has meant more to me than my relationship with you. I have often thought of it and on occasion have spoken of it to other writers. In the beginning you had every reason to be suspicious of me and you were, and I like to recall how both of us broke down the false barriers that stood between us until at last we could meet man to man and after that, free communication between us became possible. For me it was a stirring experience. That is one reason why I am so very happy that we are working together again.

Richard felt easy in his mind but he could not immediately begin the new novel. But he had learned not to fret—it would come, it was working itself out in his mind—so he filled in the time by typing and correcting some of the speeches he had been making in Europe. He then sent them off to Aswell, who was profoundly moved by the series. Nothing that he had ever read gave him such a clear view of many seemingly unrelated events that were taking place all over the world. The dedication to the tragic elite should be engraved in the hearts of men, he said. And it was more wonderful than he had hoped—he would be publishing a book of Richard's sooner than he had expected.

Taking only short trips back into Paris, Richard got down to work on the new novel alone at Ailly. By April, 1957, he had completed 644 pages of *Long Dream,* which he called *Fishbelly* after its leading character. But he was somewhat astounded and awed once again by the way that the character had seemingly taken over control of the progression of the story. It was related, in some way that he could not explain, to his aunt's death. It had opened some inner recess, like a set of Chinese puzzle boxes, each little lacquered cube opening to reveal still another. The story had nothing whatsoever to do with Paris. It was a second "autobiography" and while he had typed, or stared at the wall, forgotten episodes of his childhood had swum to the surface of his mind and assumed such importance that they compelled him to write only of a Southern experience. The characters were composites of individuals he had known as a child and those he had met in Chicago, New York and France.

Long Dream centers around an intimate father and son relationship—one that Richard had never known. Tyree, the father, is based on a businessman he had known in Jackson, a property owner who maintained his position and the safety of his family by bribing the police and the mayor. The character, Tyree, owns wooden tenements and houses of prostitution. All the while that he amasses a fortune he plays the role demanded by his environment. His son, Fish, thinks his father is a coward until after a dance hall for Negroes, owned by Tyree, burns down killing everyone inside. Fire violations have never been enforced because the pay-off is too much to lose. Police, mayor and other politicians decide that Tyree should go to jail to satisfy and silence the protesting community. But Tyree has saved, toward such a day, all the canceled checks he has given out as bribes. He will not be the scapegoat for white men as guilty as he.

Fish learns at last what his father's code of ethics and morality is based upon:

I ain't corrupt. I'm a *nigger*. Niggers ain't corrupt. Niggers ain't got no rights but them they *buy*. . . . If we niggers didn't buy justice from the white man, we'd never git any. I ain't got no rights; my papa never had any, and my papa's papa never had any; and my son sitting there ain't got none but what he can buy . . . I can't vote. There ain't no black men in office in this town. We black folks is helpless and all we can do is buy a little protection. If I'm corrupt, who made me corrupt? Who took the bribes? The law, and the law's white. . . . I didn't make Nigger Town. White men made it. Awright. I say, "Okay." But, goddammit, let me *live* in Nigger Town! And don't call me corrupt when I live the only way I can live. Sure, I did wrong. But my kind of wrong is right; when you have to do wrong to live, wrong is right. . . .[5]

Tyree is murdered by the police and Fish escapes north to take a plane to Paris. At that point Richard could not carry the manuscript further; the material had its own logic and after making six attempts to move Fish into Parisian life he gave up. The more he tried to force the story beyond that point the more it seemed to crumble away.

Richard mailed the manuscript to his publisher somewhat fearfully. He was always "scared" at the completion of a work of fiction. Aswell, very early in their friendship; reassured him. It was natural to become "scared" and it indicated merely that he was both a man of integrity and a sensitive artist. No book, not even the best of Shakespeare, was as good as it ought to be in the sense that there was always a measurable distance between the artist's vision and his realization. But it was only the good writers who knew and felt that; the hacks were never troubled by self-doubts. When they finished a book they always knew it was a masterpiece.

But this time Richard did not doubt the value of his novel; it was that he had promised one type of story and given another. What if Eddie was dissatisfied? To increase his tension he received the news from Paul Reynolds that Aswell's wife had died and that he was finding it extremely difficult to adjust his life around the void that was left. Ah, God, Richard thought. What if he had let Eddie down at a time like that?

Aswell's reaction to the novel was even more than Richard had expected. Powerful treatment of subject was what had always distinguished Richard's best writing and Aswell had had a hunch "all along" that the book was going to be a major work; he felt it even more strongly now that he had seen the manuscript. And there was an added pleasure: the story of Fishbelly in Paris had already been outlined. That would probably mean that a novel a year or every year and a half would begin to appear in the United States and reestablish Richard as one of America's leading writers of fiction.

As a burned man adds one more dollop of salve to the top of a sore Richard wrote again to ask if Aswell thought that the public would accept his ending. Once again, he had allowed his hero to solve a problem by running away. What he intended, and hoped the public would see, was that it was symbolic of those who first settled America. The white settlers had also been running away from problems which they had been helpless to solve in the environments in which they had lived in Europe. And the early Americans actually had solved their problems by running and creating a new life on a new continent. In *Long Dream* the geography is reversed but the problem is the same. Fish seeks the possibility of a new life in Paris, one which he cannot possibly find in Mississippi. Fish is a descendant of men who had not come to America voluntarily but were brought forcibly and compelled to give up their freedom for slavery.

His editor's response was that there was a great historical lesson in Fishbelly's flight and suggested that he lengthen the last sequence as Fish sits on a plane winging his way from the known, the restricted, the fearful, toward what is unknown, less restricted, and hopeful. Then, in the book to follow, Richard should just pluck Fish out of time and space, as in fact he is in the airplane, and describe him as any fellow passenger might see him; and then get inside him and into his thoughts.

The only other criticisms Richard received from the publisher were minor. They amused him for days and he would break into laughter, then walk to his desk to look at a page entitled "Offensive Words." Physiological terms were objectionable but slang was not.

A short time after the publication of *The Long Dream* Richard picked up his bundle of morning mail and glanced at the envelopes to select those he would open first. One return address pricked his curiosity: Anthony Quinn, Paramount Pictures Corporation, 5451 Marathon Street, Hollywood, California. He picked up a letter opener and neatly slit the envelope. The motion picture actor wrote that he had been profoundly moved by *Long Dream* and he hoped that Richard would not feel that he was presumptuous but he simply had to play the part of Tyree. He was so enthusiastic about a possible play that he would be glad to give advice and with or without a promise of the role he would be glad to give any assistance he could toward such a production.

After consulting his agent Richard gave permission to Quinn, who took the book to Ketti Frings, who had dramatized *Look Homeward Angel* for the Broadway stage. The playwright, who had grown up in a slum in Cleveland, was as enthusiastic as Quinn and personally identified with the characters. Martin Ritt, a friend of Quinn's, had always wanted to direct a Broadway play and they proposed the formation of a corporation.

A brilliant adaptation of *The Long Dream* was finally brought to Broadway by producer Cheryl Crawford in February, 1960. Quinn did not play the role he loved because the company could not meet his demand for a salary of $3,000 a week and a slightly lesser amount for his director friend Martin Ritt. Critics were merciless in their attacks and the play had only a brief run. Miss Frings believed that the critics had killed a fine production.

Reviews of the book itself were poor, with the severest criticism by the Negro press: Wright exaggerated the position of the Negro in the United States; conditions had changed drastically and for the better; he had lost touch with reality because he lived in France. As a result, sales were poor and the book went through only one printing.

Aswell and Reynolds had been so enthusiastic about his novel that Richard pushed his own forebodings of its reception to the back of his mind. It appeared that no matter what he wrote he would be attacked. One had to decide, early in life, what one wanted to do and then it was necessary to be hard, hard in the sense of self-discipline. And, whatever the blows, it was important to steel his emotions. Ah, but it was not easy. Yes, he thought, the United States had found a way to solve the race question; they pushed it under the rug. The black middle-class critics sickened him. Things had changed! While he had been at work on *The Long Dream* a fourteen-year-old boy, Emmett Till, had been lynched because he had whistled at a white woman in Mississippi. Richard and William Faulkner had issued a statement to the French press calling the child's death a "legal lynching." And Richard had written a letter to his Dutch translator to explain how such a horror could take place:[5a]

Such murders of blacks by whites have been and are the order of the day in the Deep South. Only the form of the murders have changed. This does not mean that the government of the U. S. wishes such to happen; the leaders of the government are against it. But what can they do? It is wise to remember that the whites of the American South are really primitive people and do not have any conception of the outside world. Of course, one can say that our government is remiss inasmuch as it waited 80 years to take a moral stand against such murders. And I'm afraid that now the government is against such not because it is inhuman, but because it hurts America's foreign policy. . . . In my childhood in the Deep South, murders such as the Emmett Till murder took place almost every week and there was not a line in the newspapers about them; today such murders become world news. This shows how little and how much has been done. At least, it is now morally wrong to kill in the South, but they still kill. At least today they really bring the murderer into court; a few years ago no white murderer of a black ever went to court for his crime . . . I'm afraid that these killings will continue to happen for a long time to come, that is, until an entire generation of old whites have died. The newer generation is developing a newer attitude. Such is life. . . . That is why I cannot live in America. Such wanton killings fill me with disgust, uneasiness, and a sense of dread. Personal appeals on my part will not help any; it is only world opinion that can check such outrages, can brand them morally for what they are. The American government today is ashamed of such, for it hurts them when they try to sell the idea of democracy to India, Indonesia. . . . Emmett Till was the color of Nehru, and how on earth could any sensible person feel that Nehru could love a nation in which human life is so cheap. A man like Nehru feels that such could happen to him if he lived in the United States! In short, the Western world pays highly when an Emmett Till is slain, and it would be wise to remember that when the people of Asia and Africa think of Emmett Till being slain, they do not think that white Americans did it, but that the WHITE MEN OF THE WEST-ERN WORLD HAVE KILLED ANOTHER MAN OF COLORED SKIN. It hurts the whole cause of the West.

There seems to be something fateful about what is happening in the world today. The West cannot practice what it preaches. Hence, Nehru turns to Russia and China, two nations that have no past of racial hatreds! C'est la vie. . . .[6]

Richard was not unprepared for an attack by a publication he considered an enemy, but it went beyond his endurance. On November 12, 1958, he wrote to his agent and asked that he read an article in that week's issue of *Time* magazine entitled "Amid Alien Corn." Among other things, the article claimed that in an interview Richard had said that the Negro problem had not changed in 300 years. The interview was a myth. It had not taken place at all.

Time's Paris office had telephoned his apartment one morning to ask for an interview. Ellen answered the telephone and when she heard who it was could barely conceal her anger. *Time* had been consistently hostile for many years and Richard had vowed never to have anything to do with any of the Luce publications. His attitude was, in part, based upon his own dealings with *Life* magazine, which, he felt, had taken advantage of him financially when he had given them permission to do a story on *Native Son* many years before. So Ellen had answered with a firm: NO!

A few days later, the same reporter called in the name of *Pen* magazine to ask for an interview but Ellen was suspicious. Again the answer was No! And this time she spoke sharply. Eventually, the article appeared and in three separate places gave fabricated quotations from Richard. Richard was furious. He took immediate action and cabled *Time* in New York City:

QUOTATIONS ATTRIBUTED TO ME IN YOUR ARTICLE AMID ALIEN CORN COMPLETELY FALSE AND FABRICATED. ASTOUNDED AT TIMES JOURNALIST ETHICS DID NOT SEE YOUR REPORTER ARE YOU APING COMMUNIST TACTICS OF CHARACTER ASSASSINATION?

A copy of the cable was sent to Paul together with a letter which described what had happened and ended with Richard's reaction to the lies:

. . . this *Time* thing goes much too far; they put words I never said or thought of saying in my mouth. I don't know law. Is not there some redress for this? That *Time* attack is worse than attacks by Southern whites. In fact, no Southern white paper has ever deliberately said I said something that I never said. The *Time* article borders on forgery. . . . I did not talk to the *Time* man at all.

Then Richard called the *Time* office in Paris and an icily controlled voice added a further fabrication: he had been interviewed and photographed by Giselle Freund, a well-known French camerawoman. What *Time* had not realized was that Giselle was a good friend of Richard's so he hung up and called her at once.

Giselle went to see Richard at his apartment within the hour. She had met him in Argentina years before and respected and admired him. Very often in the past she had taken photographs of Richard and the one used in *Time* magazine had been requested by a New York photographic agency. Giselle had not been told by the agency that they had given one of her pictures of Richard to *Time*. She sat down at Richard's typewriter and wrote a letter of denial to the Luce Corporation and gave him a copy to use in any law suit he might decide to initiate. Through his agent Richard arranged for a lawyer. He was ready to combat the entire Luce empire. They had finally gone too far; it was an invasion of his privacy. However, his attorneys advised that although he might win a suit, it would be a long, tedious case and perhaps only one dollar might be gained. And Luce held in his hands the instruments of publicity and influence which he would mobilize against Richard. He dropped the case. But later he learned from someone sympathetic toward him in the Paris office of *Time* that his action had forestalled publication of a large collection of hostile letters which *Time* had solicited with which it intended to attack *The Long Dream*.

On November 5 Richard opened a cable from his agent and gasped in shock. Edward Aswell was dead. A feeling of numbness came over him. He could only stand and stare at the large words on the page of the message. Only the day before he had written Aswell a long letter to give him a report on a new novel. He could not accept the death. While he waited for an explanatory letter from Paul he tried not to think about his friend. Aswell, who lived alone, had died alone in his house. His death was not discovered until the police broke through his door when his publishing company became worried. Paul, who lived nearby, had gone to his house on a previous Tuesday because one of his authors had been trying to reach Aswell. He had gone away after knocking because he presumed that Aswell was out of town.

The Long Dream had been dedicated: To my friends Edward C.

Aswell and Paul R. Reynolds whose aid and counsel made this book possible. Richard walked around the Luxembourg Gardens, which stretched out bleak and cold yet held a strange beauty, and thought of his editor. He would not find such a relationship again; a man like him was so wonderfully unique. Both were Southerners and both knew what the subject matter down in the South was. There was no better Southerner than an honest one, for he had a lot to face and accept. And Eddie had done that, Richard brooded. And one cannot ask a Southern white man to do more than that.

Everywhere Richard turned at the end of 1958 he encountered shocks and problems. All were serious and each demanded attention almost to the point of emotional exhaustion. A cable arrived from Alan that his mother was seriously ill in Chicago. Money was needed. Richard increased his monthly payments for her care and forced down a feeling of panic at the state of his finances. Failure of *The Long Dream* meant that the steady $500 a month would be depleted before very long. There would be royalty payments for past books but they would not equal the sure account that Paul had been able to maintain for him over the years.

Even his pleasure in the Café Tournon, just within the shadow of the giant Palais du Luxembourg, the home of the French Senate, grew dim. Madame Alazard, a dark handsome Frenchwoman, who ran the café, worshiped "Le Grand Monsieur Reeshard," and grew angry at the viciousness of the Left Bank expatriate colony toward him. Seated at tables nearby, American expatriates would speak of his books contemptuously and sneer openly if he raised his eyes in their direction. A young Israeli poet once asked:

"But why does such a great and world famous writer sit so patiently and try to answer the insults of these savage people? If Faulkner or Hemingway ever came here they wouldn't even dare ask them questions." Then the young poet quietly concluded. "But of course. It is only because he is a black man and they feel that they have the right to say what they wish to him."[7]

Bente Heeris, an eighteen-year-old girl in Denmark with whom he had corresponded, although they had never met, killed herself. *Black Boy* had moved her so deeply that she had written a thesis on Richard's work. When it was completed she threatened suicide, saying that she could not live in a world that was so inhuman, where black men could be treated like vicious beasts. This resulted in a series of letters between Richard and Bente in an attempt to turn her away from her suicidal intentions. But, at last Bente wrote saying that when he received her letter she would be dead. And she took sleeping pills. They did not work so she turned on the gas and then slashed her wrists.[8] And Bente's letter reached Richard after her death.

Resolutely, Richard continued a new novel; next year had to improve. What else could happen? The bitter cold days that opened 1959 in Paris reminded Richard of his life in Chicago. At the beginning of the second week in January still another cable was delivered. Even before he slit it open he was filled with a sense of dread. As soon as his fingers had touched the white envelope it enlivened the foreboding that had been holding his mind all morning. It was from his brother Alan. His mother had suffered another stroke. She was dead.

XXVIII

On the morning of February 16, 1959, Richard stood at the window of his study and looked out at the gray sky above the Paris chimney pots. Behind him, lying on his desk, was a final draft, 517 pages, of a new manuscript: *Island of Hallucination*. He was aware, in fact lucidly aware, that he did not feel like taking the next step. It had to be wrapped and sent airmail that day to his agent. That was why he stared out of the window so early in the morning instead of getting down to work. Never had he had such misgivings about a manuscript in his life. Not even when he had been learning to write had he been so troubled. He could think of a hundred reasons why Americans would not like the book. But it was true. Everything in the novel had happened, but he had twisted the characters about so that no one would recognize them. It was a crisis book. With the failure of *The Long Dream* he did not think that Doubleday would want to publish anything else if they disliked *Hallucination*. Suddenly, he missed Ed Aswell; his foreboding was that his new editor, Timothy Seldes, tall, slender, sandy-haired, was too boyish for his needs. Besides, Seldes came from liberal parents—Northerners—how could he understand at the depth of his old friend from Nashville. Northerners believed they were unprejudiced; that was their barrier. One first had to recognize one's prejudices in order to overcome them. When a Southerner faced himself it was right out in the open; if he broke with his past, it was a little revolution in the personality. Then he was your friend for life.

If *Hallucination* was a failure, then he would have to look around quickly to find some other way of making a living. A novel took him a year to write and if a publisher did not think he was a good investment there would be no money. Then what would happen to his family? He turned from the window abruptly, picked up the manuscript and divided it into two parts. It was too heavy to send by air in a single package. When it was ready to mail he took it to the post office and sent it to New York. Then, feeling quite cheerful, he stopped at a kiosk, bought a morning paper and went into a café for a *café crème*.

Although Paul answered with his reactions, the receipt of Richard's manuscript, by February 24—only eight days after it had been mailed from Paris—it took Timothy Seldes until March 19. Then as a good editor facing a valuable property and a manuscript he did not understand, or like, he was evasive. He wanted to discuss; he had suggestions; was it possible for Richard to come to New York? Could the book be reworked? Timothy was "somewhat hard pressed" to write Richard. There was a grave disadvantage in their relationship—they had never met and discussions by mail were difficult. The best thing would be to try to work out all of the difficulties by mail and Richard should please let him know how he *felt* about the letter. Richard's heart sickened and curled; he was used to handling by agent and editor with the delicacy and sympathy that might be extended a precious, breakable jewel. Reynolds had already written— "I wish, oh I wish that we only had Ed Aswell with us." He had no harsh words to say about Seldes; as a matter of fact, he told Richard that if and when they met he thought they might get on together. And he knew his client friend well enough to tell him that writing was in his blood and that he suspected that it would never be given up; that perhaps here and there he had overstated his case—conditions had not improved in the South but they had changed—and there would be a better reception and sale if he were not so strong in his generalizations. Richard accepted whatever Paul had to say without hesitancy because in the same letters of criticism he could add:

You cannot be too strong in the degradation that the Negro goes through in being a second class citizen just because his skin is black and being mistreated and spurned by a large part of the white race . . . [Whatever general observations he would make were with a great deal of hesitancy.] None of us think we are prejudiced in this world but any white man is prejudiced on this particular subject. I am conditioned with my background just as you doubtless are by yours and if a white man says he isn't prejudiced, he probably should have his head examined.

Wright was fifty years old. The subject with which he was treating was familiar, as intimate as the texture of his own skin upon which he gazed each morning that he shaved. Equably, he answered Seldes, telling him that he knew what it was to be up to one's neck in work, thanking him for his letter, explaining that he was not in a financial position to go to New York; and ending with a desire to rework the manuscript if it proved necessary. With open-mindedness on both sides, even by mail, the job could be done.

In April Richard went out to the estate of the "Verigoud" family, partly to prepare the way for a visit by an old friend whom he admired more than almost any other American sociologist, Dr. E. Franklin Frazier, who had written on one of Richard's favorite topics, "The Black Bourgeoisie," and partly to think through *Hallucination* once again before beginning the third volume in the sequence.

Hallucination was a hard book. It continued an early faintly hinted concept to which he had held in the hating South, during his years in the self-seeking Communist Party, and among the dislocated, near sleepwalking French intellectuals, who wandered from the bed of a third force back to that of Russian Communism each time the United States made a severe move. It was, or appeared to be, a fairly simple conviction: Negroes were human beings. But he knew it was a shattering concept when pursued to the end. The proof had shocked even Richard: black men could be as corrupt as white men. They could be, quite possibly, even more corrupt in some situations if he followed out another thesis of his—that the Negro was also special, advanced and gifted with double vision.

When he left the United States he had written five books about the black man in his own country. He prided himself that he knew his people. To his dismay, after living in Paris, he discovered that he had only a hazy notion about what happened. Naïvely, he had assumed that as soon as a black man left the States he would stop reacting racially. But it did not happen. The conditioning he had received at home was much deeper than Richard had originally thought and felt. Expatriate black men in Paris were still living mentally in black belts in the United States. When he went to Africa he discovered that, although the British had gone, Africans were still acting as though they were present. He found the same reaction among the Indonesians regarding the Dutch. All of this meant that white people had to accustom themselves to the idea that no matter how much good was accomplished immediately, the Negro's consciousness would remain just what it was for at least one more generation.

Island of Hallucination is a sequel to *The Long Dream* and describes Fishbelly's experiences in Paris. Temporarily disoriented, he discovers that he has fled death in Mississippi to find danger of a subtler, more menacing nature, one that has no color or race or nationality. The Southern white man is a pure 150 percent bastard but he is simple-minded compared to the black men he meets in Paris. Fish finds that the bitter race wars in Mississippi have prepared him in a fashion for understanding the intrigues among blacks on the Left Bank, thousands of miles from home.

Paris, as the center of the struggle between Russia and the United States, is infiltrated by agents from both sides; governments, navies, armies, air forces, embassies, international organizations have unlimited sums of money to hand out and the black man makes an ideal spy. As an outsider he has always looked on and observed, which has given him a keen sensitivity toward the functioning of the mind and personality of the oppressor. Diplomacy is not something he has to learn; all his life he has lived by subterfuge, masking his face, ferreting out information, merely to survive. As a child he has learned to watch the faces of white people on whom he was dependent to see if they would kick him, kill him or pat him on the head and give him a quarter. Thus, the faintest twitch of a lip, a shadow across the eyes, or no expression at all is a Morse code he knows how to read. His entire life has been, in a sense, a spying on white America. In Paris spying, as conducted by white men, is literally child's play to a black man.

In addition to these honed senses he has the ability to read other spies, especially if they are black. A white man never knows what a black man is thinking. As a matter of fact, his expression of that fatal weakness is always: "Can't tell one from another . . . They all look alike to me . . ." Within the separated-off black community, as in the gigantic white community, there are only a few Negroes who are exceptionally gifted or independent. Most black men know or know about all others who rise out of the mass. In Paris it is still easier because black men flock together in their strange exile to keep one another company. They need to cling together because they have lost their roots and have involved themselves in a barren round of activities. Racial vanity has been bred as a reflex defense against racial degradation; it is a racial spur in the blood. In America resentment and hate are natural and the only means for keeping intact a sense of one's own worth. But as a premise for action in another culture, Paris, such feelings are incorrect.

Fish has made his life out of the turgid feelings of living a "black" life in a white world and he is conditioned to make all judgments only in relation to his consciousness of being black. A terror he has not experienced overcomes him for a few months because French people claim the right, by their actions, to judge him as a man, separate from race. Fish has never lived on such grounds; they render him less than human because manhood in Mississippi rested upon the degree of violent hate one felt toward all white people. Even sexual experience is interwoven with his blackness. A young French girl, Yvette, daughter of a Senator, falls in love with him, but inter-course with her leaves him depressed. He wants to feel his hate and needs Yvette to turn from him; then he could feel superior. Then he could have been kind or even compassionate because his feeling of superiority would have balanced out the menace of her whiteness. Paris bewilders him because he sees only human prejudice and he can not read it; he can never discern what individual is prejudiced against which or for what reason.

In the Café Tournon, Fish meets many of his people, those men who limp on the secret, wooden leg of race, who live in a world whose sweet poison has become a kind of emotional metabolism of their nerves and brain. "Mechanical," second-generation African, missionary-educated, grandson of the executioner for a tribal chief, works for the CIA. He has been warped by white domination too but differently from Fish. Christianity has fostered in him a need to be loved by the white world. He is a member of the tragic elite and feels that he has been ripped from his soil and is withering. He describes one of the tribal rituals which his grandfather has conducted, the killing of a victim, catching his blood in a gold pan and sprinkling it on the bones of dead ancestors as an aid to the living. His grand-father believed that when the missionaries stopped the blood-letting it kept Africa from achieving her freedom. Mechanical only half believes in the customs of his tribe but Fishbelly is revolted. The hell with that kind of freedom he shouts. Fish realizes that he is a Western civilized man who is repelled by tribalism. He does not feel as lost as the African who tells him that the problem is that they have nothing to believe in; they need their own dreams which would answer their needs. Mechanical is a homosexual who confesses that it is only when white people frighten him that he acts like a woman.

When he regains his balance Fishbelly, like any typical American, sets out to make money. He becomes a businessman by looking around him to see what Americans need and then setting it up. He gets together a group of musicians and singers, who double as prostitutes, and tours Germany, providing entertainment for the American troops. Later, he watches Mechanical moving among a crowd demonstrating against General Ridgeway and pointing out the Communists to the French Sûreté. It sickens him. He is sick of Negroes selling people. A memory of his father's activities rises in his mind: he had been willing to make a scapegoat of any other black man if it would protect him. And how different, he wonders, is his own activity. He is selling women to the soldiers.

The third main character in *Hallucination* is Ned, an intellectual American lawyer who is a free man: "I'm with no bloc, group, sect, party. I'm free." It is through Ned that Fishbelly gradually understands the role of the expatriates and eventually his own character and perspective. Ned explains that the Left Bank is filled with agents from America, Russia, China, and England. Spies spy on spies. The majority of American spies are black men who hate their own country so much that they will accept money from anyone in order to remain in Europe. Fishbelly and Ned are revolted. Black men are taking funds from an organization which perpetuates the conditions of misery in the black belts and Northern slums. Many of them salve their consciences by becoming members of the non-Communist left, most often Trotskyists.

At the end Mechanical crucifies himself, by hanging, on one of the gargoyles of Notre Dame. Crucifixion is a love relationship and a weapon of psychological blackmail in its effect upon the watching white faces. Jesus suffering upon the Cross is the most vivid heritage of Western culture. Mechanical is saying: You reject me? All right, I will kill myself. That is how deeply I feel your rejection. Mechanical loved the powerful white men who hired him, despised him and rejected him.

Ned explains Mechanical's act to Fishbelly as they walk away from the towers of Notre Dame. Then he asks, whom can you blame for your troubles? And when Fishbelly admits, no one but himself, Ned says that he has accomplished something. "When you can accept responsibility for what you do, then you are starting to grow up, to be free." Such a concept of freedom is frightening. Fishbelly's recognition that he can do with himself what he likes is pained. It is the anguish of responsibility in a world where God is dead.

Hallucination was written from Richard's own observation of and experience with the United States government activities in Paris. On his initial visit to Paris, in 1946, he had been met by Douglas H. Schneider, public relations officer from the American Embassy, in two government limousines. When he moved to France permanently he drove into Paris in his own Oldsmobile and no American official visited him for several months. In his apartment on Rue Monsieur le Prince, both Embassy and State Department officials visited him with regularity. He was asked to lecture under their auspices, sometimes open and sometimes concealed, at clubs, halls, universities and auditoriums. Richard refused. Two of the men who visited him were unable to disguise their anger and hostility but a third was curious and asked, why? He explained that he could not make a speech which would give Europeans the impression that there was any democracy for the black man in America. The official responded by saying that many of his compatriots did not hold his point of view; there was one young novelist, a William Gardner Smith, who often gave lectures which they sponsored. Richard ended the conversation quietly. With a smile on his lips he answered: "What Bill Smith does is his business; but for me, it is a betrayal of our people."[1] Visits and telephone calls to Richard's apartment were so frequent that eventually he became friendly with Charles E. Cox after he had left the American Embassy and was able to arrange rapid shipment of Macy "Red Star," 16 percent rag content paper through the government offices.

As the Cold War grew more severe, and Richard persisted in speaking his mind in lectures, books and numerous interviews, the CIA took an interest in his ideas. "He was almost continuously under surveillance and they were hostile to him. Many expatriates in France work[ed] for the CIA or [were] used by them in one way or another."[2]

In May, 1954, the Paris *Herald Tribune* reported in its "Paris Diary" that more than 30,000 Americans were living in Paris and that the State Department was tightening up restrictions. The Department made it clear that they intended to confiscate the passports of any Americans it considered undesirable. A columnist, Guy Henriques, interviewed Richard for his column and was told that "in the present atmosphere in America, any American going abroad is expected to behave like an ambassador. In other words, he's not expected to voice any criticism which might reflect on American policy. If he does, then the State Department try to get him back home as quickly as possible." Miss Agnes Schneider, the elderly, distinguished-looking head of the Passport Division, was in charge of what Parisians described as the State Department's "witchhunt." She was known among American residents as "the Spider." The *Tribune* reported that Miss Schneider was assisted in her work by a team of fifty plainclothesmen snoopers who patrolled cafés and restaurants eavesdropping on their fellow countrymen.[3]

In June, 1956, Richard explained the intricacies of espionage in Paris and his own position in such an atmosphere:

. . . I do not know the day or the hour when my American passport might be taken from me and I shall be faced with being semi-stateless. . . . My position is really complicated, much more than you think. I'm not a Communist, the government can take no political objection to me; but they burn up at the idea of an independent Negro living in a foreign country and saying whatever he likes. One has got loose! I'm probably just about the only uncontrolled black men alive today and I pay for that. . . . They think I am worse than a Communist, for my writing falls like a shadow across their policies in Asia and Africa. They asked me time and time again to work for them. I'd die first! The number of Negroes in the world who are free to say what they want are far too few. . . . I will never work for anybody's government. Truth-telling today is both unpopular and suspect. Ah, God, what a world. What a poor sick world!

Oliver "Ollie" Harrington, rotund creator of "Bootsie," a syndicated cartoon, and a writer, met Richard about 1957 and they became warm friends. It was the closest relationship with an American that he had experienced in many years. The two men did not agree politically[4] but Ollie admired Richard's work and personality; ". . . they were like brothers without any words being said."[5] And, as a brother, Richard nagged at Ollie because he was too generous and trusting. He had just loaned his apartment on the Left Bank to Richard Gibson, a Negro-American writer, who arrived in Paris presumably without funds. Something about Gibson excited a feeling of distaste in Richard. He attempted to behave like a white executive, yet his high-pitched tone and head-ducking never allowed him to measure up to his imagined standard and he was half conscious of it. Richard grew more wary of the man than ever when he gossiped about almost every member of the expatriate black community. William Gardner Smith had told him that he was a close personal friend of Wright's; Smith was a Communist; another day he was a Trotskyist; still later he was an agent for the FBI or the CIA. It was not affection for Smith that irritated Wright—he had heard that the young man called him an FBI agent—but that Gibson's stories were so contradictory. Gradually, he became convinced that Gibson himself was an agent for the American government; he was extremely familiar with its operation, particularly the espionage in Germany. And when Gibson informed Richard that there was no FBI in Paris, only CIA, and that they were located in small offices throughout Paris he became ever more convinced that he was in the hire of the U.S. government.

Ollie laughed and joked at Richard's gloomy warnings, but when he returned to Paris from a visit to the country he discovered that Gibson had opened his mail, copied his signature to endorse checks, and written two letters: one to the London *Observer*, which was never published, and the other to *Life* magazine. The articles were for Letters to the Editor columns and consisted of violently pro-Communist material and an admission that the writer was himself a Communist. These were sent out over the signature of Oliver Harrington.

It placed Ollie in an exceedingly dangerous position: he might be expelled from France or even detained by the United States government as a dangerous subversive. He went looking for Gibson, and on the terrace of the Café Tournon beat him severely. As a result of the fight Gibson was hospitalized.

Eventually, the forged letter in *Life* magazine was brought to the attention of the Federal Bureau of Investigation. They, in turn, made inquiries of the French Consul, who secured the original and sent photostatic copies to the Sûreté in Paris. Gibson's handwriting on the forged letter was recognized and he was apprehended by the Sûreté on a complaint from Harrington, and he signed a lengthy confession. "Ironically, he would have been sent to a long prison term if [Richard] and [Ollie] hadn't intervened . . . to spare the Negro community a messy situation."[6]

When a friend and admirer, the Reverend Clayton Williams of the American Church of Paris, invited Richard to lecture he chose as his subject "The Position of the Negro Artist and Intellectual in American Society."[7] Before a full-house which crowded the small room to hear him he described the means by which the dominant white society in America kept black men under control. And three-quarters of the way through his speech he described the extent of espionage in Paris. The audience was stunned. It had been his intention to speak boldly; he had reached the point in life where he felt it was not worthwhile merely to hint at information he had gathered. He named names, dates and places: Negroes who could "talk Communism" were being sent into the ghettos as well as into every colony of expatriate Americans. The agent provocateur had been introduced into the Black Belt for the first time. It was, in a sense, a sign of progress. Books, mass media, developing tourism among Negroes had broken down the walls of the ghetto and the black man was in motion. The audience was so intent that hardly an individual moved in his seat. More Communism was being talked in the ghettos than ever in American history but it was a false Communism, the language of the informer, the spy. As Communism declined, the talk of Communism increased. He would go as far as to say that "most communism in the Black Belts of the United States today [was] sponsored by the American Government. . . . the most revolutionary movements in the Western world [were] government-sponsored; they [were] launched by agent provocateurs to organize the discontented so that the Government [could] keep an eye on them."

All people disliked spies, but the black spy should be viewed with some degree of compassion, Richard explained. His was a most difficult job. Social stratification was so tight in the ghetto that it was almost impossible for a black spy to fool his black brothers. "Spies, if they are to be good ones, must have what is known as 'cover stories.' Now what cover story could a black spy have?" Richard paused and smiled. "He could not possibly say that he was a stockbroker on the New York Stock Exchange; if he did, someone would call the nearest insane asylum and ask that he be taken away. Could he pose as a steel magnate? If he did, somebody would come running with a straitjacket." His audience was laughing and there were a few handclaps so he paused again before continuing. "Could he pretend that he had inherited a fortune from a rich uncle? But that could be checked in an hour to find out that no such rich uncle ever existed. . . . You see, when a Negro lands a job working for the government making $10,000 a year, that event is headlined in all the Black Belt's newspapers, so rare an event it is!"

Richard had had several experiences with spies but he selected only a few. One young man arrived in Paris and posed as an agent of an employment bureau. He sat down at the Café Tournon with Richard and sipped an aperitif, looking away from him while he described his occupation. Richard leaned forward trying to look into the man's eyes: "Just what kind of an employment bureau are you operating?" "Well, Mr. Wright, you see I'm recruiting French girls to teach the children of the Rockefellers and Fords back home," the man said glibly. "You're recruiting governesses for the rich families?" Richard was persistent. "That's right," he said eagerly. The young man thought Richard was convinced by his meditative look. Then Richard asked: "By the way, did you have anything to do with recruiting the Norwegian girl that recently married into the Rockefeller family?" "Oh, no. I wasn't in on that one," the man stammered.

Within a week most black expatriates were joking and whispering about the employment agency man. A few months later there appeared in *Ebony* magazine a photograph in praise of the governess recruiter: he was an agent of the United States Treasury Department and spoke five languages. *Ebony's* revelations of his own suspicions spurred Richard's imagination. He laughed, waved his hands, and described his intention of establishing a Paris Bureau whose job it would be to invent identities for stray black spies. It would be a good way for him to solve his financial problems because he could charge a good fee by inventing a foolproof identity for provocateurs. To protect himself, however, he would state, in writing, that the invented identities would be valid only two weeks. After all, he smiled, he could not accomplish the impossible, no matter how ardently he loved his country.

Hallucination was a crisis book and when Timothy Seldes visited him in France and suggested that the book be rewritten, and then immediately changed the subject, Richard knew that there would be no money coming in right away. He suspected that even Paul, his agent, was not enthusiastic because he wrote that he considered the novel too strong in its attack against America. The situation had changed for the better: lynching, for example, had disappeared. Well, Richard thought, and put Paul's letter on top of a stack of mail on his desk, the artist today works in an impossible atmosphere; there is no call for truth-telling. No one reading that novel could say that I am for Russia, but if they define being for America as being unable to say that America is perfect, then they can say that I'm a bad guy who is just as dangerous as a Communist. Maybe, I should not write about Negroes any more, he wondered. Not even Negroes want to listen. Nobody wants to listen. Yet, I'm convinced that I'm telling some important truths. What to do? I'd better just stop writing and find some other work.

But a visit from Dr. Martin Luther King, in March, 1959, was reassuring. King stayed at Richard's apartment and the two talked through twenty-four hours. Finally, toward the end of their long day and night, Richard asked point-blank: "Has the Negro's relationship to America changed?" And Dr. King said, "No, there has been no qualitative change. It may come, but it hasn't come yet." Richard did not always agree with King but he liked and admired him. Above all, he believed that King was an honest man. And King told Richard that he must go on writing the kinds of books that told the truth of what the black man lived. It was most important that he do so.

Richard's mind had already been moving along toward a third Fishbelly volume and he took a short tour of American Army camps in Germany to research it. At the same time he wrote to his agent to sound out the publisher for the novel, which would give a bird's-eye view of the Negro soldier abroad and then propel Fishbelly into North Africa in an attempt to come to terms with the race from which he had sprung. He would gain a dawning insight into what was happening in the world, the drama of millions of people taking their freedom and then return to America to organize an insurance company and dream of an eventual way that he could fit himself into Africa.

"When the month of June rolls around, I'll have waited six months to get Mr. Seldes' reactions. That is a long time to wait on a publisher. Yet I don't see much sense in pushing the man," Richard wrote to his agent. In the meantime, would Paul inquire whether or not Doubleday or a paperback publisher would be interested in a book about French Africa. De Gaulle had taken power and Richard, who was friendly with Michael Bokanowski, one of the Ministers of Government, had assured Richard that he could go into French Africa with government consent. The Society of African Culture, which Richard had helped to set up and organize, would pay some of the expenses of such a trip. Dr. Mercer Cook, who was in charge of the Society's Paris office, seemed enthusiastic and promised to write John A. Davis, executive secretary of the organization in New York.

While he waited for an answer from his agent and another from John Davis, Richard received a telephone call from Ben Zevin, president of World Publishing Company, and they met for lunch at La Méditerranée. Zevin, whose company had published a cloth-bound reprint edition of *Uncle Tom's Children,* listened intently to his plans for another trip to Africa. When Richard stopped speaking Zevin said: 'If that trip's to have a book I buy it."[8] His spirits rose. Everyone seemed to feel that it was an exciting project. But when he reached home there was a letter from his agent: Doubleday was interested but would pay only $2,500 toward the trip. The most careful estimates Richard had been able to make indicated $10,000 as a minimum. Then Dr. Cook telephoned to say that the Society of African Culture could not pay for such an expensive trip.

Feeling gloomy, Richard contemplated his shrinking bank account. He was beginning to feel closed in; every project he attempted seemed to fall apart. And when Editions Mondiales, which had purchased *The Long Dream,* decided not to bring out the novel friends told Richard that American government pressure had forced the firm to give it up. Almost convinced that he would have to take a job teaching or working in some field suitable to his knowledge and write as a sideline, he spoke of his dilemma to his friends Alva and Gunnar Myrdal. They suggested that he move to India, where Mrs. Myrdal was Swedish Ambassador. George and Dorothy Padmore asked him to come to Ghana, where his old friend was a member of the government. Richard wrote to Prime Minister Nkrumah and offered his services as a teacher to young Africans, but there was no reply. And he offered his services to an old friend, Dr. Eric Williams, who had become Premier of Trinidad and Tobago. Again, there was no answer from a man he had helped, advised and comforted when Williams had been fired from the Caribbean Commission.[9]

The Congress for Cultural Freedom offered to pay Richard for a trip to New Delhi to speak on Tolstoy. He refused, saying that he was too busy fighting issues in the Western world to go into Asia and try to sell its brand of pretense. The Congress had paid Richard's expenses and $500 for each article he brought back from the Bandung Conference in 1955. But even then he had been suspicious of the wealthy Congress, which published four magazines: *Preuves* in France; *Encounter* in England; *Cuadernos* in Spain; and *Monat* in Germany. He had written to his agent that it was a semi-official agency with the indirect backing of the State Department. When he accepted its money it was with a strict agreement that he was not covering the African-Asian conference for it; he would go as a freelance writer; the Congress would have the right to publish his articles but without censorship; and he reserved the right to publish the material in the form of a small book.

He was met in Jakarta by members of the Congress, together with P.E.N. club officials and Mochtar Lubis, editor of the *Indonesia Raya,* an independent Socialist daily. Lubis, who was anti-Sukarno,[10] introduced Richard to a Miss Beb Vuyk, an Indonesian-Dutch journalist. The fat woman with a yellow complexion and narrow eyes behind round colorless plastic-rimmed glasses impressed Richard as being somewhat opportunistic. He assumed that she worked for the Congress for Cultural Freedom and she was vigorously pro-American; but at the same time she professed to be revolutionary and concerned with freedom for Asia and Africa. Indonesian intellectuals distrusted her because she was always in and out of the American Embassy and they wondered what she might be reporting to the United States government. Beb Vuyk was eventually expelled from Indonesia and began to write a series entitled "People I have Known" for *Vrij Nederland.* Two of the articles were about Richard and Miss Vuyk claimed in them that Richard had stayed at the American Embassy in Indonesia; that he had told her that the American Ambassador was a "slave driver"; that she had taken him to dinner with a white American family and he was uncomfortable in the presence of whites; that he was a short, fat, little man whose primary interest in life seemed to be eating good food. When he did some quiet investigating in Paris he was informed that Miss Vuyk, indeed, had worked for the Congress for Cultural Freedom.

Always a nagging worry at the edge of his mind was the continual French political crisis. Time and again he had heard Speakers of the Sénat announce that France was on the verge of civil war. He had watched near chaos envelop Paris prior to de Gaulle's speech in the Assembly in May, 1958. Armed police, silent in their vans, and shock

troops of the Compagnie Républicaine de Sécurité had surrounded
Parliament while others took up positions in the Tuileries and the
Place de la Concorde. Sirens blared along the Seine and the police
menaced the populace, driving them back from the entire area
around the House of Parliament. He had seen nation-wide strikes
and the declaration of a state of emergency. Movements of people
and vehicles were regulated; security zones were established; curfews
were ordered and there were house searches and censorship of the
press. He had given his support to his friends Jean-Paul Sartre and
Simone de Beauvoir in the Comité d'Action et de Défense Républicaine, which organized a demonstration in opposition to de Gaulle.
Over a quarter of a million men, women and children had joined the
protest march lining up at the Place de la Nation and distributing
leaflets:

General de Gaulle's last declaration leaves no doubt; it is a defiance to
the workers and the people of all France. The question is not now one of
either government or a constitution but of our most elemental liberties.
Freedom of speech, of public assembly, of unions and their right to strike
is today menaced by military power.[11]

Richard had worried when his friend Jean-Paul Sartre published
an article in *L'Express* entitled "The Constitution of Contempt."
Sartre was called a traitor to his country and over 5,000 war veterans
had marched down the Champs-Elysées shouting "Shoot Sartre!"
France appeared to be sinking each day, each hour, and Richard
feared there would be a Fascist dictatorship.

While Richard was with his family he did not worry excessively—
he could take care of them, and he had a secret feeling that France
was an elastic country which would weather anything—but when he
went away to lecture or write a book in another country their well-
being nagged at him. He alerted his agent to be ready to respond at a
moment's notice if Ellen wired or phoned and to pay down cash at
any airline or steamship company designated and get his family out
of Europe.

A decision by his daughter to take the exhaustive competitive
examinations in two disciplines at Cambridge University made up
Richard's mind overnight. Julia, who at seventeen had grown into a
lovely, slender girl with the same haunting eyes she had as a baby,
worshipped her father. "She lived to please him; but most of the time
he was not even aware of it and of how sensitive she was. And he
loved her too. He loved both of his children but it was a nervous,
somewhat possessive love. They were *his;* that was a part of his love.

And he was busy and often impatient with them. He just did not really have the dope on being a father." Julia, who looked very much like her father except that she had a greater delicacy of bone structure, had graduated with honors. In the auditorium of the Sorbonne in the presence of dignitaries of France, including the Minister of Education, Julia, who had sat for French and English, was awarded an English prize in the Concours Générale, which was a country-wide contest among the terminal classes in the lycées. Only three prizes were awarded to students, following their final tests, in all of France. Shortly after final examinations, when she was not quite seventeen, she was received as a candidate by both Oxford and Cambridge universities.

Richard was fond of England and its green countryside; and the English people had a certain irreducible decency about them not found in other people. Julia was certain that it was what she wanted and he did not intend to let his young daughter leave the family so early. As soon as his mind was made up he thought about the move and convinced himself that the British had refused to allow themselves to be stampeded into hysteria in the Cold War atmosphere of Europe. And, he thought, France still teeters on the verge of tragic events. Nothing is really settled here, notwithstanding de Gaulle's coming to power. Well, I've decided to live in a self-respecting country.

Cautioning his family and his agent to keep it secret that they were going to move, and elated by the need for silence—so the Bokanowkis, his good friends, who were fierce patriots would not be offended—he drove to Paris from Ailly in August, 1959. At the office of the British Consul he filled out application papers for English residence. Within a few days, Reginald Butler, the British Home Secretary, told Richard that England would accept him, providing he could show proof of solvency.

A little sad to lose the lovely country farm, Richard put it up for sale and transferred his funds from Switzerland to a British banking house. On Cromwell Road, in South West London, they settled into a large flat and arrangements were completed for Julia's entrance to Cambridge as a Greek and French scholar. Rachel was entered in a French lycée. Richard had been granted a three-month visitor's permit and assured that his status would be established as a permanent resident within that period.

Weeks passed but no word came about their permanent visa and Richard worried. What could be wrong? Every time he telephoned about it he was told that it was simply held up temporarily. Eventually, he was informed that his premanent residence visa had been rejected. Alarmed, he called his friend John Strachey, one-time Minister of Defense in the Labor government, and was told that some error had been made, probably by a minor functionary. Through Strachey's influence an interview was finally given to Richard at the Home Office, where he was met by a red-faced, spluttering official who refused to explain the denial of the visa. He was rude, raised his voice, and said, the answer is No! Richard protested that he had already settled his family and pulled up most of his roots in France. All that the man would give him was a thirty-day extension of his visitor's permit, providing Richard would agree to leave the country without publicity at the end of that time. His family could remain; he would have to leave. Richard refused to sign any statement but continued to question the officer. Suddenly the man threw Richard's passport violently to the floor and walked away. Silent, Richard stooped and picked it up. He was trembling all over. Rage made him feel blinded for a few minutes, then he turned and left the building.

An investigation was instituted by John Strachey, but when he could not receive any satisfactory answers he brought the question up on the floor of Parliament and asked for a clear statement of policy from his government. Each time his questions were parried.[12] Reginald Butler, in a face-to-face confrontation, would give no reasons for the refusal. An investigation was promised but Strachey's influence and that of other Englishmen could not change the decision and Richard was unable to discover the reasons behind the denial.

He had his own ideas about the British government. He was bitterly angry: England did not want articulate Negroes who attacked colonialism or capitalism to live in her country. She could not prevent Jamaicans and Trinidadians and Africans from entering the country unless she endorsed a racist policy—something she could not possibly do and retain any semblance of a democracy before the rest of the world. Probably England had been pressured by the United States. He could not do much damage living in France, where the language was foreign, but they did not want him to live in an English-speaking country where everyone—the man in the street— could understand and perhaps sympathize with his point of view.

Richard's rage extended as far as Canada. When he was asked to participate in a series of broadcasts he wrote to Oliver Swann at the Reynolds' office:

At this moment, I do not wish to participate in the series. . . . I find myself constantly under attack—both me and my books—by the white West. I lift my hand to fight Communism and I find that the hand of the

Western world is sticking knives into my back. That is a crazy position. I don't want it. The Western world must make up its mind as to whether it hates colored people more than it hates Communists or does it hate Communists more than it hates colored people. . . . I have had some bitter experiences with the British, and Canada is a part of the British Commonwealth. Why should I aid a people who hold toward me an attitude of disdain? I asked the British the right to live in England to educate my children there, and they were nasty, evasive, and downright racist about it. . . . Of course, one needs money, but I'm willing to sacrifice the money and be honest about it.

*We fret, we feel frustrated, but things are moving
on the broad scale. We must never forget that . . .*

XXIX

With a sigh, part satisfaction and part fatigue, Richard relaxed in his
new apartment at 4 Rue Regis and gazed at his three rooms. Rue
Regis was one of the shortest streets in Paris, on the Left Bank, in the
Sèvres-Babylone neighborhood. The apartment, located on the
ground floor of the building, included a large cellar in which
Richard intended to organize and store manuscripts, letters, photographs, magazine and newspaper clippings and folders of scribbled
notes. Seated on the bright green couch, which was one of the items
he had removed before disposing of the old apartment on Monsieur
le Prince, he could look across the large living room and into his
study beyond an arched doorway. On the opposite side from where
he sat another archway led to a small bedroom. Above the graceful
curve of each opening he had hung huge beaten brass serving platters
which he and Ellen had purchased in the Flea Market in 1946. A
large glass-doored bookcase containing Richard's leather-bound
copies of his own writings, including translations in Japanese,
Hebrew, Braille and Bengali, faced him on the wall opposite the
couch. A painting by a young friend who claimed to be the natural
great-grandson of Percy Bysshe Shelley hung with the rest of his
collection on the white walls. The white-tiled coffee table standing
close in front of the couch was covered with books he was currently
reading. He had just discovered *Mandingo,* by Kyle Onstott, a novel
based on slave period documents. He had been instrumental in
persuading his publisher to translate it into French. It was a book
that everyone had to read because then they would understand what
had happened to the American dream. Next to *Mandingo* lay a slim

book of haiku poetry which he read over and over. The style of these Japanese poems of three lines, constructed according to a rigid pattern of syllables, excited him more than anything he had read in years. He had to study it and study to find out why it struck his ear with such a modern note.

Everything in the apartment was in order except his office, and he had begun to work on that. He looked through the archways at the book-lined room and the large oak table covered with manuscripts, which served as his desk. A tall revolving bookcase next to the old table held whatever he might need for current work. Shifting his body comfortably, he eased down on the couch until his head rested against the green velour. He stretched out an arm and his hand touched one of the two large square-shaped bundles which a typist had finally delivered. Each package was wrapped in brown paper and tied with heavy cream-colored cord. Again, he sighed. That was one job that he had put aside for years. He was glad that it had been finished. Now he had everything except novels in duplicate for his files. What a lot of work, he thought. How many million words had he written since Jackson, Mississippi? Well, he had just gotten started. He had a great deal more to say and he knew how to say it without some of the earlier hesitation.

The sound of footsteps leaving the neighboring bistro of Monsieur Vallette, a silent colossus of an Auvergnian, entered the room and left abruptly. It was a quiet, tiny street lined with miniature art galleries and antique shops, and he was glad that there was not too much noise. He had not lived on the ground floor for many years. There was something wonderful about being alone in a silent apartment. His mind went to his wife and two children in London in the new apartment he had purchased. They would be fine, he assured himself: the girls in school and Ellen busy with her literary agency.[1] A faint smile turned the corners of his mouth upward when he thought of his helpless, sometimes impractical wife. A businesswoman. And a good one. Why, she had once overpaid her income tax. But, then, was he any more practical? The same year (1945) he had underpaid $377.36, more than double Ellen's $110. But, ah, God, it was good to be alone. His nerves had been all raw the past year and Ellen could not seem to control the children. There was always tension in the house and she knew he could not work under such conditions. And the children sometimes seemed actually antagonistic to him. To their own father! Wonder whether all children go through these stages? But they would be all right. Julia was melancholy and desperately sensitive, something like her mother, but then so was he. She would learn to guard that vulnerable core and discipline herself to hold at a distance the things that hurt her too much. And she could write; it was good, too. All that was needed was that she finish at the university and decide whether writing was what she wanted to do. Then she would have to sweat it out as he had.

Rachel, in some ways, was more like his family—the Wilsons—even though she resembled her mother. She had always known her own mind; at two years of age she had been as willful and as dramatic as a Duse. He had never been able to hold out against her teasing defiance. How beautiful she was. She was harder and tougher than Julia; had already learned to armor her painful sensitivity; and she had just turned eleven, three weeks before, on January 17. Both girls would be fine and when they grew up they would be good friends with their father. There was so much he could tell them, help them with; it was much more than he had ever had; and he would never take them back to be hurt by the jungle of America. But, now, he was very tired. He did not want to drive himself as hard as he had on the last novel. On the new one he would take it more easily.

The day after Rachel's birthday he had mailed off to his agent a bundle of short stories which he had been writing over the years; they amounted to about 50,000 words and some 300 pages. He was satisfied with them. He might be all wet, but he had seen some paperback collections of short stories and these made a not-too-disrespectable group. He had been right, too, because Paul had liked them very much and had found a publisher. Several months earlier, when Bill Targ had seen Richard in Paris at lunch, he had expressed intense interest in the short stories and in all of Richard's future writings. The thought of World Publishing brought Richard to his feet and he went into his study and removed the cover to his battered typewriter. Seated at the Underwood he typed rapidly with two fingers. Negotiations with World were conditional:

Dear Paul:
    Yes, go ahead and make a deal with World, BUT ONLY ON CONDITION THAT BILL TARG IS MY EDITOR. . . .

Richard had met William Targ in Chicago when Targ owned a bookshop on Chicago Avenue and Clark Street. It had been a hangout for young novelists, poets, artists, and intellectuals, many of them members of the John Reed Club. Although he had usually been somewhat shy and quiet in his presence, Richard had taken an affectionate liking to Bill and they had established a friendship later in New York, when they lived a few blocks apart in Greenwich Village. In a description of Bill, Richard explained that he was always more interested in psychological landscapes than in physical ones. Something in the landscape of Bill's face had been a clue to him of a sensitiveness almost equal to his own. And he was honest. He felt safe with Bill; he felt Targ would not lie if it killed him. And Bill had become editor-in-chief at World and had published *Color Curtain,* the book on Bandung, which had gone into two printings.

When he completed the letter to Paul, Richard folded it into a thin airmail envelope and sealed and stamped it. He would mail it later. First, he would lie on the couch to rest. Ah, God, he was weak, kept weak, with only about 50 percent of his old energy. It was almost time to take another dose of bismuth. What a bore. It was the first time in his life that he disliked taking medicine. And he had to avoid spices, fried foods and anything fermented. He had decreased the number of cigarettes to a pack a day and limited himself to tea instead of coffee. But how raw he was inside. Must be the massive doses of sulfa, emetine, arsenic, 3,000,000 units of penicillin and all the bismuth. But he was cured of the amoebas he had picked up somewhere in Spain, Africa or Indonesia.

Richard was slowly learning to be ill. That was the hard part; it was the first serious illness he had ever had. There had been one case of pneumonia, when he was twenty, then the usual tonsillectomy to see if it would alleviate the colds and sore throats he got in Paris; and there had been a simple hernia operation after the trip to Africa. But it was difficult to sit or lie still. All his life, when he had wanted to move, he had just told his body to go, and it went. Now, it was different. When he told his body to move, it hesitated. And that sometimes made him angry clear through. Well, he thought, the worst is over. With periodic checkups over another year it would probably be safe to say that there would not be a recurrence of the tenacious organisms.

A few months before Richard had made the attempt to live in England he had become ill and spent three weeks in the American Hospital in Neuilly. The diagnosis of amoebic infestation had been made but the treatment did not help. Richard was convinced that he had been given the wrong medicine. His weight dropped eighteen pounds and he grew steadily weaker. Just to rise from the bed in the morning made him break out into a cold perspiration and shiver all over. Finally, someone recommended to him a specialist in tropical disease, a Russian refugee named Dr. Vladimir Schwartzmann.

In spite of his terrible feeling of ennui, Richard went to see Schwartzmann with a joyous sense of anticipation. He was supposed to be the finest man in his field and his name was prophetic, Richard thought: Black Man. He must be a good doctor and Richard chuckled down in his throat at his own joke. But an eerie feeling struck him when he entered the doctor's office. Lying on his desk, as if he had just put it down, was a copy of *White Man, Listen*. Schwartzmann was of medium height, quite thin, clean shaven, with a high forehead because his dark blond hair was receding, and pleasant, rather ordinary features. Only his eyes were unusual. They were deep, and gray-blue with a hypnotic quality. Schwartzmann asked Richard if he had written the book, touching it with his slender fingers, as he asked the question. He explained that as a Jew he was very enthusiastic about anti-racist literature and had purchased Richard's book before he knew he was to become a patient. It was an admirable study and his enthusiasm was so great that he would not charge for his treatments.

For several months Dr. Schwartzmann treated Richard with an array of medicines and finally pronounced him cured, but tests would have to be given for a two-year period to be certain he was really well. He also started a series of vitamin B12 injections and doses of bismuth. The doctor introduced him to his father and the three men occasionally ate dinner together. But the oftener he met Schwartzmann the more puzzled he became about the doctor's personality. He was a strange man; Richard did not really know what was disturbing about him. Something was bothering him, Richard pondered. But I don't think it has anything to do with me. He has a problem, I can sense that. Then he sent it from his mind—well, we black men are always bothered by emotionally hurt whites who feel that they wish to identify with us. But there was something between him and the doctor that created tension. Sometimes he felt hypnotized and always he felt uneasy and smiled and laughed more than ever when he was in the doctor's presence.

Spring came and Richard was feeling better under Schwartzmann's care when he suddenly had a relapse. An acute pain gripped his intestines and a resurgence of the old weakness spread all through his body. He could barely drag himself from the bed. The doctor said that it was nothing to worry about; it was a relapse. But what caused the relapse? Richard asked Schwartzmann. The doctor replied that it was a general reaction and the pain had been caused by colic. He administered a sedative, vitamins C and B12, and told Richard to rest. Following the three-week treatment with vitamins Richard was not back to normal but he had regained enough strength to go outdoors, drive his car and take care of small errands. A woman came in every day to clean the apartment and he cooked for himself a light diet. His spirits began to lift because he thought there was progress.

But the bad times when he was afraid to go out of doors made him feel that his nerves would go to pieces.

On April 7, Richard left the doctor's office in good spirits. He was cured. The pain he suffered in his lower abdomen was not serious, the doctor had said. It was simply a spastic condition in the intestines. Perhaps soon he could go to the Bokanowskis' in Normandy and get the poison of Paris out of his system. Strange, he thought. He had asked his doctor a few weeks before if he could go to the country at the end of April and he had said no, it might overtire him, he should remain in the city. And, now, the doctor had asked: "Say, I'm going to Holland for a medical conference. Why don't you come along? It'll be good for you."[2] Richard had answered that he did not know, after all, he was only a tiny bit better. He would see. Then Schwartzmann chided him about his sensitiveness to everything in the world and Richard did not answer. He laughed nervously and thought to himself: "He fails to understand that if one has the capacity of joy, one has also the capacity to suffer. And I have the capacity of both in large measure. Too large."[3]

Richard left Paris on April 21 with Dr. Schwartzmann and his father. He was feeling much better and had gotten back to work on a new schedule. After sleeping under a sedative for ten hours he got up in the morning and all through the day he worked. If he grew weak, he lay on his bed for fifteen minutes or so until his strength returned. There was no pain in his stomach; in fact, he was surprised that such a powerful illness had given so little pain. The decision to drive to Leiden had been made when the doctor mentioned, in passing, that there was really no urgent reason for him to attend the medical conference. He simply had to meet an American doctor in Noordwijk, on the seacoast near Leiden, who was bringing him money for his research work. How odd, Richard thought. Why would he receive money from America in such a peculiar fashion. Maybe that was why he had so few patients and yet needed no fee from him. He had to find out what was happening.

But, driving into the lovely city of Leiden with its canals and flowers on a Friday night, Richard was ready to collapse. Irritation and hostility bubbled in his nerves toward the doctor and his father. Neither had helped him drive the whole distance. And he was a sick man. It did not seem fair. Ah, well, he thought again: the doctor is a good man and we are almost there, then I can rest.

Richard spent Friday and Saturday night in Leiden, which was packed with people celebrating Bulb Sunday, while the doctor and his father went to meet the American. He had wired Madame

Margrit de Sabloniere, his friend and translator, to arrange hotel accommodations and she met him when he arrived. Margrit was alarmed at his appearance. He looked wretched after the long drive and she had not seen him since he had lost eighteen pounds. Richard's large eyes drooped and lacked their usual luster; a line between his eyebrows had deepened and there were other lines running downwards from each side of his nose toward a firmly compressed mouth. Worst of all, he seemed utterly tense, wound to a fine thread which she felt might break in two at any moment. The following day, Saturday, after his night's rest Richard felt better and when he reached Margrit's home he began to unwind. What a warm home, and house, he thought. And that canal flowing eternally past the windows. There were what seemed to be hundreds of plants, all in pots, some blooming and others beginning to show threads of color among the green pungent leaves as they began to open. What a comfort it was to have Sis Margrit. She was the sister he had never had and had always wanted. And she fought for his work like a tiger.

Margrit, a handsome woman, tall and large-boned, with a compassionate face and blue keen eyes, was a writer, lecturer and translator. Married to a businessman, she had always been interested in African culture and literature. When she had first read Richard's books their power and ideas almost literally gave her a shock. She wanted to translate this work and the desire grew stronger when she looked at the earlier Dutch translations, which were not too well done. Richard's publisher in Holland, Sijthoff, was conservative but commercially minded and Margrit received permission to translate *The Outsider*. Suddenly, Sijthoff demanded that she cut thirty-two pages from the last ninety in the proofs. In a diplomatic way, Margrit avoided doing so by an arrangement with the printer. They simply added two more lines to each page and it was not detected by Sijthoff. When Richard learned that the publisher had demanded cutting he was furious and developed an immediate aversion for the man. And as a result of that first episode he demanded that Margrit be named his only translator in Holland. He was confident that she understood his point of view and would protect his books. Gradually, they had become intimate friends and Margrit watched over him and his whole family from her house on the canal in Leiden. Ellen and Julia and Rachel had gone to visit, and when Richard became ill, Margrit sent tea, biscuits, candy and a medication named Korvan. Later, unasked, she sensed that he was in financial difficulties and offered to send money.

Richard returned to Paris, leaving Leiden on Sunday afternoon after a luncheon at Margrit's, with Dr. Schwartzmann and his father. When he asked his doctor whether he had met the American doctor, who was to bring him money, Schwartzmann smiled noncommittally and made no answer. It was still a mystery, but Richard felt too ill to pursue the subject. And when they reached Paris he suffered a relapse. This second relapse brought a new decision: he would measure his strength and work out a way to live with his illness. He was not rich in physical energy anymore. Yet, when he was sitting still he felt quite normal. It was baffling. While lying against the pillows one afternoon he picked up the small book of Japanese poetry and began to read it again. A tingle began in his nerves and brain more intense than anything he had experienced for several years, not since he had begun to write *The Outsider* and *Island of Hallucination*. To the fifteenth- to seventeenth-century haiku form he would try to bring the life and consciousness of a black American. Lying back on his pillows and scribbling with pen or pencil, whichever his fingers touched first, he began to write the small poems. They poured out like a flood and formed in his brain asleep and awake. Everything he observed or had experienced began to shape itself in a natural flow into a poem. Within a few months he had written 4,000. As they grew in number he attached the pages to a steel frame so that while lying in bed he could refer to the earlier ones quickly. Repetition was easy and care had to be exercised because the poetry was not as simple as it appeared. The writing of haikus required enormous skill and discipline. They seemed to answer the rawness he felt, which had, in turn, created a sensitivity that ached. Never had he been so sensitive, as if his nervous system had been exposed to rough air. All his nervous energy was harnessed by the haikus. But the frames on which the hand-written poems were strung became too heavy for him to hold and he hired a stenographer to type them, seven to a page. When he held them and could carry them around in his hands he felt extraordinary pleasure. They weighed only a pound or two. What crazy things I think of, he mused. "Yet, the physical weight of those haikus is an important thing to me." They were such fragile things, like spider webs. "They may not be worth a damn." But he began an agonizing job of selecting 800 from the 4,000 to make into a small book.

> A balmy spring wind
> Reminding me of something
> I cannot recall.

The green cockleburrs
Caught in the thick wooly hair
Of the black boy's head.

Standing in the field,
I hear the whispering of
Snowflake to snowflake.

It is September
The month in which I was born,
And I have no thoughts.

While he was engrossed in the poems Richard's health improved steadily and he looked forward to a summer in the country. The blue Paris sky began to intensify and change color as the sun grew brighter and stayed overhead longer each day. There were many places he could stay in Normandy, but he wanted to be alone. Many people were boring and wasted his time. He explained what he felt to Margrit: ". . . I'd like to be alone, as much alone as possible. Have you taken solitude for your friend? I have. When I'm alone and wake up in the morning, with my world of dreams close by me, I write without effort. By noon, I've done a day's work. All else, after that, is gravy, as the Americans say."

At last, by June, he had weeded out what he thought were the best haikus and Richard mailed them to Bill Targ for an opinion. A moment after they were mailed he felt a flash of guilt. He had not even mentioned the poems to his agent and had automatically sent them to Targ because they had lunched together in March and he asked to see them.[4] What would Paul think if he heard that a manuscript he knew nothing about was over at World? Rushing home, he typed a letter to his agent:

Listen, today I've sent to William Targ of World Publishers a ms. of poems. Now I did not send you this little ms. first (it runs to 80 pages) because I feel that it has no commercial value. And I don't know if you would want to handle poetry or not. The ms. was not submitted to World, but sent to Targ as my personal friend for his reaction. . . . Targ is an old friend of mine and has good judgment. Have you met him yet? You'll like him.

These poems are the results of my being in bed a great deal and it is likely that they are bad. I don't know. But don't get worried that I'm going daft. I'm turning back to fiction now. . . .[5]

June and July in Paris were cool and at Moulin d'Ande, Saint Pierre du Vauray Eure, along the Seine, where Richard went to stay, it was cold. And there was rain, rain, rain but he had an oil stove in his room and each morning made a fire to dry up the humidity. He rested and he was almost content. Some days he felt gloomy and depressed, but his nervousness had decreased and he was sleeping ten and twelve hours a night without sedation. On sunny days he walked along the Seine, which was a purer blue than in Paris and once he decided to fish. Unfortunately, he caught a small fish within a few minutes and its gaping mouth and wildly lashing tail were revolting. He took the hook out of its mouth and threw the small gilled creature back into the river.

In August he recognized the beginning of a compulsion toward working out a new idea and he put the novel in the center of his mind and thought about it day and night. He welcomed the obsession but decided not to sit at the typewriter for a week or two until he was less tired. Writing was not only mental and emotional work, but physical work also. But the ideas worked out more quickly than he had thought possible and he sat down to the Underwood and began banging it out morning and night. It made him feel much better. Somewhat surprised, he examined his new strength: writing for him must act as a therapeutic measure. He wrote piles of letters saying no, no, no, to introductions, essays and articles. Funny, he thought, how saying no frees one. "Now, I'm free with white sheets of paper before me and a head full of wild ideas, ideas that excite me. Maybe writing with me is like being psychoanalyzed. I feel all the poison being drained out." The theme had him by the throat[6] and by the end of August he had reached page 300 of a first draft and it flowed on and on. Again, he was awed and slightly astonished by the writing process and the seeming ease with which ideas worked themselves out.

A slow drizzling rain was falling on September 6 when Richard began to pack for his return to Paris, but he was happy and excited. Julia was arriving on the 15 to stay for a week; then friends from England on the 16; friends from Australia on the 17; friends from Nashville on the 25; and Dorothy Padmore, whose husband had died, was arriving from Ghana via Russia. He wanted to put his dusty apartment in order and have the rain spots washed off the windows.

Three days after Julia's arrival Richard became ill again. It was diagnosed by Schwartzmann as a liver upset with no relation to his amoebic sickness. The antibiotics he had to take lowered his vision and he placed a new light over his desk. But his doctor assured him that the liver upset was only a temporary setback. Whatever gloom he was feeling lifted miraculously when Julia decided to stay in Paris. "I want to be with Daddy," she wrote to her mother. Richard watched his daughter and kept silent while she made a decision about her future. They had long conversations for the first time on literature and art and politics. He was enormously pleased and satisfied with his slim daughter. People, in his opinion, meant only so much as they could project out of themselves, and his daughter did not escape that judgment. It was a good sign that she no longer talked only of herself, for he felt that when people talked of themselves incessantly it indicated that something was wrong. Finally, Julia made up her mind: she would remain in Paris and attend the Sorbonne and the British Institute. She did not want to go to Cambridge and would return to London, pick up her school records and enter school in the fall. Hurrah! her father cheered silently. She had made it on her own. That was a good thing. He watched her growing calm and confident and he wanted to write to Margrit about his lovely daughter.

"She's wonderful," he wrote, ". . . she seems quite happy and confident that she made the right decision. I like for her to come and have coffee with me and we talk about things in general. . . . Julia has been a great help; I feel that she likes to help me . . . she had a hard inner struggle about Cambridge and I feel that she is in a much better mood now that she has given it up."[7]

For a few days following Dorothy Padmore's visit Richard's spirits dipped again. When they talked about Africa he worried that Nkrumah did not have the intelligence to grasp the magnitude of what was fighting him and his people. Dorothy was suffering. She felt that the Prime Minister was too isolated from his people, surrounded by Party officials and that the British CID and the American CIA were working with his opposition to remove him from power. His Pan-Africanism was too great a threat. It hurt Richard to watch Dorothy hiding her bitterness. The government gave her barely enough to live on and nothing else. All of the archives of the revolutionary struggle were in her keeping but after her husband's death she was cast aside.[8]

A few days after Dorothy left Paris Richard's spirits soared when he opened a package from Bill Targ of World which contained jacket proofs and posters advertising *Eight Men*. Proudly, he put a poster up in his living room. An accompanying letter from Targ explained World's enthusiastic plans for an extensive advertising campaign for *Eight Men*. Some of his financial worries began to lift and he grew more sanguine about the future: there was so much to do; he would go to Africa again; he wanted to see Cuba—something was happening there that was new and exciting—Sartre was going to bring out a book; he would finish the short novel on which he was working and begin the third volume of Fishbelly.

During September a very old friend, whom he met first in Chicago, came to see him with his wife. Arna Bontemps shared with Richard a secret; their early mutual exposure to the Seventh-Day Adventists. Moreover, Richard's grandmother had been a member of Arna's minister-brother-in-law's church. Richard never tired of talking about the peculiarities of that religion. Arna was full of new anecdotes and the two men had an intimacy whose nuances were as if they had shared a portion of their childhood. Happily, almost joyously, he took the Bontemps' to meet many of his friends and when their reservation at the Grand Hotel expired he found them a place on Rue Regis, near his apartment.

At the end of September he enjoyed a visit from Herbert Hill, member of the faculty at the New School in Greenwich Village, and national labor secretary of the National Association for the Advancement of Colored People. Richard had met Hill years before, when he lived on Lefferts Place in Brooklyn. He had been a very young, enthusiastic man, with a shock of straight black hair, and Richard always remembered him ducking his head slightly when he entered a room because he towered well over six feet in height. Herbert wanted Richard's suggestions and advice on a book he was planning on the writings of Negroes from 1940 to 1962, and Richard agreed to write an introduction for *Soon, One Morning*. Toward the end of Herbert's visit Richard's stomach began to nag at him again, but he insisted upon taking him to the Gare Montparnasse. In the French manner, Richard embraced Hill before he stepped onto the train.

Again, depression fell on Richard's spirits; when would he feel really well? It lifted when he received his telephone call from Ellen. They had arranged that one day she would call Paris and the alternating one he would call London. She had taken over as his literary representative in England and had already received an enthusiastic response from four different publishers. All of these Ellen turned over to Rose, who was Reynolds' subagent. She was in bubbling spirits and if she sold his books there would not only be money but perhaps eventually they would keep the 10 percent commission to an agent in the family. And they made plans for his wife to handle his work in France, the Eastern countries and Holland. He was gleeful when he hung up the telephone. He had never trusted that man in Holland anyway.

Margrit was alarmed when she received a letter from Richard on

October 25: X rays showed inflammation of the stomach and the doctor had discontinued the massive doses of bismuth. His intestines were healed but something in his stomach needed attention. He was tired, now. When he tried to type, sweat started all over his body. Margrit must not worry; she had helped him a lot, more than she knew. How wonderful that was and how wonderful it remained.

"We fret, we feel frustrated, but things are moving on the broad scale. We must never forget that."

The evening of November 8, Richard spoke before a huge and rapt audience in the American Church in Paris. The speech had been so successful that he considered making a short book of it. Reverend Clayton Williams told him that he had never heard so much excited and appreciative comment. When he returned home he looked rather wistfully at the bottle of champagne friends had brought and put it aside. It was forbidden; he could have nothing fermented. Well, he thought, and poured a little whiskey into a glass, he would save it for friends.

A few days after his speech at the Church Richard came down with the grippe and ran a high fever. His high temperature continued until at last Dr. Schwartzmann began injections of 1,000,000 units of penicillin daily. Within a few days his fever left him and he got out of bed and sat on the green couch in the front room. Inertia gripped him and the fever had stirred up his sensitive intestinal tract so the doses of antibiotics were continued. Julia and friends came every day to shop and prepare meals and he began to feel better. He called Hélène Bokanowski and made arrangements to go to Croisilles, packed his bags, and then promised Dr. Schwartzmann that he would go into the clinic for a checkup before he left.

A cold gray sky covered Paris on November 25; it had been drizzling for several days. Richard dressed carefully in a gray suit, white shirt, and tie for the trip to the clinic. The effort was exhausting and he lay down on the bed, its foot facing the doorway, and Julia covered her father with a quilt. When the doorbell rang, he lifted his head from the pillow expecting to see Dr. Schwartzmann but it was another visitor: a man he had not seen for over fourteen years. The big man poked his nose into the door of the room and without salutation, as if he had seen Richard the day before, Langston Hughes guffawed: "Man, you look like you are ready to go to glory!"⁹ Richard burst into laughter and pushed aside the quilt to step out of bed. He explained that he was going for a checkup in a few minutes and the two men made plans to meet when he returned. Schwartzmann arrived, but before Richard left he turned back into his study and picked up a copy of a play he had translated into

English. He had fallen in love with *Papa Bon Dieu,* by Louis Sapin, and had retitled it *Daddy Goodness.* It was a wise folk tale, ironic and full of laughter. "Man, it's right up your alley," Richard exclaimed to Hughes. "Read it and see what you can do about its production in America." Then Julia helped her father into his topcoat and saw him into the car.

At the Clinique Chirurgicale Eugéne Gibez, Richard entered a private room and began a series of tests for the amoeba. All of the tests were negative. The amoebas had disappeared and the stomach upset had been caused by the case of grippe. His liver was in order and blood pressure, temperature and weight were good. Happily, Richard picked up the telephone and placed a call to his wife in London. Now, he would get to work again on a long fictional work. The city made him feel numb with fatigue but he was leaving the following day. It would be good to get among trees and fresh air again.

During the evening of November 28 Richard sat in a large armchair and read all of the newspapers. He felt very happy and calm but at about ten o'clock when he became tired he climbed into the high narrow bed. Thank goodness, he thought, there wasn't anything seriously wrong and most of the annoyances of the last half year were out of the way. He would go into the green countryside and work fourteen and fifteen hours at a stretch; then he would get into the car and roll to Rouen or some other place to sit and drink a beer or a cognac. His nurse entered the room, rustling in her starchy uniform, and they talked for twenty minutes. Richard told her stories until she became breathless from laughter and at last she said good night. A few minutes before eleven o'clock Richard placed the book he was reading on the metal-topped bedside table. It was time to go to sleep. Big day tomorrow, he mused. Apparently, before he turned out the light over his bed a sharp pain stabbed his body and he reached out his right hand for the signal light.

Three minutes later the floor nurse came out of another patient's room, looked up the hallway and saw Richard's light. She walked quietly in her rubber-soled shoes to his room and entered. Richard lay on his back, his head turned toward the door, an apologetic smile on his lips as though to excuse himself for disturbing her. Before he could speak he simply seemed to fall away; his face smoothed of lines.

Richard Wright was dead at fifty-two years of age.

When Ellen arrived from London the following day and went to the hospital with Julia, they were taken below ground to the clinic mortuary where Richard lay encased in "snow." His face was serene but someone had placed a spray of flowers in his clasped hands. It seemed so incongruous there against his still chest that Ellen and Julia exchanged glances—words were not necessary—and Ellen removed it. The following day Ellen came to the clinic again, bringing with her a copy of *Black Boy*. When she approached the body of her husband to place the book at his side she saw that his hands, so tightly clasped the day before, had opened and lay lightly below his heart as if a complete relaxation had taken place.

On a gray and steadily drizzling December 3, 1960, Richard's body was cremated at the Père Lachaise crematory. Next to his body as it slid into the flames lay the copy of *Black Boy*. After a long wait Ellen and Julia followed an urn, carried by attendants on a gray velvet palanquin, to a creche in the Columbarium Père Lachaise. Creche number 4596 stood open, awaiting the silent procession. A moment after the urn was placed into its niche Ellen placed her right hand into the opening for a second; the urn still radiated the heat from its contents and she had a fleeting impression that she had again come into contact with the warmth of her husband's body.

Later, in her father's empty study, Julia sat with his haikus. Finally, she picked up a pen and wrote: "This is Daddy."

> Burning out its time,
> And timing its own burning,
> One lonely candle.

Notes

Chapter I
"It's them goddamn rebels . . ."

1. Jesse T. Wallace, *A History of the Negroes of Mississippi, from 1865 to 1890* (Clinton, Miss. Thesis, PhD. Columbia University, 1928), p. 23.
2. Frederick Douglass, *Life and Times of Frederick Douglass, Written by himself, and His Early Life as a Slave, his Escape From Bondage, and his complete History to the Present etc.* (Hartford, Conn.: Park Publishing Company, 1884), p. 611.
3. In *Black Boy* Wright incorrectly listed the name as Vinson. Correspondence in the National Archives, Washington, D.C., shows the name as Vincent; he served in the Navy and not the Army as his grandson had remembered.
4. Richard Wright, *Black Boy* (New York: Harper & Brothers, 1945), p. 122.
5. *Ibid.*, p. 89.

Chapter II
Richard is born, 1908

1. *Black Boy*, pp. 3, 4, 5, 6, and confirmed in conversation with Richard Wright.
2. Unpublished ms., *Freedom's Lonely Song.*
2A. *Ibid.*, p. 7.
3. David L. Cohn, *Life & Times of King Cotton* (New York: Oxford University, 1956), p. 232.
4. *Ibid.*, p. 233.

Chapter III
Memphis, Tennessee, Dread and distrust . . .

1. Wright believed that his mother transferred her emotional longings to him when Nathan deserted the household. There was a Calvinistic emphasis on the denial or control of emotion, particularly in front of strangers, which resulted in violent explosions at home. He sensed under Ella's hysteria a sexual deprivation, which made him uneasy. "We were too close and yet too far apart. Sometimes she made me feel so guilty for her blighted life that I wanted to run away." He admitted that her excessive preachments stemmed from her fear that he would get into trouble. Alan Wright told the author that his brother's great interest in people and personalities, which he believes was owing to the fact that Richard was "a born poet, writer and critic," caused him to be in constant difficulty with playmates, parents

and other members of the family even as a tiny child. A creative individual was in great danger in the South.
2. *Black Boy*, p. 26.

Chapter IV
Terror . . . some natural force

1. *Black Boy*, p. 40.
2. *Ibid.*, p. 48.
3. Scipio A. Jones, *The Arkansas Peons*, a brief reviewing the case for presentation to the Supreme Court of the United States. Unpublished, given to the author by L. C. Bates, editor/publisher of *The Arkansas State Press*, Little Rock, Ark.
4. Richard Wright, *The Long Dream* (New York: Doubleday & Company, 1958), p. 25.
5. Wright told the author this story, adding that relations between white women and black men were common in the South. They usually ended in disaster.
6. *Black Boy*, p. 68.
7. *Ibid.*, p. 65.

Chapter V
A somberness of spirit

1. *Black Boy*, pp. 76, 77.
2. *Ibid.*, p. 87.
3. Wright thought that he had attended three private schools but could only remember two: the Seventh-Day Adventists' and the orphanage, Settlement Home.
4. Across the street from the school is a cemetery and in it is a large statue of Jim Hill, who played a part during Reconstruction. He was known in the community as an appeaser who had been an Uncle Tom and sold the black man's birthright to politicians who denied them the vote in Jackson. When Richard Wright was a teenager Hill was a community joke—he was the white man's hero not the Negro's.
5. Richard Jordan, "Squilla," is Griggs in *Black Boy*. During preliminary work on that book Wright went to Chicago to talk to Jordan, who gave him detailed information about trains and work as a porter. Jordan died an alcoholic and Richard's reaction was: "My brilliant young friend was wasted by society—just thrown down the drain."
6. "Big Boy Leaves Home" contains a description of the creek in which Wright swam with his friends.
7. Bigger Thomas in *Native Son* was patterned on the real Bigger Thomas of Jackson.
8. A permanent horror remained in Wright all his life at the lynching of Bob Robinson. His brother, Carl T. Robinson, attended Howard University Law School and Richard visited him a number of times in Washington, D.C. Time and again, in conversation and in his fiction, he described Bob's lynching. It appears in *Long Dream*, *Black Boy*, "Big Boy Leaves Home" and other unpublished stories. "One lynching is the mutilation and murder of countless black men north and south," Richard told the author.

Chapter VI
The white South has never known me . . .

1. *Black Boy*, p. 157.
2. *Ibid.*, p. 162.
3. Joe C. Brown letters. *The Negro Vanguard* by Richard Bardolph (New York: Vintage Books, 1961) lists Giles Hubert as a foreign services officer—Chief of Educational Mission in Afghanistan. He also served in India.
4. *Ibid.*
5. Arthur Leaner later changed his name and became a well-known disc jockey and radio personality.
6. *Black Boy*, p. 222.
7. *Ibid.*, p. 227.

Chapter VII
Chicago seemed an unreal city . . .

1. Most of the material in this chapter is from the last third of *Black Boy*, which Richard Wright gave to the author, who printed it for private circulation.
2. Maggie was not afraid; she had lived in a large city, Detroit, and Wright admitted that he had read his own fears into his aunt.
3. *Black Boy*, p. 54.
4. Last third of *Black Boy*, see above. p. 4.
5. *Ibid.*, pp. 16, 17.

Chapter VIII
". . . as though offering libations of forgiveness to my environment."

1. Last third of *Black Boy*, p. 23.
2. *Ibid.*, p. 27.
3. Description given to the author by Richard Wright.
4. H. F. Gosnell *Negro Politicians* (Chicago: University of Chicago, 1935), p. 39.
5. Last third of *Black Boy*, p. 39.
6. *Ibid.*, p. 41.
7. "We later found out that he was talking to spirits in another world."
8. The name for the new business was Richard's suggestion.
9. After Richard Wright became a well-known writer he often wrote to Joe C. Brown asking about Leaner and whether Arthur "had the idea that in his writings he too was being tricky and using underhanded methods for getting ahead."
10. Last third of *Black Boy*, p. 50.
11. Wright wrote a protest of the episode (which was not published) entitled *Hymn to the Rising Sun* after Paul Green's title.

Chapter IX
All my life I had been full of a hunger for a new way to live . . .

1. St. Claire Drake, "Hide My Face?" in *Soon, One Morning*, ed. by Herbert Hill (New York: Alfred A. Knopf, 1963).
2. Jan Wittenber is portrayed in *Native Son* as Jan Erlone. Wright jokingly used "Erlone" to signify his affection toward Wittenber. He said that he *alone* during that period, although a cultural whip for the Party, was a man of humanity, capable of a depth of understanding not found in many white comrades.
3. Essay by Richard Wright in *The God That Failed*, ed. Richard Crossman (New York: Harper & Brothers, 1950).
4. Richard Wright, "I Have Seen Black Hands," *New Masses*, 1934.
5. Last third of *Black Boy*, p. 58.
6. *Ibid.*, p. 73.
7. *Ibid.*, p. 71.
8. Wright said that Waldo Frank's writing was important to him because of its lyricism and social analysis and the portrayal of the tragedy of racial hatred in *Holiday, City Block, Dawn in Russia*. He saw in the work a desire similar to his own for a communal life.
9. Wright was reading E. M. Forster. He admitted that he was not the most affable of comrades because he was always busy writing.
10. Richard Wright, notes for a preface to *Uncle Tom's Children*, unpublished. Copy in the files of the author.
11. Last third of *Black Boy*, p. 85.
12. Daniel Aaron, *Writers on the Left* (New York: Harcourt, Brace & World Inc., Avon Library edition 1965), p. 315.
13. Trachtenberg was not Turkish. Jack Conroy gave the author the following story:

"When I attended the first American Writers' Congress in New York in 1935 somebody told me that Trachty and other party pundits had cornered Theodore Dreiser and took him to task about some recent statements he had made which seemed anti-Semitic. Dreiser, sweating profusely and mopping his face repeatedly with a handkerchief (a habit of his), suddenly shouted 'Get that goddam Sicilian out of here before he sticks a knife in my back!' "

14. Last third of *Black Boy*, pp. 83, 84.
15. *Ibid.*, p. 84.
16. Daniel Aaron, *Writers on the Left*, p. 173.
17. Richard Wright, "Joe Louis Uncovers Dynamite," *New Masses* XVII, Oct. 8, 1935.
18. Wright was at work on two novels: *Tarbaby's Dawn* (originally *Tarbaby's Sunrise*) and *Lawd Today*. *Tarbaby* was not published.
19. Wright said that a few months after his refusal an anti-Communist black man he knew joined the Party to make the trip.
20. Actually the term existentialist (which Sartre deplored) did not yet exist but developed after World War II. Richard Wright was, in a sense, antecedent to the French existentialists.
21. Boris Souvarine, *Stalin*, translated by C. L. R. James (New York: Longmans, Green, & Co., 1939), p. 626.
22. Several trials were held by the Party. One in the spring of 1931 in New York concerned August Yokinen, an immigrant Finn who belonged to the Party and earned his living as a janitor for the Finnish Workers Club in Harlem. One evening, at a dance sponsored by the Club three Negroes appeared and were treated with a lack of courtesy. The Party ordered an investigation and all club members expressed their regrets except Yokinen. It was suggested that Yokinen neither understood nor spoke more than a few words of English and probably did not know what was happening. However, the Party staged a public trial to publicize its position on the Negro. On March 1, 1931, a "Workers Court" convened in Harlem and was attended by 1,500 people. Clarence Hathaway acted as prosecuting attorney and Richard Moore, head of the Negro department of the International Labor Defense, acted as defense attorney. Alfred Wagenknecht, a veteran Communist, served as judge. A workers' "jury" of fourteen voted unanimously to expel Yokinen despite his plea for mercy. Information on this is from Irving Howe and Lewis Coser's *The American Communist Party* (New York: Frederick Praeger, 1962), pp. 209–211.
23. Last third of *Black Boy*, p. 113.
24. Conversation with Richard Wright in Wading River, Long Island, N.Y., the summer he left for France. He had been under severe criticism by liberals and other leftists who demanded to know why he stayed in the Party after the trials in Russia and the abrupt change of line when Russia was attacked by Germany.

Chapter X
New York, 1937

1. This detailed description of his arrival in New York via train and the journey on the IRT was given to the author by Richard Wright. Mrs. Wright says that actually it is a fiction and that her husband drove in a car to New York with friends.
2. Richard Wright, *Blue Print for Negro Writing*, *New Challenge* II, Fall 1937. Information of this period in this section is from Wright, Benjamin Davis and James Ford.
3. James W. Ford and William L. Patterson worked out of the Harlem Bureau. Richard Wright told the writer that Ford was "Earl's [Browder] Uncle Tom" and that he was always attacking Ben Davis. Ellison told the author that Richard said that Ford and Patterson made life "hard" for Davis and were contemptuous of Richard, who "hated the two men." Ellison also told the author that he was never a witness to their conflict.
4. Ellison wrote the author that Wright seemed to require opposition and "dwelled

upon the antagonism of fellows who were little more than newsboys who delivered the *Daily Worker*."

5. Ellison explained his great interest in Wright prior to their meeting: "I had been reading lots of modern poetry and works on its technique, and this was the first time *I* had found the spirit and techniques of modern poetry present in a Negro writer."

6. Ellison told the author that he "had been interested in sculpture only for a year, while I had been playing and studying music from the age of eight. At the time I was trying to get back to Tuskegee to complete what would have been my senior year. I had played in bands and orchestras during grade and high school and college, and in high school I was student leader (conductor) of the band, held first chair in the trumpet section of the orchestra, and was also student conductor of the Tuskegee band. . . . During the first year (1937) I knew [Richard], I studied for a while with Wallingford Reigger at the Downtown Music School."

7. From Ralph Ellison regarding his apprenticeship with Richard Wright: ". . . as for writing, I had been playing with words in the form of verse since the 11th grade in high school but had no idea of becoming a writer. Nevertheless, there are quite a number of people at Tuskegee and a few now living in New York who knew of my interest in literature and its techniques. And I have two texts on the techniques of poetry enscribed and given to me by a faculty member at Tuskegee long before I met Wright."

8. Ralph Ellison, *Shadow and Act* (New York: Signet, The New American Library, 1966).

9. After "Hymies Bull" Ralph Ellison wrote some 200 pages on a novel, part of which was later published in *Direction,* but he was unable to finish it. The piece was "Slick Gonna Learn" but this and other stories he was writing convinced him that they were "too *un*formed, and as a musician who had studied *The Harmophonic Forms of Musical Composition* [he] didn't know why [his] stories weren't working, but [he] had, nonetheless, an acute feeling for their incompleteness and lack of resonance. . . ."

10. *Daily Worker,* July 15, 1937.

11. Richard Wright, "There Are Still Men Left," unpublished notes.

12. *Ibid.*

13. *New Masses,* XXXIX, June 17, 1941.

14. Richard Wright to Paul Green, Dec. 21, 1941.

15. This document by Wright is approximately 1,500 words. It urges dissemination of facts for the purpose of clarifying public opinion among Negroes to demonstrate their inescapable stake in the war; a dissemination of facts to the colored peoples of the world acquainting them with the advantages of the democratic way of life as opposed to the fascistic, Nazi, and Japanese militaristic systems. The proposal outlines a plan of propaganda through radio, church, schools, Negro press, writers, actors, painters, musicians, slogan buttons, emblems, broadsides, posters, etc. By this time *Native Son* had been published as well as its adaptation into a play. He added new lines to the play and modified the speech of the Communist attorney to include an expression of the willingness of Negroes to fight in the war.

Chapter XI
I love my people . . .

1. Horace Cayton, at that time journalist for the Pittsburgh *Courier,* was one of the people who gave this information to Wright. Cayton also mentioned it in his column written in response to an attack against Wright by Ben Davis after he left the Party.

2. Interview of Richard Wright, *Afro-American,* Jan. 13, 1945.

3. "Richard Wright and Antonio R. Frasconi: Exchange of Letters," *Twice a Year,* XII–XIII, (1945).

4. Among some white reviewers was the notion that Wright was a "natural" writer without knowledge of why and how he used technique to obtain certain effects. He became so irritated one day that he wrote the essay "How Bigger Was Born" (*Satur-*

day Review of Literature, June 1, 1940), to demonstrate how consciously he had gone about writing *Native Son.* He told the author that the reason white critics insisted upon the "natural" theory of his work was sheer bigotry, perhaps unconscious, but flowing from a deep-rooted conviction that Negroes could be clever, like performing monkeys, but that they had not the capacity to master a literary style.

5. *Shadow and Act,* Ralph Ellison expounded the ideas of the young Negro critic Edward Bland.

6. Richard Wright, notes for a preface to *Uncle Tom's Children,* unpublished.

Chapter XII
Native Son

1. *Daily News,* Jackson, Miss. April 26, 1938.

2. Three letters were written by Mrs. Roosevelt: to Eugene Saxton, March 4, 1938, commenting on *Uncle Tom's Children* and asking when she might write it up in her column; to Richard Wright, August 30, 1938, stating she would be happy to sponsor him for the Guggenheim, and another to him in February, 1939, when he received the award, she wrote congratulating him on its receipt.

3. Richard Wright, "How Bigger Was Born," *Saturday Review of Literature,* June 1, 1940. This was not written, of course, until after publication of *Native Son.*

4. *Ibid.*

5. "Daltonism" is a medical term for a form of blindness. Dr. Fredric Wertham, a friend of Wright's, persuaded him to submit to analysis briefly to determine the unconscious determinants in *Native Son.* See Wertham's article in *The Journal of Criminal Psychopathology,* Vol. VI, No. I, pages 111–116, July 1944. Richard was curious about psychoanalysis but extremely skeptical. He said it might be true that Wertham was correct and that he had used the name Dalton to signify color blindness, but Dalton was also the name of a street near where he had lived in Jackson.

6. Richard Wright, *Native Son* (New York: Harper & Brothers, 1940), pp. 74, 75. Wright said Negroes often wished that liberals would stop greeting them with sticky kisses and just accept them as individuals.

7. In 1937 Wright visited Ted Ward at the Oakland Manor Hotel in Chicago to read the first act of Ward's play *Big White Fog.* Richard said it was "epic." Following publication of *Uncle Tom's Children* Richard visited Chicago again but saw Ward only briefly. Ward writes that "a friend had called it to my attention that Wright had not hesitated to pirate the title of my play 'Big White Fog' for use in his 'Fire and Cloud,' as being an original observation of his hero's conception of the race's position in the surrounding white world. I did not know at the time how unscrupulous he was capable of being, so I did not say anything about it, but he sensed that I was cold toward him and soon went about his business. Despite my knowledge of his piracy, however, I think I must have taken it merely as a personal slight due to Wright's desire to get ahead, his drive to say something important about the life of our people."

8. Mack Parker, taken from a jail and lynched, many years after Wright wrote his story, was dragged down a flight of stairs by his heels, his head bumping the metal grids on each stair.

Chapter XIII
Dhima or Ellen?

1. "I thought he was a splendid looking creature," Ellen Wright told the author.

2. Ellen Wright's birth was not immediately registered and when it was recorded it was put down as Sept. 3. In checking records, years later, she discovered that she had actually been born on Sept. 4, the same day as her husband though years later.

3. Letter from Theodore Ward.

4. Richard Wright to Lawrence Martin, Feb. 5, 1940.

5. Letter from Theodore Ward. Wright took Ralph Ellison to meet Dhima and Utis, supposedly to get his opinion. Ellison was noncomittal because he felt that Richard was already very much in love and he had "shared Dick's concern about an earlier marriage [intention]."

6. Theodore Ward "got kicked out of the house [in Brooklyn] for nearly setting [it] afire by falling asleep with a burning cigarette." He moved to the Douglass Hotel and Richard followed shortly after.

7. Wright had been going with another girl and invitations were sent out for their wedding. When they went for blood tests it was discovered that the girl had congenital syphilis. Richard broke off the relationship at once. Ellison said that he was worried that the girl might become a life-long invalid like his mother. The incident haunted Richard and many years later became the basis for a novelette *A Father's Law* (unpublished). The story's hero is tormented by the notion that he "killed" his ex-fiance by abandoning her and ruining her life.

8. Wright took Jean Blackwell (Mrs. Jean Hutson, Curator, Schomburg Collection, New York Public Library) to the stage play *Of Mice and Men*. Richard's pained enjoyment was a revelation to her. She says that during agonized moments of the play Richard beat his chest with his fists. It had never occurred to her that emotional agony could be enjoyable and the experience opened areas of understanding in the young girl which she has never forgotten. Mrs. Hutson also told the author that Richard seemed to assume that she was in love with him although they were merely friends. After his marriage to Dhima he sent Jean friendly notes to reassure her ego, which, of course, she did not need but thought of as an example of his kindness.

9. Ralph Ellison does not believe that Wright had any such qualms. He had known many white women, however, both Theodore and Jean Hutson say that he consulted them about these fears. He told Mrs. Hutson that "Probably none of my friends will speak to me for marrying a white woman."

10. Richard Wright, *The Outsider* (New York: Harper & Brothers, 1953). This passage has been quoted because Richard told the author that it corresponded exactly with attitudes he held toward his mother. Richard said that his devotion to his mother was so intense that it had to be attacked as an enemy if his own personality was to survive.

11. Calvin C. Hernton, *Sex and Racism in America*, Doubleday, 1965, suggests that the taboos in relation to white women resulting in extreme peril may stimulate the black man in pursuit as a new frontier in the American tradition. "Indeed it is this sort of spirit or 'guts' that has made America a great nation. The rugged individualist, the man who transcends the chains of background and provincialism to surge ahead toward new frontiers is an American hero." And Hernton's remarks, particularly that there seems to be a mutual conspiracy between white women and black men, was a concept held by Wright in the late '40's.

12. Conversation with Ellen Wright.

13. Ellen Wright has never forgotten Richard's statement: It was crushing and "after someone says something like that, what is there to say? I just felt a complete hopelessness."

14. Wright told the author that *Life* magazine paid him 50 percent less than they would have paid a white writer.

15. Wright was almost ashamed to admit that he had never read *Up From Slavery*. He had escaped being educated in Negro institutions and never got around to reading those books which everyone was supposed to read. He did know that the greatest split among educated Negroes of a generation or so ago was over Washington's proposals.

16. Wright was surprised when he received a check from *Harper's Bazaar* for $200. He had written the story five years before and laid it aside thinking it had no sales value. He said, "The story is not so hot, as stories go." A friend of his who was collecting material for an anthology asked for a short piece and he gave him "Almos' a Man." When the anthology was not published the friend sent it to

George Davis at *Harper's*. Richard asked his agent to deduct $20 commission since normally he would have handled the sale of the story.

17. Ralph Ellison said that Wright went to Mexico to escape the attacks by the Communists. He also wanted to escape what he felt was a war hysteria building up in the United States.

18. Richard Wright, MS originally entitled *Little Sister* and then *Maud* (unpublished). It was intended as a social commentary on the role of women in American society. Its heroine whitened her skin by taking arsenic wafers orally. In 1940 he had completed 960 pages and finished the novel before he left the Communist Party in 1942. The last third disintegrates into a story consistent with Party mentality. The first two-thirds is extraordinary.

19. Steinbeck later came to the conclusion that he had been wrong in his judgment and the two men became friendly.

20. When Wright met Orson Welles and worked with him he observed him closely. Welles' genius fascinated him and he said "he is not a man but some kind of creative engine."

21. Paul Reynolds Jr. submitted a list of playwrights to Wright, who said that he wanted only Paul Green. Green had been accused of "artiness" but Richard dismissed the criticism. What was important to Richard was that Green possessed a knowledge of the Negro and his life, great skill as a playwright, and the integrity to portray Bigger Thomas as he had been written.

22. Ralph Ellison and his first wife, Rose, had been living at 25 Hamilton Terrace on the ground floor rear and gave up their apartment with its terrace and boxes of rambler roses reluctantly. It was an act of friendship. They hoped that Dhima and Richard might become reconciled if given a chance to see one another. The apartment they shared with Dhima rented for $56.00 a month and was not luxurious even in 1940. But Richard, nevertheless, felt that it was his money that paid for the apartment. If he had asked, Ralph could have shown him the rent receipts with his portion listed but it never occurred to him to do so. The estrangement from Dhima had been growing for many months and by the time he reached New York he was utterly disinterested and in a mood to be critical of anyone who made an arrangement with a person who had become a stranger to him.

23. When the reconciliation failed Dhima moved out of the apartment, causing an abrupt hardship for Ellison and his wife.

24. When Richard and Ellen Wright went to obtain visas in Paris he was asked the last name of his ex-wife. He could not remember and hissed across the room to Ellen, "What was her name?" Neither could remember so Ellen said, "Just put Cooper or Smith, put anything."

Chapter XIV
Ellen and Julia

1. Ellison wrote for the *New Masses* but never joined the Party. "I wasn't on the make in that sense. I wrote what I felt and wasn't in awe of functionaries and published where I could. I only wanted to be a writer, not a leader of anything or a politician." He was perhaps the only writer the Party paid for articles. When he told them that he would not write unless he was paid—"I was surprised. They paid." He received fifteen dollars for the article on the National Negro Congress.

2. Gunnar Myrdal, *An American Dilemma* (New York: Harper & Brothers, 1944).

3. Book of Ruth 1:16.

4. Ellison says that after an intimate involvement in bringing Richard and Ellen together again they did not tell him of their marriage. Richard was in one of his secretive periods, "a conspiratorial mood. When he told something to me in utter confidence telling me not to tell anyone else and I soon discovered he had told others the same thing. Some of the things I couldn't care less about even as gossip." Visiting at their home on Revere Place, Ellison deduced their marriage by stray remarks.

5. Wright became an expert photographer; he and Ellen designed a combination bed, desk and bookcase unit which A. D. Bates, a Harlem furniture maker, constructed.
6. Oliver Evans, *Carson McCullers, Her Life and Work* (London: Peter Owen, 1965).

Chapter XV
Black Boy

1. Margot Johnson to Richard Wright, Dec. 30, 1937. Horace Cayton, in *Anger and Beyond*, tells a story that Richard did not reach Miss Watkins' office at all, having been offended by an elevator operator who told him to take the freight elevator—the only means of entrance—which he interpreted as racial prejudice. The episode is not true, but it is not impossible that Richard may have told such a story to Cayton, since he loved to spin out real and imagined stories for friends.
2. Regarding Miss Watkins, Ellen Wright said, "Dick fled in horror from her after a short association to take refuge with Reynolds."
3. Wright arranged a gift by Paul Reynolds, Jr., of Dunbar's letters to the Schomburg Collection in Harlem.
4. Reynolds wrote to Wright on March 2, 1939: "I would be prepared to say without hesitation that Bigger is not only the equal but superior to the protagonist in Theodore Dreiser's AMERICAN TRAGEDY."
5. Reynolds would approach the job of street-cleaner with the same devotion and sober attention.
6. Full account of this trip is in notes prepared for a speech on Negro Literature (unpublished).
7. Horace Cayton in his autobiography, *Long Old Road* Trident Press (1965) describes a trip South with Wright. During the night he saw that he was lying in his berth fully clothed and awake. At Cayton's question Richard answered: "When I'm down South, I want steel between me and those white folks, not just a cloth curtain."
8. Unpublished MS given to the author by Richard Wright. The material was in part an intended lecture on "The Literature of the Negro in the United States" which was in part published in *White Man, Listen!* (New York: Doubleday & Co., 1957).
9. An episode concerning Richard and Uncle Hoskins (*Black Boy*, pp. 45–47) was based on an incident told him by Ralph Ellison. Ellison's father had been teasing him and was actually going into the river for sand to make a sandpile and had not realized his son's terror.
10. Wright had "waking dreams of the images of his life, distorted by secret pressures of desire and dread—a desire to probe and reveal and a dread of what he would find." He also said that he distrusted psychoanalysis because he knew "what was eating at [him] well enough and [he] could make [his] way above water as long as no storms arose and swept [his] boat over. He said, "I feel strong, wonder is that because I'm really a weak man. Do weak men feel that they are strong?"
11. Wright liked John O'Hara's work. He said *Butterfield 8* had excellent characters but their destinies were poor and trivial. *Pal Joey* reminded him *of Dostoevsky's Poor People.* When he read *Joey* he thought he might rewrite *Lawd Today*, recasting the novel in the form of twenty letters. He did not rewrite it, however.
12. This was a favorite expression of Wright's after he read an article by Zora Neal Hurston in *American Mercury* entitled "The Pet Nigger System."
13. Wright told some friends that he had accidentally blundered into the heart of the race question at Fisk but admitted to the author that he had known the touchiness of his subject for many years.
14. Wright called his ideas on fear "a pet theory" and said that fear came first, then dread, then self-hatred and finally hostility toward the white man.
15. There was a paper shortage at Harper. It eventually farmed out the printing of *Black Boy* to World Publishing Co., which, according to Wright, had "millions of reams of paper."
16. Last third of *Black Boy*.

17. Wright broke from the Communists early in 1942, about the end of February. One morning he simply told Ellen: "For God's sake, let us quit. I have had it. And let's make a definite break." He spoke to the author of his "rage and pain" when Cleo Wright, a Mississippi Negro, was lynched in 1942. The Party did not attack the lynchers for the brutal murder but simply accused them of obstructing the war effort. The *Daily Worker* claimed that the lynching was a conscious act of sabotage toward the military program of the country. Richard denied this and said the mob was the usual Southern mob concerned only with mutilating and killing a Negro and had nothing to do with war and sabotage. He had usually been able to put up with attacks against himself, but the attack on A. Philip Randolph and this attitude toward a lynched young man was something he could not endure. He said that the Party behavior during this period was worse than the Dies Committee.

18. Edward C. Aswell, Wright's editor at Harper and then Doubleday, told him that *Black Boy*'s prepublication sale was 30,000, the highest, next to one other book, in the history of the firm.

19. Congressional Record, 79th Congress, First Session, Wednesday, June 27, 1945, Issue #128, Vol. 91.

Chapter XVI
How many understand how they make us feel and live . . .

1. Richard Wright, unpublished Diaries.
2. Horace Cayton & St. Clair Drake, *Black Metropolis* (New York: Harcourt, Brace & Co., 1945).
3. James respected Drake's academic achievements but told Wright before the meeting not to get into senseless argument that would lead nowhere and might disrupt the working out of the book.
4. Although this section is from Wright's Diaries, it is unlikely that Horace Cayton, who is a sophisticated, highly cultivated man, was intimidated by the fact that Mrs. Norman was white, rich, and beautiful. For some years Horace was friendly with both men and women who were able to contribute millions to charitable causes; among these was Mrs. Clara Florsheim, wife of the well-known shoe man. Also, he had been Dr. Louis Wirth's assistant at the University of Chicago and then director of the South Parkway Community Center. It was Cayton, too, who introduced Richard to Marshall Field. And Cayton's first wife, Bonnie, was a fellow university student in Seattle, a white girl.
5. Richard Wright, unpublished Diaries.
6. *Ibid.*
7. Gunnar Myrdal, *An American Dilemma*, p. 1004.
8. The author was present at this meeting, and others relating to the magazine, took notes, typed up material for Wright and James.
9. Described to the author by Richard Wright.

Chapter XVII
World War II

1. The Schomburg Collection of Negro Literature and History, a branch of the New York Public Library. This is a reference and research library devoted to Negro life and history and is considered one of the most important centers in the world for the study of the Negro. International in scope, it covers every phase of Negro activity, wherever Negroes have lived, and its materials range from early rarities to current happenings and from Mississippi to Timbuctoo. The nucleus of the collection is the private library assembled by Arthur A. Schomburg, a Puerto Rican of African descent. In 1926, the Carnegie Corporation of New York purchased Schomburg's collection from him and presented it to the New York Public Library. Today its materials have been expanded and it serves as a major resource to those seeking documentation about the Negro, his past, and present activities. (This description is from the Schomburg Collection's brochure.)

2. Actually, Ralph Ellison enlisted in the Merchant Marine because a friend had informed him that there was a shortage of cooks. He did not intend to be Jim-Crowed in the Army, but he was willing to do his part in the War.

3. Wright told the author that the draft board refused Dr. Wertham's letter. Ralph Ellison told the author that a woman on the draft board whose husband was a member of the Communist Party hounded him until "Old Man Bailey, a Negro," told him that since he was in the Merchant Marine just to go back to sea.

4. Richard Wright, unpublished Diaries.

5. Fredric Wertham, *Headlines and Pictures*, "Harlem Pioneers With Mental Clinic," July, 1946.

6. Ralph Ellison told the author that there was no question of his needing psychiatric help. He was never under analysis at any time. Dr. Wertham simply arranged for a physical examination at Queens General Hospital.

7. Richard Wright, "I Tried to be a Communist," *Atlantic Monthly*, Aug. 1944 & Sept. 1944.

8. Richard Wright, unpublished speech, given to the author by Wright, portions of which he used later in *White Man, Listen!* and in the introduction to *Black Metropolis*.

9. Richard Wright to Gertrude Stein, Oct. 29, 1945.

10. Richard Wright, Introduction to *Black Metropolis* by St. Clair Drake & Horace R. Cayton.

Chapter XVIII
To live in this land is to breathe poison each day . . .

1. Richard Wright, unpublished Diaries.

2. Wright met his landlord, who was a liberal, sometime after he had moved into the new apartment. The man told him with enthusiasm, unconscious of his bigotry, that he had advised his Negro maid to write the story of her own life. "Then she will be famous like Richard Wright and she, too, could live in a nice apartment in the Village."

3. One morning Wright was facing a trip to Brooklyn or Harlem when the author arrived at the apartment on Charles Street. He was angry but he was not scowling or obviously showing his irritation. There was an aura in the room of rage and tension. Finally, he told Ellen that he might as well get it over with, but he damn well resented traveling so far to spend time on a haircut. The author blurted out the question: "Why travel so far? Go down to the corner for a haircut . . ." Richard answered: "Yes, And get my throat cut? I just lay down in that white man's chair and he would put that razor across my throat and tell me, 'Nigger, get the hell out of here.'"

4. Richard Wright, unpublished Diaries.

5. *Ibid.*

6. Richard Wright, "I Choose Exile," unpublished article. Written for *Ebony* magazine but rejected as too severe an attack against the United States.

7. *Ibid.*

Chapter XIX
Dear Richard,
 It is obvious that you and I are the
 only two geniuses of this era . . .
    —Gertrude Stein

1. Wright had taken so many new authors and directed so much material her way, Dorothy Norman made him an editor for *Twice A Year*. It was an honorary title inasmuch as he did not do any technical work for the publication.

2. The author.

3. Quoted by Douglas H. Schneider.

4. Wright was told later that several Communist reporters were present "intent upon

determining to what degree I'd lie about the Negro's status in America! I disappointed them!"

5. Richard Wright to Gertrude Stein, April 12, 1946.
6. Richard Wright, "I Choose Exile."
7. Wright said that these were Gide's words.
8. Gertrude Stein to Richard Wright (May, 1949). Carson McCullers remembers Richard Wright reading *Melanctha* at Middaugh Street and roaring with laughter.
9. William James, *The Philosophy of William James* (New York: Random House, Modern Library Edit., 1953, p. 128.
10. This section on Gertrude Stein is based on notes made by the author during long conversations with Richard Wright after his return from France in 1947.
11. Wright did not read Henry Miller until 1945, when he decided "to see what everyone was gabbing about."
12. Richard Wright to Gertrude Stein, April 12, 1946.

Chapter XX
I feel certain that she knows already much more than she knows she knows . . .

1. The WASP was the author.
2. Richard Wright, unpublished Diaries.
3. The author took Julia to Bergdorf Goodman. It was one of several such experiences with Wright's daughter.
4. Richard Wright, unpublished and untitled notes for a speech.
5. Among liberals there was a general fear that Fascism might engulf the United States. Henry Wallace, in one of his campaign speeches for the Presidency, said, "Nazis are running our American government, so why should Russia make peace with them?" From *Henry Wallace, The Last Seven Months of His Campaign* (Americans for Democratic Action, 1948) .
6. Richard Wright, "I Choose Exile."
7. A large number of people in the United States and in Europe believe that a campaign was instituted against Wright and an attempt made to destroy his reputation and obfuscate the power of his ideas. He was vilified publicly and privately when many lesser American authors were treated with respect in reviews, anthologies, books of criticism. Until recently his works were not listed in any major encyclopedias including the *Encyclopaedia Britannica*. Among the critics, one of Wright's few consistent defenders was Irving Howe. Recently, Lerone Bennett, Jr., editor of *Ebony* magazine, wrote in his book *Confrontation: Black and White* (Johnson Pub. Co., Chicago, Ill.) , "Richard Wright performed an act [by writing *Native Son*] of leadership that affected race relations as much as any act of any protest leader. For Wright's achievement lay, precisely, in this: He named the problem. And the problem, once named, was not and could not be experienced again in the same way."

Many people argued that Wright should not leave the United States: "How can he write so far from his subject matter?" etc. Richard said that if a writer did not have enough experiences out of which to imagine and create by the time he reached twenty years of age then he should give up. Dorothy Norman told the author that many white writers asked her to use her influence to keep Wright in the United States. "His fight is here," they claimed. "He will be spoiled." Mrs. Norman was appalled by their chauvinism.

Chapter XXI
But I am filled with the details of living . . .

1. Wright was bored with the ceremony of leave-taking, eager to be on his way to new adventures. He had spent the last three days at the home of George Davis, who did not see him off at the boat. Richard said he was grateful to George and that he liked him for his "slightly melancholy disposition, the hallmark of a sensitive man."
2. After reading the MS Ellen Wright wrote the author: "In French, an hôtel can also mean a private home or mansion and is often distinguished from the other kind of

hotel by referring to it as an 'hôtel particulier.' Thus Odette Lieutier occupied the first two floors of a mansion, actually belonging to a titled person. It was in her sizeable duplex that we had two rooms set aside for us, giving on to a vast formal garden."

3. Richard Wright, *The Jackal,* unpublished.
4. Carson and Reeves McCullers.
5. It was Carson McCullers' third stroke, of which Richard was not aware. Her first stroke occurred in 1940, when she was only twenty-two or twenty-three years of age. A valiant woman, she continued with her work as soon as she was able.
6. Reeves McCullers committed suicide in 1953, despite an anguished love for his wife who did all she could to help him.
7. Horace Cayton in *Anger, and Beyond* describes an experience with Wright on a subway just after he had had a tooth pulled. Richard talked about nerve endings and the intricacies of dentistry until Horace became angry. He was in pain, and asked: "How did you learn all this stuff?" Richard answered: "Well, there's nothing to it. I just picked up a book on dentistry."
8. Richard Wright, unpublished Diaries.
9. *Ibid.*
10. *Ibid.*

Chapter XXII
I choose exile . . .

1. Richard Wright to Gertrude Stein, March 28, 1946.
2. Last third of *Black Boy*.
3. Conversation with Richard Wright. The phrase regarding lynching is from Chester Himes' *Lonely Crusade*. It expressed Wright's feelings precisely.
4. These pages combine conversations with Richard Wright in Paris, some of the direct quotations with portions of his Diary, particularly his first opinions of Sartre and de Beauvoir. Comments on where Richard differed from the existentialists are the author's own from lengthy talks with him.
5. Richard Wright to Dorothy Norman, Feb. 28, 1948, March 9, 1948. Published by Mrs. Norman in her magazine *Twice a Year*, 1938–1948, 10th Anniversary Issue. Wright's reactions toward Belgium, England, Italy, are from this publication. Wright exaggerated the membership of the Communist Party when pressed for actual figures by the French. It made him feel defensive of his country; he could not explain that such hysteria and fear arose from only a handful of "mostly old people" Communists.
6. Wright was not convinced of any danger at this time because he had received a twenty-seven page telegram (see below) from Vladimir Yermilov, a Russian critic, comparing *Native Son* to the work of Dostoevski. Also, Wright's books were enormously popular in the Soviet Union. Ellen Wright wrote the author: "I do not recall that he went so far as to obtain plane tickets from Cook's. In fact, our plan was not to return to the U.S. at all, but to keep in readiness a packed trunk, extra gas provisions, and thus be in a position, if the situation called for it, to cross one or more borders, *in the car,* depending on the general European situation. Dick was extremely attuned to what was happening here, as you could imagine he would be. This does not mean of course, that Nello [C. L. R. James], also aware of the political climate, might not have offered him the advice you mention, i.e., to return to the U.S. I can say with absolute certainty he never would have entertained the notion, short of Europe going up in flames." Nevertheless, in a letter to his agent, Paul Reynolds Jr., and to his friend, Chester Himes, Wright confessed that he was purchasing tickets to put in his wallet in the event the Russians occupied Paris. However, as Mrs. Wright states, he may not have purchased them because later he wrote Reynolds to stand ready to send money to Ellen Wright for plane or boat fare should she request it when he was away from France.
7. Richard Wright, letters to Dorothy Norman.
8. Richard Wright to Margrit de Sabloniere, Sept. 18, 1960: "The Congo mess is merely

a dress rehearsal for the dismemberment of Nigeria. Africa and the nationalist movements are under attack from one end of the continent to another."

9. Richard Wright letter to Dorothy Norman.
10. Richard Wright, "I Choose Exile."
11. *Ibid.*

Copy of a cable from Moscow to Richard Wright, Dec. 28, 1942, from Vladimir Yermilov. Original was given to the author by Richard Wright and is presently in her files.

My dear Colleague:

I have not had the pleasure of a personal acquaintance with you and know you only through your remarkable books but certain circumstances encourage me to write this letter to you the circumstances are to some extent of a personal nature I am aware that you have commented favorably on the modest work I have done on the subject of Dostoievsky the opinion expressed by a writer whom I love and who as I gathered from my reading of your Native Son himself pays tribute to Dostoievsky is of great significance to me in the days of the great patriotic war we are fighting against the German barbarians I continue to think about Dostoievsky and re-read his works in a new day the word should not be taken in the literal sense it was more often in my mind I re-read him when I was marching in the ranks of the peoples guard and while I was learning to use a rifle and throw hand-grenades I re-read him while fighting German incendiary bombs on the roof of the nine storied building that houses the writers club in a quiet Moscow sidestreet opposite the famous Tretyakov Gallery during nights when the darkness was criss-crossed with tracer bullets and hideous with the scream of demolition bombs it was on one of these nights that I was what I call re-reading Dostoievsky with a friend we were standing on the roof recalling how Versilov in the Adolescent dreamed of the future happiness of mankind we talked of the time when having destroyed Hitler and with him the very possibility of war mankind liberated and at peace again would celebrate holidays of the solidarity of the democratic nations and peacetime tracer-bullets would serve as an impressive antiwar firework display just at that moment a German lightweight high explosive bomb struck the roof not ten paces away and destroyed the writers libraries on all the upper floors in one of these there was a volume autographed by Dostoievsky I should like to ask you dear colleague do you too re-read Dostoievsky these dangerous but majestic days and what do you think about him now don't you agree that is living a new life in our time his genius is seen in this among other things that he sensed in the history atmosphere of his time the portents of new and terrible threat to mankind the threat of a return to savagery to the desolation cynicism and brutishness of Stavrogin and Smerdykov and of the loss of all moral and cultural values all his life long Dostoievsky fought against the idea which almost all his characters speak and the essence of which is defined by Raskolnikov as follows it lies precisely in this that by the law of nature people are divided in general into two categories that is to say into material that serves solely for the purpose of begetting others like itself and into people properly speaking the masters to whom everything is permissible and the slaves with whom everything is permissible this is the essence of the idea that Dostoievsky abhorred you know that the pro-Fascist ideologists have attempted to represent him as a forerunner of Nietzsche or as sharing his views they might with the same degree of accuracy have asserted that the author of a code of laws formulating the nature of crime is the criminal's predecessor or shares his views from Dostoievsky's standpoint the opinions expressed by Raskolnikov Ivan Kara-mazov and others are precisely the crime that calls for ruthless punishment Dostoievsky's hero yielded for the time being for a number of complex reasons to the influence of the morals of the masters was not a tyrant nor a beast in human form but a man who having come into contact with the moral of the brute recoiled in horror and loathing and strove to find the way back to himself the very character of the hero in this case lays particular stress on the utter incompatibility of the brutish morals of the masters with any humanity whatsoever in one of his letters Dostoievsky remarked that Raskolnikov was obliged to give himself up obliged in order that he might return once more even though perishing in penal servitude to contact with people the sense of isolation of disunitedness from mankind which he felt immediately on committing the crime tormented him German reactionary writers like Nietzsche and Spengler lauded the isolated the superman who prided himself upon his isolation and disunitedness as though foreseeing that writers of this kind fond of a sounding phraseology would be bound to appear Dostoievsky gave a very florid formulation of the ideas he abhorred in the legend of the Grand Inquisitor Ivan Karamazov expresses opinions that differ in no way from that which led Raskolnikov to his crime at the back of Ivan's declamation on the subject of the handful of the elect who rule the human herd on the basis of miracle mystery and authority at the back of Ivan himself Dostoievsky discerns one thing alone the human semblance of the smirking mask of that super-lackey Smerdayakov Smerdyakovism is the essence of the morals that had a temptation for Raskolnikov and Ivan Karamazov there was a purpose in Dostoievsky's making Smerdyakov the double the spiritual and even physical brother of Ivan Karamazov for Smerdyakov carried out the practical conclusions that were the outcome of Ivan's idea regarding the superman to whom all is permissible so before ever German reactionary literature brought forward the character of the superman this same conception was presented in Russian literature as a super-lackey Dostoievsky hated Prussian militarism its influence on literature and philosophy in Germany he says in a writer's diary the sense of national self-satisfaction has reached the point of triviality even science has begun to savour of chauvinism over and over again he asserted that a small section of mankind cannot own the rest of humanity as a slave the Hitlerite band has expanded to incredible proportions all the wild German prejudices regarding Germans being the elect it has corrupted the German Burgher with poisonous nonsensical propaganda about Germans being elected to become the master people and to own the rest of mankind like a slave this has led to an orgy of the most abominable cynicism ever known a cynicism beside which Smerdyakovism pales to the destruction by Fascist hordes of millions of innocent people women children and the aged to an orgy of torture to that nightmare of which the great Russian writer warned mankind so long ago in our day when the freedom loving nations of the world have joined forces for the struggle against the Hitlerite clique of super-lackeys who call themselves by the flattering title of supermen do we not think differently and with a new feeling of the genius Feodor Dostoievsky who is equally respected by Russian and American literary men I don't know about you but I know that what is dearest of all in Dostoievsky to me at present is that place in the Brothers Karamazov where Ivan infects with the force of his protest and indignation Aloysha mildest of men preacher of forbearance meekness and submission Dostoievsky's best-loved hero he ought to be shot whispers Aloysha in reply to Ivan's question as to what was to be done with a landowner who set his dogs on a peasant boy this whisper is more audible than any shout dearest of all to me in Dostoievsky at present in his appeal for immediate revenge for every tear shed by a tormented child and for how many children's tears has Hitler's band of tormenters and cannibals been responsible but the hour of retribution is at hand the past year has been the year when we came closer to victory may the New Year be the year of victory and revenge may there not remain a single childish tear that has not been avenged we shall live solely for victory and revenge in the name of love and beauty in the name of the happiness of all mankind permit me dear colleague to send you my New Year's greetings—yours respectfully, Vladimir Yermilov.

Chapter XXIII

I must make this film . . .

1. Chenal was considered one of the three most important directors in Paris.
2. Harold Hecht to Paul Reynolds, Jr., March 10, 1947.
3. Mark Marvin Theatrical Productions planned to form Canada Lee, Inc., with Lee,

Marvin and Alexis de Gunzburg to produce a French and English language version of *Native Son*. Directors being considered were Jean Renoir, Julien Duvivier, Jules Dassin, Edward Dymytrk. In a letter of Nov. 5, 1948 they stipulated the following changes to be made in the book:

"We insist that any and all political connotations now in the novel and the written play be converted into non-political, disaffiliated humanitarian motivations. Knowing the author, I feel certain he will welcome these changes in the picture version."

They did not know Wright very well. He refused and continued to refuse all offers which would "water down or dilute" the ideas in the book, no matter what sums of money were offered. Also, his agent advised him that the firm was shaky financially

4. The thousands of letters received by Wright would form a human-interest book. A majority of his mail came from white Southerners, praising his honesty and often asking for his advice. The range was wide, from advice as to how to start a pearl fishery to a professor of mathematics, who had a severe heart attack and asked for guidance and perspective.

5. Wright carried this still further and thought up tunes to be used as background for bodies swaying from tree limbs.

6. Wright loved gadgets, but essentially the Ediphone was to listen to the rhythms of speech and speed his own production. A portion of the work could be typed by a secretary or by Ellen while he continued on to the next chapter.

7. Conversation with LeRoy Haynes is the source of direct quotes and the secret of his Southern "greens" which he said amused R.W.

8. Jack Conroy to the author, Jan. 16, 1967.

9. Richard Wright to Paul Reynolds, Nov. 29, 1948. Richard believed that Green had been overpaid because he said that he had written a major portion of the play and yet on film rights Orson Welles took 33⅓ percent, Green 35 percent, which left less than 32 percent for Wright to share with his agent.

10. Re: "the boys from Chicago" see Bob Thomas, *King Cohn. The Life and Times of Harry Cohn* (New York: G. P. Putnam's Sons, 1967). During Kim Novak's romance with Sammy Davis, Jr., Cohn called upon "friends in Chicago" whose attorney paid a visit to Davis in Las Vegas. He was given an alternative to breaking off his relations with Miss Novak or being unable to find employment in any nightclub in the country. Davis chose to earn his living and severed all connections with Miss Novak. Miss Wallace was not yet the "property" represented by Miss Novak, but her career was ended to any substantial degree after her appearance in *Native Son*.

11. Wright insisted that Paul Reynolds subtract his usual 10 percent for his efforts on the film. He also asked him to subtract the cost of numerous cables which went back and forth. This was typical of Richard. There were times when Ellen sold articles or short stories in Europe without the help of his agent and he always paid a percentage to Reynolds.

12. Senator Charles E. Potter, *Days of Shame* (New York: Coward-McCann, Inc., 1963).

13. In conversation, the late Walter Gould's partner, Sidney A. Mayers, denied this. Mayers claims that Wright requested a 35 mm film and when offered a 16 mm refused it. Whatever the facts may be, to this day, Ellen Wright has no copy of the film in *any* version or millimeter.

Chapter XXIV
The black existentialist and the white Freudian . . .

1. Richard Wright, *Jackal* and *Maude,* or *Little Sister,* unpublished.

2. Written in 1951. Over ten years later James Baldwin took this theme as his own and startled the American public.

3. Wright pondered the significance of this story for months.

4. Ben Burns turned an article down and later incurred the wrath of Wright and his agent when he attacked him in an article for *The Reporter* (Mar. 8, 1956). Burns,

who had been a personal friend, stated that Richard had poisoned the mind of Europe and bordered on the subversive. Richard made no reply to the article but said: "If I do not have enough friends left in the USA to defend me from attacks such as that, then it is just too bad for me." Later Burns became connected with *Male* and *Stag* magazines and requested "The Man Who Lived Underground" from Richard. Richard refused. Reynolds backed him up and said he would not sell a line of Richard's to Burns for even a thousand dollars.

5. Richard Wright, *The Outsider* (New York: Harper & Brothers, 1953).
6. Wright planted the seed for a call at his apartment by David Schine. Seated with Chester Himes in a café frequented by Americans, Richard looked around and then said that everything spoken there was sent back to the McCarthy Committee. Chester laughed and Richard said he would prove it. He raised his voice slightly and described an easy method by which to transmit secret messages to the U. S. A writer would send certain page numbers of his MS and on those pages sprinkled in dialogue would be the code information. A month later, when Richard had forgotten the entire episode, Schine paid him a visit at his apartment. Schine questioned him as to how he numbered his MS pages. Richard felt he would burst with laughter but he kept a calm face and very soberly explained to Schine, "Well, I just number them 1, 2, 3, 4, and on through to the end of the story."
7. Jack Conroy wrote the author that what was amazing to him was that people in Chicago were not so surprised at what Wright wrote as by the fact that he could write at all. It was an unconscious prejudice. Some of the attitudes toward his knowledge and use of existentialism held these same overtones.
8. New York *Times,* Mar. 18, 1953.
9. In *Outsider* the breast uplift operation, p. 51, was actually performed on a friend of the Wrights. He was so shocked that he awakened in the middle of the night thinking about it. The Book-of-the-Month Club episode was also something that actually occurred. Wright sent his own name, a fictitious one, and gave Joe C. Brown's address. For months Joe hid the books and bills from his aunt and kept them for Richard. When lawyers wrote threatening letters the two young men were alarmed and Richard sent in a nonexistent change of address There are many other personal experiences throughout the novel.
10. Richard Wright, *Savage Holiday* (New York: Avon Publications, Inc., 1954).
11. John Fischer had become Wright's editor at Harper. Edward C. Aswell had gone to McGraw-Hill.

Chapter XXV
Black Power . . .

1. Richard Wright, Introduction to George Padmore, *Pan-Africanism or Communism?* (London: Dennis Dobson, 1956).
2. C. L. R. James, "George Padmore," *Tribune* (London) Oct. 2, 1964.
3. Kwame Nkrumah, *Ghana* (London: Thomas Nelson & Sons, 1957).
4. Richard Wright, unpublished Diaries. Madame Pandit was the first Indian woman to hold the post of Provisional Minister and later Ambassador to the United Nations General Assembly.
5. Kwame Nkrumah, *Towards Colonial Freedom* (London: Heinemann Ltd., 1946).
6. Conversations with George Padmore, Kwame Nkrumah and Richard Wright are the sources for this information. A detailed description of "The Circle" may be found in *The Autobiography of Kwame Nkrumah* (London: Thomas Nelson & Sons, 1957).
7. Called "Negritude" in the United States.
8. Richard Wright to Paul Reynolds, Sept. 4, 1953.
9. Richard Wright, *Black Power* (New York: Harper & Brothers, 1954).
10. Richard Wright's title *Black Power* anticipated the slogan of Stokely Carmichael by thirteen or fourteen years.

11. Although there was never an open clash, Wright did not like his editor, John Fischer.
12. Wright appreciated Harper president Frank McGregor's stand on *Black Power*. He felt that many publishers would have been afraid to publish the book. The McCarthy hearings opened April 22, 1954, at the time of McGregor's letter to Richard.
13. Angus & Robertson letter to Innes Rose, Reynolds' representative in London, Jan. 5, 1955.
14. Not until 1966 did a book appear on this theme: *The New Elites of Tropical Africa*, edited by P. C. Lloyd, Oxford University Press, London, 1966. Also, in 1966 Kwame Nkrumah was overthrown. (Julia Wright, her husband, Henri Herve, and their baby Ellen Amah, were working in Ghana for Nkrumah. They were taken from an airport bus at bayonet point and held briefly. Refuge was given the young family at the Cuban Embassy in Ghana until they were permitted to leave the country). Many years before Nkrumah was overthrown, Wright became critical of his leadership, feeling that he had isolated himself from the masses which had placed him in office. But Wright believed that Nkrumah had to be supported because with all of his weaknesses he was the strongest leader in Africa. George Padmore, before his death, told Richard that he was afraid that a united states of Africa would take at least another twenty-five years. He also told him that the British sent in agents to stir up trouble for the Pan-Africanists and that they were assisted by the CIA. *Black Power* was forbidden in Nigeria and Wright was told that it was the U.S. government that had made the ruling. It was also Wright's conviction that the U.S. was trying to "make a deal with Russia that neither side would have atomic bases in Africa. . . . In Africa, the Americans are buying all the blacks who offer themselves, and they are stupid enough to think that they are winning a continent in such a foolish fashion."
15. Richard Wright, *White Man, Listen!* (New York: Doubleday & Co., Inc., 1957). This book consists of lectures Wright made in Europe after his return from Ghana.

Chapter XXVI
Pagan Spain

1. Richard Wright, *Pagan Spain* (New York: Harper & Brothers, 1957).
2. *Ibid.*
3. *Ibid.*
4. *Ibid.*

Chapter XXVII
I want to assume an attitude that places me wholly on the side of feeling in life . . .

1. Ellen Wright told the author that the Bokanowskis had nothing to do with the obtaining of their Carte de Séjour. Unasked, she says, they were suddenly offered a ten-year card when they went to renew their three-year permit. Yet, in a letter to Reynolds, Wright said that the Bokanowskis had been influential in securing his special permit.
2. Conversation with Ellen Wright. Neighbors with whom the author talked in Normandy constantly mentioned Wright's smile. It was "the sign of a *good* man," they insisted.
3. Richard Wright, speech at the American Church, Paris, Nov. 1960.
4. Richard Wright, "Good Big Black Man," in his collection *Eight Men* (New York: World Publishing Company, 1961. For many years Wright wrote and sent short stories to Reynolds and originally planned a book to be entitled *Ten Men.*
5. Richard Wright, *The Long Dream* (New York: Doubleday, Ace Star edition, 1958).

5A. Emmet Till's murder for "wolf-whistling" at a white woman (in 1955) shook Richard violently.

6. Richard Wright to Margrit de Sabloniere, Nov. 28, 1955.

7. Ollie Harrington, "The Last Days of Richard Wright," *Ebony* magazine, February, 1961.

8. Mrs. Heeris, Bente's mother, later visited Wright in Paris to thank him for his concern for her daughter. She told him that his letters had given her daughter happiness and comfort for a time.

Chapter XXVIII
Island of Hallucination . . .

1. Wright had a great deal more to say than the author has included about Smith's conduct in Europe. Source for Smith is Richard Wright.

2. Name withheld.

3. *Herald-Tribune,* Paris Edition, May 14, 1954. Ellen Wright wrote the author that Miss Schneider "was for many years, notorious for her tight control, passport-wise, concerning Americans, especially those who were unattached to American companies or governmental agencies, but simply were here because they preferred it to America. . . . They got Ollie's [Harrington] passport by the ruse of asking him to come in for some reason or other and to bring his passport along. I'm fairly certain that Ollie guessed what their maneuver was in advance, but the fact was they did confiscate it and he was deprived of it for many years. In Dick's case, they knew he'd have to come in for renewal and they decided in favor of this ploy. Since both his and mine expired at the same time, we presented ourselves and whereas it worked smoothly for me, old Agnes, once she took possession of Dick's, announced she'd have to clear with Washington before issuing a new one. Naturally, Dick was prepared for this, and in an oblique way, let her know that if his new passport wasn't forthcoming in a certain short delay, he would apply to the French authorities for the necessary traveling papers and in general blast it to the press for all it was worth. The threat of this adverse publicity seemed to have worked because within no time at all Dick was summoned to the Embassy to pick up his renewed passport, with Agnes Schneider oozing with all the charm she could muster for the credit of the State Department."

4. Harrington is presently employed by East Berlin Radio.

5. Conversation with Ellen Wright.

6. Ollie Harrington, "The Last Days of Richard Wright," *Ebony* magazine Feb. 1961. Richard made other attempts to prevent the deterioration of black expatriates, primarily by forming organizations. It was his conviction that disintegration set in unless one was anchored by serious work or by politics. One organization he established arose when a young nurse, Margaret Cleveland, came to ask him for help. She had been refused employment at the American Hospital in Neuilly and claimed it was on racial grounds. When Richard investigated, he discovered that her accusations were apparently justified. He had also learned from friends, Chester Himes and others, that they had been refused rooms in small hotels and pensions on the Left Bank for racial reasons. He formed the Franco American Fellowship in 1950. Assisting him were William Rutherford, an American who had worked in Africa; Daniel Guérin, a French writer; and Colette Lacroix, Legon Buford, Jean Maho, Daniel Moss, LeRoy Haynes, Wendell Jeanpierre, Don Harris, Walter Nichols, Pierre Cahn, Edward Myers. American members residing in the U.S. were James Ivy, Gordon Parks, Jimmy Davis, Frances Dorsey, Minto Cato, Roy Eldridge. The Preamble of the organization reads:

"This group exists to serve the mutual and personal needs of its members; to promote social and cultural relations; and to heighten the consciousness of its members in relation to the urgent issues confronting the world today. It proposes to attain these ends by dedicating its energies to an elucidation of the problem of human freedom amidst modern industrialization; to combat the deepening and extension of racist ideas and practices from whatever quarter they spring; to urge the spread of the principles of fundamental education among the non-industrial peoples of the world; to lend encouragement and support to all minorities and exploited groups in their aspirations and struggles for freedom; to promote interest in the relation of modern art, literary, plastic, and musical, to the consciousness of contemporary man; to an exposure of all those mental habits which tend to solidify racial, class, social, religious, and national divisions between men; to support those impulses which seek to express a creative concept of human freedom; to reaffirm the common identity and destiny of humankind, and the internationalism of the human spirit."

Membership was open without further qualification to any and all persons subscribing to the stated aims.

7. The entire speech may be found in the American Library in Paris. The catalogue description reads as follows: *Typescript of a tape recording of a speech by Richard Wright in Nov. 1960.* Whereabouts of the original tape is not known. A transcript of the speech is in the files of Richard Wright in the home of his widow, who is executor of his estate. Another copy is in the files of the author in New York.
8. Wright sent off a letter to his agent immediately after his meeting with Zevin stating that he would not consider working with World Publishing Co. unless his friend William Targ was his editor. Mr. Targ was editor-in-chief and a vice-president at World.
9. Ellen Wright told the author that Dr. Williams wept and finally fainted at a restaurant table in Paris after he was discharged from the Caribbean Commission. At a later date Mrs. Wright asked Williams why it was that so many leaders turned on the men who had educated them and helped them to power. "Why is there a pattern that seems to be set up when people are in the struggle for emancipation? You and Nkrumah and Kenyatta and others were idealists, some of you spent time in prison, you struggled and you relied upon people like Padmore, Dick and C. L. R. [James]. But the minute you took power these people were an embarrassment. You could never have succeeded on the level of strategy or political understanding without people like these." Mrs. Wright's analysis of patterns of betrayal was similar to that of Camus in *The Rebel,* that the successful rebel was in danger of becoming the bureaucrat of the revolution.
10. Lubis later spent time in jail and finally left Indonesia. The author has been informed that he is now in Red China.
11. Part of a leaflet issued by Comité d'Action et de Défense Républicaine.
12. Documented in *Hansard,* the British equivalent of the U.S. *Congressional Record.*

Chapter XXIX

We fret, we feel frustrated, but things are moving on the broad scale. We must never forget that . . .

1. Simone de Beauvoir and Nelson Algren are among Ellen's clients.
2. Richard Wright to Madame Margrit de Sabloniere, April 7, 1960.
3. *Ibid.*
4. Targ reluctantly returned the haikus and told Wright that unfortunately, in his judgment, they were not marketable.
5. R.W. letter to Paul Reynolds, March 2, 1960.
6. Richard Wright, *A Father's Law,* unpublished.
7. Richard Wright to Margrit de Sabloniere, Oct. 8, 1960.
8. This comes from Wright's own letters; however Ellen Wright wrote the author, "Dorothy continued to work after George's death, and received a handsome salary. She lived in a beautiful home, rent free, set in the midst of sweeping lawns and gardens. She was able to pay for the services of a gardener, a steward and a chauffeur who drove her around in her car which was a gift from the President. She may even have received a widow's pension befitting the wife of George Padmore. It is true, in a certain sense, that she felt 'cast aside.' You know, of course, of the continual power

struggle, during George's lifetime, with him as the main target. However, since he had the President's support and protection, she too could make her weight felt, and very effectively, for the most part. After his death, she had only the President to support her. When I was in Ghana in 1964, she was seeing Nkrumah almost daily, was researching for him in preparation for his book, *Neo-Colonialism—The Last Stage of Imperialism,* was actively involved in creating an archive, etc. She was, in fact, a Presidential Assistant. So, all in all, I'd go along on her being 'cast aside' if it's in a relative sense."

9. Conversation with Langston Hughes.

Bibliography

FICTION

"The Voodoo of Hell's Half Acre," *Southern Register* (Jackson, Miss.), 1924. (Precise date unknown—no copy available.)

"Superstition," *Abbot's Monthly Magazine*, II (April 1931), 45–47, 64–66, 72–73.

"Big Boy Leaves Home," in Alfred Kreymborg et al., eds., *The New Caravan* (New York, 1936), pp. 124–158. Included in *Uncle Tom's Children.*

"Silt," *New Masses*, XXIV (August 24, 1937), 19–20. Included in *Eight Men* (1961) under the title "The Man Who Saw the Flood."

"Fire and Cloud," *Story Magazine*, XII (March 1938), 9–41. Included in *Uncle Tom's Children* (1940).

Uncle Tom's Children: four novellas. New York, 1938. 317 p.

"Bright and Morning Star," *New Masses*, XXVII (May 10, 1938), 97–99, 116–124. Included in *Uncle Tom's Children* (1940 edition). Published in book form in 1941 (New York, International Publishers, 48 p.).

"Almos' A Man," *Harper's Bazaar*, LXXIV (Jan. 1940), 40–41. Included in *Eight Men* under the title "The Man Who Was Almost a Man."

Native Son. New York, 1940. 359 p.

Uncle Tom's Children: five long stories. New York, 1940. 384 p.

Native Son, the Biography of a Young American. A Play in Ten Scenes. By Paul Green and Richard Wright. New York, 1941. 148 p.

"The Man Who Lived Underground," *Accent*, II (Spring 1942), 170–176. Enlarged version in Edwin Seaver, ed., *Cross-section 1944* (New York, 1944), pp. 58–102. Included in *Eight Men* (1961).

"L'Homme qui tua une ombre," *Les Lettres Françaises* (Oct. 4, 1946), translated by Andrè Villars. See "The Man Who Killed a Shadow" (1949).

"The Man Who Killed a Shadow," *Zero* (Paris), I (Spring, 1949), 45–53. Included in *Eight Men* (1961).

The Outsider. New York, 1953. 405 p.

Savage Holiday. New York: Avon, 1954. 220 p.

"Big Black Good Man," *Esquire*, L (Nov. 1957), 76–80. Included in *Eight Men* (1961).

The Long Dream. New York, 1958. 384 p.

Eight Men. Cleveland and New York, 1961. 250 p.

Lawd Today. New York, 1963. 189 p. [Although published posthumously *Lawd Today* was probably written sometime between 1935 and 1937.)
"Five Episodes" (from an unfinished novel), in Herbert Hill, ed., *Soon One Morning* (New York, 1963), pp. 140–164.

POETRY

"Rest for the Weary," *Left Front,* No. 3 (Jan.–Feb. 1934), 3.
"A Red Love Note," *Left Front,* No. 3 (Jan.–Feb. 1934), 3.
"Strength," *The Anvil,* No. 5 (March–April 1934), 20.
"Child of the Dead and Forgotten Gods," *The Anvil,* No. 5 (March–April 1934), 30.
"Everywhere Waters Rise," *Left Front,* No. 4 (May–June 1934), 9.
"I Have Seen Black Hands," *New Masses,* X (June 26, 1934), 16.
"Between the World and Me," *Partisan Review,* II (July–August 1935), 18–19. Reprinted in *The Partisan Reader* (1934–1944), ed. William Phillips and Philip Rahv, New York, 1946, 218–219.
"I Am a Red Slogan," *International Literature,* IV (April 1935), 35.
"Ah Feels It in Mah Bones," *International Literature,* IV (April 1935), 80.
"Red Leaves of Red Books," *New Masses,* XV (April 30, 1935), 6.
"Spread Your Sunrise," *New Masses,* XVI (July 2, 1935), 26.
"Transcontinental," *International Literature,* V (Jan. 1936), 52–57.
"Hearst Headline Blues," *New Masses,* XIX (May 12, 1936), 14.
"Old Habit and New Love," *New Masses,* XXI (Dec. 15, 1936), 29.
"We of the Streets," *New Masses,* XXIII (April 13, 1937), 14.
"Red Clay Blues," *New Masses,* XXXII (Aug. 1, 1939), 14. In collaboration with Langston Hughes.
"King Joe" (Joe Louis Blues), OKEH Record No. 6475, Oct. 3, 1941.

NONFICTION

Books

12 Million Black Voices: A Folk History of the Negro in the United States. Photo direction by Edwin Rosskam. New York, 1941. 152 p.
Black Boy; a Record of Childhood and Youth. New York, 1945. 288 p.
Black Power; a Record of Reactions in a Land of Pathos. New York, 1954. 358 p.
Bandoeng, 1.500.000.000 d'hommes. Trans. Hélène Claireau. Paris, 1955. 203 p. Preceded the American edition.
The Color Curtain; a Report on the Bandung Conference. Cleveland and New York, 1956. 221 p.
Pagan Spain. New York, 1956. 241 p.
White Man, Listen! New York, 1957. 190 p.

Magazine Articles and Reviews

"Joe Louis Uncovers Dynamite," *New Masses,* XVII (Oct. 8, 1935), 18.
"Two Million Black Voices," *New Masses,* XVII (Feb. 25, 1936), 16.
"A Tale of Folk Courage" (Review of *Black Thunder,* by Arna Bontemps), *Partisan Review and Anvil,* III (April 1936), 31.
"Letter to the Editors" (In Defense of Meyer Levin), *Partisan Review and Anvil,* III (June 1936), 30.
"Between Laughter and Tears" (Review of *These Low Grounds* by Walter

Turpin, and *Their Eyes Were Watching God,* by Zora N. Hurston), *New Masses,* XXV (Oct. 5, 1937), 22–25.

"Blueprint for Negro Writing," *New Challenge,* II (Fall 1937), 53–65.

"A Sharecropper's Story" (Review of *I Was a Sharecropper,* by Harry B. Kroll), *New Republic,* XCIII (Dec. 1, 1937), 109.

"Adventure and Love in Loyalist Spain" (Review of *The Wall of Men,* by William Rollins), *New Masses,* XXVI (March 8, 1938), 25–26.

"High Tide in Harlem," *New Masses,* XXVIII (July 5, 1938), 18–20.

"Lynching Bee" (Review of *Trouble in July,* by Erskine Caldwell), *New Republic,* CII (March 11, 1940), 351.

"How 'Bigger' Was Born," *Saturday Review,* XXII (June 1, 1940), 17–20. Also published in book form, New York: Harper, 1940, 39 p. (Enlarged version).

"I Bite the Hand That Feeds Me," *Atlantic Monthly,* CLV (June 1940), 826–828.

"Rascoe-Baiting," *American Mercury,* L (July 1940), 376–377.

"Inner Landscape" (Review of *The Heart Is a Lonely Hunter,* by Carson McCullers), *New Republic,* CIII (Aug. 5, 1940), 195.

"Forerunner and Ambassador" (Review of *The Big Sea,* by Langston Hughes), *New Republic,* CIII (Oct. 24, 1940), 600.

"Greetings," *New Masses,* XXXIX (Feb. 18, 1941), 14.

"The Negro and Parkway Community House," (pamphlet) Chicago, April 1941. 4 p.

"Not My People's War," *New Masses,* XXXIX (June 17, 1941), 8–9, 12.

"I Support the Soviet Union," *Soviet Russia,* Sept. 1941, 29.

"What You Don't Know Won't Hurt You," *Harper's Magazine,* CLXXXVI (Dec. 1942), 58–61.

"I Tried To Be a Communist," *Atlantic Monthly,* CLXXXIV (August 1944), 61–70; (Sept. 1944), 48–56. Included in Richard Crossman, ed., *The God That Failed.* New York, 1949.

"Richard Wright and Antonio Frasconi, an Exchange of Letters. Wright to Frasconi," *Twice a Year,* No. 12–13, 1945, 256–261.

"American Hunger," *Mademoiselle,* XXI (Sept. 1945), 164–165, 299–301.

"Psychiatry Comes to Harlem," *Free World,* XII (Sept. 1946), 49–51. Reprinted in *Twice a Year* (1946–1947) under the title "Psychiatry Goes to Harlem."

"How Jim Crow Feels," *True Magazine,* Nov. 1946. Reprinted in *Negro Digest,* V (Jan. 1947), 44–53.

"Discrimination in America," *Twice a Year,* No. 14–15 (Fall 1946–Winter 1947).
—"Urban Misery in an American City. Juvenile Delinquency in Harlem," 339–345.
—"A World View of the American Negro," 346–348. Published as "Lettre sur le problème noir aux U.S.A. Paris, 20 Juin 1946," in *Les Nouvelles Epîtres,* Paris, 1947, Epître xxxii.
—"Psychiatry Goes to Harlem," 349–354.

"Richard Wright nous presente *Black Boy,*" *L'Ordre* (Paris), 15 Janvier 1948, p. 3. Reprinted as an introduction to "American Hunger," in Whit Burnett, ed., *The World's Best,* New York, 1950, p. 303.

"Littérature noire américaine," *Les Temps Modernes,* No. 35 (August 1948), 193–220. Included in *White Man, Listen!,* 1957.

"Preface" to "Human, All Too Human," by E. F. Frazier, in *Présence Africaine,* VI (Janvier–Mars 1949), 47.

"Introducing Some American Negro Folk Songs," *Présence Africaine,* VI (Janvier–Mars 1949), 70.

"L'homme du Sud" (William Faulkner), *France Etats-Unis*, Décembre 1950, 2.

"Richard Wright Explains Ideas about Movie Making," *Ebony*, VI (Jan. 1951), 84–85.

"Les Noirs Américains et la France," *France Observateur*, No. 56 (3 Mai 1951). Printed in *Crisis*, LVIII (June–July 1951). 381–383, under the title "American Negroes in France."

"Derrière l'affaire McGee," *Le Droit de Vivre* (Paris), 15 Mai 1951.

"The Shame of Chicago," *Ebony*, VII (Dec. 1951), 24–32.

"What Is Africa to Me?" *Encounter*, III (Sept. 1954), 22–31. Included in *Black Power* (1954).

"Deux Portraits Africains," *Preuves*, No. 45 (Nov. 1954), 3–6.

"Vers Bandoeng via Seville," *Preuves*, No. 53 (Juillet 1955), 6–9. Incorporated in *The Color Curtain* (1956).

"Le Congrès des hommes de couleur," *Preuves*, No. 54 (Aout 1955), 42–48. Incorporated in *The Color Curtain* (1956).

"Indonesian Notebook," *Encounter*, V (August 1955), 24–31. Incorporated in *The Color Curtain* (1956).

"Le monde occidental à Bandoeng," *Preuves*, No. 55 (Sept. 1955), 44–55. Incorporated in *The Color Curtain* (1956).

"Tradition and Industrialization, the Plight of the Tragic Elite in Africa," *Présence Africaine*, No. 8–10 (Juin–Nov. 1956), 347–360. Included in *White Man, Listen!* (1957).

"Neurosis of Conquest" (Review of *Prospero and Caliban*, by O. Mannoni), *Nation*, CLXXXIII (Oct. 20, 1956), 330–331.

"De la Côte de l'Or au Ghana," *Preuves*, No. 75 (Mai 1957), 11–14.

"Le Noir est une création du Blanc," *Preuves*, No. 87 (Mai 1958), 40–41.

"Spanish Snapshots: Granada, Seville," *Two Cities* (Paris), No. 2 (July 1959), 25–34.

"The Voiceless Ones" (Review of *The Disinherited*, by Michel del Castillo), *Saturday Review*, XLIII (April 16, 1960), 21–22.

"Le Jazz et le Désir," Les Cahiers du Jazz, No. 4 (1961), 53–54.

NEWSPAPER CONTRIBUTIONS

"Negro Writers Launch Literary Quarterly," *Daily Worker*, June 8, 1937, 7.

"Young Writers Launch Literary Quarterly," *San Antonio Register* (Texas), July 10, 1937, 4.

"Butcher Who Attacked Negro Boy Is Fired," *Daily Worker*, July 15, 1937, 2.

"Negro, with 3-Week-Old Baby, Begs Food on Streets," *Daily Worker*, August 4, 1937, 3.

"C P Leads Struggle for Freedom, Stachel Says," *Daily Worker*, August 9, 1937, 2.

"Huddie Ledbetter, Famous Negro Folk Artist," *Daily Worker*, August 12, 1937, 7.

"Communist Leader Warns on Harlem Tiger Stooges," *Daily Worker*, August 13, 1937, 4.

"What Happens at a C P Meeting," *Daily Worker*, August 16, 1937, 6.

"Pullman Porters to Celebrate 12th Year of Their Union," *Daily Worker*, August 19, 1937, 3.

"Scottsboro Boys on Stage Is Opposed," *Daily Worker*, August 21, 1937, 3.

"Born a Slave She Recruits 5 Members for Communist Party," *Daily Worker*, August 30, 1937, 2.

"Harlem Women Hit Boost on Milk Price," *Daily Worker*, Sept. 3, 1937, 3.

"Insect Ridden Medicine Given in Hospital," *Daily Worker*, Sept. 4, 1937, 5.

"Mrs. Holmes and Daughter Drink from the Fountain of Communism," *Daily Worker,* Sept. 7, 1937, 5.

" 'Horseplay' at Lafayette Fun for Children and Grown-Ups Alike," *Daily Worker,* Sept. 11, 1937, 7.

"Harlem Spanish Women Come Out of the Kitchen," *Daily Worker,* Sept. 20, 1937, 5.

"10,000 Negro Vets in New York Silent, But They're Talking Up at Home," *Daily Worker,* Sept. 23, 1937, 4.

"Big Harlem Rally for China Tonight," *Daily Worker,* Sept. 27, 1937, 4.

"2 American Negroes in Key Posts of Spain's Loyalist Forces," *Daily Worker,* Sept. 29, 1937, 2.

"Randolph Urges Parley between CIO-AFL Unions," *Daily Worker,* Sept. 30, 1937, 3.

"Bates Tells of Spain's Fight for Strong Republican Army," *Daily Worker,* Oct. 1, 1937, 2.

"Negro Youth on March: Says Leader," *Daily Worker,* Oct. 7, 1937, 3.

"Opening on Harlem Project Homes Shows How Slums Can Be Wiped Out in New York," *Daily Worker,* Oct. 8, 1937, 5.

"See Biggest Negro Parley Since Days of Reconstruction," *Daily Worker,* Oct. 14, 1937, 5.

"Negro Tradition in the Theater," *Daily Worker,* Oct. 15, 1937, 7.

"Harlem, Bronx Sign Competition Pact," *Daily Worker,* Oct. 19, 1937, 5.

"Harlem Negro Leaders Back Mayor for Liberal Views," *Daily Worker,* Oct. 20, 1937, 5.

"Browder Warns of Growth of Fascism in Latin America," *Daily Worker,* Oct. 23, 1937, 5.

"New Negro Pamphlet Stresses Need for U.S. People's Front," *Daily Worker,* Oct. 25, 1937, 2.

"Harlem Leaders Rap *Amsterdam News,* Stand for Mahoney," *Daily Worker,* Oct. 30, 1937, 6.

"Harlem Vote Swings Away from Tiger," *Daily Worker,* Nov. 2, 1937, 3.

"Negro Leaders Hail Victory of ALP at New York Polls," *Daily Worker,* Nov. 4, 1937, 5.

"ALP Assemblyman Urges State Control," *Daily Worker,* Nov. 8, 1937, 1.

"Negro Social Worker Hails Housing, Education in Spain," *Daily Worker,* Nov. 12, 1937, 2.

"ALP Assemblyman in Harlem Hails Unity of Labor at Polls," *Daily Worker,* Nov. 18, 1937, 2.

"Walter Garland Tells What Spain's Fight against Fascism Means to the Negro People," *Daily Worker,* Nov. 29, 1937, 2.

" 'He Died by Them,' Hero's Widow Tells of Rescue of Negro Children," *Daily Worker,* Dec. 6, 1937, 1, 6.

"Harlem East Side Honor Hero Who Died in Rescue of Negroes," *Daily Worker,* Dec. 7, 1937, 4.

"Ban on Negro Doctors Bared at City Probe," *Daily Worker,* Dec. 15, 1937, 1.

"Gouging Landlord Discrimination against Negroes Bared at Hearing," *Daily Worker,* Dec. 15, 1937, 6.

"James W. Ford Celebrates 44th Birthday," *Daily Worker,* Dec. 23, 1937, 4.

"Santa Claus Has a Hard Time Finding Way in Harlem Slums," *Daily Worker,* Dec. 27, 1937, 4.

"Every Child Is a Genius," *Daily Worker,* Dec. 28, 1937, 7.

"Reader's Right: Writer Asks Break for Negroes" (Letter to the Editors), *New York Post,* April 5, 1938, 20.

"Statement in Support of Browder and Ford," *Daily Worker,* Sept. 30, 1940, 15.

"What Do I Think of the Theater," *N.Y. World Telegram,* March 22, 1941.

"Letter to Sender Garlin," *Daily Worker,* Feb. 10, 1942.

"Gertrude Stein's Story Is Drenched in Hitler's Horrors" (Review of *Wars I Have Seen,* by Gertrude Stein), *PM,* March 11, 1945, m. 15.

"A Non-Combat Soldier Strips Words for Action" (Review of *The Brick Foxhole,* by Richard Brooks), *PM,* June 24, 1945, m. 16.

"Two Novels of the Crushing of Men, One White, One Black" (Review of *Focus,* by Arthur Miller, and of *If He Hollers Let Him Go,* by Chester Himes), *PM,* Nov. 25, 1945, m. 7, m. 8.

"*Wasteland* Uses Psychoanalysis Deftly" (Review of *Wasteland,* by Jo Sinclair), *PM,* Feb. 17, 1946, m. 8.

"Dans le monde entier je sais reconnaître un nègre du Sud . . ." *Paris Matin,* 27 Juin 1946, 1–2. Incorporated in "How Jim Crow Feels" (1946).

"American G.I.'s Fears Worry Gertrude Stein" (Review of *Brewsie and Willie,* by Gertrude Stein), *PM,* July 26, 1946, m. 15-m. 16.

"E. M. Forster Anatomizes the Novel" (Review of *Aspects of the Novel,* by E. M. Forster), *PM,* March 16, 1947, m. 3.

"A Junker's Epic Novel on Militarism" (Review of *The End Is Not Yet,* by Karl von Unruh), *PM,* May 4, 1947, m. 3.

"L'humanité est plus grande que l'Amérique ou la Russie," *Franc Tireur,* 1 Décembre 1948, p. 3.

"Comrade Strong, Don't You Remember?" (Letter to Anna Louise Strong), *N.Y. Herald Tribune* (European edit.), April 4, 1949.

"Letter to Axel Lonnquist," *N.Y. Herald Tribune* (European edit.), Dec. 19, 1956.

MISCELLANEOUS—INTRODUCTIONS TO BOOKS, LETTERS, SKETCHES, ETC.

"The Ethics of Living Jim Crow, an Autobiographical Sketch," *American Stuff,* a W.P.A. Writers' Anthology, New York, 1937, pp. 39–52. Included in the 1940 edition of *Uncle Tom's Children.*

"Portrait of Harlem," in *New York Panorama,* (edit. Writers' Program of W.P.A.), New York, 1938, pp. 132–151. Unsigned.

"Introduction," in Howard Nutt, *Special Laughter,* pp. ix–xii, Press of James Decker: Prairie City, Illinois, 1940.

"Letter to International Publishers," a preface to *Bright and Morning Star* (see Fiction), dated April 1941, p. i.

"Forward," in Morris V. Schappes, *Letters from the Tombs,* pp. v–vi, Schappes Defense Committee, New York, 1941.

"Introduction," in Nelson Algren, *Never Come Morning,* pp. ix–x, New York, 1942.

"Introduction," in J. Saunders Redding, *No Day of Triumph,* p. i, New York, 1942.

"A hitherto unpublished manuscript by Richard Wright being a continuation of *Black Boy,*" edited by Constance Webb, New York, 1944. Photo-offset, private circulation, numbered copies. Includes "American Hunger" (1945) and "Early Days in Chicago" (1945).

"Introduction," in Horace R. Cayton and St. Clair Drake, *Black Metropolis,* pp. xvii–xxxiv, New York, 1945.

"Early Days in Chicago," in Edwin Seaver, ed., *Cross-section,* New York, 1945, pp. 306–342. Included in *Eight Men,* 1961. (See fiction).

"Introductory Note to 'The Respectful Prostitute,'" in *Art and Action, A Book of Literature, the Arts, and Civil Liberties* (10th Anniversary Issue, *Twice a Year,* 1938–1948), New York, 1948, pp. 14–16.

"Two Letters to Dorothy Norman," in *Art and Action* (see above).
  —Letter dated Feb. 28, 1948, pp. 65–71.
  —Letter dated March 9, 1948, pp. 72–73.

"Richard Wright," in Richard Crossman, ed., *The God That Failed,* New York, 1949, pp. 115–162. Text of "I Tried To Be a Communist" (1944).

"Préface," in Chester Himes, *La Croisade de Lee Gordon,* pp. 7–8, Paris, 1952.

"Introduction," in George Lamming, *In the Castle of My Skin,* pp. ix–xii, New York, 1953.

"From Richard Wright," in Donald Gallup, ed., *The Flowers of Friendship. Letters Written to Gertrude Stein,* New York, 1953. Letter dated May 27, 1945, pp. 379–380.

"Introduction," in George Padmore, *Pan-Africanism or Communism,* pp. 11–14, London, 1956.

"Au lecteur francais," in *Ecoute, Homme Blanc!* (*White Man, Listen!*) trans. Dominique Guillet, Paris, 1959, pp. xv–xxxvi.

"Foreword," in Paul Oliver, *Blues Fell This Morning,* pp. vii–xii, London, 1960, and New York, 1961.

"Introduction," in Françoise Gourdon, *Tant qu'il y aura la Peur,* Paris, 1961, pp. 1–3.

Index